KISSINGER
PORTRAIT OF A MIND

KISSINGER

PORTRAIT OF
A MIND

Stephen R. Graubard

W·W· NORTON & COMPANY · INC ·

New York

COPYRIGHT © 1973 BY W. W. NORTON & COMPANY, INC.

First Edition

Library of Congress Cataloging in Publication Data

Graubard, Stephen Richards.
    Kissinger: portrait of a mind.

    1.   Kissinger, Henry Alfred.   I.   Title.
E840.8.K58G72   973.924'092'4 [B]   73–1888
ISBN 0–393–05481–0

Excerpts from pp. 1, 2, 3, 4, 5, 95, 96, 177, 178, 179, 185, 187, 206, 216, 286, and 298 in *The Necessity for Choice* by Henry A. Kissinger Copyright © 1960, 1961 by Henry A. Kissinger By permission of Harper & Row, Publishers, Inc., and Chatto & Windus Ltd.

Henry A. Kissinger, *Nuclear Weapons and Foreign Policy* (New York: Harper & Brothers, for the Council on Foreign Relations, 1957).

A Troubled Partnership by Henry A. Kissinger. Copyright 1965 by the Council on Foreign Relations, Inc. and used with permission of McGraw-Hill Book Company.

A World Restored: Metternich, Castlereagh, and the Problems of Peace, 1812–22 by Henry A. Kissinger. Reprinted by permission of Houghton Mifflin Company.

PRINTED IN THE UNITED STATES OF AMERICA

1 2 3 4 5 6 7 8 9 0

For my brother

CONTENTS

PREFACE

There has been no one like Henry Kissinger in a high governmental position in the United States at any time in its history. Kissinger's career is unusual in at least three respects: He is an intellectual, who spent the greatest part of his adult life in a university, reflecting and writing about foreign affairs, criticizing the performance of those actively responsible for American policy, and offering alternatives; he is a scholar, who has never been satisfied to live entirely within the academy or by the academy's rules, believing that a larger experience was available outside and that it would be a mistake to ignore it; he is a European—sensitive to tradition and history, accepting of the possibility of tragedy—but also an American, aware of certain forms of power, not infrequently preoccupied with moral issues.

It is curious that all attention has been given to what Kissinger has done since he joined the Nixon administration, and that so few have thought to inquire into what he proposed before he went to Washington. This book is based on the very simple proposition that there is a link between the two, between what Kissinger wrote in the 1950s and 1960s and what he has been doing since January 20, 1969. The record of his thought is open; anyone may consult it. His actions are only partially known; many years must elapse before they are entirely revealed. This, in my view, makes only more imperative the consulting of the knowledge that is available.

My purpose has not been to write a biography of Henry Kissinger. While I have no doubt that such a book would generate great interest in many quarters, I am not persuaded that it would serve any of the objectives that I think to be crucially important at this time. I have written about Kissinger in the way I have, not because I know more, and choose out of friendship to say less, but because I think that the matters I have treated are essential to an understanding of the man. My interest has been to explain what he argued for, and I have done so, quite frequently, in his own words. I have examined seriously and analyzed in the following pages everything that Kissinger wrote and published prior to his taking public office. I have not chosen to compare his writings with those of his professional colleagues; others may wish to do that. I have, however, tried to say something about the institutions that shaped him, the individuals who mattered to him, the events that in one way or other made it possible for him to acquire the knowledge and experience that made his public career conceivable. I am persuaded that he could not have made his way without the stimulus and support he received, but also that it is impossible to understand his life without giving the greatest attention to his thought.

Kissinger, like de Gaulle, probably always believed in his own destiny; his American education almost certainly taught him the necessity of never saying so publicly. He spent a great part of his adult life writing for Americans, trying very self-consciously to instruct them in the fundamentals of international relations and policy-making in a thermonuclear age. He, in turn, was molded by his American experience, in ways that are not always recognized. Kissinger's career—and not only the one that began on January 20, 1969—is a testimonial to American possibilities. It is not, however, a Horatio Alger tale; Kissinger is very much the product of twentieth-century America.

I am grateful to many people for help in writing this book. Needless to say, no one of them is responsible for any part of it. For reading the manuscript, and giving me the benefit of their criticism, I should like to thank Graham Allison, Jr., Geno Ballotti, François Bourricaud, and Martin Meyerson. Each of them knows how grateful I am. To other friends, who listened to one or other of the chapters, or spoke about the manuscript with me, and who knew Henry Kissinger, I am also beholden; I would mention particularly Hélène d'Andlau, John and Jill Conway, Elizabeth Epstein, Stanley Hoffmann, and Eric Weil. Daniel Bell, Eleanor Farrar, Gerald Holton, Hilda de Rothschild, and Peter Wolkonsky encouraged me in other ways, not least in their understanding of what I was trying to do. Many of the individuals mentioned in the book are known to me personally; at one time or other, I have spoken to many of them about Kissinger. Since this was never intended to be a biography, I saw no reason to approach each of them for an interview; in a few instances, however, I felt some desire to do so. I should like to record my thanks to William Y. Elliott, Caryl Haskins, Fritz Kraemer, Herbert Marcovich, and Nelson Rockefeller. Finally, a word of thanks to my secretary, Bonnie Harris. Her willingness to take responsibility for successive versions of this manuscript, and to do so cheerfully and efficiently, meant a great deal to me. So, also, did the enormously helpful comments of my publisher, Donald Lamm.

Cambridge, Massachusetts   S. R. G.

INTRODUCTION

Henry Kissinger's life can only be understood by those who are prepared to acknowledge its ironies and its contradictions. The man reputed to be secretive never made a secret of his opinions; they are to be found in almost any reasonably well-equipped library. The man who made his way through intellect, and through the power of words, knew many years before he went to Washington to serve under Richard Nixon the limited authority of each. Had history not told him this, the experience of watching the Kennedy administration would have given him all the lessons he required. Enjoying his success as a scholar—a success that probably exceeded his expectations—he found that such achievement did not ultimately satisfy. His books, as he realized from his royalty statements, sold remarkably well; this did not persuade him that many of his theories were at all congenial to those whom he most wished to influence. A man who was quintessentially of the twentieth century—a victim of European persecutions and a beneficiary of uniquely American opportunities—Kissinger was generally regarded as someone who hankered after the glories of an earlier age. He would have been happier, some said, in the time of Metternich or Bismarck, about whom he had written. Had Kissinger published his undergraduate reflections on the age of Pericles, some of the same people would have been tempted to declare him a latter-day Athenian. They would have been stopped only by their unwillingness to pay him that compliment. When Kissinger was called a Metternichian or a Bismarckian, no tribute was intended.

Kissinger's secret visit to Peking in 1971 did a great deal to establish his reputation as a man of mystery; he saw no more reason to challenge a characterization that flattered him than to take issue with those that were intended to be wounding. The truth, in fact, was considerably more complex; its discovery, however, depended on a knowledge of the man, particularly of his mind. The evidences for that are abundantly available in his voluminous writings, which contain a faithful rendering of his thoughts on all those issues that have been important to him. It would not be too much to say that they offer a portrait of his mind. As such, they are invaluable for anyone who has the patience to explore them. It is in no way surprising that they are so immensely rich. Kissinger, as an adult, gave himself unstintingly to his writing. It was the activity that occupied him most completely, consuming the greatest part of his always abundant energies and providing him with many satisfactions. Anyone who has observed Kissinger pore over successive drafts of one of his manuscripts, starting with a badly handwritten foolscap version, and ending with last-minute revisions of a typed text that has generally circulated among friends and passed through three or four revisions, is aware that writing was never a chore that he took lightly. The results of that vast expenditure of time and energy are available to anyone who wishes to consult them. Foreign offices and embassies have almost certainly done so; the mass media have not been equally diligent. They have, in fact, been singularly uninterested in Kissinger's ideas; when, on rare occasions, they have wished to represent them, they have done so in a largely stereotyped and inaccurate fashion. The hundreds of profiles, backgrounders, biographical essays, and news stories that have appeared concerning Kissinger are filled with speculation on every conceivable subject; few show any substantial familiarity with his thought. We are constantly told that he is cerebral and intelligent, one of the most gifted men to enter the public service in recent decades. What better way, one would think, to judge a man's intelligence than to read his books and articles? They were not, after all, the scribblings of a wayward youth.

During an academic career that stretched over a decade and a half, Kissinger wrote four books and numerous articles. These are as much the product of his mind as anything that he has done from that day to this. To ignore them, or to underestimate their importance as a device for understanding him, is to show an innocence about both his argument and his life. From 1947 to 1968, Kissinger lived in an academic environment, first as a student, then as a member of the faculty. He ignored Harvard in his undergraduate days, being too busy with his studies; as he came to know the institution better, he found that he liked it less. He experienced all the pettiness endemic to communities where power is negligible and ambition is rife, and complained constantly of the lack of generosity among those whom he had to deal with. He knew also the pleasures of the academic world, particularly those that permitted him to pursue his studies in ways that he wished to do. He belonged to a self-confident university and a vigorous discipline, both constantly changing to take advantage of new opportunities. He entered the field of strategic studies before the subject was so designated, and remained in it long enough to know that a number of full-time researchers throughout the country thought him a popularizer—a term of abuse in scholarly circles. Though some could in fact claim a technical proficiency in the subject that made his own knowledge seem superficial by comparison, Kissinger never thought to imitate them. He believed in what he was doing, and saw no need to copy the more abstruse formulations of others. Nor was he at all tempted to exchange his university connection for one that would take him to a research institute where he would be free of the distraction of students. Where he was indebted to others, he was quick to acknowledge it; most often, it was to persons like himself, brilliant generalists, who were unwilling to be bound by narrow technical interests.

Kissinger, in any case, rejected the idea that his principal interest was strategy. For him, strategy was part of a larger discipline, and he thought it unfortunate that so few inside or outside the area of strategic studies admitted the necessity of seeing the field within a larger intellectual frame. Kissinger's own "system," insofar as it can be called that, depended on the proposition that there was a necessary interrelation among diplomacy, military strategy, and domestic politics. Because he thought it impossible to dissociate one from the other—and believed that many of the country's foreign policy failures derived from the mistaken attempt to do so—Kissinger found it as natural to study weapons systems as bureaucracy; for him, ideology was no less important than psychology; both depended on a view of history that emphasized the possibility of choice, the need for doctrine, and the centrality of leadership.

Kissinger was a professor and not a journalist; he felt under no obligation to comment on every major happening or to judge the foreign policy performance of every administration. His concern, however, was always to be concrete, and this led him to relate his theories to specific actions of governments. Certain kinds of questions constantly recurred: what general principle lay behind a specific policy; how had the policy come to be adopted; were other options considered; why had they been found wanting; why were certain others not thought of? Kissinger's methods involved him in historical research but he never pretended to be a historian; his concern was overwhelmingly with the present, but principally as a device for indicating the possibilities that might also exist in the future.

Written in the 1950s and 1960s, his works provide a running commentary on the foreign policy achievements and failures of three presidents —Harry Truman, Dwight Eisenhower, and John Kennedy. No one of the three—had he read Kissinger—would have been especially pleased with the judgment rendered. On Johnson, Kissinger was virtually silent. That may have been his most damning verdict. Had Kissinger never written certain of his articles and books before he joined the Nixon administration, they would never have been written. For Kissinger never wrote simply to set the record straight; his concern was always to effect policy. When he found fault with the Eisenhower administration, he offered alternatives; when the Kennedy administration, despite its frenetic activity and massive publicity, achieved so little in the field of foreign policy, he expressed his reservations and indicated options that were not being pursued.

All this is part of the public record; neither private correspondence nor top-secret documents need to be consulted for those who want to know what Kissinger thought about Eisenhower, Kennedy, or any number of other American leaders. There has, in fact, been scant interest in the subject; instead, all attention has been riveted on what Kissinger wrote about two nineteenth-century European statesmen, Metternich and Bismarck. The ignoring of one set of texts in favor of another is always interesting; what makes it particularly so in this instance, however, is that many who have chosen to describe Kissinger's views on nineteenth-century statesmanship show only the most superficial familiarity with what he in fact said. Simple notions circulate about why Kissinger is reputed to have "liked" Metternich and Bismarck, and why each was his hero. Indolence may explain why Kissinger's 350-page book on Metternich, which includes a number of fairly difficult passages and demands at least a minimal historical interest, has not always been carefully read; it will not explain, however, why anyone who has not read it should wish to write about it. As for Kissinger's views on Bismarck, even indolence will not excuse those lapses. To the extent that Kissinger made his views known on the Prussian leader, his opinions may be gleaned from a rapid perusal of a single article of thirty-five pages.

Why, then, the distortions? Because many who have bandied about the terms Metternichian and Bismarckian to explain Kissinger's own views have little interest in his historical judgments and are concerned only with his political actions and those of the President he serves. They write as political pamphleteers; when they use terms like *Realpolitik*, with its slightly sinister connotations, they intend to suggest an ideological affinity between Kissinger and the "reactionary autocrats" who ruled Germany and Austria in the nineteenth century. The fact that Kissinger himself expressed serious reservations about Bismarck's policies is irrelevant to them; they much prefer to make him out to be Bismarck's disciple, perhaps even his heir. As for Metternich, why, they seem to ask, should one be bothered with all those convoluted Kissingerian arguments? It saves a great deal of time and trouble simply to enroll Kissinger under the Metternichian banner. Knowing how to deal with his portrayal of Castlereagh, Britain's Foreign Secretary in the early nineteenth century, poses certain problems for those who wish to feign familiarity with Kissinger's writings but refuse to read his works. The temptation to ignore the subject entirely is overwhelming. There is probably no loss in this; Castlereagh never served as a bogeyman for Americans; he bears only a superficial resemblance to the truly evil geniuses, Metternich and Bismarck; besides, he does not even qualify as a German!

There would be no reason to dwell on these distortions if they did not reflect a basic misconception of the nature of Kissinger's interest in nineteenth-century diplomacy, and, more specifically, of his interest in statesmen like Metternich and Castlereagh. Kissinger did not approach them as a nineteenth-century schoolboy would have approached the study of Plutarch's *Lives*, imagining that he would find models worthy of emulation. Kissinger would have been naïve indeed to imagine that imitation of either Metternich or Bismarck was desirable or possible. His purpose in studying their lives was not that he wished to become like them; he had no conceivable reason for being interested in adopting their methods. He studied them because they gave him a perspective from which he could more effectively examine the problems of his own time. It was the twentieth century that interested Kissinger; particularly, the issues that grew out of the introduction of thermonuclear weapons.

It is curious that so much attention has been lavished on European figures who are almost mythological for most Americans, and that no comparable effort has been made to consider Kissinger's evaluations of men like Churchill and de Gaulle, Stalin and Khrushchev, Dulles and McNamara, who are active presences. The evidence is overwhelming that very few are aware that Kissinger ever wrote about any of these men. That his opinions were unconventional, and that he evaluated their strengths and weaknesses differently from many who were obliged to deal with them, is only the beginning of a story that is largely untold because Kissinger's works are so relatively unknown.

Rarely does a major figure arrive on the American political scene who is able to point to anything he has said or written that will give even a hint of what he is likely to do in high public office. It is difficult in the United States today to have a very precise sense of the intellectual and moral qualities of many of those who have achieved national prominence. The public learns about its leaders largely through information disseminated by the mass media. They are judged most often by intangibles: by what others say about them; by the associates they bring with them (often individuals as obscure as they are); by the impressions they create in those highly structured situations that test their theatrical gifts and their physical stamina even more than they do their character. Even when, as in a few isolated instances, they appear to have distinctive points of view, discoverable in the *Congressional Record* or in some other such place, it is impossible to know whether one is reading the ghostwritten effort of a bright administrative assistant or whether the individual is in fact the father of the thought ascribed to him. We live with shadows, sometimes successfully limned in by conscientious news reporters. Occasionally —very occasionally—someone arrives on the scene who has actually recorded what he thought, and deposited the record in a public place where all may have access to it. To know what a public man has thought —and to know it at the time he holds office—is to be privileged; this situation is so uncommon that it would be churlish to ignore the opportunity it offers.

Yet it has been ignored in the case of Henry Kissinger. A file filched from Kissinger's office in the White House would probably whet the appetite of every journalist in the country; journalists would endure almost any hardship to scrutinize such materials. Granted that "secret" documents do have a special attraction, and that some, at least, are significant not only for the light they throw on the mind of the President's National Security Adviser but also for information they may give about governmental policies more generally, is it not legitimate to ask whether a preoccupation with "confidential" materials has not made too many American journalists (and too many others as well) insufficiently attentive to the vast stores of information available in the public domain?

The question is not intended to be rhetorical. In the case of Henry Kissinger, the failure to consider his published work seriously has had unfortunate consequences: it has contributed to a perpetuation of a view of foreign policy which makes everything seem to depend on the will of individual leaders. The romanticization of Kissinger himself would never have proceeded as far as it did if there had been a more adequate knowledge of his works. Implicitly and explicitly, Kissinger was always asking about the durability of solo performances; he knew how much the individual could and must do; he also knew what he could not do.

A more intimate knowledge of Kissinger's writings might have made it easier for others to anticipate many of the foreign policy developments of recent years, making it possible for them to look somewhat more critically at the various "spectaculars" that were being produced. The news itself was so overwhelming that there was little disposition to stand apart from it and give it the serious scrutiny that it deserved. There has been no one like Henry Kissinger outside the government since 1969, offering relentless criticism of American foreign policy, and doing so free of personal rancor. Kissinger, in short, has been handicapped by not having his own "Kissinger" outside the governmental bureaucracy.

There is, however, another reason to regret that studies of Kissinger have been so lame, informed, when they were friendly, by an almost maudlin sentimentality, or, when they were hostile, by a vicious destructiveness, which has only too often concealed a general ignorance about the fundamentals of his life. Neither has served to emphasize sufficiently those aspects of Kissinger's life that are unique and deserve mention. A knowledge of these factors would go far to explain why his career could only have developed as it did in the United States.

It is well to recall how modest were Kissinger's educational accomplishments when the war liberated him from his New York refugee ghetto and launched him into a wider world. His Army service gave him his citizenship in several senses; it introduced him to a country he would not otherwise have come to know so quickly; it permitted him to see his old country under circumstances that compelled him to be compassionate. His important formal education began only when he was twenty-four; not every major university in the world would have been so understanding of his circumstances, or so ready to let him run free, with just enough supervision to give him a sense of what the intellectual life was all about. In these years, as a virtual recluse, Kissinger acquired the rudiments of an education that was to serve him for the rest of his life.

Graduate studies provided him with new opportunities—to build novel institutions with very limited resources, and to do so in such a way that permitted both him and others to benefit. The International Seminar and the journal *Confluence* were Kissinger's institutional bequests to Harvard; they may be considered as a partial repayment for what Harvard gave him in his undergraduate years. In almost no other country in the world, whatever the personal relations of a graduate student with his professor, would it have been possible for two such institutions to be created. They depended on that unique American assumption that anything may be tried—if only on a very *ad hoc* basis—when someone is prepared to devote time, and no one in authority raises serious objections.

It was in New York, however, that Kissinger was to have an even more important experience—one that took him out of his academic shell and brought him into touch with all sorts of people whom he felt instinctively drawn to. The Council on Foreign Relations did much to make an important book possible; its more lasting contribution, perhaps, was to give confidence and encouragement to an awkward and lonely individual who knew how much he needed to feel something other than the dreary competitiveness of Cambridge, Massachusetts. And then a no less vital link developed with Nelson Rockefeller, soon to be elected Governor of New York, but at the time working to delineate with others an America that did not then exist. The Special Studies Project of the Rockefeller Brothers Fund was a very American enterprise; American in its optimism and also in its assumption that men of good will would almost certainly agree about the ends that a good society should seek.

Within a decade of his return from military service in war-ravaged Germany, Kissinger was on his way to receiving a permanent position on the Harvard faculty, with every reason to expect that other honors and opportunities would also come his way. There was a brief period of part-time service in Washington in 1961 at the time of the Berlin crisis, and then Kissinger resumed his Cambridge professorial life. Again, it is easy to forget how uniquely American that Cambridge academic life was. It was heavy with obligations, but filled with freedom. Kissinger could write on precisely what he wished; foundation and other funds permitted him to travel constantly; there were almost daily telephonic communications with men in high places in Washington, and a constant stream of visitors from the United States and abroad; a secretarial staff stood ready to take his dictation and type the latest draft of a manuscript that had already gone out to friends for their criticism; there were unique library resources, and these could always be supplemented by the clipping files and other facilities of libraries like those of the Council on Foreign Relations. Everything that could exist to make the life of a scholar congenial and agreeable existed in the Harvard of that period. It was easy to forget that such resources did not exist for British, French, or German colleagues. There were, however, also certain frustrations, many of them less uniquely American than the advantages mentioned. Academic communities, even when they appear most open, risk becoming provincial places; the politics of a university, for anyone who enjoys the real thing, can only appear as an adolescent's game. In the great European capitals, like London or Paris, a university professor can, if he wishes, live somewhat apart from the academic world, sharing in a larger social life. This was not quite so easy for someone in Cambridge, even for someone prepared to travel to Washington or New York once or twice a week.

The professorial regimen seemed to make less sense for Kissinger during the years 1964–1968 than it did at any other time. There was a new awareness of how limited were the opportunities to have influence on government from the outside. In the United States, the illusion existed in certain disciplines that positions as consultant, adviser, and the like gave substantial influence. Kissinger knew better. Though he was increasingly restive in these years, there were few external signs of his unhappiness. In Harvard, one of the last refuges of the entrepreneurial system, no one paid very great attention to what was happening to him. Colleagues were scarcely aware that he was writing less; what interested them, obviously, was what they themselves were doing.

And then, in the spring of 1968, an unexpected opportunity came; Nelson Rockefeller, after first declining to seek the Republican nomination for the presidency, agreed to run. Kissinger was his foreign policy adviser; Kissinger worked as if the nomination itself depended on his efforts. That aim was unrealizable; Rockefeller had come in too late; Nixon had gone too far to be derailed, even by a combination of Rockefeller and Reagan forces. This, however, was not the way that either Rockefeller or

Kissinger saw the matter. If they aimed for an impossible goal, the campaign gave Kissinger the opportunity to formulate a series of foreign policy statements that he believed to be more significant than any that had ever been produced for a party contender. After Rockefeller's loss, tentative feelers from the Nixon camp were made in Kissinger's direction. Did Kissinger want to join Nixon's campaign staff? He indicated that he had no interest in doing so.

It was quite another matter, however, when the President-elect, in November, asked Kissinger to visit him in New York at his Pierre Hotel headquarters. After two long private meetings, Kissinger was offered the position of Assistant to the President for National Security Affairs. Kissinger knew that he could not refuse it; he had no desire to do so. Having for well over a decade tried to tell others what they ought to be doing in the area of foreign policy, he welcomed the opportunity to try his own hand at it.

Kissinger's life had many characteristic twentieth-century features; it was busy, agitated, and filled with frustrations. In the end, Kissinger, like the man whom he went to serve under, belonged nowhere. He was very much the child of his age, whose career was quite literally made possible by the fact that he was prepared to think the unthinkable, and reflect on how a new arms technology made obsolete the diplomacy and politics, not to speak of the defense, of an earlier day. He lived in a society that no longer placed insuperable barriers in the way of someone like himself, born a Jew, and a refugee to boot, who had to make his way without the advantage of family connections or financial resources. Kissinger had no illusion about why his progress had been possible; others, with less talent, would have gone as far much more easily. He traded on his principal resource—his intelligence. It was remarkable that he was able to maintain so much of his natural reserve and independence in a race where there were such powerful incentives to join the academic club, adopting its values and beliefs. His mind and industry were his principal assets. His great insight, however, which he owed to his study of history, was that mind had its own limitations. It was not an absolute weapon; the intrinsic difficulties of the tasks that government confronted would not suddenly succumb to the power of intelligence. He knew that mind had brought him to where he was; he knew that it might carry him even further. He was too intelligent to believe that it would ultimately give him the "perfect peace" that Americans had been seeking from the time they first came to the New World. Kissinger remained a European among Americans; an American among Europeans.

KISSINGER
PORTRAIT OF A MIND

1

The Early Years
Learning to Choose

Henry Kissinger was not a professional historian; he did not think of himself as such; others did not so regard him. He did, however, read history, and his interest in the subject went beyond what was common among Americans of his generation, even among those who shared his wartime experiences and his preoccupation with foreign affairs and international relations. How did Kissinger come to develop his interest in history? Had he been born in 1914 or 1915 rather than in 1923, and had he completed under the Weimar Republic a traditional *Gymnasium* education, with its heavy emphasis on philosophy, history, and ancient languages, his knowledge would have been attributed to a superior German educational system. As it was, he arrived in the United States with only the rudiments of a European education.

As a boy of fifteen, he was scarcely aware of any educational lacks. In Germany, he had attended a *Realschule*, where he had shown great aptitude in all his studies. In New York, at George Washington High School, he proved to be no less successful. By every conventional American academic standard, Kissinger was a superior student. If colleges did not press scholarship funds on him when he graduated from high school in 1941, and if no teacher thought it imperative that he be selected out for special higher educational opportunity, it was because such things did not happen in the United States, at least not in the vast public secondary-school system of New York where there were hundreds of students each year with perfect or near-perfect grade records. Kissinger's parents, like many others in the city, had to decide whether to send their son to a city college full time and forgo certain income that he would otherwise earn or press him to attend evening session, so that he might be employed full time. They opted for the second course, claiming that the economic plight of the family made any other solution impractical.

Kissinger enrolled for evening courses at City College and began to study accounting; he worked during the day, for a time in a downtown Manhattan factory. Whatever the glories of full-time undergraduate study at the old City College—so frequently described by some of its more successful alumni—these were scarcely experienced by the overworked crew that checked in each evening to pursue college studies on a part-time basis. Kissinger felt that he spent his days in an industrial factory and his nights in an educational factory. The first provided him a modest income that he shared with his family; the second, he and his parents assumed, would one day give him the credentials that would enable him to pursue a professional career with the possibilities of a more substantial income. The family's horizons extended no further than that. Their son was at college for one reason only—to improve his prospects in life; in the insecure refugee world of the early 1940s, that translated into economic improvement. Nothing that happened to Kissinger during those years encouraged him to read more widely; his historical interests were as underdeveloped when he was twenty as when he arrived in New York as a boy of fifteen.

Kissinger was liberated from this life by the accident of war. The United States Army drafted him in February 1943, and he soon found himself in infantry basic training at Camp Croft, South Carolina. Kissinger had never been south of the Mason-Dixon line; he had never lived away from his family; he knew nothing of American life outside the refugee neighborhood in upper Manhattan where he spent his late adolescence. In Camp Croft, near Spartanburg, Kissinger gained the first impressions of an America that his high-school history textbooks had not prepared him for. As his letters home indicated, he found the experience immensely exhilarating. He was a solitary figure who observed and listened. South Carolina was more of a "new world" for him than New York had ever been. So, also, was Lafayette College, in Easton, Pennsylvania, where he was sent in September 1943, after a summer at Clemson College. The A.S.T.P. (Army Specialized Training Program) was one of several World War II educational schemes that permitted soldiers, selected on the basis of intelligence-test scores, to be trained in colleges at government expense in subjects that the Army thought useful. The program had the incidental advantage of keeping open a number of colleges that might otherwise have closed their doors for lack of a sufficient number of civilian male students. Kissinger spent more than six months at Lafayette College in a special engineering program. It added nothing to his knowledge of history; it did, however, give him a new appreciation of his qualities as a student. Several Lafayette College professors singled him out for special attention; he was clearly their ablest student. This idyllic period came to an end quite suddenly, largely because of the urgent military need for greater numbers of front-line soldiers. Kissinger, and many others who had expected to remain somewhat longer in the Army's special educational programs, were rushed back to Army camps to prepare for service in one or other of the active theaters of war. Kissinger, in April 1944, found himself assigned to the 84th Infantry Division at Camp Claiborne, Louisiana.

The move proved to be a fortunate one for Kissinger. At Camp Claiborne, he met Fritz Kraemer, a private like himself, a German, but not a Jew, who had left Germany voluntarily. A great deal has been made of Kraemer's contributions to Henry Kissinger's education. The reports, while somewhat exaggerated, contain the kernel of a truth that must be insisted on. Kissinger gained immensely from knowing someone who was well educated by European standards and who could make him aware of his own serious academic limitations. Kraemer was generous to a fault; he thought that the young Kissinger had immense intellectual capabilities; he knew that he grasped even the most complex matters easily and that he listened attentively. These were important qualities for a man who himself liked to talk, and who imagined that he had found a worthy auditor in the young Jewish boy who was already beginning to lose his command of the German language. Kraemer talked incessantly; he insisted that the conversation be carried on in German. The two became inseparable They could not have been more different. Kraemer, already thirty-five, belonged to a German world that Kissinger had never known; he was a devout Christian who regarded Nazism as an abomination. Much preoccupied with himself and with his "philosophy of life," he quoted from books that Kissinger had never read and developed idealistic arguments that he had never heard. The older man believed that he was educating the callow youth, though he only dimly perceived the nature of the influence he was exerting on Kissinger. Kraemer's two earned doctorates—his knowledge of Latin, Greek, and several modern languages, not to speak of philosophy, history, and law—impressed the young man. More important by far, however, was the fact that Kissinger had not previously met any German who had *chosen* exile, and who had done so for political and moral reasons. Kissinger's whole refugee experience had been with men and women who had been forced to flee; they had not chosen their destiny. He was immensely impressed with someone who had. He admired what he knew to be Kraemer's courage; he enjoyed his resilience and his bravado. While he could not fail occasionally to be put off by Kraemer's bombastic and overbearing qualities, these seemed to be very minor defects; they could be dismissed as the harmless quirks of an obviously eccentric personality. Kissinger liked Kraemer because he had made a moral choice; that, in his mind, showed character. Kraemer, in talking about himself, insisted always that he was beholden to no one; the young Kissinger almost certainly believed him. He looked on him as a free man.

The six months in Camp Claiborne were very important ones for Kissinger; so, also, were the six months of combat in Western Europe and the assignment which made him, a staff sergeant in the Counter-Intelligence Corps, virtual commander of a small town outside Heidelberg. He enjoyed very substantial authority in Bensheim and used it judiciously. Demobilized in May 1946, Kissinger remained in Europe as a well-paid instructor at the European Command Intelligence School at Oberammergau, where he was immensely successful in instructing military officers for their occupation duties. He studied carefully the materials prepared for the course and drew heavily on what he had learned in administering a war-ravaged area in the difficult period immediately following the elimination of Nazi power. He was clearly more able than most of the men who sat before him. He also knew, however, how little he knew; it was important that he return home to be educated. Kraemer intervened again, told him that a "gentleman" did not seek a degree from City College, and implored him to apply elsewhere. Kissinger wrote to Harvard in the spring of 1947, was accepted almost immediately, and began his studies there the following September as an undergraduate.

Harvard was an exciting university in the years immediately after World War II. The G.I. Bill of Rights brought great numbers of World War II veterans, some as old as or older than Kissinger, to begin or continue studies interrupted by the war. For almost the only time in Harvard's history, adults and adolescents mingled in the same classes, instructed by men whose experience of life had been considerably enlarged by a war that had led them to unlikely assignments in distant parts of the world. There was an air of expectancy and urgency in Cambridge during those first postwar years; many, and not only those who were married and felt keenly their family responsibilities, acted as if they ought to make up for lost time. They thought themselves already very late in the race; it did not seem right for them to linger too long in a tranquil university world that appeared bustling only to those who had known it first in the 1930s. Kissinger lived very privately during the whole of his undergraduate years. He made no lasting friendships with other students; he seemed scarcely aware of the extraordinary range of people gathered in Cambridge. He was preoccupied not so much with preparing for a career as with learning how to learn. For the first time in his life, Kissinger experienced the exhilaration that came from habitual reading and writing; he became something of a recluse.

Henry Kissinger was fortunate in his tutor, William Y. Elliott. Something of a legendary Harvard figure even before the war, Elliott tried to give the handful of students who came under his personal charge each year a taste of the experience he had known himself as a Rhodes scholar at Balliol College, Oxford. Though a senior professor—said to be one of the two most powerful men in the Government Department—and free to offer any courses that he wished, Elliott remained faithful to his Oxford memories, and elected always to teach a certain number of undergraduate students, whom he met individually in weekly tutorial sessions. He followed procedures that were common in the two ancient English universities: students were asked to read one or more books for each tutorial session; they wrote short essays and generally discussed what they had read or written. Kissinger reveled in the relationship; he admired Elliott's erudition and valued his criticisms. The weekly reading assignments ranged over a vast intellectual terrain; Elliott never seemed surprised by Kissinger's ability to read everything that was assigned to him and to come back asking for more. Before many weeks had passed, Kissinger knew that he wanted to continue with Elliott, and that he would be privileged indeed if Elliott consented to serve as his tutor when he came to write his senior honors thesis. Kissinger was impressed by Elliott's vigor, passion, and forthrightness; even more by his courtliness, generosity, and readiness to discuss any intellectual issue that Kissinger raised. Elliott was anything but a pedant; certain qualities that made him suspect to many of his colleagues made him immensely attractive to the young Kissinger. It was difficult to know precisely what Elliott's interests were; he taught political theory, but had a deep interest in international relations and in domestic politics. He was a consultant to the House Committee on Foreign Affairs in Washington when Kissinger first came to know him; he was generally absent from Cambridge a number of days each week. When in residence, his students had easy access to him. Kissinger took advantage of the situation. He found Elliott an articulate and forceful man, precisely the kind of man he wished to study under. He wanted to please him, and thought he could do this best by showing intellectual venturesomeness.

Kissinger's senior honors thesis—a long 377-page typed manuscript —which contributed to the Government Department's decision to institute new rules governing the permissible length of undergraduate theses, was a testimonial to what Kissinger had learned from Elliott. Few undergraduates would have been prepared to undertake so massive an assignment; few professors would have encouraged them to do so. Elliott pressed Kissinger to read widely, and he saved him from the protectionist academic mentality that made particular texts and problems seem appropriate only to specific disciplines, while others were declared inadmissible. Kissinger's thesis was spirited; it brought together two philosophers who were thought dubious in many academic quarters with a third who inhabited everyone's philosophical pantheon. Kissinger wrote on Oswald Spengler, Arnold Toynbee, and Immanuel Kant. His thesis was entitled "The Meaning of History: Reflections on Spengler, Toynbee and Kant." In uniting the three, Kissinger challenged any number of academic orthodoxies; another tutor might have suggested that his student show greater intellectual fastidiousness and discrimination. Kissinger discussed all three because they served his purposes. He did not much care whether they were really comparable figures, and even less whether they were academically respectable. He realized, of course, that he had produced a gigantic tome, and that not everyone would be prepared to read all of it; for those who cared only about the central argument, Kissinger provided a set of directional signals indicating the subsections that might be omitted. There were four principal parts: "Spengler: History as Intuition"; "Toynbee: History as an Empirical Science"; "Kant: History and Man's Experience of Morality"; and a final section entitled "The Sense of Responsibility." The work was highly complex; the prose excessively labored; the argument exceedingly personal. In addition to writing about his principal authors, Kissinger thought it necessary to consider Aristotle and Homer, Virgil and Dante, Milton and Spinoza, and dozens of others who in one way or another seemed relevant to his concerns. Kissinger had attended course lectures faithfully; he had learned substantially from many of those who had spoken in the crowded Harvard lecture halls. Notes that would have served others only until a final examination was safely negotiated had been made a permanent part of his intellectual store. Much of what he learned at Harvard was incorporated into a thesis that pretended to deal with selected philosophies of history since the eighteenth century; it was, in fact, a kind of personal testament.

Kissinger wrote the thesis with great deliberateness. While he immersed himself in the works of his three principal authors, he used each to illustrate his own philosophy, which he never stated but which was implicit throughout. The work was passionate, original, and very idiosyncratic. It is difficult to render its quality except through a number of direct quotations. They may suggest why Kissinger was not entirely like other of his undergraduate contemporaries, even in the Harvard of the immediate postwar period. Thus, for example, Kissinger could write: "Life is suffering, birth involves death. Transitoriness is the fate of existence. No civilization has yet been permanent, no longing completely fulfilled. This is necessity, the fatedness of history, the dilemma of mortality." Kissinger's preoccupation with life and death was not simply a morbid reflection on what had happened to himself or his family, or the millions of Jews who had been even less fortunate, meeting their end in Nazi concentration camps. His concern was with historical change more generally, and not only with the phenomenon of decline in the twentieth century, which he took to be a brutal and tawdry epoch. Kissinger wrote: "Though aging in a culture is not analogous to physical decay, it does bear a similarity to another problem of existence, the process of disenchantment. Just as the life of every person exhibits a gradual loss of wonder at the world, so history reveals an increase of familiarity with the environment, a tired groping for a certainty which will obviate all struggles, a quest for a guarantee of man's hopes in nature's mechanism."

It was this quest for certainty—for technical solutions to the immensely complex problems of human existence—that so much offended the young Kissinger. He had no sympathy for what he regarded as the engineering approach to the dilemmas of life. In a whole series of intensely personal statements, he wrote mockingly of those who imagined that they were able to reduce everything to formulas, that all problems were solvable, and that good will would cause injustice to be abolished and peace to reign. The quality of his argument may be given in any of a hundred quotations; the following is not untypical. Kissinger wrote: "But what is the greater delusion, the Golden Age or the belief in infinite material progress? As the enchantment of an inwardly remote nature is dissipated and the cold materialistic intellect replaces the sentimentality of the romantic, life emerges as but a technical problem. The frantic search for social solutions, for economic panaceas testifies to the emptiness of a soul to which necessity is an objective state, not an inward condition, and which ever believes that just a little more knowledge, just one more formula will solve the increasing bafflement of a materialistic surrounding. And it is forgotten that matter can defeat only those who have no spirituality to impart to it."

Kissinger refused to place himself either in the camp of the determinists or in the camp of those who insisted on the complete freedom of the will. He accepted the laws of necessity even as he insisted on the need for action. He showed his intense commitment to a philosophy that made the individual the responsible agent: "Reason discloses objective necessity, the inexorability of causal laws, the linkages which enable man to master his environment. They present life as a technical task and instill a manipulatory attitude. In their sphere they may achieve tremendous successes. The physicist has opened vistas of worlds which even the fatuous optimism of the late nineteenth century would scarcely believe. But a knowledge of objective necessity has definite limits. It is confined to a naturalistic mechanism in which the scientist does not directly participate." Kissinger's concern was with action; ultimately, with the individual. He wrote: "But action derives from an inward necessity, from the personal in the conception of the environment, from the unique in the apprehension of phenomena. Consequently, objective necessity can never guide conduct, and any activity reveals a personality. Reason can help us understand the world in which we live. Rational analysis can assist us in developing institutions which make an inward experience possible. But nothing can relieve man from his ultimate responsibility, from giving his own meaning to life, from elevating himself above necessity. . . ."

Kissinger esteemed Oswald Spengler for having understood "the fatedness of historical events," and for recognizing "the disenchantment that accompanies a civilization's growth," but Spengler had not gone far enough; Spengler, Kissinger wrote, "did not grasp that inevitability is a poor guide and no inspiration. . . . Success and failure are relative attributes, meaningful only in retrospect and never finally decided. But the attitude which accompanies activity testifies to a character, to the intrinsically unique which man imparts to objective necessity."

Kissinger's concluding paragraphs perfectly sum up his view of history, at least as he conceived history when he was a senior at Harvard College. He wrote: "Is man doomed to struggle without certainty and live without assurance? In a sense that is so. Man cannot achieve a guarantee for his conduct. No technical solutions to the dilemmas of life are at hand. That is the fatedness of existence. But it also poses a challenge, an evocation of the sense of responsibility to give one's own meaning to one's life. Ethics must always reside in an inward personal state, in a personal recognition of limits." Realizing how easy it was to detect the factors that determined specific events in the past, Kissinger insisted on believing in the indeterminacy of the future; he wrote: "The past is dead and ruled by necessity, but freedom governs the future." Finally, he wrote: "Life involves suffering and transitoriness. No person can choose his age or the condition of his time. The past may rob the present of much joy and much mystery. The generation of Buchenwald and the Siberian labor-camps cannot talk with the same optimism as its fathers. The bliss of Dante has been lost in our civilization. But this merely describes a fact of decline and not its necessity. Man's existence is as transcendental a fact as the violence of history. Man's actions testify to his aspirations which stem from an attitude of the soul, not an evaluation of conditions. To be sure these may be tired times. But we cannot require immortality as the price for giving meaning to life. The experience of freedom enables us to rise beyond the suffering of the past and the frustrations of history. In this spirituality resides humanity's essence, the unique which each man imparts to the necessity of his life, the self-transcendence which gives peace."

Henry Kissinger's undergraduate thesis was thought to be excellent by those in the Government Department who judged it; he received his bachelor's degree *summa cum laude*, an honor reserved for very few at Harvard College. The recognition, while gratifying, posed a problem for Kissinger: Did he wish to persist with further studies of the same kind, dealing essentially with philosophical ideas, perhaps in the area of political theory, or ought he to strike out and do work of a very different order in graduate school? Kissinger knew himself sufficiently well to realize that his undergraduate thesis had served the purpose intended; it had contributed to remedying at least some of the large deficiencies in his education that he knew existed. Harvard College had been Kissinger's *Gymnasium*; it had given him a liberal-arts education. He had been privileged to have that education not when he was an adolescent—however precocious —but when he was an adult and could appreciate fully the extraordinary texts that were placed before him. Kissinger, in 1950, a man of twenty-seven, was ready to prepare for a profession.

His announced intention was to become a professor. To achieve that objective, it was necessary for him to secure a Ph.D. degree. As a *summa cum laude* graduate of Harvard, he started with one large advantage in the Government Department: he would not have to prepare for the so-called general examinations; he could begin to think almost at once of a dissertation. His department had the reputation for being rather liberal in allowing its students ample choice in their selection of a dissertation subject; many fastened on a very contemporary problem. Kissinger was not even tempted by that possibility. Instead of dealing with a major international crisis since 1945, or with some other crucial twentieth-century foreign policy issue, he chose to analyze the European world order in the first decades of the nineteenth century. His choice of subject was very deliberate. He was saying, in effect, that he did not agree with those who insisted that Hiroshima marked the end of an epoch, certainly the end of an era in international relations. If the atomic bomb had changed all state relations, then the study of diplomacy and politics in the nineteenth century became a form of antiquarianism. Kissinger argued precisely the opposite. Without denying the importance of the development of atomic arms—indeed, while insisting on their critical significance for the peace of the world—Kissinger argued for the continuing importance of history. Like Thucydides, whom he quoted, Kissinger believed that the present, while never replicating the past, must inevitably resemble it; so, also, must the future. The task of the historian was to determine where the similarities lay and what the differences were. These concerns were to remain central with Kissinger throughout his academic career.

As a graduate student he moved rapidly toward an intensive study of international relations. In the relations between states, he believed, lay the future peace of the world and the destiny of the human race. Just as he

and interests that they lacked. States were not mollified by other states' choosing to regard them as other than they really were. State interests were intimately linked to their power, and power was a complex compound, consisting, of course, of military capability and economic resources, but depending ultimately on one other crucial element—the quality of the political leadership. Kissinger's nineteenth-century studies led him to emphasize four absolutely essential components of state power: prevailing political and strategic perceptions; internal support for specific policies; relations with other states—allied, neutral, or enemy—and the character of the leadership and its capacity to achieve the objectives that it decided upon. The state, unlike the individual, could not be said to have a natural life span. The question of its life or death was a function always of specific decisions taken; there was no way to prove that a specific risk, averted, would have compromised the life of the state.

The atomic bomb, in Kissinger's mind, had not destroyed the "revolutionary" world of Napoleon. Because the events of the early nineteenth century did not engage American sentiment in anything like the way that more recent happenings did, they provided an extraordinary opportunity for analysis. Everyone in the 1950s thought himself to be something of an expert on Franklin Roosevelt. To enter into that period would have been to trespass on the preserve of many who had interests to defend. Their own reputations depended on a certain view being maintained. Kissinger had no interest in meeting such opposition head on. It made much better sense for him to inquire about men who did not have so many "protectors"—who, in fact, had none. The object of the exercise was to learn. Kissinger was creating an analytical system; its originality lay in its insistence that diplomacy, strategy, and domestic politics were inseparable; but more than that, that individual action at the highest levels of government determined whether a state lived or died. Kissinger was too much a child of the twentieth century to doubt that the second possibility was always present.

2

On Metternich and Castlereagh
Writing for Himself

Henry Kissinger completed his doctoral dissertation in early 1954; it appeared as a book under the title *A World Restored: Metternich, Castlereagh, and the Problems of Peace, 1812–1822*, in October 1957, following hard on the publication of his better-known work, *Nuclear Weapons and Foreign Policy*. The Metternich manuscript was rejected by a number of publishers before being accepted by Houghton Mifflin; its publication was further delayed by a strike which kept the pages, printed in Great Britain, from reaching the United States. There were no such delays and no such problems with *Nuclear Weapons and Foreign Policy*. The Council on Foreign Relations, having commissioned the study, recognized its importance and pressed for early publication; an arrangement with Harper guaranteed that this would be done, and done quickly. Few who read *Nuclear Weapons and Foreign Policy* were at all aware of Kissinger's other interests; not many who read that book thought it necessary to look also at *A World Restored*. Had they done so, they would have noticed at once the extent to which Kissinger made use in the nuclear weapons volume of insights drawn from his early-nineteenth-century researches. He had used his years as a graduate student at Harvard to great advantage. Some of the most important concepts in *Nuclear Weapons and Foreign Policy* derived from the prolonged, almost leisurely study that Kissinger had made of diplomacy and politics in the Napoleonic era.

A World Restored was not a typical American doctoral dissertation;

13

nor was it at all characteristic of the dissertations completed at Harvard at the time. It was in fact a very personal document—almost a dialogue between Kissinger and himself. Kissinger had managed to adopt an unconventional analytical scheme—which might easily have been dismissed as bizarre—and had then proceeded to use his method to reach conclusions that effectively contradicted most of the traditional analyses of Metternich, Castlereagh, the Congress of Vienna, and the period following on Napoleon's final defeat. Kissinger understood only too well the reasons why Metternich was held in such low repute by American academics who looked upon him as a reactionary—in the words of one of the classic textbooks of the period, "the self-appointed spokesman of the reactionary forces of the day"—but he was not much deterred (or influenced) by such opinions. Kissinger had no interest in rehabilitating the reputation of Austria's greatest nineteenth-century statesman; nor was he under any illusion that his doctoral dissertation could have accomplished that purpose even if he had set out to do it.

Kissinger's interest was not in a historical personage, Metternich, but in the problems that Metternich was compelled to deal with. He chose the Napoleonic period because he believed it resembled his own. The book, while technically about Metternich and Castlereagh, was, as its subtitle indicated, a study of war, peace-making, and peace-keeping. These subjects interested Kissinger precisely because they encouraged him to reflect on the relations between foreign policy and domestic political structure, and on the role of ideology in international relations during a revolutionary era. While studying actions involving Austria, Great Britain, Russia, Prussia, and France in the first decades of the nineteenth century, Kissinger was largely preoccupied with the implications of these events for understanding an unstable international order in the middle of the twentieth century that involved the United States, the Soviet Union, Great Britain, France, and Germany. He was sufficiently respectful of academic tradition not to draw the analogies too explicitly, but they were never absent from his mind.

Some will say that a university system that encouraged such latitude in its students could not be all bad. Kissinger was able to pursue a fairly unconventional subject in a quite eccentric fashion because of the peculiar strengths of the university in which he was enrolled. The strengths of Harvard are almost always inaccurately represented; they are thought to reside wholly in an incomparable faculty and in unrivaled library and laboratory resources. Without disparaging the importance of such resources, it must be said that Kissinger, like many other graduate students, profited less from them and a good deal more from others that were considerably less tangible. Specifically, Kissinger profited from Harvard's institutional vanity and self-confidence; he profited from the near proximity of contemporaries who knew more about the subject than he did, or, even when they knew less, were prepared to argue with him about his conclusions; finally, he profited from an instructional system that did not require professors to pretend to know more than they did or to intervene where it made better sense for them to remain aloof. Kissinger's dissertation could not have been written in many other universities in America, not because the others lacked a library of the distinction of Harvard's, but because they had neither the tradition nor the self-assurance that permitted them to let many of their students run free.

This is precisely what Henry Kissinger did during his years as a graduate student at Harvard. It was during this period that he emerged from his self-imposed isolation. He began to meet a number of his contemporaries; he taught in one of the introductory social science courses; he organized the International Seminar and founded a quarterly journal, which he named *Confluence*. He was as conscientious a student as he had ever been. As soon as he found a professor to act technically as his "adviser," he was free to proceed. In a more conventionally organized department, questions might have been raised about the appropriateness of the subject Kissinger chose for his dissertation or about the research procedures that he intended to employ. Neither question was even bruited in the Government Department, which, in the early 1950s, was a loose confederation of several disparate disciplines, presided over by men who did not much interfere with what their colleagues consented to.

Kissinger had every reason to approve of an academic system that offered the possibilities of such independence. Yet from time to time he asked himself whether he had chosen the right profession. As an undergraduate he had thought seriously of going into either law or medicine; he had gone so far as to take premedical courses, believing that he might one day wish to apply to medical school. That prospect no longer beckoned, but law continued to have a fascination for him. He wondered whether a legal degree would not provide a scope for action that could never be hoped for with a doctorate in international relations. The life of the graduate student, as he looked about him, seemed fraught with difficulties; it was joyless, narrow, and seemingly removed from many of the things that most interested him. Was this a warning of what the academic profession held in store for him? Did he really care to spend the rest of his life in a university environment? Ought he to persist with his graduate studies in the Government Department? In the end, he decided to do so, in part because the prospect of a professorial career had a very special appeal for someone born in his circumstances in Germany, and also because he intuited, correctly, that he could mold his life as an American academic in ways that would permit him to live as he wished to.

These facts are important because they draw attention to certain of the salient characteristics of university life in Cambridge when Kissinger was enrolled as a graduate student. The formal instruction in international relations was minimal; the interest in Germany as a whole in the academic community was relatively restricted; Austria under the Habsburgs was virtually *terra incognita*. Kissinger was not bothered in the slightest by the absence of very great interest in his subject; it may even be argued that he was helped by the general ignorance. Very methodically, he went through all the published primary sources that had to do with Metternich and Castlereagh. In the beginning, he expressed some doubts that the secondary literature on the subject would teach him very much. His friend and fellow graduate student, the late Klaus Epstein, whose immense erudition he admired and who read the whole of his manuscript, persuaded him that it was impossible to write about Metternich without reading the whole of the secondary literature; others persuaded him that the same was true for Castlereagh. He followed his friends' injunctions; in a very deliberate fashion he set about to read the major secondary works on his subject. When he came to prepare his annotated bibliography, he listed the hundred or more books that he had consulted; only a handful were the works of American scholars. The greatest number of these he found ephemeral; of one he wrote: "A well-written, occasionally brilliant book, but too thin for serious research"; of another he said: "Another trivial war effort, drawing the obvious comparisons between Britain's experiences with Hitler and with Napoleon." Was this, then, an early demonstration of Kissinger's reputed arrogance? Not at all. The American books were bad; others, written primarily by German and British scholars, when they were good, were praised. Was Kissinger thinking then of becoming *the* American expert on Metternichian diplomacy? Nothing could have interested him less. To carve out a scholarly domain, and then appropriate it against the claims of other rival scholars, had no great appeal for him.

Kissinger chose to write about Metternich and Castlereagh because he believed that he might educate himself through a study of their careers. In theory, any other graduate student in the Government Department might have selected the same subject and gone about studying it in much the same way. In fact, that was not likely. Kissinger's major resource was his intelligence; beyond that, however, he had another incontestable strength: he was prepared to experiment with a method that had not been tried. He knew that others thought sufficiently well of him to permit him to do what he wished. No one came forward to tell him that he had not consulted all of Castlereagh's papers. In a less self-confident and less self-sufficient academic environment, someone would have reminded Kissinger that Sir Charles Webster, before sitting down to write about Castlereagh, had ransacked the archives of London, Vienna, Berlin, Leningrad, Hanover, and Paris. Did Kissinger believe that he could approach his subject by simply using resources available in Widener Library? No one at Harvard insisted that Kissinger write a dissertation that would satisfy traditional scholarly canons. Or, to put the matter more accurately, Harvard's self-confidence permitted its professors to savor the delicious experience of believing that scholarly canons were precisely what they declared them to be.

Kissinger was given the freedom to roam. His work was largely unsupervised. No one pressed him to do it in a particular fashion or to hasten its completion. No one pretended that it would alter earlier interpretations of the subject, and that the more traditional analyses would be displaced. Kissinger was left to work out his intellectual problem in precisely the manner he thought appropriate. In the end, he was writing mostly for himself. There was no one waiting for the book to roll off the presses; no one pretended that it would cause a great stir. It is difficult to imagine a set of circumstances more auspicious for a young man whose purpose in writing was principally to instruct himself.

What, then, had Kissinger learned? Many things, and almost all of them had some relevance to the contemporary world. Kissinger started with an exploration of how peace might be secured. Persuaded that peace could not be made the *objective* of foreign policy, he argued that it was the bonus that followed from a properly conceived and intelligently executed policy. He was not being ironical when he opened his book with the observation that "those ages which in retrospect seem most peaceful were least in search of peace." In any international system where peace was the primary objective, Kissinger wrote, every state within the system was at the mercy of the most ruthless, since there was a maximum incentive to mollify the most aggressive state and to accept its demands, even when they were unreasonable. Such situations could only produce massive instability and insecurity.

Since the object of an international system, according to Kissinger, was stability, the problem was to devise methods to achieve it. In Kissinger's mind, stability depended on there being "a generally accepted legitimacy," an international agreement "about the nature of workable arrangements and about the permissible aims and methods of foreign policy." Kissinger developed a distinction that he never abandoned in any of his later writings; he contrasted two types of international orders: he called one "legitimate," the other "revolutionary." They were very distinct categories for him; the statesman who confused one with the other, or imagined himself to be living in one when he was living in the other, would certainly commit diplomatic blunders. Kissinger acknowledged that war might occur in a legitimate order; he insisted, however, that such war would be limited, and that diplomacy would be an option. His definition of diplomacy was simple: "the adjustment of differences through negotiation." States that accepted a particular international order as legitimate were in a position to negotiate their differences. When, however, a state maintained that the international order was illegitimate, diplomacy was excluded. Such a state was revolutionary; in challenging the established international order, it was asking, in effect, for the existing order to be set aside and for another to be put in its place.

In theory, Kissinger was writing about problems that confronted European statesmen early in the nineteenth century; in fact, he was probing the nature of the international system of the mid-twentieth century. Together with many others, he was asking whether the Soviet Union should be viewed as a "revolutionary" power. That, for Kissinger, was the one question that could not be safely ignored. Did the Soviet Union accept the "legitimacy" of the existing international system or did it hope to replace that system? Kissinger had little sympathy for those who justified Soviet behavior by pointing to the unhappy experiences of the 1920s and 1930s, which had made their leaders suspicious and insecure, and which now called for sympathy and understanding. Without even alluding to those who argued, for example, that Russia's preoccupation with defensible frontiers reflected its tragic history in the period after the Russian Revolution, Kissinger explained that feelings of insecurity were inevitable in any international order made up of independent states. Insecurity, he explained, was as endemic to a state system as mortality was to a human system. It was in the nature of things for states to feel threatened; there was nothing unusual in this. What interested him, however, and what he believed to be significant, was the refusal of certain states to be reassured. Their demand was for "absolute security"; in Kissinger's mind, an untenable demand. A state that insisted on "absolute security" was a "revolutionary" state; were its demands to be satisfied, then every other state would be totally insecure.

Negotiation would be impossible in any international order that harbored a "revolutionary" state; diplomats might meet, but there was little likelihood of meaningful agreements being reached. In effect, Kissinger implied, diplomats would be speaking different languages. Non-revolutionary states, however, found it difficult to admit this; they preferred to believe, Kissinger wrote, that they could get along with "revolutionary" states. All that was required was "good faith" and a "willingness to come to an agreement." They would not accept the impasse for what it was; they wanted to believe that the "revolutionary" state was simply exaggerating its position so that it might achieve certain tactical gains. Confident that limited concessions would in time produce a "thaw," which would contribute to a willingness to discuss fundamental issues, they insisted that the end result would be agreement. Non-revolutionary states, Kissinger wrote, found it hard to accept the proposition that other states could have "unlimited objectives," and that these objectives were non-negotiable. The idea that "revolutionary" states had no interest in adjudicating differences—that their principal purpose, in fact, was to subvert loyalties—was difficult for a non-revolutionary state to accept. When an international system included a "revolutionary" state, and when that state was powerful, Kissinger explained, an arms race or war was the general result.

Reflecting on the Napoleonic Empire as it appeared in the year 1812, Kissinger saw that it had successfully destroyed earlier European concepts of legitimacy but that its own survival was not assured. As he explained, its success depended on its capacity to impose its will on peoples who had been militarily defeated. What happened, however, if those people did not accept their defeat as final? It was not a foregone conclusion that Europe would permit itself to be organized through force. How, then, would it be organized? In Kissinger's view, two men—Metternich and Castlereagh—provided the principles that eventually created the new European equilibrium. Kissinger did not suggest that the achievement depended simply on the intuitive powers of these men. For their conceptions to gain acceptance, it was important that they be tailored to the needs of their own countries. Those needs were not identical. In any international system—as in any alliance—divergent needs had to be compromised. Great Britain and Austria were very different kinds of states. Kissinger was led to develop another of his fundamental distinctions—between what he called an "island" power and a "continental" power.

Great Britain was the island power; Austria was the continental power. This was more than a matter of geography; Kissinger saw two distinct mentalities; each perceived foreign policy issues in a very different way. Although Kissinger was reluctant to speak of the twentieth century in a book that pretended to treat only the nineteenth, there was a clear implication that the United States, at least until the early 1950s, was the island power. Its definition of security had to be different from that of a continental power. So, also, in the nineteenth century, as between Castlereagh and Metternich, there could never be a complete meeting of minds. Their interests were fundamentally incompatible. It was impossible that either one would liberate himself sufficiently of his preconceptions to adopt those of the other; nor was it at all clear that to do so would contribute to the creation of a stable international order.

Castlereagh fashioned a policy suited to the needs of an island power. Great Britain, because of basic geographic factors, considered itself endangered only when overt aggression occurred, when the threat of the whole Continent's falling under the influence of a single individual could be adduced. Austria, because of its geographic situation in the heart of Europe, could not afford to take so sanguine a view of incidents that might in time affect its security. It dared not wait for aggression to take place; its permanent interest was to forestall upheavals. While Kissinger thought geography to be significant in determining a state's image of itself, he refused to see it as the only important factor. In his view, the domestic structure and the internal politics of a state were no less important. The statesman who ignored the internal weaknesses of his society or exaggerated its strengths, whether measured by the determination of the people or their unity, neglected the rudiments of his political profession.

Great Britain, the island power, was absolutely secure in its constitution; ideological currents across the Channel, however powerful, could not possibly threaten that constitution. Austria, one of the great feudal survivals, was a polyglot kingdom, harboring many nationalities at different levels of civilization. Its domestic institutions were fragile; in a time of growing nationalism, the existence of the Austrian Empire seemed an offense to all who believed nationalism to be the wave of the future. Austria, acutely aware of its vulnerability, did not dare allow social unrest to raise its head anywhere. A conflagration, once started, might not easily be controlled. Kissinger raised the question of how two states with such diametrically opposed interests could be persuaded to subordinate their differences in favor of a common policy. Britain, because of its own geography and stable political structure, was being reasonable when it insisted on a policy of "non-interference" in the internal affairs of other states; its own security was so absolute that it saw no need for a guarantee that other states would preserve a particular political complexion. Austria had no such advantage; its security was immediately affected by events that occurred elsewhere; it made sense for Austria to argue for a "generalized right of interference." Two quite distinct national interests—each comprehensible and reasonable—were not easily joined; Kissinger showed, however, how the two came eventually to be compromised.

Kissinger was certain of one thing: the stable international order that Metternich and Castlereagh imposed on Europe created conditions that allowed for a century of peace. He thought that to be no mean achievement, but it did not prevent him from recognizing the price exacted for the advantage Europe came to enjoy. In the nineteenth century, Kissinger wrote, Europeans came to believe that they were in a position to enjoy every benefit—material prosperity, disarmament, and permanent peace. This, he said, was a "millennial faith"; it had no great appeal for him, particularly when he reflected that the end of the "age of innocence" was World War I, a conflict of unparalleled brutality and destructiveness.

Kissinger, in sounding this tragic note, and in suggesting that the individual, even as he realized his ambitions, only lost what he aspired to, expressed himself in an idiom that was to become increasingly common in all his writings. Kissinger was not in any sense a student of the classics. His works, however, came to be filled with references to Greek tragedy; a number of images, borrowed from Greek texts, constantly recurred. He saw man often achieving what he set out to accomplish, only to find in the end that the accomplishment was empty. Metternich, on one level, achieved the kind of victory that any Austrian leader would have prized. His success guaranteed the survival of the Empire for a season; ultimately, it also contributed to the Empire's demise. Kissinger made the same judgment some years later when he came to write about Bismarck. There were no permanent victories in human affairs.

Given his view of the nature of human experience, and his insistence on the importance of leadership, Kissinger's analyses of individual leaders were generally complex, filled with nuance. Occasionally, as with Metternich, they were also ambiguous, intentionally so. Kissinger portrayed Metternich as the quintessential eighteenth-century man—cool and cultivated, rational and clever. He saw him as "a Rococo figure, complex, finely carved, all surface, like an intricately cut prism." Kissinger wrote: "His face was delicate but without depth, his conversation brilliant but without ultimate seriousness. Equally at home in the Salon and in the Cabinet, graceful and facile, he was the *beau ideal* of the eighteenth-century aristocracy which justified itself not by its truth but by its existence. And if he never came to terms with the new age it was not because he failed to understand its seriousness but because he disdained it. Therein too his fate was the fate of Austria." For those who imagine that Metternich was Kissinger's own *beau ideal*, passages of this sort ought to inspire caution. Kissinger wrote of the "methods of almost nonchalant manipulation that he [Metternich] had learned in his youth," and expatiated on his deviousness and guile. He was a man born too late who felt only contempt for the tawdry civilization in which he was obliged to live out his days. Given Austria's desperate situation, he did what he could to preserve the state, but in the end he failed. His failure, in Kissinger's mind, was linked to his success. While he had been able to stem the tide, he was powerless to avert the final catastrophe. He did not understand the need to accommodate Austria to new forces in the world. He imagined, wrongly, that the international system could be permanently accommodated to Austria's needs.

Kissinger admired Metternich's intelligence; he was impressed with his skills as a negotiator; he realized that neither could guarantee the future security of the Austrian Empire. What, in Kissinger's mind, were Metternich's strengths? First, he was a realist; those who opposed him were almost all visionaries. Second, he aspired to be a statesman; he had a precise notion of what statesmanship consisted of; in Metternich's mind, it involved understanding the "science of the interests of states." That science, like any other, had its laws; they were discoverable and governed the international universe in much the same way that physical laws governed the natural universe. Such an idea was entirely congenial to someone who looked on the universe with eighteenth-century eyes. Metternich was much hated in his time; not everyone, Kissinger explained, took kindly to either his "smug self-satisfaction" or to his "rigid conservatism." That did not detract, however, from his remarkable diplomatic capabilities, which, according to Kissinger, were of a high, though not perhaps of the highest, order. Kissinger saw Metternich's genius as being "instrumental" rather than "creative"; in short, "he excelled at manipulation, not construction." His eighteenth-century bias imposed other limitations; as Kissinger explained, "his rationalism frequently made him mistake a well-phrased manifesto for an accomplished action." Kissinger thought him a "mediocre strategist but a great tactician," and he particularly prized his "sensibility to nuance."

Metternich, in Kissinger's mind, had one profound insight; he knew Napoleon to be a "revolutionary," and realized that it was impossible to satisfy such a national leader. Nothing—neither compromise, concession, nor alliance—would satiate Napoleon's hunger. Metternich acknowledged that Napoleon might, through the use of force, succeed one day in conquering the world. He did not believe that he would ever succeed in holding it. Metternich never underestimated his adversary, but this did not lead him to believe that Napoleon's victories would be permanent. Metternich's major interest, Kissinger wrote, was to devise a policy that would guarantee Austria's survival. Nothing less than that was at stake.

Believing that Napoleon could not be bought off—that no alliance with France would serve to protect Austria's integrity—Metternich set out on a course that was intended to achieve two results: the defeat of Napoleonic France and the survival of Imperial Austria. Few Europeans would have thought such an outcome to be possible. In their minds, France represented power and the future; Austria, by comparison, seemed weak and anachronistic. Metternich accepted the fact that France and Austria represented antithetical forces in the Europe of his time; it was not probable that both could survive. Metternich concluded, therefore, that Napoleon would have to go. How, then, was he to achieve that feat? Through cunning, patience, and manipulation. Austria needed to assume the lead in organizing an alliance against France, and had to do this surreptitiously and carefully. A false step that raised Napoleon's suspicions would almost certainly cause the edifice to collapse. A master diplomat was called for; one who knew the art of handling many different negotiations simultaneously. He had to know Napoleon's mind, and neither underestimate nor exaggerate its qualities. Finally, and perhaps most important, the operation required a legitimating principle: Metternich discovered that principle in the concept of *peace*.

According to Kissinger, the operation was hazardous, but Metternich was more than equal to it. Recognizing that the fundamental weakness of the Napoleonic Empire was the absence of a guaranteed legitimate succession, and knowing Napoleon's anxiety to repair that deficiency, Metternich conceived of the supreme service that his own Emperor could make to the Emperor of the French. A marriage between Napoleon and the daughter of the Holy Roman Emperor would finally legitimize the Corsican *parvenu;* Metternich hastened to prepare all the arrangements for the happy event. In reflecting on the negotiations that led to the royal betrothal in 1810, Kissinger saw the irony of the situation. Just as many of Napoleon's enemies refused to believe that the French Emperor's policy was one of "unlimited objectives," preferring to see him as an eighteenth-century ruler who could be reasoned with, and just as this had led to their continuous defeats, so, now, Napoleon totally misconstrued the nature of dynastic relations. He believed that marriage with the daughter of the Austrian Emperor gave him certain guarantees in respect to Austria's policy. Nothing could have been further from the truth, particularly at a time when someone like Metternich controlled Austria's foreign policy.

Metternich knew in 1812 that Napoleon was planning an invasion of Russia. How would Austria respond? According to Kissinger, there were only three options: alliance with Russia, alliance with France, a policy of armed neutrality. Each option carried substantial dangers. Russia was a highly unstable partner; she had betrayed her Austrian ally on at least one previous occasion. Why should Austria risk a repetition of that experience? Besides, to become the ally of Russia was to invite a French attack on Austria, with possibly catastrophic results. Alliance with France carried other no less considerable risks; Austria's moral position in Europe would be jeopardized; though the policy might serve Austria's self-interest, it would never win the approval of the rest of Europe. As for armed neutrality, that policy could prove immensely expensive. Required to choose, Metternich opted for a limited alliance with Napoleon. Kissinger was only too well aware of the moral ambiguities of Metternich's choice, but he knew that it served Austria's interest. Among other things, it meant that Austria was spared the danger of a French invasion; also, she was spared the necessity of having to arm herself. Napoleon, anxious to have Austrian support, agreed to supply an Austrian auxiliary corps of 30,000 men. In return for a minimal engagement, Austria was promised very substantial advantages, including the promise of territorial gains when Napoleon defeated Russia.

If Napoleon succeeded, there would be no risk to Austria. If he failed, Russia could be expected to press Austria to abandon her alliance and join a general European coalition against Napoleon. Whatever happened, Austria stood to gain. In fact, it was the second scenario that came to be played. Almost as soon as the news of the French debacle in Russia reached Vienna, the first of several initiatives came from St. Petersburg; the Tsar urged Austria to abandon the French alliance and join the Allies in making war on Napoleon. Metternich refused even to entertain that possibility; he explained to the Russians that a state "whose very existence depended on the recognition of the sanctity of treaty relations could not simply break an alliance." Metternich had no desire to see Napoleon defeated in the name of nationalism. A multi-national state like Austria could not survive if legitimacy came to be associated principally with the idea of national self-determination. If Austria was to join a coalition formed against Napoleon, it had to join that coalition on terms that took account of its own principles.

Kissinger, surveying Metternich's policies, found them "deliberate and cunning." While they were scarcely understood by others, Metternich knew what he was doing. But the risks were enormous; "one wrong move," Kissinger wrote, "might mean disaster and loss of confidence might spell isolation." Metternich was trying to organize an alliance based on principles acceptable to Austria. To do this, Austria had to appear a neutral in the European struggle, interested only in the restoration of peace. In the end, Metternich accomplished what he set out to do; Austria, in Kissinger's words, "attained the Supreme Command of the Alliance . . . deflected the war from its territories . . . based the Coalition on the Cabinets and not on the peoples and thereby . . . assured a peace, the legitimization of which was consistent with her continued existence." Of all this, Kissinger wrote: "It was not heroic, but it saved an empire."

How did Metternich manage to do this? His first problem was to slip out of the position of being France's ally and to become a neutral; he hoped to use his position as a neutral to establish his credentials as a mediator, and, ultimately, to emerge as the peace-maker. His purpose was to negotiate between Napoleon and his enemies. This had to be done in such a way that Napoleon would never be able to say that Austria had broken its pledges or had betrayed its alliance with him. Behind the façade of peace-making, Metternich had another purpose—to lay the basis for a new coalition against Napoleon, which would satisfy Austria's internal needs.

In insisting on this last point, Kissinger introduced a theme that was to be central in all his later writing. The foreign policy of a state, Kissinger believed, had always to take account of its domestic structure. Austria's foreign policy had to be specific to itself; as a multi-national state, where sovereignty did not reside in the people and where the principle of national self-determination was suspect, the most urgent need was for an international order that respected the rights of a state like Austria to survive. Metternich knew that Austria could never survive as a nation; there was no Austrian nation. The international order had to take account of the legitimating principles that made a state like Austria possible.

The problems for Britain were totally different. In comparing Castlereagh with Metternich, Kissinger cared less about the personal idiosyncrasies of either and more about the foreign policy options that two such very different states could choose from. The fact that Castlereagh was solid, ponderous, and pragmatic, while Metternich, in Kissinger's mind, appeared as elegant, facile, and rationalist, was much less significant than the fact that one had to consult the interests of an island power while the other had to develop a policy appropriate to the interests of a multi-national continental state. Earlier British policy had led to the country's becoming isolated; Kissinger wrote of "the ordeal of a decade of isolation," and suggested that the country had no wish to repeat that experience. That, however, did not alter the fact that the Channel was a true defense; continental wars did not touch London in the way that they affected Vienna. Also, Kissinger explained, Britain's parliamentary constitutionalism was not endangered by the prevailing revolutionary ideology in anything like the way that Austria's multi-national monarchy was threatened. The legitimacy of the Austrian state—its survival—was challenged by a doctrine that claimed that only states based on nationality were legitimate. When Great Britain joined a coalition to fight France, her concern was not with a revolutionary doctrine, which she cared very little about, but with Napoleon's very concrete aspirations to universal rule. British statesmen, unalterably opposed to any arrangement that allowed the Continent to be controlled by a single state, believed traditionally that such control would jeopardize their own security. The British nightmare, Kissinger explained, was a peace that excluded Britain from the Continent. The continental nightmare took a very different form; it was "permanent revolution."

In theory, both Metternich and Castlereagh were opposed to revolution; in fact, they saw revolution from quite different perspectives. Castlereagh, as the spokesman of an insular power predominantly concerned with devising methods to protect Europe against future military aggression, wished above all to act as a mediator. Despite the general characterization of Castlereagh by liberal historians and critics as a die-hard conservative, Kissinger thought him a man of moderation who worked diligently to defeat any proposal that implied a concern with vengeance. The British were dogmatic and unyielding on only one issue: they would not compromise their maritime rights, which they thought to be essential to their security. They hoped that British intervention on the Continent would be a rare event, occurring only in response to some extraordinary emergency. When and if such a danger did exist, they wanted Britain to intervene with substantial force; otherwise, Britain ought to stay free of continental squabbles. Such a doctrine, Kissinger wrote, was entirely suited to an island mentality.

So long as the principal problem was to defeat Napoleon, the full extent of the gulf that separated Castlereagh's vision of the future from that of Metternich was not apparent. Metternich's purposes sometimes seemed mysterious to Castlereagh, who prided himself on his reputation for "plain dealing," but the fact that the two viewed the world from fundamentally different perspectives was not generally recognized. Metternich was involved in highly complex maneuvers that few in Europe divined. In public, he continued to speak of the necessity of peace; behind the scenes, he tried to persuade the Austrian Emperor of the need to create a powerful Austrian army. Metternich understood exactly what he needed to do to influence his own Emperor. His greatest gift, however, according to Kissinger, was not that he knew how to treat with his own Emperor, a simple but stubborn man of modest endowments, but that he knew how to deal with Napoleon. Metternich never made the mistake of other of Napoleon's enemies in underestimating the enormity of his goals. Napoleon had known how to exploit the shortsightedness of others; he had no opportunity to do this with Metternich, who entertained no illusions about his intentions. Metternich was not at all awed by the French Emperor; he believed that he could be defeated through diplomacy. There was some irony in the situation; Napoleon had conquered because he had fought by rules that his adversaries thought to be impossible. Metternich now compassed the defeat of Napoleon by diplomatic maneuvers that Napoleon did not even recognize for what they were.

By insisting that his only purpose was to serve as a mediator, and that his only interest was peace, Metternich succeeded in allaying Napoleon's suspicions. The French Emperor believed in Austria's sincerity; it seemed inconceivable to him that a father would choose to make war on the husband of his daughter. Napoleon clearly knew very little about the habits of kings. The more serious error, however, was Napoleon's failure to perceive the likely consequences of a new war with the Allies. According to Kissinger, Napoleon lived with three illusions: first, that he would quickly defeat the Alliance and that this would bring about a rapid disintegration of the coalition; second, that he could have peace with Russia at any time he chose; finally, that while he could not count absolutely on Austrian assistance, there was a good prospect of the Austrians' remaining neutral. Napoleon was mistaken on all three counts. Metternich, faithful to his pose of being simply a mediator, continued to press an armistice on all the belligerents. No one of them entirely understood his game. The Austrian Emperor was himself only partially aware of what Metternich intended; the Allies, even less informed, were suspicious. If they agreed to an armistice in the end, it was mostly because they believed they might gain from a respite. Having succeeded to that point, Metternich pressed on; he came forward with an offer of peace terms that he called reasonable. The Allies resisted; they argued that Metternich's terms scarcely provided the security they had been fighting for. They wanted to ask for better terms, having no comprehension of the game Metternich was playing. He believed that Napoleon would reject *any* terms. Therefore, there was no danger in offering him terms that were generous. Napoleon would certainly spurn the offer, and this would prove his intransigence. Metternich knew what he was doing; as Kissinger explained, while "the Allies were stating conditions of peace," he was "elaborating a cause of war."

Kissinger used the episode to illustrate a theory that he thought had relevance to negotiations more generally. His interest was not only in a tactic once used by Metternich against Napoleon. Kissinger was contrasting negotiations that proceeded in a stable international order, where all states accepted the same rules, and negotiations involving a revolutionary power whose principal interest was to change the rules. In a stable international order, Kissinger implied, where agreement could be expected, it made sense to put forward maximum demands; these would certainly be pared down in the course of negotiations. When, however, the adversary was a revolutionary state, and one knew that the prospects of agreement were minimal, it made sense to offer modest terms. These would almost certainly be rejected, and the state offering such terms would be credited in the international community with moderation. Kissinger was saying that in a stable international order demands were made seriously, in the expectation that they would be negotiated. Where a revolutionary state was involved, demands were made principally for psychological reasons. One did not expect them to be taken seriously.

Kissinger recognized that there was some risk in what Metternich did. Had Napoleon been genuinely flexible, had he seen the game that Metternich was playing, he might have seized on the terms and agreed to them. Metternich had no reason to worry; as Kissinger explained, the idea that there is ever "perfect flexibility in diplomacy is the illusion of amateurs." For Napoleon to have acted other than he did, Kissinger wrote, would have meant that he had ceased to be Napoleon. Metternich's demand was not simply for the cession of specific territories; he was asking Napoleon to desist from supporting revolutionary policies. Napoleon could never agree to that. In the end, Napoleon was destroyed, Kissinger wrote, because he could not recognize limits. He made every mistake that Metternich expected him to make.

Metternich accomplished his objective; he showed that Napoleon's purpose was war, not peace, and that even the most favorable terms would not tempt him. A new Allied coalition was formed against Napoleon; Austria, originally France's ally, became France's enemy, and the whole operation was conducted with such consummate skill that not even Napoleon could claim that Austria had violated its treaty commitments. That, in Kissinger's mind, was no small achievement. Metternich's next problem was to know how to treat with his new allies.

The Tsar wanted the war against Napoleon to be a war of national liberation. Austria did not favor such a war; Metternich insisted, in Kissinger's words, that it be a "cabinet war for the equilibrium." This was the only kind of war that coincided with Austria's interests. Kissinger wrote: "Philosophers may quarrel with the moral stature of this policy, but statesmen can study it with profit." A multi-national state like Austria could not fight a national war; a financially exhausted state like Austria could not fight a long war. Because Austria's survival depended "on a recognition of limits, on the sanctity of treaties, on legitimacy," Metternich insisted on an alliance policy that placed none of these things in jeopardy. Lacking a firm popular base, the Austrian state could only depend on diplomacy for its survival. Metternich chose the only weapon that was available to him. He used it well.

Kissinger refused to believe that a state was capable of pursuing *any* policy, and that the choice depended simply on the will of individual leaders. Austria, in fact, had remarkably few options; no state was ever likely to have very many. Diplomatic skill was shown in the capacity to choose well between the few available options. As a multi-national state trying to survive in an age of nationalism, Austrian statesmen knew that they could never rely on public opinion for support. Diplomacy was Austria's appropriate arm, but not everyone knew how to use diplomacy. Metternich did; carefully preparing his moves, knowing his purposes before he set out to achieve them, he sought the widest possible moral consensus. He succeeded in correctly estimating the intentions of his adversary; he knew how to treat with his allies; he was able to achieve the extraordinary feat of identifying "the domestic legitimizing principle of Austria with that of the international order." He imposed on the international system a set of principles congenial to Austria.

While the new coalition was being formed, Austria, in a very calculated fashion, excluded Britain from any major role in the negotiations. This served only to increase Britain's suspicion of Austria. Metternich was well aware of what he was doing. He did not believe that Britain would understand or support Austria's quest for moderate peace terms. Had Britain intervened, she would probably have spoiled Metternich's game. It was better to leave her out; Kissinger wrote: "A power which has never suffered disaster finds it difficult to comprehend a policy conducted with a premonition of catastrophe. The attempt of a less favored ally to hedge its risks cannot but appear to it as the outgrowth of a decadent cleverness." Britain would never have sympathized with what Austria was trying to accomplish. So far as the British were concerned, the political and military problems were simple. As Kissinger explained, the "island power," secure in its frontiers, simply asked that other states be less Machiavellian, and that they proceed to do what the military situation called for. Austria's obligations were clear— she ought to join the war at once, and make her contribution to pushing Napoleon from his imperial throne. Such a policy, Kissinger wrote, made eminently good sense for Britain; it made no sense at all for Austria. The British position, which was superficially so open, forthright, and decisive, in fact provided no important diplomatic options. As Kissinger explained, "a power which is absolutely committed has no negotiating position."

While Castlereagh deplored what he conceived to be Austria's "irresolution," Metternich showed all of his habitual shrewdness; he was already looking beyond the war to the peace that would one day be negotiated. While Metternich understood that Britain's only interest was to prevent a single power from dominating the Continent, he did not believe that Austria ought to be preoccupied with that problem to the exclusion of all others. He was already beginning to reflect on what Russia might do after the Allies were victorious. Castlereagh, with his eye fixed on the one enemy, Napoleon, believed that Europe's problems would come to an end with Napoleon's defeat. Metternich knew better; while he never forgot Napoleon, he showed himself exceedingly wary of Tsar Alexander. The prospect of Russian penetration deep into the heart of Europe filled Metternich with foreboding. If Russia took territories in Poland that Prussia hoped to have, the results could be dangerous for Austria. Thwarted in Eastern Europe, Prussia might conclude that it was in her interest to become a major power in Germany. Alternatively, deprived of defensible frontiers in the East, she might easily fall under the influence of Russia. Neither prospect filled Metternich with glee.

Castlereagh's foreign policy views, by contrast, were few and simple: the Continent had suffered terribly under Napoleon; its most ardent desire was to be liberated from the Napoleonic yoke. That could be achieved only through military victory. When Napoleon was defeated, Europe would again be peaceful. Castlereagh refused to believe that Russia (or any other Allied state) could aspire to other objectives. France, the disturber of the peace, had to be militarily quelled; that seemed to be more than a sufficient policy objective for Great Britain. Castlereagh thought that Russia was a "satisfied" power, and that the key to peace would be cooperation between Great Britain and Russia. Only after Castlereagh came to the Continent and began to be more knowledgeable about European politics did he begin to wonder whether the doctrine he expressed so confidently at Westminster was in fact true. Slowly, but very perceptibly, he began to moderate his views. The question which he found unsettling but could not avoid was whether it was not Austria, more than Russia, that had the greatest interest in restoring the European equilibrium. Castlereagh did not shed immediately certain of his residual suspicions concerning Austria, but the first seeds of doubt were planted. Meanwhile, many of his colleagues at home, who had sent him abroad because of their misgivings about Allied policy, remained as suspicious as ever. They were interested in only two things: that France be defeated and that Antwerp be awarded to a friendly power. They had no interest whatever in Italy, Germany, or Poland, distant places that posed no threat to a country protected by the English Channel.

Kissinger wrote of "the crisis of the coalition"; his chapter might have been subtitled "The Education of Castlereagh." Metternich had been the principal architect of the Alliance; it now fell to Castlereagh to defend the Alliance when success threatened its existence. When Castlereagh first came to the Continent, he acted as any one of a half dozen other British statesmen might have done; suddenly, he was required to do a good deal more. The seriousness of the choices that confronted him is suggested by Kissinger's remark that these tested him even more than "heroic persistence in adversity" would have done. Britain was being asked to "generate its own objectives," and not simply to react to those created by others. Kissinger wrote of Britain's being required to "fashion a new interpretation of reality." The "island power" was being forced into the world, and that was never a comfortable position. This was not what Britain had bargained for when she went to war against Napoleonic "tyranny," Kissinger was almost certainly reflecting on the United States in the twentieth century when he wrote in this way. He made his point even more explicit when he suggested that "island powers" generally refused to admit "that wars may be produced by intrinsic causes"; they wished to believe that wars originated in "the malice of wicked men." The concept of a "power with no unsatisfied claims" was highly congenial to the insular mentality. It provided the final justification for converting wars into "crusades" so that the wicked influences that had caused them in the first instance might be chastised.

When Castlereagh left London, his colleagues were interested in only one thing—the defeat of Napoleon and his replacement by the legitimate king, Louis XVIII. Castlereagh himself harbored another wish—

that he might serve as a mediator between the squabbling Allies. Kissinger could not restrain his irony when he wrote: "If the war had been caused by bad faith, good will was to provide the remedy." It all seemed very easy; it was not to prove so. Allied unity had been relatively easy to achieve when Napoleon was strong; it was not easy to maintain when Napoleon was faltering and every state looked only to its own future. As Kissinger explained, when an enemy was so weakened that every state imagined it could stand alone, a coalition was at the mercy of its most determined member. A year earlier, when Austria's armies had been essential to the coalition, Metternich's diplomatic abilities were universally praised; that situation no longer existed. The Tsar believed that he could defeat the French armies singlehandedly; Austrian collaboration no longer seemed so necessary to him. He considered talk of a negotiated peace with Napoleon to be treasonable; there was only one way to bring the French Emperor down, the Tsar argued, and that was to defeat him in battle. Alexander, according to Kissinger, had captured the legitimating principle that went under the name of "the common effort." The Tsar spoke in an idiom that had vast appeal; as Kissinger explained, "war has its own legitimacy and it is victory, not peace." When Metternich argued for one more effort at negotiation, he only provoked suspicion. Few were prepared to applaud what seemed to them to be an inexplicable and strange timidity. Kissinger said: "Moderation in an hour of triumph is appreciated only by posterity, rarely by contemporaries to whom it tends to appear as a needless surrender."

Metternich's fine distinctions were not likely to have very great appeal for the British. Yet, as Kissinger pointed out, the distinctions he insisted on went to the heart of the matter. Metternich and Alexander were bickering over *the* fundamental issue: the conditions of a stable international order. The Tsar believed that if the war could be converted into a moral crusade against Napoleon, and if the Allies remained loyal to each other, there were no other problems. Metternich recognized that these were not sufficient guarantees of a stable order. He insisted on an explicit statement of war aims, arguing that such a statement would serve to guarantee the new equilibrium, and he opposed Alexander's candidate for the French throne, the Prince Royal of Sweden, the former Marshal Bernadotte.

Given these differences, and given the weakened condition of Napoleon, it was questionable whether the Alliance would be able to hold together at all. Fear of the French Emperor no longer served as a unifying force, and there was no other to take its place. A great deal depended on Castlereagh; if he conceived Great Britain's interests narrowly, and thought only as many of his colleagues did in the House of Commons, the possibility of Russia's becoming a predominant power on the Continent was very real. If he took a broad view of Britain's interests, and decided to strengthen Metternich's hands, in Kissinger's view, he would greatly improve the chances of a stable equilibrium being realized in Europe. Castlereagh and Metternich met several times privately to discuss the future of the coalition. The conversations showed substantial differences between the two, but each knew how much he depended on the other, and each began to think of the wisdom of making a number of concessions to the other. While Castlereagh clearly preferred a Bourbon restoration, believing that this would create the maximum security against renewed upheaval in France, he was prepared to support Metternich in his plan to make one final approach to Napoleon.

These negotiations proved futile. Napoleon never understood what concessions were required at a particular moment; when the military situation favored him, he tended to make impossible demands; when it went against him, he showed some interest in accommodating himself to the wishes of the Allies, but found, not surprisingly, less interest on the other side. Alexander, during the whole period, made it perfectly clear that nothing would satisfy him except a successful military campaign that brought Napoleon to his knees, with the Russian armies entering Paris in triumph. Alexander's insistence on the need for total victory almost caused the Alliance to break up. Austria, in Kissinger's words, was unwilling to accept "a march into infinity." Metternich worried about the vacuum in power that such a policy would produce, but even more that the war would end in revolution, the one result he was absolutely determined to avoid. Kissinger wrote: "Austria was more afraid of the open road to Paris than of Napoleon's army."

Metternich realized that he had no option but to try to isolate Russia within the Alliance. That policy called for great diplomatic skill. Metternich planned his actions as carefully as he had done when he established his credentials as a mediator, expecting the mediation to fail. He asked the Tsar for a statement of his war aims. Alexander replied that he intended to take Paris, summon an assembly of notables, and ask them to choose the future ruler of France. Alexander claimed to be unconcerned with whether the assembly chose one candidate rather than another. He intended to appoint a Russian governor to rule Paris, and the governor was to be made responsible for supervising the elections. The Tsar thought these terms reasonable, given the military effort that the Russians had made in the war against Napoleon. Kissinger's comment was: "The Tsar was proposing nothing less than to be appointed arbiter of the fate of Europe."

Metternich had no intention of approving such an "appointment." The war had not been fought to give France a new government; its object, in his view, had been to restore the international equilibrium. Metternich had no interest in consulting the French people; he thought the issue was a dynastic one, and he objected to the idea that a government acquired its legitimacy through popular approval. Were that standard to become universal, the House of Habsburg would not survive for a day. He made it clear to Castlereagh that Austria was prepared to leave the coalition and make a separate peace if Alexander was not restrained. Castlereagh's position was difficult; if he did nothing, he risked seeing Austria withdraw from the coalition; if he pressed Alexander to accept Metternich's terms, he risked offending the Tsar. The second hazard seemed to be the lesser one. Castlereagh agreed to press the Tsar to obtain an armistice on the basis of an agreement that would restore the pre-war boundaries, the so-called "ancient limits."

In the end, Austria agreed that Russia might continue her military advance on Paris, but only under certain conditions. Kissinger suggested that these negotiations were immensely important; in his words, they ended "the halcyon days of hope when protestations of eternal friendship were taken as the guarantee of eternal stability." More than that, Kissinger wrote, they led to the "recognition that the problems of peace, although less exhilarating than those of war, have their own logic and that they alone justify the suffering of nations." The most important result, Kissinger said, was that "the Allies had lost their illusions, the most painful crisis in the life of men as well as of nations, and [had] survived."

Any reasonable man would have realized that the time had come to make peace. Napoleon, having achieved his legitimacy through charisma and force, could not believe that his misfortunes were caused by his own inadequacies. He much preferred to believe that they were caused by the malice of others. Napoleon, in Kissinger's mind, was defeated by his own stubborn pride. Metternich tried desperately to control the situation and to save Napoleon; he was unable to do so. Kissinger wrote: ". . . while Napoleon was experiencing the boundaries of power, Metternich was learning the limits of manipulation, that spirits once called forth cannot be banished by an act of will. Metternich had never intended more than the limitation of Napoleon's power, if only because the overthrow of *any* dynasty was a dangerous symbol for Austria. Because he needed a strong France, Metternich now attempted to reverse the fate of which he had himself been the agent, to demand of Napoleon what he must have known was impossible, the recognition of limits. And just as in Greek tragedy the warning of the oracle does not suffice to avert the doom because salvation resides not in knowledge but in acceptance, so now Napoleon disregarded Metternich's entreaties, not because he failed to understand their arguments but because he disdained them." A revolutionary, according to Kissinger, "finds it easier to destroy himself than to surrender." Metternich made one final effort; "like an exasperated professor," Kissinger wrote, he sought to bring Napoleon back to a sense of reality.

He failed. He could not have succeeded. Metternich was appealing to the one sense that revolutionaries lack—a sense of reality.

The drama played itself out; when Alexander entered Paris in triumph, Metternich and Castlereagh stayed behind in Dijon. They knew what they were doing; at the moment of "liberation," foreign armies of occupation might seem welcome; years later, men recalled only the humiliation they had suffered. Metternich's victory was no less great for his not being in Paris to celebrate it. Legitimacy had triumphed—both on the battlefield and in Paris. Alexander personified the victory, but Metternich had conceived it.

Kissinger, having written a historical narrative to the moment of the Allied victory, suddenly changed his style and set down certain general observations on the nature of war, peace, and peace-making. While, with one exception, all the references were to events of the Napoleonic era, Kissinger's comments lose much of their import if they are read simply as judgments on the past. Kissinger used his nineteenth-century case study to justify setting down a number of foreign policy maxims. There may be an advantage in enumerating them, though Kissinger himself chose not to do so. He said:

1. "Although every war is fought in the name of peace, there is a tendency to define peace as the absence of war and to confuse it with military victory."

2. "To discuss conditions of peace during wartime seems almost indecent, as if the admission that the war might end could cause a relaxation of the effort."

3. "The logic of war is power, and power has no inherent limit. The logic of peace is proportion, and proportion implies limitation."

4. "The success of war is victory; the success of peace is stability. The conditions of victory are commitment, the condition of stability is self-restraint."

5. "The motivation of war is extrinsic: the fear of an enemy. The motivation of peace is intrinsic: the balance of forces and the acceptance of its legitimacy."

6. "A war without an enemy is inconceivable; a peace built on the myth of an enemy is an armistice. It is the temptation of war to punish; it is the task of policy to construct. Power can sit in judgment, but statesmanship must look to the future."

7. "These incommensurabilities are the particular problems of peace settlements at the end of total wars. The enormity of suffering leads to a conception of war in personal terms, of the enemy as the 'cause' of the misfortune, of his defeat as the moment for retribution."

8. "The greater the suffering, the more the war will be conceived an end in itself and the rules of war applied to the peace settlement. The

more total the commitment, the more 'natural' unlimited claims will appear. Suffering leads to self-righteousness more often than to humility, as if it were a badge of good faith, as if only the 'innocent' could suffer."

9. "Each peace settlement is thus confronted with the fate of the enemy and with the more fundamental problem whether the experience of war has made it impossible to conceive of a world *without* an enemy."

10. "Whether the powers conclude a retrospective peace or one that considers the future depends on their social strength and on the degree to which they can generate their own motivation."

11. "A retrospective peace will crush the enemy so that he is *unable* to fight again; its opposite will deal with the enemy so that he does not *wish* to attack again."

12. "A retrospective peace is the expression of a rigid social order, clinging to the only certainty: the past. It will make a 'legitimate' settlement impossible, because the defeated nation, unless completely dismembered, will not accept its humiliation."

13. "There exist two legitimacies in such cases: the internal arrangements among the victorious powers and the claims of the defeated. Between the two, only force or the threat of force regulates relations."

14. "In its quest to achieve stability through safety, in its myth of the absence of intrinsic causes for war, a retrospective peace produces a revolutionary situation."

The men who negotiated the post-Napoleonic settlement, Kissinger wrote, avoided "the temptation of a punitive peace." Against those who criticized the Vienna settlement, and who dwelt on its "reactionary" features, Kissinger set his aim: the Vienna negotiators accomplished what any group of statesmen needed always to do. They succeeded in creating an international order that prevented general war for a century. Metternich aimed for "equilibrium and not retribution, legitimacy and not punishment." Castlereagh was singled out for special praise. Kissinger emphasized Castlereagh's insistence on moderation while his countrymen clamored for punishment and vengeance. The statesmen at Vienna were reasonable even with respect to Napoleon; Kissinger wrote: "The early nineteenth century was not yet a period which measured the extent of its triumph by the degree of personal retribution exacted."

No peace settlement, Kissinger explained, could totally satisfy any one party. If one state was totally satisfied, this meant that every other would be totally dissatisfied. Where a permanently disaffected state existed, there would always be an incentive to upset the established order. The object of negotiators had always to be the securing of a voluntary agreement by all the parties to abide by a specific accord and to undertake to work within its general boundaries. A "legitimate" international order existed when these conditions were met. Just as internal order implied a "preponderance of authority," so international order implied a "balance of forces."

Kissinger went out of his way to discount the common historical interpretation that gave Talleyrand principal credit for inventing the concept of "legitimacy," and that made the French Foreign Minister appear to have been the arbiter of Europe. Kissinger, believing that such accounts were vastly exaggerated, wrote: "It is a legend spread by those who confuse results and causes and by professional diplomats wont to ascribe to mere negotiating skill what can be achieved only through the exploitation of more deep-seated factors." The judgment is important because it reiterated Kissinger's insistence that diplomacy was not a game played by intelligent men but an activity that invariably reflected real forces that had to be brought together. "Legitimacy" was not a phrase invented by a luminous intelligence; it was a concept that expressed a power situation that existed, and that diplomats were able to use in their negotiations.

Kissinger believed that the hero of the Congress of Vienna—if such a term had any meaning at all—was Castlereagh. British opinion, inside and outside Parliament, was concerned with only one issue—France. No other foreign policy question exercised the nation. Because Castlereagh had come to understand that the future stability of the Continent depended on there being no serious rivalry between Austria and Prussia, which could only permit Russian influence to grow in the heart of Europe, with Holland being left defenseless, he arranged, through a series of complicated maneuvers, to prevent such rivalry from developing. Posterity, Kissinger wrote, insisted on seeing Vienna as a struggle between reform and reaction. Nothing, he said, was further from the truth. The statesmen at Vienna sought to replace the Napoleonic reliance on force with a set of international agreements that depended on a "sense of obligation." There had to be a "consensus on the nature of a just arrangement"; otherwise, there would be no possibility of a stable international order, which alone guaranteed peace.

Castlereagh, without a conspicuous historical example to guide him, and with a nation clamoring for vengeance against France, particularly after Napoleon's escape from Elba, stood firm in his belief that a punitive peace would never serve Britain's interests. Kissinger recounted all the military arguments that were used to justify a harsh peace; Castlereagh was moved by none of them. Kissinger admired his resolution, but also his intelligence in rejecting the military arguments. He made his own position very clear when he wrote: "And, as always in such periods, final recourse was had to military considerations, as if the military component of security had a morality of its own, as if the reliance on purely military considerations was not itself a symptom of the abdication of policy."

Castlereagh, acknowledging the serious opposition to his policies, wrote two memoranda to explain why the whole idea of "absolute security" was chimerical. To emphasize so totally the importance of physical security, Castlereagh said, was to lose all sense of the importance of moral considerations. While everything was being done to assemble physical force to restrain the defeated enemy, insufficient thought was given to how to maintain the resolution—the will—to make that force effective. Castlereagh insisted that foreign policy could not be conducted if every short-range shift in public opinion was given attention and respect. Kissinger thought that it was "a measure of Castlereagh's growth as a statesman that the most implacable foe of Napoleon, fifteen months earlier, should now emerge as the advocate of a peace of harmony." Castlereagh's differences were not only with his own countrymen but with members of the coalition itself; there were many in Europe who insisted on harsh terms. While certain concessions had to be made to these powerful advocates, the peace treaty that finally emerged was not vengeful. France did not become a permanently dissatisfied power, and Kissinger believed that Castlereagh deserved the major credit for that achievement. By Kissinger's own standards, it was no mean accomplishment.

If the Vienna settlement deserved praise, Kissinger had reservations about the machinery established to enforce it. Neither the Quadruple Alliance, largely Castlereagh's handiwork, nor the Holy Alliance, Alexander's romantic and mystical conception, achieved its intended purposes. Kissinger treated both as flawed mechanisms. He understood how Alexander had come to invent his Holy Alliance. What, however, had possessed Castlereagh to invent his plan for periodic congresses? Before he came to the Continent and became immersed in its affairs, Castlereagh's only interest was to secure a peace that would guarantee Europe against French aggression. That seemed to be the whole of his ambition. After some experience with the Continent, Castlereagh, in Kissinger's words, became "the victim of a temptation encountered by many statesmen of great Coalitions." He came to believe in the "mythology of Coalitions," which made the diplomacy leading up to the war seem "overly subtle, petty and a contributing cause to a climate of distrust." Worse still, Castlereagh had "come to see the unity of purpose inspired by a common enemy as the normal pattern of international relations"; he had forgotten how hard it had been to achieve unity among the Allies. Castlereagh wanted to believe that "confidential relationships" produced harmony; Kissinger suggested that they expressed harmony and did not produce it. Given his convictions, Castlereagh found it natural to urge the Allies to remain in intimate contact so that every question touching the security of Europe could be jointly considered. The "conference system," which was to exercise a certain authority in Europe over the next seven years, developed out of Castlereagh's vision. The British scarcely comprehended what Castlereagh had in mind; they imagined that his purpose was simply to fashion another instrument that would serve to keep France in check.

Kissinger's reservations about the Quadruple Alliance are perhaps most eloquently expressed when he explained that Castlereagh was not the only man in Paris "aiming at unattainable perfection." That also was Alexander's dream. There was, however, a substantial gulf that separated the pragmatic Castlereagh from the mystical Alexander. Kissinger had no interest in comparing the two. But he did recognize the utility of comparing two categories of men—those whom he called "prophets" and those whom he called "statesmen." Alexander clearly belonged to the first category; Metternich and Castlereagh to the second. What, then, were the major differences between them? Kissinger wrote: "The statesman lives in time; his test is the permanence of his structure under stress. The prophet lives in eternity which, by definition, has no temporal dimension; his test is inherent in his vision. The encounter between the two is always tragic, because the statesman must strive to reduce the prophet's vision to precise measures, while the prophet will judge the temporal structure by transcendental standards. To the statesman, the prophet represents a threat, because an assertion of absolute justice is a denial of nuance. To the prophet, the statesman represents a revolt against reality, because the attempt to reduce justice to the attainable is a triumph of the contingent over the universal. To the statesman, negotiation is the essence of stability, because it symbolizes the adjustment of conflicting claims and the recognition of legitimacy; to the prophet, it is the symbol of imperfection, of impure motives frustrating universal bliss."

Alexander achieved his aim; he imposed his Holy Alliance on the others. For him, it was a "transcendental happening." Metternich was not equally moved; he accepted the Holy Alliance as one more device that might be useful in maintaining the European equilibrium. The two alliances, Kissinger wrote, in the end destroyed their architects; Castlereagh failed because he sought to institutionalize an intuition that went beyond the experience of the British nation; Alexander failed because the international order could not sustain such a mystical construct.

Metternich was the one statesman who never dreamed of "reforming the ethos of his people." Kissinger thought this to be perhaps his greatest weakness. Aware of the rigidities of Austria, he did nothing to alter them; his principal accomplishment was to construct an international order that would accommodate Austria and leave its peculiar institutions untouched. He believed that the political struggle was over and that the social struggle was about to begin; he imagined that he could use the tactics he had employed against the political revolution to defeat the social revolution. He expected "to defeat his opponents not by constructiveness but by patience, not by transcending but by outlasting them." Metternich, the conservative, was trying desperately to learn how to navigate in the new revolutionary currents. Napoleon had been defeated, but the social revolution went on. When the social order was stable, Kissinger wrote, opposition to it could be ignored or assimilated. When, however, it was fragile, every shock registered. The essence of a revolutionary age, Kissinger said, was its "self-consciousness"; political life lost its spontaneity; the existing pattern of obligations was challenged. A stable order, Kissinger explained, was preoccupied with *duty;* a revolutionary period was preoccupied with *loyalty,* "where the act of submitting the will acquires a symbolic and even ritualistic significance, because alternatives seem ever present." The concept of loyalty, inevitably, became a means for achieving a group identity.

The conservative always found himself in a difficult position in a revolutionary age. Metternich would have preferred to remain silent; he felt compelled to answer and to act. His conservatism was different from that of Edmund Burke, who denounced revolution in the name of history. Metternich denounced revolution in the name of reason; revolution violated the structure of the universe. Metternich had little sympathy for those of his contemporaries who wasted their lives in constructing ideal constitutions. All states were subject to laws, Metternich insisted, and these were their true constitutions. No one, not even the king, had the right to transgress laws. Constitutional guarantees, Metternich argued, provided no protection against state power; only the self-restraint of those in positions of authority could give any meaningful protection. Metternich, according to Kissinger, met his revolutionary adversaries on their own ground; his appeal, like theirs, was to reason. This was what made their contest so bitter. The revolutionaries could not abide to see a conservative use rationalist philosophy for such nefarious ends.

Metternich's historical view was a mélange of the opinions of others; it owed a certain amount to Burke. He believed that revolution destroyed the "natural" balance between the forces of conservation and destruction. Until sometime in the sixteenth century, Metternich imagined, these forces had been in balance. The invention of printing, the development of gunpowder, and the discovery of America—these were the events that produced a major crisis in the West. The Reformation, in Metternich's mind, only served to complete the process; it overturned the moral system and exalted the individual over the forces of history. A new kind of man appeared in Europe—the revolutionary—the "presumptuous man," in Metternich's words. Kissinger recognized that what Metternich hoped to make preposterous through his use of irony others would find entirely acceptable.

Kissinger asked whether a spirit, held to be so widespread, with such deep roots, could possibly be defeated. If the middle class was as potent as

Metternich implied, how could it be bridled? Castlereagh and Burke
would have argued for cooptation; the middle class ought to be seduced
with power; that was not a remedy calculated to appeal to Metternich,
who much preferred to strengthen the forces of order—the conservative forces—which would then be used to beat down the forces of destruction. Metternich insisted that the defense of existing institutions,
whatever their defects, was in fact possible. He believed that the overthrow of any part of the established order would have great symbolic
importance, and that it could threaten the whole edifice. Therefore, every
part had to be protected.

Kissinger expressed the most serious reservations about Metternich's
wisdom in all of this. Those who have made Metternich Kissinger's nineteenth-century hero have been careless in their reading of his book. Writing of Metternich, Kissinger said: "It was a futile contest, a *tour de force*
leading to self-destruction, this effort to bring about change through order and to identify order with tranquility in the middle of a revolutionary
period. It was really, despite its protestations to the contrary, an effort to
recapture a lost innocence, a quest for a period when obligation was
spontaneous, an aristocratic notion of government as the reciprocal execu-
tion of duties. The 'Metternich system' answered the question of the
cause of revolution, but it gave no indication of how to cope with it once
it had occurred. It spoke abstractly of its readiness to reform but it never
discussed what specific measures it would consider appropriate. As late as
1851 Metternich could give no better advice to his successor, Schwarzen-
berg, than to strengthen the landed aristocracy, as if the middle class
could still be crushed. The assertion that revolutions were always the fault
of government, that only action could conserve, was unexceptionable.
But in practice it led to a vicious circle, because Metternich, although
not opposed to reform in principle, wanted it as an emanation of order,
while his opponents desired the same thing in the name of change. The result was a stalemate, a triumph of form over substance." Kissinger saw
Metternich as pursuing "a never-ending quest for a moment of tranquillity,
for a suspension, if only for an instant, of the flux of life." Such a quest was
doomed to fail. Kissinger saw a certain grandeur in the failure, but he
never doubted that it was a failure. To spend one's life, in Metternich's
words, in "shoring up decaying buildings," was not a pursuit worthy of a
statesman.

When he left office in 1848, Metternich said that he expected men
would say that he had "carried the monarchy away" with him. He
denied this; on the contrary, he said: "No individual has shoulders strong
enough to carry an Empire; if states disappear, it is because they lose faith
in themselves." Kissinger found in this statement the ultimate expression
of the conservative dilemma. The conservative's task was not to defeat

revolution but to forestall it; the fact of revolution—its having happened—proved that the values that supported the traditional regime were no longer vital. A revolution could not, Kissinger said, be defeated by conservative measures. A traditional order, once broken, could only be restored by what Kissinger called "the experience of chaos," the experience of disorder.

Metternich did not understand this. He had several options to choose from; he chose none. Neither ministerial responsibility nor the devolution of authority into various legislatures in different parts of the Empire was thought to be possible. Metternich dismissed them almost too casually. He imagined that there was only one safe course for the Empire, which was to keep the prevailing system intact, with all authority continuing to be vested in the Emperor. Acknowledging the strength of nationalist feeling, Metternich believed that some decentralization of the administration might serve to reduce tensions. Kissinger expressed his disdain for so obviously inadequate a solution to Austria's problems. Confronted with several possibilities—though each involved substantial difficulties—Metternich confused bureaucratic reform with statesmanship.

The failure was grotesque. Kissinger used it as an excuse for broaching a subject that he was to return to many times later. The Austrian Empire, he wrote, looked increasingly for determinacy of calculation; the illusion was created that this could be achieved through bureaucratic norms. While Austria ought to have been making every effort to adjust itself to changing conditions, its only interest seemed to be safety. Bureaucracy, with its promise of routine, satisfied the deep craving for security. Austria pursued what Kissinger thought to be a disastrous policy in attempting to resolve its complex domestic political problems with purely administrative solutions.

Metternich sometimes asked himself whether he ought not to have tried to force the administration into other directions. He reassured himself by saying that he would never have succeeded. Prevented from governing or administering, he became the Empire's principal diplomat. In Kissinger's view, he concealed Austria's weaknesses, delaying the inevitable collapse of the Empire as long as possible. Required to minister to an ailing patient, he did what any competent physician might have done. That, in Kissinger's view, was not enough. He judged a statesman by his ability to conceive of alternatives. In his view, Metternich accepted too easily the situation he found himself saddled with; Kissinger wrote: "Those statesmen who have achieved final greatness did not do so through resignation, however well founded. It was given to them not only to maintain the perfection of order, but to have the strength to contemplate chaos, there to find material for fresh creation." By those standards, Metternich fell considerably short of Kissinger's ideal.

from pursuing its objectives elsewhere in Europe during the period when Austria was involved in putting down the revolution in Italy. Was it totally inconceivable that Russia would use Austria's involvement to excuse her own emergence as the principal advocate of nationalism? Russia had a great deal to gain from adopting that pose. If Russia chose not to adopt it, what would prevent France from doing so? France, the "traditional protector" of the Italian states, might well be called on to help the Italian revolutionaries against Austria's armies; it was not a foregone conclusion that France would resist such a call. France might conclude that there was a great deal to be gained from identifying herself with the liberal and nationalist movements of Europe. There were, however, other even more practical reasons for resisting Castlereagh's suggestions: Austria had only about 20,000 troops available for an Italian campaign; it was by no means certain that an army of that size would be sufficient.

If Metternich ignored Castlereagh's injunctions and demanded instead that there be an Allied operation against Naples, that policy involved other risks. First, certainly, was the risk of offending Britain, and even of pushing Britain out of the Alliance. That prospect terrified Metternich; he knew how necessary Britain's friendship was to Austria. Every action involved some risk. Metternich concluded that his first objective had to be the engaging of Russia in a joint action. Even the defeat of the Neapolitan revolution seemed less urgent to him than the need to involve the Russians; the alternative was to open the possibility that Russia would emerge as the principal advocate of nationalism. As between losing Russia and losing Great Britain, Kissinger explained, Metternich concluded that it was less hazardous to lose Britain. When, therefore, the Tsar proposed a five-power meeting at Troppau, Metternich quickly agreed. His purpose, Kissinger explained, was to "paralyze" Alexander by calculated and ardent embraces. Systematically, he communicated reports to the Tsar of conspiracies that were being hatched everywhere in Europe. Paris was represented as the center of a vast network of revolutionary activity. Metternich succeeded in making the Tsar believe that the events in Naples were simply the harbinger of revolutionary outbreaks that would soon threaten the whole of Europe.

When the conferees gathered in Troppau, Metternich, in Kissinger's words, had emerged as "the conscience of Europe." The Tsar was entirely converted to his point of view; he admitted his earlier errors, and asked only to be permitted to serve in putting down the revolutionary danger. Metternich, as always, showed himself extremely adroit. Fully confident of Russian support, he now moved to mollify the British. He agreed that a state had no right to interfere in the domestic affairs of another state unless situations there were producing results that were likely to have an adverse effect on the international world order. When internal circumstances in one state threatened the security of another state, there was a right of intervention. In effect, Metternich asked for a doctrine of non-interference, framed in such a way as to justify his intention to over-throw the revolutionary forces in Naples. Kissinger thought that he ac-complished a remarkable *tour de force;* he achieved virtually everything that he wanted. Castlereagh was not fooled by what Metternich had done, but he chose to remain silent; to do otherwise was to bring into the open the growing gulf between Austria and Britain on the question of the right of interference in the internal affairs of other states.

Troppau, in Kissinger's view, was Metternich's most successful diplo-matic venture. In converting the contest between Austria and Naples into a European question, he successfully concealed the incongruities of Aus-tria's own anachronistic domestic structure. The anomalous principles that guided Austria's internal life were now translated into the interna-tional sphere, and they were made to appear entirely reasonable. Russia was neutralized; Metternich, compelled to choose between isolating Rus-sia or dominating her, chose the tactic of domination. After Troppau, Metternich was the Tsar's principal political confidant; even the Tsar's own ministers did not enjoy an equivalent status with their royal master.

Metternich succeeded, Kissinger wrote, because he "gambled on the tangibility of psychological factors." Metternich committed the Tsar to an anti-revolutionary crusade, in effect "embroiling him with all those movements his previous ambiguities had encouraged." Metternich be-lieved that the "key to success in diplomacy was freedom of action, not formal relationships." He sought this for Austria—the "freedom of ac-tion" that a country like Britain enjoyed as the free gift of geography. That freedom, however, for a continental power, Kissinger wrote, was to arrange its commitments in such a way that its options were always greater than those of any potential rival. The policy, Kissinger wrote, "required cool nerves, because it sought to demonstrate Austria's indis-pensability by the calm acceptance of great risks, of isolation, or sudden settlements at Austria's expense."

Castlereagh objected to the Troppau declaration, arguing that a general right of interference violated the fundamental law of Great Britain. Kis-singer sympathized with Castlereagh's position, but found it one of "tragic obtuseness which refused to recognize that common action was no longer possible, not through anyone's fault, but because the insular and the Continental conceptions of danger had become incompatible." He also knew that "Castlereagh could not admit this, however, without denying himself." Castlereagh's final speech in Parliament was a powerful defense of the Alliance. He never succeeded in persuading the British public, which continued to think of an alliance as a group of states organized to defend themselves against a specific enemy. In the absence of an obvious foe, Castlereagh's policy never acquired domestic legitimacy. That was part of his tragedy. But there was more.

Metternich, meanwhile, showed all of his accustomed skill. When, in the last days of the Laibach conference, news came of a revolution in Piedmont, Metternich acted immediately; he knew that the Tsar fully supported him. The Piedmont revolution was rapidly quelled. Kissinger explained that the successful defeat of two revolutions in campaigns of less than two weeks might have been thought a fairly remarkable performance. One would have expected the Austrian people to be pleased. Many were not; they asked whether Metternich had not taken unnecessary risks. Some thought him to be the Tsar's tool. Metternich had never expected to be understood or admired. Still, Kissinger could not avoid commenting on the irony of the situation; he wrote: "At the height of his triumph, while Europe looked to him almost as its Prime Minister and three monarchs would not take a step without him; after two crushing victories, Metternich was aware not of power, nor of glory, but of weakness, of danger, of impending disaster. Nothing could have made clearer that the Central Empire was doomed than the pessimism of its Foreign Minister at the apogee of his career. Unwilling to adapt its domestic structure, unable to survive with it in a century of nationalism, even Austria's most successful policies amounted to no more than a reprieve, to a desperate grasping to commit allies, not to a work of construction, but to deflect part of the inevitable holocaust. For this reason Metternich's policy was diplomacy in its purest sense, a virtuoso performance of an essentially instrumental kind, whose very skill testified to its ultimate futility, to the fact that the Central Empire, which required stability above all, could survive only through a *tour de force*."

If all the revolutions of 1819–1820 had occurred simultaneously, the Austrian Empire might have collapsed a century before its final decline. Later crises that took place in the Balkans and in Greece carried the threat of unilateral Russian action; it was not preordained that the Tsar would abstain from taking action. Metternich wanted to obviate that possibility; at the conference planned in Verona, he hoped to terminate once and for all the threat of unilateral Russian action in the Balkans. He hoped that Castlereagh would attend the meeting and support him in this policy. The British Foreign Secretary agreed to come, still holding fast to the idea that a united Europe was possible. He never came; becoming suddenly deranged, he took his own life. The conference system had never developed as Castlereagh had intended that it should. The "jockeying for position," which prevented action in one corner of Europe being taken except by the threat of intervention in another, was not what Castlereagh had hoped for. The Alliance had known precious little unity since the defeat of Napoleon. Castlereagh went to his death persuaded that he had been a failure. In his last meeting with the King, Castlereagh is reported to have said: "Sir, it is necessary to say good-bye to Europe; you and I alone know it and have saved it: no one after me understands the affairs of the continent."

Castlereagh's dream of a Europe "united by self-evident requirements of harmony" came to nothing. Yet there had been some real accomplishments, and Kissinger felt some obligation to take note of them. For a century, Europe was spared a major war; after Britain withdrew from the Alliance, Austria, Russia, and Prussia organized a common policy; no power on the Continent was in a position to challenge them. Violence, Kissinger explained, was virtually precluded by the relations that subsisted between these three European states.

Kissinger entitled his final chapter "The Nature of Statesmanship"; this permitted him to reflect more generally about certain ideal types—the statesman, the revolutionary, the prophet. Castlereagh's death was represented as a severe blow to Metternich. So long as Castlereagh served as British Foreign Secretary, Britain maintained close links with the Alliance. Metternich knew that he could count on Castlereagh, particularly in difficult situations. With Castlereagh gone, Austria's friendship with Russia ceased to be one option among several, and became an absolute necessity. Metternich's bargaining position was substantially weakened; Russia knew that Austria could not survive without her. Kissinger wrote: "It is thus that the gods revenge themselves by fulfilling our wishes too completely. Metternich had now achieved all he sought. . . . But he was also prisoner of his myth, for he no longer dared to destroy Alexander's faith. Confronted by a suspicious Britain, he was obliged to flatter the Tsar's craving for crusades—and in the process to transform British reserve into hostility." Kissinger added: "What posterity has associated with the entire post-Vienna period, the doctrinaire adherence to the status quo at almost any price, really dates from the death of Castlereagh." Metternich knew what he had lost; he recognized that Castlereagh was absolutely irreplaceable. As he wrote: "An intelligent man can make up the lack of everything except experience. Castlereagh was the only man in his country who had experience in foreign affairs."

In comparing Metternich and Castlereagh, Kissinger recognized their differences, but insisted that each was concerned with maintaining a European equilibrium. That had never been the intention of either Napoleon or Alexander, whom Kissinger considered revolutionaries, though of very different kinds. They believed that Europe could be united by an act of will; Napoleon, the conqueror, aimed at universal dominion; Alexander, the prophet, hoped for a reconciled humanity. Kissinger saw the prophet as someone searching for perfection. But perfection implied uniformity; Kissinger wrote: "Utopias are not achieved except by a process of levelling and dislocation that erodes all patterns of obligation." Both the conqueror and the prophet sought eternity. According to Kissinger, the conqueror looked for "the peace of impotence"; the prophet looked for "the peace of bliss."

The statesman remained suspicious of all such efforts, knowing that the survival of the state depended on its being prepared at all times for the worst contingency. No statesman could permit himself to become entirely dependent on the good will of another sovereign; it was too hazardous, a sort of invitation to irresponsibility. The statesman knew that he could not escape time, that his duty was to reflect always on accident and contingency. There was no way for the statesman to avoid the necessary tension between organization and inspiration. The prophet had no concern with organization; he expected organization to be dissolved in a moment of transcendence. The statesman found all such ideas chimerical. He wished for inspiration and knew the importance of issuing a call for greatness, but he also accepted organization, realizing that mediocrity was the usual pattern of leadership.

According to Kissinger, Castlereagh and Metternich sought stability, not perfection. Both believed in the "balance of power"; both accepted the fact that no international order was secure without the institutionalization of certain physical safeguards against aggression. Their definitions of security differed. How could it be otherwise, given the differences between the two states? Britain recognized no enemy once Napoleon had been defeated; neither liberalism nor nationalism seemed dangerous to men who lived in London. The conference machinery invented by Castlereagh was used cynically by Metternich, principally to repress social revolution. Metternich, the last eighteenth-century diplomat, knew how to manipulate; according to Kissinger: "He had the great advantage over his adversaries that he knew what he wanted; if his goals were sterile, they were also fixed." How many who have written about Kissinger's views on Metternich recall (or know) this judgment? Yet it is part of a larger analysis which seeks to credit Metternich with extraordinary diplomatic skills, even as it accounts him a failure. Metternich, Kissinger explained, was effective because he was persuasive, but also because he was plausible. His success, however, also guaranteed his failure. To advocate the status quo in a revolutionary epoch was simply to reinforce the tendency for Austria's domestic structure to become even more rigid, until, in Kissinger's view, that structure virtually petrified. Metternich's diplomacy was only a mask to conceal his failure; Austria was an anachronism in a time of nationalism and liberalism. Metternich's diplomatic skills were so impressive that few recognized that the greater number of Austria's fundamental problems remained unresolved. In Kissinger's view, this was the triumph of "manipulation," and not of "creation." What ought Metternich to have done? Kissinger made no effort to conceal the enormity of the task, given the structure of the state and the character of the Emperor, but the effort to adapt, to loosen Austria's ties with her past, ought to have been made.

Metternich's "marvellous diplomatic skill," Kissinger wrote, "enabled Austria to avoid the hard choice between domestic reform and revolutionary struggle." But diplomacy, Kissinger insisted, was "not a substitute for conception"; Metternich's extraordinary gifts concealed "that what seemed the application of universal principles was in reality the *tour de force* of a solitary figure." Kissinger faulted Metternich for his "smug self-satisfaction with an essentially technical virtuosity which prevented him from achieving the tragic stature he might have had, given the process in which he was involved." Kissinger found in Metternich a "bittersweet resignation," which he recognized as having a certain grandeur, but this was a quality of a distinctly secondary kind. Kissinger wrote: "Men become myths, not by what they know, or even by what they achieve, but by the tasks they set for themselves." Metternich was ideally suited to conducting negotiations according to the eighteenth-century rules of diplomacy; those rules were not always useful in a revolutionary age. Kissinger did not say that Metternich's achievements were insubstantial, only that his objectives were too limited. "There was about him," he wrote, "an aura of futility." The eighteenth century had been persuaded that knowledge was power; events in the nineteenth century proved the inadequacy of that maxim. The death of one man—Castlereagh—deprived Metternich of many of his options. Prussia, which he imagined would sustain his new order, in the end helped to destroy it, and the agent of the destruction was not someone from the middle class but Otto von Bismarck, who came from the most traditional segment of Prussian society. Kissinger wrote that Bismarck "completed the futile revolutions that Metternich had tried to master."

Castlereagh, Kissinger said, was defeated by ignoring his domestic structure; Metternich was defeated by being too conscious of its vulnerability. Neither event was predestined. Kissinger had little sympathy with those who doubted that the statesman had a significant role to play in defining and realizing specific options. Decisions were made by individuals; while they were in part determined by external circumstance—geography, national character, resources, and the like—such factors never entirely defined the range of possibilities that existed. Every major decision involved an *estimate*, which, in Kissinger's mind, depended on a "conception of goals," which was another way of saying that "no policy is better . . . than the goals it sets itself." Kissinger hoped to draw attention not only to the need for goals but also to the necessity for choice and action. Facts could never tell the statesman what he ought to do;

they might guide him in deciding what he chose to do. "The test of a statesman," Kissinger wrote, "is his ability to recognize the real relationship of forces and to make this knowledge serve his ends. That Austria should seek stability was inherent in its geographic position and domestic structure. But that it would succeed, if only temporarily and however unwisely, in identifying its domestic legitimizing principle with that of the international order was the work of its Foreign Minister. That Great Britain should attempt to find security in a balance of power was the consequence of twenty-three years of intermittent warfare. But that it should emerge as a part of the concert of Europe was due to the efforts of a solitary individual."

A statesman, Kissinger insisted, was not a philosopher. He could not be judged simply by the quality of his conceptions. The statesman had to be able to implement his vision, and to do that required him to know how to cope with the "inertia" of his material. Other states could not simply be manipulated; they had to be reconciled. Diplomacy, because it depended on persuasion, could only succeed where there was substantial agreement, generally on the "legitimizing principle" that governed international behavior. Kissinger saw both Castlereagh and Metternich as extraordinary diplomats, though their gifts were of very different kinds. Castlereagh knew how to reconcile conflicting points of view; his empirical approach gave him other important advantages. Metternich managed to achieve a remarkable dominance over his adversaries; he knew how to define a moral framework in such a way that concessions made to him did not appear as surrenders but, in Kissinger's words, "as sacrifices to a common cause."

But all such success would have been impossible without solid domestic support. The securing of that support, Kissinger implied, was the absolutely essential prerequisite of policy-making. Metternich had great difficulties at times in securing approval for his policies in Austria. Kissinger found this not at all surprising; as he explained, "the spirit of policy and that of bureaucracy are diametrically opposed." Policy is by definition "contingent"; its success, Kissinger wrote, "depends on the correctness of an estimate which is in part conjectural." Bureaucracy, on the other hand, was concerned overwhelmingly with "safety"; its success was its "calculability."

Kissinger, in contrasting policy-making with bureaucracy, made no secret of his preference for the former, though he recognized and insisted on the necessity of both. In a series of bold statements that had obvious applicability to the problems of the early nineteenth century but that took on particular urgency because they so openly demonstrated an interest in the problems of the twentieth, Kissinger wrote: "Profound policy thrives on perpetual creation, on a constant redefinition of goals. Good administration thrives on routine, the definition of relationships which can survive mediocrity. Policy involves an adjustment of risks; administration an avoidance of deviation. Policy justifies itself by the relationship of its measures and its sense of proportion; administration by the rationality of each action in terms of a given goal. The attempt to conduct policy bureaucratically leads to a quest for calculability which tends to become a prisoner of events. The effort to administer politically leads to total irresponsibility, because bureaucracies are designed to execute, not to conceive."

Most governments, Kissinger argued, were organized primarily for the conduct of domestic policy. Since domestic policy involved essentially the implementation of social decisions, where the concern with technical feasibility was paramount, there was no spill-over from such policy formulation to that required in the area of foreign affairs. Kissinger suggested that those who conduct foreign policy with habits acquired in the domestic field will generally tend to judge performance more by mistakes and catastrophes avoided than by goals and opportunities realized. A society, he explained, was capable of only a finite number of decisions, largely because its values were relatively fixed; the bureaucracy, in theory, could be depended on to carry out any decision that was administratively feasible. That, however, did not mean that social goals could be defined bureaucratically. There was a real danger in trying to do this, Kissinger wrote, because it confused two essentially different processes. Decision-making depended on a conceptual ability and a degree of responsibility that the bureaucrat could not possibly have. Metternich and Castlereagh were in a position to plan policy as long-range national strategy. Because they remained in office for so many years, they were able to relate measures to each other, and not press for individual measures, any one of which could be called rational.

States were obliged to play in an international arena; citizens knew mostly what they learned from domestic experience. As a result, there was an almost perpetual incentive to make foreign affairs conform to the principles of national life. Within the nation, there would be agreement about the nature of justice; such agreement was not always obtainable in the international community. Where one state insisted on its own principles being observed and all others being denied, there was no possibility of peace. Where competing systems of legitimacy were proclaimed, agreement would rarely result; even where it was achieved, states would find it difficult to secure domestic support for the agreement. Kissinger was saying, in effect, that it was rare for an international accord which had treated a significant and complex problem to receive widespread domestic support in very differing societies.

The tool of domestic policy, Kissinger wrote, was bureaucracy; the tool of foreign policy was diplomacy. Bureaucracy expressed a unified will, which was being applied effectively; diplomacy was a more tenuous process, depending on contingency and nuance. In the end, Kissinger said, it was not at all surprising that a "powerful, if subconscious rebellion against foreign policy" often occurred in many countries. Foreign policy demanded too many compromises. For a state's domestic concept of "justice" to be debated and modified in international adjudication was too upsetting an experience for many citizens. They much preferred their domestic experience, which was known, and which they were able to relate to directly. Foreign policy did not touch actual experience; it dealt with a potential experience—war—and the purpose of statesmanship was to prevent that experience from becoming actual. Foreign policy was a highly ambiguous undertaking; Kissinger was not at all surprised that so many societies chose to believe that the sharp practices of foreigners were depriving them of their birthright.

Statesmen, Kissinger wrote, were in an almost impossible situation; ". . . they know the future, feel it in their bones, but are incapable of proving the truth of their insights. Nations learn only by experience; they 'know' only when it is too late to act." Statesmen, he insisted, had to act before their intuition was made actual; this necessity made them suspect to many ordinary citizens. Kissinger believed that statesmen all too often shared the fate of prophets; they were denied honor in their own day and seen as farsighted only by later generations. Kissinger thought of the statesman as an educator; his duty was to "bridge the gap between a people's experience and his vision, between a nation's tradition and its future." This was never easy; both Castlereagh and Metternich failed, according to Kissinger's criteria. Castlereagh so far outdistanced the experience of his people that he neglected to achieve a domestic consensus; Metternich was so determined to make his policy coincide with the experience of his people that he doomed himself to sterility. The task of conducting foreign policy was so inherently difficult, Kissinger believed, that only conservatives or revolutionaries were capable of discharging its responsibilities. The conservative was effective because he understood the experience of his people and was able to carry them along with him. The revolutionary succeeded because he knew how to transcend experience, identifying the just with the possible, and winning favor for his views through his charisma. Statesmanship, Kissinger concluded, "involves not only a problem of conception but also of implementation, an appreciation of the attainable as much as a vision of the desirable." It was in the nature of things that states could only experiment with one interpretation at a time; they were incapable of rerunning the experiment to see how it would have worked had another option been taken. This, Kissinger wrote, "is the challenge of history and its tragedy; it is the shape 'destiny' assumes on the earth. And its solution, even its recognition, is perhaps the most difficult task of statesmanship."

Kissinger wrote his dissertation because he wanted a degree that would enable him to pursue a particular profession; he wrote it also because he wanted to educate himself in a specific discipline: international relations. Those who characterize Kissinger as a Metternichian do not intend any compliment in the remark; if they were fully aware of what Kissinger had written about Metternich, they would realize the full extent of their insult. Metternich was not Kissinger's hero; nor, for that matter, was Castlereagh. Both were men of great talent whom Kissinger esteemed for specific actions that showed their high level of competence at particular historical junctures. In the end, both failed; their failures, in Kissinger's mind, were attributable to their own shortcomings—not least, their intellectual shortcomings. Kissinger wrote about them not because he had a romantic vision of a conservative statesmanship that had once ruled Europe and had known how to make diplomacy work. Kissinger never implied that this was the last moment in history when men knew how to conduct foreign policy. On the contrary, his objective was to explain why they had failed, and how their failure could be attributed to specific actions they had themselves taken. Kissinger admired Metternich for his ability to shape a coalition capable of defeating Napoleon; he then went on to question his rigidity and his unwillingness to risk certain things to achieve reform in an Austrian Empire that was becoming increasingly anachronistic. Kissinger applauded Castlereagh for insisting on a peace that did not seek retribution; he questioned his naïveté with respect to the Quadruple Alliance that he foisted on Europe; even more, he criticized him for his failure to gain parliamentary support for his policies. Both men were in the end defeated, and a great part of their defeat was attributable to events that they were themselves in a position to control. Some things, however, they, like other men, were incapable of either controlling or predicting. Kissinger knew and emphasized the importance of accident in history. Who could have predicted that Castlereagh would take his own life? Who could have told Metternich how to prepare for that contingency? It was unpredictable, and Metternich suffered as much as anyone because it happened. The reputation that Metternich gained in the years after 1815 remained with him always. It prevented many liberals —historians and others—from studying his life with any objectivity. Kissinger found it not at all uncongenial to try to do precisely that. Because his purpose was to analyze—and not to apportion credit or blame—he found the intellectual exercise enormously stimulating. It taught him lessons that he retained for the rest of his career, the most important of which was his conviction that foreign policy was an infinitely more complex pursuit than domestic policy, and that it could never be studied (or conducted) independently of domestic policy.

3

On Nuclear Weapons

and Foreign Policy

Writing for Others

A World Restored was an eclectic work—half history, half intellectual autobiography, it could be read on several levels. While representing itself as an analysis of early-nineteenth-century European diplomacy, it was, in a more fundamental sense, an extended essay on the nature of statesmanship. Kissinger's preoccupation with the theme was long-standing; those who encountered him first in the early 1950s were quickly made aware of the consuming nature of his interest in political leadership. Whether speaking of Truman, Churchill, or Adenauer, or listening to someone else interpret the strengths and weaknesses of these or any of a dozen other world leaders, he showed a keen appreciation of political talent. While many who crossed his path during these years shared his interests, and enjoyed the interminable discussions about politics, others chose to discuss matters that were considerably more wide-ranging. It was never very apparent how much Kissinger absorbed from these conversations; he was too good a listener to show boredom. His overwhelming concern was always with the *problems* of international politics; years later, when he came to know personally a number of the political leaders of Europe, he dwelt on individual eccentricity and repeated stories about individual encounters—it was obvious that Kissinger enjoyed telling these stories quite as much as his listeners enjoyed hearing them—but such matters never formed the staple of his conversational diet. Kissinger spoke mostly in a rather serious vein, very often about problems that he was writing about; almost never about purely domestic or local political happenings.

Even as a graduate student, when the temptations to be preoccupied with Harvard were overwhelming, Kissinger sought his friends outside. He never entirely accepted the role of being a student; nor did he try to imagine himself in the role he would one day occupy: that of being a professor. Kissinger knew many of those who were to become his professional colleagues; his relations with most of them, while cordial, were never really intimate. Academic politics bored him; he almost never discussed the subject, and belonged to none of the coteries that formed either in his department or in Cambridge more generally. His interest was Europe—not the Europe of professors who very occasionally made their way over on sabbatical leave to do research or lecture, but the Europe of politicians, concerned with very concrete contemporary political problems.

Early in 1951, he and William Y. Elliott began to lay plans for an institution that developed into the Harvard International Seminar. This was the first, and in certain respects the most important, of several university innovations for which Kissinger could claim a substantial share of credit. His loyalty to the International Seminar was total; as late as the mid-1960s, when other obligations might easily have provided an excuse for abandoning an enterprise that required a great deal of time and effort, Kissinger continued to meet with the participants in the International Seminar in much the way he did a decade earlier. The continuing relation was not fortuitous; Kissinger knew how much his participation meant to the life of the Seminar; he also knew what the Seminar contributed to his own political education, and how much pleasure it gave him. The indebtedness was reciprocal; Kissinger owed a debt to those foreigners who came to study in Cambridge; few who came would have been able to conceive of the International Seminar without him.

The International Seminar provided an opportunity for young men and women, mostly between the ages of twenty-five and forty, originally from Europe but later from every part of the world, to come to the United States as the guests of the Harvard Summer School, and to spend eight weeks in a special program of study that Kissinger created for them. Today, when international travel has become routine, it is difficult to recall the situation of the early 1950s. A whole generation of men and women, who had come to their maturity in the late 1930s or during the war itself, had been prevented from traveling. Whether they lived in the bombed-out cities of Germany and Italy or in the less heavily scarred centers of the Continent or England, they knew the world outside Europe mostly by report. The expense of foreign travel, particularly to the United

States, prevented very many of them from seriously contemplating such a journey. The habit of American travel had, in any case, not been common in Europe before the war; there was no tradition that made it indispensable for every well-educated European to think of the United States as a country to visit. While European newspapers spoke increasingly of American happenings, and while the United States presence in Western Europe took new forms, particularly after the inauguration of the Marshall Plan and the founding of NATO, the character of the American colossus remained obscure. Nor was the image greatly clarified by Soviet and Communist propaganda, which dominated discussion in so many quarters. The information available to Europeans about the United States generally came from a limited number of politically inspired European or American sources. Few Europeans enjoyed any direct access to the United States.

In founding the International Seminar, William Elliott and Henry Kissinger sought to make some contribution toward changing this. Elliott's position as Director of the Harvard Summer School made the experiment possible; Kissinger's personal involvement gave form and substance to the idea. Their plan was a rather modest one: to invite to the United States a number of young foreigners, no longer students, already embarked on their professional careers, who were prepared to come to Harvard for a summer. Though there was never an explicit statement that preference would be given to men and women pursuing active careers as journalists, politicians, civil servants, and the like, as against those who were more obviously academically inclined, such a bias did exist. Kissinger, concerned also with the membership of the humanities group, took special pains to attract promising poets, artists, critics, and writers; it never occurred to him that he was scanting scientists.

The experiment was launched so late in the spring of 1951 that virtually all members in the first year were Europeans who had already come to the United States on their own. In subsequent years, participants were chosen specifically for the Seminar, and efforts were made to extend the search for suitable candidates to countries outside Europe. All this was accomplished with a minimum of bureaucratic machinery, and a minimum of expense. Application forms were sent out to the more obvious foreign university addresses; American cultural attachés and other Embassy personnel were solicited for names, and a special effort was made to ask always for recommendations from those who had already attended the Seminar. Several hundred personal letters were written every year; word of the existence of the Seminar spread, and, in a remarkably short time, the Seminar office in the Harvard Yard was receiving inquiries from every part of the world. The application form was deceptively simple. Letters of recommendation weighed heavily; the Seminar, in predicting a successful career rather than insisting on evidence of it, selected from a pool of relatively obscure persons. Kissinger chose the participants himself, seeking the advice of close friends. Three or four Seminar members generally came from the United Kingdom, a delegation that almost always included a backbencher from the House of Commons; an equal number were generally selected from France and Germany. Other European countries might have one or two members chosen from the many that applied; later, when Asians came in good number, Japan, Korea, the Philippines, India, and Pakistan were usually represented. In the first years of the Seminar, many who attended were older than Kissinger himself, and held positions of greater responsibility. Feeling himself to be in the presence of his contemporaries, he treated many as valued friends only weeks after he met them.

The Seminar's procedures and practices were an amalgam of *ad hoc* devices, whose underlying principle seemed to be frugality. Europeans who imagined America to be Puritan must have had all their expectations confirmed by their first Harvard experiences. In the unreformed Harvard of the 1950s and early 1960s, dormitories were sex-segregated; a policeman stood guard during the summer session to guarantee that no male would enter the sacred precincts set aside for females. It never occurred to anyone that foreign guests, of whatever age or distinction, should not live precisely as American undergraduates did, or as an American schoolteacher did who chose to attend the Harvard Summer School for educational credits. Harvard, in the summer, was an "open university," and accommodated everyone who paid a registration fee and took one or more courses. It seemed entirely natural that a British M.P. or a French member of the Cour de Comptes, once he had abandoned his tie, jacket, and reserve in the stifling heat of a Cambridge summer, should be lunching with American teen-agers in the cavernous Harvard Union. Anyone at all familiar with how many of these men and women lived in their own countries would have predicted total disaster for the Seminar. In fact, it worked admirably.

A great deal of the credit for the Seminar's success must go to Kissinger himself. While he studiously avoided becoming involved in anything that had to do with the "lodging and feeding" of his guests, he took an interest in everything that had to do with the planned educational program. The special Seminar sessions that met twice a week were important, and Kissinger made the greatest effort to secure the help of able colleagues. Year after year he recruited assistants—sometimes persons senior to himself in rank and age—to take one or both of the principal groups. In the afternoon, twice or three times a week, the Seminar met to receive a distinguished visitor who would talk informally about some aspect of American life. Kissinger felt a special obligation to chair these meetings, and to join in the questioning that followed. Frequently, before the closed Seminar sessions, Kissinger would lunch with his invited guest, asking eight or ten of the Seminar participants to join him. The talk that began at the Faculty Club frequently spilled over into the afternoon. Kissinger felt no compunction about asking anyone to address the Seminar. There were no honoraria in the early years; the pleasure of speaking to a lively group of foreigners seemed a sufficient inducement. Kissinger often asked a member of the Harvard faculty to attend. David Riesman, Arthur Schlesinger, Jr., and McGeorge Bundy were frequent guests; so, also, were national figures like Eleanor Roosevelt and Walter Reuther; critics and writers like Thornton Wilder and John Crowe Ransom; journalists as different as James Reston and William Buckley.

Kissinger made himself available to Seminar members in his minuscule, simply furnished office in the Harvard Yard several days a week. In the evening, he and his wife entertained Seminar participants in their home; the talk would go on for many hours, politics being the principal subject. Seminar participants, from the day they arrived, knew that they owed their summer in Cambridge to Kissinger. They admired him for his intelligence, but also for his industry. In just under eight weeks, summer after summer, Kissinger became personally acquainted with dozens of men and women whose names he had not known six months earlier. Inevitably, some were more interesting to him than others; he, in turn, could be a fairly forbidding personality to shy or inarticulate men and women who did not share his political interests.

After only a few years, Kissinger's network of foreign friends— persons in the prime of their political or professional lives—was unrivaled. No American could boast acquaintance with a more diverse group of European and Asian intellectuals; few had such intimate knowledge of the political situation abroad, as described by a great variety of political informants. If Kissinger gave his guests some slight introduction to the complexities of American life, they reciprocated with invaluable insights into their own countries. Many of the Seminar participants became his friends, and corresponded regularly with him. When he traveled abroad, he knew personally hundreds of men and women in various parts of the world; it seemed entirely reasonable that he avail himself of the hospitality they offered. Many a journalist, politician, and civil servant thought it a singular honor to be asked by Kissinger to effect an introduction to someone whom he was anxious to meet. Kissinger was not just another American visitor, but someone who had demonstrated extraordinary dialectical skills in a great variety of Cambridge encounters. Former Seminar members—particularly those who knew him best—realized that he would work hard at any interview they arranged, and that their own reputations would not be diminished by the encounter. It is difficult to exaggerate the help that Kissinger received from his International Seminar friends.

In March 1952, Kissinger became the editor of a new journal, entitled, appropriately enough, *Confluence*. Again, William Elliott, in his capacity as Director of the Harvard Summer School, stood behind the effort. The first number, published in a format that was both inexpensive and unimaginative, dealt with a cosmic theme—"What Are the Bases of Civilization?" Later issues were more modest, dealing with subjects as different as education, the mass media, religion, ideology, and the problems of the nuclear age. At a time when politics divided Europe, isolating most intellectuals in narrow ideological conventicles, Kissinger thought of a journal that transcended these boundaries; he published without reference to them. *Confluence* began as a dialogue between Europeans and Americans; in time, it extended its purview to Asia, though Western Europe and the United States remained its major intellectual focus. Many of the essays were ephemeral; a number had great distinction. Kissinger, with exceedingly modest resources, managed to produce a journal that belonged neither to the left nor to the right, and that published poets and novelists, both famous and obscure, together with philosophers, historians, and political scientists of diverse intellectual leanings, and politicians— liberal, socialist, and conservative. A journal that published Reinhold Niebuhr and Enoch Powell, Alberto Moravia and André Malraux, Karl Jaspers and Joyce Cary, Denis Healy and Walt Rostow, Victor Weisskopf and Bertrand de Jouvenel could not be said to belong to any identifiable political or professional group. Kissinger spread his net as wide as the times permitted him to. He was never able to penetrate the Soviet world, but he made the greatest efforts to seek out the greatest variety of opinion in those places where he was free to go.

When Kissinger ceased to be a graduate student, he could look back on two unique experiences; he had been instrumental in founding the International Seminar and *Confluence*. He knew that their continued operation and vitality depended very largely on him, and that they had contributed as much to his education as anything that he had ever done. Unlike so many of his contemporaries in graduate school, Kissinger did not measure time by when he gained his doctorate or when he started to teach. His life in 1952, when his dissertation was only half finished, was not substantially different from what it was three years later. Academic credentials did not provide Kissinger with the opportunities or the associations that he prized. While many senior members of his department seemed scarcely aware of his presence, let alone of what he was doing, newspaper editors in Frankfurt and Paris vied for his time. There was nothing very conventional in Kissinger's graduate-student experience.

In 1955, a new association, of a very different kind, became important to him. Gordon Dean, formerly head of the Atomic Energy Commission, in writing the Foreword to Kissinger's book, *Nuclear Weapons and Foreign Policy*, told how the Council on Foreign Relations in 1954 had "called together a panel of exceptionally qualified individuals to explore all factors which are involved in the making and implementing of foreign policy in the nuclear age." Gordon Dean, selected to chair the panel, met with the group for many months. After almost a year, Kissinger was asked whether he would join the group as its study director. The appointment proved to be the most important event in Kissinger's adult life, second only to his decision to enroll at Harvard. Neither the Council nor Kissinger recognized the full potentialities of the appointment. Nor, for that matter, did Gordon Dean know what he had done. As he explained, "We asked Dr. Kissinger, fully exposed to the facts and the views of the group, to write a book for which he alone would be responsible, and we ended our deliberations fully respectful of each other and with a final exhortation: 'Good luck, Dr. Kissinger. If you can make anything out of the efforts of this panel we will be eternally grateful.' " Kissinger was given the opportunity to write a book. The Council had given numerous other men at other times the same opportunity. Their works, most frequently, had fallen dead from the presses. The Council's list of publications was long; there were not many titles that had brought great fame to their authors. The Council's record in this respect was no different from that of other similar organizations.

But what precisely was the Council on Foreign Relations? Many knew it principally through its quarterly journal, *Foreign Affairs*, which was founded soon after World War I, and by the late 1930s had established itself as the most prestigious American publication dealing with foreign policy. The journal enjoyed a great reputation in New York and Washington; important political figures both in the United States and abroad sometimes used it to disseminate their foreign policy views. That certain of the articles were ghostwritten sometimes obviously so, did not really matter. To know that a Prime Minister or Foreign Secretary wished to have his name associated with a particular policy was more important than whether or not he had written the article himself. The journal was well edited, and while it could never be called exciting, it had the merit of reaching men who were known to be influential. Kissinger, beginning in the middle 1950s, published extensively in *Foreign Affairs*. He felt a great indebtedness to its editor, Hamilton Fish Armstrong, and to the managing editor, Philip Quigg. *Foreign Affairs*, however, was only the Council's public face; Kissinger's greatest debt was to the Council as it existed for its members.

The Council on Foreign Relations, in the mid-1950s, was "unreformed"; it was a men's club, to which only United States citizens were eligible; half its membership lived or worked in the New York area; the other half were scattered throughout the world, with the preponderant number on the East Coast, many temporarily or permanently based in Washington, D.C. Having some interest in foreign affairs was mandatory for someone proposed for Council membership; actual experience in an important governmental position, civilian or military, generally helped advance a candidate's election prospects. In the New York area, where so many leading bankers, lawyers, and business executives had at one time or other held a major governmental post, the Council's membership list read like a Who's Who of former high governmental officials. It included also a number of foundation executives, professors, and journalists. Many of the names were familiar; the greatest number had at one time or other held a position that gave them some public exposure. Some were simply very wealthy men, recognizable as such. Whether in or out of government, intending to return or having no such interest, most members professed to some interest in foreign affairs. It was useful for them to have access to an organization like the Council. They enjoyed the opportunity to meet each other there, and felt more in touch with the outside world through the distinguished foreign guests invited by the Council to speak in meetings that were always "off the record." The organization was ideally suited to the needs and interests of men who did not have daily access to governmental information, who were generally located in or near New York, and who enjoyed the reality or illusion of believing that foreign affairs was a compelling subject.

The Council's practice during the year (except for the summer months) was to invite members to meetings two or three times each week to hear prominent American or foreign dignitaries speak. Depending on the fame of the speaker—and, to a lesser extent, on his subject—as many as several hundred Council members might come to the Council's house on East 68th Street on a late weekday afternoon to listen to the Council's guest. The meetings were brief; a speaker rarely addressed the Council for more than forty-five minutes, and there was generally some time left for discussion. Despite the pledge of secrecy, few men ever chose to use the Council to elaborate policies that were new and that they wished to air. The Council was not a place for thinking out loud. The talks were sometimes factual, generally of a kind that could be delivered anywhere in the world before a group of knowledgeable men, assembled to discuss a topic whose principal configurations were known. Where the individual was unusually candid or brilliant, there was some possibility of interest being sustained for the whole hour. Where these qualities were lacking, the talk might be desultory, with the general discussion (which was no more than a question-and-answer session) showing the same dull pattern. Since members were free to leave immediately after the talk, and since train schedules to suburban New York and Connecticut communities often governed departures quite as much as the intrinsic merits of the presentation, it was impossible to gauge the success of a meeting simply by the number who stayed to the end.

Given the quality of many of the meetings, both speakers and Council members must occasionally have asked themselves whether they had not participated in a purely ceremonial affair. For many, it did not seem to matter. Speakers were generally gratified by those who came to hear them. No Foreign Secretary, Minister of Finance, Prime Minister, or President, coming from abroad and looking at the list of those in attendance, could fail to believe that New York's financial elite had turned out. As for Council members, they frequently came out of curiosity about the person scheduled to speak, sometimes out of friendship for him, and very often simply to register their interest in foreign affairs. Those for whom foreign affairs had an economic, scholarly, or journalistic interest had reason enough to come. Many others simply came to see friends in a setting that was always congenial.

In addition to the afternoon meetings, the Council sponsored small dinners and lunches to which a selected number of Council members were invited. An effort was made to bring together those members who had the greatest reason to be interested in the specific activities of the invited speaker. At the dinners, particularly, the pace was somewhat relaxed; the speaker, sitting at his place at table, might address the group informally for forty-five minutes or an hour, with general discussion following. Dinners generally started at 7:00 P.M., and they were expected to end by 9:30 P.M. Again, these were not occasions that generated heated debate or argument, but they did provide a very useful way for Council members to take measure of their guest. The mood was almost always informal, even when the speaker occupied a great position in his own country.

For most members, these activities exhausted the services that they expected the Council to provide. A few made use of the Council's excellent library, and a number belonged each year to one or other of the special study groups that the Council organized on specific topics, in which participation was restricted to invited members. The study groups varied greatly both in their quality and seriousness; men who gathered late in the afternoon, after a full day in the office, were not generally in the best condition to discuss seriously complex foreign policy issues. Still, the intelligence and articulateness of individual members often made certain of these study groups, which met once or twice a month, agreeable occasions. A great deal depended on the chairman of the group; even more important, perhaps, was the participation of members of the Council staff; they prepared papers for the meeting and kept many of the groups going.

It was Henry Kissinger's great good fortune to become associated with a very distinguished group that provided assistance to him of a very special kind. *Nuclear Weapons and Foreign Policy* was Kissinger's book; it would not, however, have been written in the way that it was, or have achieved the renown that it did, but for the Council's sponsorship. The group included a number of extraordinary individuals—men whom Kissinger would not otherwise have met. Their range of interests made them ideal interlocutors for Kissinger. They were the first men Kissinger had met with extensive governmental experience at the highest levels; a number were men of great scientific and technological learning who understood the new weapons systems as few others in the country did. Kissinger's study group included, among others, Hamilton Fish Armstrong; Hanson Baldwin, military editor of the New York *Times;* Lloyd Berkner, research physicist and scientific administrator, expert in radar and electronics; Robert Bowie, most recently of the State Department, soon to be appointed director of the Harvard University Center for International Affairs; McGeorge Bundy, dean of the Faculty of Arts and Sciences of Harvard University; William Burden, financier, formerly Assistant Secretary of Commerce for Air; Thomas Finletter, former Secretary of the Air Force; General James Gavin, famed commander of the 82nd Airborne Division, later ambassador to France; Roswell Gilpatric, lawyer, former Under-Secretary of the Air Force, later Deputy Secretary of Defense; Caryl Haskins, research scientist, president of the Carnegie Institution of Washington, consultant on research and development to the Secretaries of State and Defense; Joseph Johnson, president and trustee of the Carnegie Endowment for International Peace; Air Force General James McCormack, Jr., vice-president of the Massachusetts Institute of Technology, later chairman of the Communication Satellite and the Aerospace Corporations; Paul Nitze, former director of the Policy Planning Staff of the Department of State, later Assistant Secretary of Defense for International Security Affairs and Secretary of the Navy; Frank Pace, Jr., former Secretary of the Army, chairman of General Dynamics Corporation; James Perkins, vice-president of the Carnegie Corporation, later president of Cornell University; Don K. Price, Jr., vice-president of the Ford Foundation, later dean of the Graduate School of Public Administration at Harvard; I. I. Rabi, Nobel Prize-winning physicist, member of the President's Science Advisory Committee, vice-president of the International Conference on the Peaceful Uses of Atomic Energy; David Rockefeller, of the Chase Manhattan Bank; Oscar Ruebhausen, attorney, friend and adviser to Nelson Rockefeller; General Walter Bedell Smith, former Under-Secretary of State, ambassador to Russia, and director of the Central Intelligence Agency; Carroll Wilson of the Massachusetts Institute of Technology, formerly general manager of the Atomic Energy Commission; and Arnold Wolfers, historian, professor of international relations at Yale University. The group combined extraordinary intellectual resources with very disparate kinds of experiences, in and out of government.

A more advantageous position for a young man, little known at the time, could scarcely have been invented. Kissinger could use the group as a sounding board for his own ideas, without, in the words of its chairman, Gordon Dean, feeling any obligation to heed its advice. Had Kissinger been given no greater help than this, it would have been reason enough for him to feel indebted to the Council. Actually, he was helped in other ways also. By agreeing to become study director, and choosing to live in close proximity to the Council, he had a unique opportunity to appreciate the quality of its staff, and particularly of its Executive Director, George Franklin, Jr., to whom he felt particularly close. Kissinger spoke frequently of his gratitude to a staff that treated him with great gentleness and consideration. Their principal concern seemed to be to make his life easier. While no one of them could claim to have made a major contribution to his intellectual development, their solicitude and friendship counted for a great deal; they were as much responsible for his book as those who had served in the study group.

Kissinger met at the Council a number of men who in another age would simply have been called "gentlemen." Some were men of great wealth, who, because they lived in the United States, thought it necessary to do something to justify their existence. Having no experience of the competitive strife of either the business or the academic world, they were capable of a kind of generosity that touched Kissinger deeply. He never forgot the moral support that these men gave him, and never underestimated its importance for his personal growth.

Kissinger's life in New York was exceedingly difficult; he worked sixteen and seventeen hours a day, and wrote innumerable drafts of a book that never acquired the grace of his earlier study. It did, however, enjoy another distinction: it had authority; it might just conceivably command a hearing. At the Council on Foreign Relations, Kissinger chose a relatively unconventional topic, and proceeded to treat it in a rather idiosyncratic way. Kissinger's doctoral dissertation was a work largely written for himself, a sort of intellectual exercise. *Nuclear Weapons and Foreign Policy* was never intended to be that; it was meant to be read, particularly by those who held responsible positions in the United States at the highest governmental levels.

Kissinger opened his book with a chapter entitled "The Challenge of the Nuclear Age." For those who knew his doctoral dissertation, there were no surprises in the chapter. It started with a reference to Nemesis, the goddess of fate, who sometimes punished man by fulfilling his wishes too completely. Never before had man enjoyed such a superabundance of physical power; in fact, Kissinger said, man's problem had always been to increase the amounts of physical power available, but the discovery of nuclear energy had changed all that. Man now had an "excess of power," and everything depended on his "ability to use it subtly and with discrimination." If, as Eisenhower had said, the power of the new weapons meant that "there is no alternative to peace," this did not answer the question of how peace could be secured and maintained. The new conventional wisdom, Kissinger wrote, was that the weapons themselves had imposed a sort of universal nonaggression treaty; since war was no longer thinkable, diplomacy was the only alternative. But, Kissinger said, diplomacy had been traditionally linked to the possibility of war. If, in the past, a negotiation had failed, the situation did not simply return to what it had been at the time that the negotiation began. The threat of war served as an inducement to negotiation. If all this was now changed, Kissinger wrote, then the international system was "at the mercy of its most ruthless or its most irresponsible member." There was no longer any penalty for intransigence. Taking up a theme he had developed in his studies of the Napoleonic era, he expanded it to consider its applicability "in a revolutionary period like the present."

Kissinger wondered whether certain statesmen would not be so obsessed with the power of nuclear weapons that they would make almost any concession to avert war. While, in theory, such an attitude would contribute to diminishing the possibilities of war, Kissinger asked whether it would not lead the two major revolutionary powers—the USSR and Communist China—to take actions that jeopardized the survival of other states. The United States, he thought, was confronted with an awesome challenge, until it understood the issues it was prepared to fight over, and possessed the requisite means to achieve its objectives, It could not develop policies that in fact reduced the risks of aggression. The most imperative need was to understand what the new weapons technology had done to alter traditional military options, and what effect nuclear weapons would have on America's diplomatic and political choices. These were not problems that could be delegated to a group of military officers who, in theory at least, understood the potentialities of the new weapons systems. There was, quite obviously, a military dimension to the problem, but Kissinger thought it to be almost secondary. The challenge, in his mind, was intellectual and political.

The United States desperately required a strategic doctrine suited to its defense needs. In Kissinger's view, this involved first and foremost a precise understanding of what constituted a *threat* to American security. The United States, the "island power" of the twentieth century, living apart from the Eurasian continent, had long believed that two oceans pro-

vided military safety; there were no hazards that could not be prepared
for in time. Like the United Kingdom in the first decades of the nineteenth century, the United States imagined that it could remain aloof
when aggression took place elsewhere; once it determined that its own
interests were adversely affected, it could enter the fray and depend on
its great productive capacity to make up for lost time. There were no unacceptable risks in being dilatory; the life of the state did not depend on a
close watch being kept of the slightest changes in the world power balance. Those states that worried over every tiny incident were thought
to be alarmist; Americans wished that they would be more calm; in their
view, they were only contributing to a destabilization of the international
order. For Americans who lived with these illusions, European diplomacy
seemed a rather dubious game, a degenerate activity that had no interest
for the United States. It was very agreeable to believe in America's virtue,
and to imagine that the country was spared by its history and geography
from having to live as other states did. Kissinger saw no point in perpetuating this myth; unlike Woodrow Wilson, he believed that "the differences between our approach to foreign policy and that of the European
states was primarily a matter of degree."

In Europe, where the growth of power for one state quickly created a
problem for others, there was only a small "margin of safety." The
United States had not traditionally been in nearly so exposed a condition;
as Kissinger explained, ". . . because many other states had to be attacked
long before the threat to our security became apparent, we could always
be certain that some powers would bear the brunt of the first battles and
hold a line while we mobilized our resources." This, Kissinger wrote, had
led the United States "to develop a doctrine of aggression so purist and
abstract that it absolved our statesmen from the necessity of making decisions in ambiguous situations and from concerning themselves with the
minutiae of day-to-day diplomacy." That condition, however, no longer
obtained. The new weapons systems had abolished America's invulnerability; the polarization of power in the world had reduced America's traditional margin of safety. America's survival in the atomic age depended
on its capacity to recognize aggression early, and to know how to react
to it. As Kissinger explained: "In the nuclear age, by the time a threat has
become unambiguous it may be too late to resist it."

America was accustomed to thinking of aggression in terms of rapidly
moving armies crossing national frontiers; events of that kind, Kissinger
wrote, were not likely to occur in the atomic age. The United States
needed also to revise its thinking about what constituted a significant
accretion of national power. Had any country in the past tried to add to
its power through territorial expansion in the way that the Soviet Union

had done through its acquisition of nuclear weapons, war would have been the inevitable consequence. In the atomic age, however, where large accretions of power occurred within a national state, principally through technological change, an arms race was the usual result. Kissinger thought that the diffusion of nuclear weapons was probably inevitable; he expected a number of states to achieve nuclear capability within fifteen years.

The great hazard, in Kissinger's mind, did not derive from the power of these weapons but from the uncertainty he felt about the American capacity to respond to the political and psychological challenge that they posed. The nuclear age, Kissinger wrote, was "the age of internal subversion, of intervention by 'volunteers,' of domination through political and psychological warfare." The United States, because of its own peculiar historical experiences, was almost prevented from knowing how to cope with the problems of such a world. Americans preferred unambiguous threats; they invented the concept of all-out war to meet overt aggression. When such aggression occurred, Americans felt morally secure in resisting it. Americans were so habituated to thinking in these terms that they could not imagine any other type of Soviet offensive. They believed that they had an effective military policy when they were in a position to threaten the Soviets with all-out war should the Soviet armies move. There was no reason, however, Kissinger explained, for expecting the Soviets to accommodate the Americans. Why should the Soviets embark on a thoroughly unambiguous aggressive military venture when they could achieve their objectives by other, less hazardous operations?

In Kissinger's view, the United States was extremely vulnerable both to Soviet maneuvers and to Soviet propaganda. In the absence of an all-out Communist attack, American leaders would be compelled to interpret Soviet truculence as stemming either from their having totally misunderstood the American position or from the power of malevolent individuals or groups within the Soviet hierarchy. Americans, Kissinger said, were not likely to believe that the policies were calculated and deliberate; they would search always for "reasonable motives" to explain what would otherwise appear to be irrational acts. Thus, for example, Americans wanted to believe that the Russians were interested principally in developing their own country, or that they were preoccupied with expanding their international trade. These seemed to be reasonable objectives; Soviet propaganda cooperated with those who wished to put the best possible face on Soviet motives; "peaceful coexistence" was an ingenious slogan, precisely attuned to the needs of the moment. It called for an abeyance of belief, for a refusal to credit what was so obviously happening in the world. Americans, searching always for evidence of a "shift" in Soviet policies, even when they found none, generally chose to remain silent; some argued as if the so-called nuclear stalemate had been produced by Soviet thermonuclear capability, and by the development of a long-range Soviet delivery system. Kissinger took a very different view; the stalemate, in his mind, had existed since the Americans had exploded their bomb over Hiroshima; even when the United States enjoyed a nuclear monopoly, he said, "we never succeeded in translating our military superiority into a political advantage." Why? Because the United States never correctly perceived the advantages that atomic weapons gave. Holding to its antiquated notion that total victory was the only meaningful objective, and remembering what the Russians had done in resisting Hitler, the United States was rendered impotent by both strategic and humanitarian considerations. The years of atomic monopoly were wasted. Kissinger was not nearly as certain as others were that the American "bomb" had kept the Soviets from taking over the whole of Europe. Given the losses that the Soviets had suffered in World War II, they were not in a very favorable position to undertake vast new military ventures. As Kissinger explained: "Not even a dictatorship can do everything simultaneously." However, even if it could be demonstrated that the American atomic monopoly did have some influence in preventing a greater expansion of Soviet power, what impressed Kissinger was that even during the period when the American monopoly was total, the Soviets managed to consolidate their control in Eastern Europe, the Chinese Communists were able to take over mainland China, and the Soviet nuclear stockpile was able to grow to impressive proportions.

In Kissinger's mind, this was evidence of American failure. There was nothing inevitable in any of these developments. Why had they occurred? Because, according to Kissinger, "we added the atomic bomb to our arsenal without integrating its implications into our thinking." Why? "Because we saw it merely as another tool in a concept of warfare which knew no goal save total victory, and no mode of war except all-out war." Americans, believing that war and peace were separate and distinct, imagining that military and political goals were equally distinct, were incapable of knowing how to use the new weapons diplomatically. Even the urgency of regulating the use of the atom was not correctly perceived. American policy became entirely defensive; Kissinger wrote: "We possessed a doctrine to repel overt aggression, but we could not translate it into a strategy for achieving positive goals."

At the time of the Korean war, when the United States recognized that aggression could be stopped only by military means, American leaders refused to "use the weapons around which our whole military planning had been built." Kissinger wrote: "The gap between military and national policy was complete. Our power was not commensurate with the objectives of our national policy, and our military doctrine could not find any intermediate application for the new weapons." The problems that the United States had been unable to resolve when it enjoyed a nuclear monopoly were still unresolved. The Soviet nuclear capability, then, did not produce the problem; it simply added an additional factor—the psychological one—to a number that had always existed. If the United States was unwilling to risk war with the Soviets when they were unable to retaliate with anything like equal power, there was no great likelihood of such risks being run when the Soviets possessed a nuclear capability and a delivery system.

Given the power of modern weapons, and given the likely consequences of their use, there was every incentive to avoid an all-out conflict, particularly when one considered the civilian casualties that would be incurred everywhere, including in the cities of America. The new weapons of war, Kissinger wrote, threatened "social disintegration," as much for the victor as for the vanquished. The Soviets, according to Kissinger, knew that so long as they presented their challenges in something less than an all-out form, the Americans, whatever their protests, would not respond with a nuclear attack. It was impossible for the United States to go on insisting that any overt act of Soviet aggression would provoke an immediate American use of atomic power. First, the United States would almost certainly never go that far; second, there was no reason for the Soviets to be so clumsy, acting in a way that provoked such a response. Kissinger feared that even the smaller states would soon cease to believe in American power, sensing its unreliability. The United States had developed an extraordinary weapons system; it was not at all clear what purposes it served, or whether it would in fact deter indirect aggression.

Kissinger stated his position very succinctly when he wrote: "Given the power of modern weapons, it should be the task of our strategic doctrine to create alternatives less cataclysmic than a thermonuclear holocaust." A faulty strategic doctrine had always inhibited action by policymakers. Kissinger was reminded of the French example in the 1930s: the French General Staff had greatly exaggerated the military capabilities of Nazi Germany; in doing so, they developed a military doctrine based on two premises, both false: only all-out war was possible; France could win such a war only by staying on the defensive. The creation of the Maginot Line—a vast network of fortresses—became the principal object of military policy. According to Kissinger, the "penalty for doctrinal rigidity was military catastrophe." The United States, in his view, faced a comparable dilemma. It could not go on with plans that presumed that the only kind of war conceivable in the atomic age was all-out war. Kissinger looked for a strategic doctrine that provided some room for diplomacy—indeed, the maximum room for diplomacy—and that recognized the atomic age as providing not only risks but opportunities.

The United States was going to have to learn what other countries had known for a long time; in Kissinger's words, "how to relate the desirable to the possible and above all how to live with possible catastrophe." To be obliged to acknowledge the country's vulnerability was not going to be easy. Nor would it be easy for a nation that had won two twentieth-century wars through abundant resources and a superior technology to admit that wars could be won also through other strengths, including, very significantly for Kissinger, the strength that came from a superior strategic doctrine. Because, according to Kissinger, Americans were "more comfortable with technology than with doctrine," there had been a massive failure to reconsider strategic questions. Every service—the Army, the Navy, the Air Force—had been given a specific mission, together with the arms necessary to defeat the enemy's military units on the ground, at sea, or in the air. The integration of the services was hastened by the development of the long-range airplane and ballistic missiles capable of carrying atomic warheads. Integration, however, Kissinger wrote, was no substitute for an agreed-upon strategic doctrine. There was still too great a tendency to make decisions only when a crisis threatened, as, for example, with the Korean war. Alternatively, strategic decisions were too often reached on the basis of cost.

Kissinger treated with contempt the military promise of "more bang for a buck," but reserved his most serious criticism for the Strategic Air Command, with its insistence on "pure" doctrine. SAC set out to prove, Kissinger said, "that there exists a final answer to our military problem, that it is possible to defeat the enemy utterly, and that war has its own rationale independent of policy." Kissinger thought the SAC doctrine naïve; the fact that it gained congressional support so easily meant that the other services were encouraged to develop an analogous all-out doctrine. At a moment in history when the American interest was to develop strategic doctrine that allowed for various kinds of offensive actions, and that made possible "intermediate applications" of America's military strength, there was an enormous incentive to follow the SAC example and try to win funds by promising total victory. Kissinger thought this a tragedy; it simply prevented the United States from developing strategic doctrines that brought its military power into some sort of balance with its willingness to use that power.

American strategic thought, Kissinger wrote, was still dominated by the nation's experiences during World War II. The country chose to believe that a new war would probably start with a surprise attack on the

United States. What the Japanese had accomplished at Pearl Harbor the Soviets might try to do again, with even more catastrophic consequences for the country. American leaders, who were increasingly preoccupied with preventing such a "sneak attack," began to depict the horrors of such a surprise attack even before the Soviet Union had either the weapons or a delivery system capable of inflicting it. Kissinger, in criticizing this preoccupation with surprise attack, stressed the damage it was doing to the United States. While Americans worried about Soviet bombs falling on their cities, the Soviets were free to pursue their preferred forms of aggression—"internal subversion and limited war." The United States, unwittingly, was placing itself in a posture not too different from the one that France placed itself in before the Nazi menace. While the United States built its Maginot Line in elaborate SAC bases, the Soviets planned offensives that would never call forth these forces; many of the Soviet offensives were not even primarily military. The Soviets, according to Kissinger, were seeking to neutralize the United States "psychologically," and to do this in such a way that no single Soviet provocation ever seemed sufficiently grave to warrant an atomic response.

The American doctrine of massive retaliation was, in Kissinger's view, a gigantic error. Although many credited John Foster Dulles with inventing the doctrine, Kissinger suggested that it had existed in the minds of many responsible Americans long before it came to be officially proclaimed. American military and foreign policy were based on the premise that the Soviets would attack openly, and that every effort should be made to prevent this, or, if that failed, to stop the Soviet advance with an all-out American atomic response. A vast network of foreign alliances was built up; this was justified primarily in terms of the bases these countries provided for American military forces.

Kissinger deplored what he called the "abstractness" of America's diplomacy, neatly separated from an equally abstract military policy. The country still seemed to believe that the purpose of diplomacy was to make peace, while the purpose of war was to achieve victory. During the years when the United States enjoyed its atomic monopoly, opportunities had existed for making imaginative diplomatic forays—thus, for example, Kissinger asked whether it would not have made sense for the United States to open discussions on unilateral disarmament, thereby showing its determination to keep the world peaceful—but no one was prepared to be that venturesome.

America's atomic monopoly was thought to be a question of military strategy; unilateral disarmament was considered a domestic policy issue. No one thought to link the two. General George Marshall, he noted, had said that "he would be reluctant to risk American lives for purely political objectives." Kissinger's comments on Marshall were intentionally muted; so, also, were his reservations about Dean Acheson, but no one reading *Nuclear Weapons and Foreign Policy* could fail to note that Acheson was not for him a towering figure, possessing a vision that others lacked, but a Secretary of State who expressed rather uncritically the opinions that formed the prevailing orthodoxy. Acheson, like so many of his contemporaries, accepted the policy of containment. According to Kissinger, that policy "was based on the assumption that military strategy and diplomacy represented successive phases of national policy: it was the task of military policy to build strength and thereby to contain Soviet aggression. After containment had been achieved, diplomacy would take over." Since United States power could reveal itself fully only when the United States or its allies were attacked, and since Kissinger did not expect the Soviets to attack, he wondered how American superiority would in fact be demonstrated. Even if the Soviets acknowledged American military superiority, why would this lead them to negotiate? It seemed more reasonable to expect that they would seek to erode America's strength or bypass it.

Kissinger found fault with the containment doctrine also because he believed that it adversely affected America's relations with its allies. If all-out war was the only possible response to overt Soviet aggression, then there was no role for America's allies to play. If their existence was threatened, the United States promised to retaliate with atomic weapons. There was nothing for them to do but wait. Worse still, in his view, it provided no incentives for Soviet concessions. What possible motive would the Soviets have for compromising on certain issues, such as those involving the unification of East and West Germany or the international control of the atom? Kissinger wrote: "In short, our posture was bellicose enough to lend color to Soviet peace offensives, but not sufficiently so to induce Soviet hesitations."

When the United States, in 1950, found itself compelled to intervene militarily in Korea, it had no doctrine or strategy suited to the occasion. It was forced to improvise. The Truman administration, Kissinger implied, worried too much about what the Soviets might do. American leaders, he wrote, acted as if only the United States had reason to fear the prospect of all-out war. There was just as much cause for the Soviets to be frightened by that prospect, but American policy dwelt always on the necessity of avoiding a catastrophe. The Soviets were given an immense psychological advantage; in Kissinger's words, "we [the United States] tended to be more aware of our risks than of our opportunities; in fact, in our eyes even opportunities became risks."

The Korean war was kept limited, Kissinger wrote, not because Americans had come to believe in limited war, but because any other policy, it was thought, carried the risk of Soviet intervention and the possibility of all-out war. MacArthur, Kissinger said, argued as if the United States could do anything it wished in Korea without any danger of Soviet intervention; his opponents argued as if the Soviets were simply waiting for an opportunity to intervene, and that one false step would mean the end. Both were wrong; all the arguments were too abstract. The alternatives posed were far too absolute, Kissinger wrote; the idea that there was no middle ground between stalemate and total victory was a mistake. While the Soviets would certainly not have permitted "an unambiguous defeat of China in an all-out war leading to the overthrow of the Communist regime," this did not mean, according to Kissinger, that "the U.S.S.R. would risk everything in order to forestall any transformation in our favor, all the more so as our nuclear superiority was still very pronounced." Had the Chinese armies been pushed back to the narrow neck of the Korean peninsula, some very positive results might have followed. The Chinese, Kissinger explained, might have begun to question the worth of their Soviet alliance; it was not a foregone conclusion that the Soviets would have rushed to the help of the Chinese. The Americans stood to gain a great deal from even a partial Chinese defeat.

The Truman administration, according to Kissinger, never understood this. It acted as if its whole concern ought to be to reassure the Soviet Union, lest the Russian Communists act militarily in response to even a partial American success. The United States acted, Kissinger wrote, "as if every move were equally open to the Kremlin." The divorce between force and diplomacy was complete. For Kissinger, the Korean war was one of the earliest applications of the doctrine of containment. Objectives were never fixed; they fluctuated wildly, and they depended always on the military position of the moment. The only reason that the war ended when it did was that China was literally unable to invest additional resources, while the United States was psychologically unprepared to do so. But even at that moment, the United States, according to Kissinger, made a fundamental mistake. By agreeing to halt military operations entirely, it virtually removed any Chinese incentive to make a definitive peace. As a result, there were "two years of inconclusive negotiations." The mistake had been to divorce force from diplomacy—in Kissinger's words, this caused "our power to lack purpose and our negotiations to lack force."

The mistakes that the United States made in Korea were also made in its dealings with its allies. Insisting, in Acheson's words, that "we work absolutely hand in hand with our allies," and that this be true for all questions where the "danger of war may be created," the Truman administration invented a policy calculated to inhibit American action. It was not very likely that America's European allies would believe that their own security was fundamentally affected by events in Korea. Given their own vulnerability to Soviet forces, they were certain to look with very great suspicion on any policy that carried a substantial risk. Kissinger did not say that they were "wrong" to think in this way; only that it tended to make them "look at the Korean war from the perspective of their vulnerabilities rather than from that of strategic opportunities." Nor did Kissinger suggest that the United States ought to have taken much greater risks; only that many more options existed than were admitted. The country was made to feel that there was no intermediate position between total war and stalemate, or, for that matter, between complete allied support and neutrality. Such a definition of the options, in Kissinger's view, only reinforced the orthodox view that the principal deterrent to Soviet aggression was the American nuclear arsenal, and that every effort had to be made to prevent the United States from becoming involved in essentially peripheral engagements.

The United States, in Kissinger's view, had not learned the correct lessons from its Korean involvement. Nor, for that matter, had it learned anything from the Soviet success in the nuclear field. American leaders, faithful to their "Maginot line mentality," continued to imagine that the new Soviet nuclear capability could be restrained by superior American weapons in greater numbers. They missed the essential point, which, according to Kissinger, was that the doctrine of massive retaliation simply did not make sense any longer. Given existing Soviet capability, and given its prospects for growth, a nuclear stalemate was likely. That stalemate, according to Kissinger, would develop not so much from equal power as from a common assessment of risks. The great danger to the United States, he said, was not from surprise attack, which he called "the greatest threat" but also "the least likely danger." American security, he said, depended on its capacity "to combine physical and psychological factors, to develop weapons systems which do not paralyze our will, and to devise strategies which permit us to shift the risks of counteraction to the other side." That single sentence contained the kernel of Kissinger's argument.

Kissinger knew that mutual terror might provide the peace that was hoped for; he was too innately cautious a man, however, to rely only on the balance of terror. He wanted several options, suited to quite different contingencies. Before he could develop these, he knew that it was essential to discredit the prevailing strategic orthodoxy, which remained powerful and which continued to accept the inevitability of total war. While dubbing the all-out war strategy "the esoteric strategy," he recognized its hold on the American imagination. Most Americans continued to believe that a total defeat of the enemy, resulting in his being rendered entirely impotent, was the desired end of any war. Kissinger reminded his readers that such a course of action was almost always costly and not generally necessary. A state might choose to surrender before its total defeat, precisely because the cost of continued resistance was excessive, given the objectives being contested. Kissinger suggested that while military strength determined the physical outcome of war, political purposes dictated the price belligerents were prepared to pay for victory.

While Americans considered all-out war to be "normal," Kissinger insisted that it was exceptional—in fact, "esoteric." All-out war signified "the abdication of political leadership"; or the existence of a schism so deep that nothing except the total defeat of an enemy seemed to be a sufficient reason for the fighting. Total war had never been common; it had occurred during the sixteenth and seventeenth centuries, when there were irreconcilable religious conflicts, and, again, during "the cycle of wars beginning with World War I." It was during World War I, Kissinger wrote, that "a gap appeared between military and political planning, which has never been bridged." The political leaders abdicated their responsibility; they did not know how to translate military objectives into peace aims that made an armistice possible before the enemy was totally humiliated. Total victory was expected to bring total security; in fact, it only created new tensions.

Total war, as the twentieth century came to know it, was conceivable only because it was technologically possible to produce a substantial surplus, which could be set aside for the making of war. Poorer economies could not afford the luxury of all-out war. Such war presupposed a willingness to defeat an enemy totally, destroy his political institutions, and administer his territory. These obligations posed no great problem for a country like the United States during World War II; its industrial capability was such that it could have both guns and butter while the fighting was going on; when the war ended, and Germany and Japan lay in ruins, the tasks of occupation were not really burdensome.

The doctrine of "all-out war" held no terror for Americans; their historical experience told them nothing of the horror that such war inflicted. If the United States was to learn about the hazards of such war, it could do so only by an act of intuition. Kissinger believed that Americans would have to make the effort to imagine the terrors of total war if they were to be spared its reality. In the atomic age, the destruction in all-out war would be such that no country was likely to retain "either the physical or physiological resources to undertake the administration and rehabilitation of foreign countries." Victory in all-out atomic war would be Pyrrhic; even the victor would be devastated. Kissinger recalled that the decline of Europe began during World War I; there were no victors; the only beneficiaries of an atomic conflict—if there were any—would be those states that had managed to stay aloof.

There would never again be a time when the United States would be invulnerable to attack, or a time when the United States could count on others to stem aggression while it proceeded to build up its own military forces. In the atomic age, the forces-in-being at the time of the initial attack were all-important. Neither side could win unless it succeeded in destroying the whole of the enemy's force-in-being before that force was used. Since the United States had explicitly repudiated the idea that it might attack first—and had in fact refused to do so when it enjoyed a nuclear monopoly—Kissinger believed that its options were effectively limited to a strategy that aimed at avoiding defeat. This might not be possible; maintaining an air defense that would, in Kissinger's words, be "capable of reducing the enemy blow below the level of catastrophe" was not very likely; if it was achieved, however, the United States would probably use its retaliatory power to achieve maximum destruction within the USSR. It was to be hoped that the existence of America's retaliatory force would deter a Soviet all-out attack in the first instance, avoiding a military scenario that could only spell catastrophe for both powers.

Kissinger, while acknowledging the vulnerability of the United States, did not believe that the Soviets intended an all-out attack in the near future. His optimism, insofar as it could be called that, was based on his judgment that the Soviet long-range air force was not yet sufficiently strong, and that if the American civilian population was vulnerable, so, also, was the Soviet population. He thought it important to propose measures that would continue to deter the Soviets; the dispersal of the Strategic Air Force, an effective civil defense organization, and new anti-submarine capabilities were all urgently required.

His chief concern, however, was not with surprise attack but with another kind of eventuality, about which few Americans were greatly concerned. Kissinger put his position very succinctly when he wrote: "The nuclear stalemate may prevent all-out war. It will not deter other forms of conflict; in fact it may even encourage them. The side which can present its challenges in less than an all-out form thereby gains a psychological advantage. It can shift to its opponent the agonizing choice of whether a challenge which explicitly stops short of all-out war should be dealt with by total retaliation." This theme, so modestly introduced, was to become an overwhelming preoccupation for Kissinger. The United States was so preoccupied with surprise attack, or with a massive Soviet invasion of Western Europe, that it refused to take seriously any other type of Soviet incursion. When any occurred, the first impulse was to do nothing; failing that, there was a great concern to take the least possible risk, avoiding any action that might lead to any kind of military confrontation.

Americans vacillated between two positions: imagining that the Soviets were capable of anything, and insisting that they were peace-loving. The

American faith in negotiations was almost childlike. There was, Kissinger said, a notion "that diplomacy can settle disputes through the processes of negotiation, detached from the pressures which otherwise shape international intercourse." Too few Americans gave thought to the really crucial questions of "what kind of military superiority is strategically significant, and what strategy can give an impetus to policy rather than paralyze it." The United States, in 1957, was in much the same position it had been in at the end of World War II. The problem was not to invent a better bomb, or to strive for a technological breakthrough, though there was no reason to disparage those possibilities, but to discover whether a relationship could be established between force and diplomacy—in short, between arms buildup, arms control, alliance policy, and diplomatic negotiations with the Soviet Union.

For years the country had been fed a propaganda diet in which the concept of massive retaliation figured as the only conceivable response to Soviet aggression. Yet, as Kissinger pointed out, the threat did nothing to "avert the Korean war, the loss of northern Indo-China, the Soviet-Egyptian arms deal, or the Suez crisis." He made no effort to conceal his meaning; he wrote, "A deterrent which one is afraid to implement when it is challenged ceases to be a deterrent." All recent Soviet and Chinese aggression, Kissinger wrote, had taken place in areas where the American "commitment of resources was small or nonexistent: Korea, Indo-China, and the Middle East." There was no reason to expect that situation to change, and it was folly to imagine that the Americans would continue to respond to such challenges with the threat of all-out war. Even were such a threat to be made, it would not be believed; were it to be carried out, Kissinger wrote, the country would be guilty of bringing about its own suicide. The prospect was not for rash action but for inaction; it was this that Kissinger found most disturbing. He wanted to develop a strategy that would free the United States from having to choose between mutually unsatisfactory options—"between all-out war and a gradual loss of positions, between Armageddon and defeat without war." Kissinger, in searching for a new strategy, asked whether "limited war" did not provide a viable military option for the nuclear age.

The country claimed to have no great experience with limited war; many thought it an "aberration," not a policy calculated to provide strategic opportunities. Kissinger argued precisely the opposite. Distinguishing between four broadly different types of limited war, he looked first at conflict between secondary powers, such as Israel and Egypt, or India and Pakistan. These wars were limited even when there was some danger of intervention by a major power. A second type would find the Western powers or the Soviet bloc fighting a clearly inferior state, where there was no hazard of outside intervention. An American action in Latin

America or a Soviet action in Eastern Europe would qualify as a limited war in this sense. Then, as a third type, he mentioned a war that began between a major power and a minor power but threatened to spread; he chose as an example the Anglo-French action in Egypt in 1956. Finally, he described a limited war between the major powers. This was the most explosive type of limited war. If it could in fact be kept limited, there was some reason to hope that other kinds of limited wars could also be kept limited.

Kissinger believed that the American preference for an all-out war strategy reflected deep national needs. Writing in an idiom reminiscent of what he had said in *A World Restored*, he asked whether the all-out war strategy was not an "attempt to resolve by force the frustration produced by the fact that foreign policy seems much less tractable than domestic policy." Domestic policy, Kissinger said, was "limited only by technical feasibility," and, in a democracy, "by the sense of justice of the majority of the citizens." Foreign policy, in contradistinction, he wrote, "is limited not only by technical feasibility, but also by the sovereign will of other states which may have different criteria of justice and incompatible conceptions of their interests." Kissinger asked whether the "predilection for all-out war" might not represent "an effort, perhaps subconscious, to transform foreign policy into an aspect of domestic policy, to bring about a situation abroad in which the will of the other nations, or at least that of the enemy, is no longer a significant factor."

Kissinger took great pains to define his concept of limited war; too many believed that it involved nothing more than a decision to refrain from using specific weapons. Kissinger emphasized its political and psychological dimensions; he wrote: "A limited war . . . is fought for specific political objectives which, by their very existence, tend to establish a relationship between the force employed and the goal to be attained. It reflects an attempt to *affect* the opponent's will, not to *crush* it, to make the conditions to be imposed seem more attractive than continued resistance, to strive for specific goals and not for complete annihilation." He acknowledged that limited wars would be more difficult to plan than all-out wars, involving greater subtlety and uncertainty. Limited war, for Kissinger, had one essential characteristic—it was political; in his words, "essentially a political act." Limited war ought not to be perceived as a "small all-out war." To think of it in those terms was to miss its essential quality. Kissinger made his point most explicitly when he wrote: "The prerequisite for a policy of limited war is to reintroduce the political element into our concept of warfare and to discard the notion that policy ends when war begins or that war can have goals distinct from those of national policy."

In the past, limited war was possible because "there existed a political framework which led to a general acceptance of a policy of limited risks." That framework no longer existed. The Soviet bloc, Kissinger wrote, accepted neither the existing international order nor the legitimacy of the domestic structure of non-Soviet states. The Soviet bloc, in short, was "revolutionary," in the same sense that Napoleon had been. A rapidly changing arms technology and the existence of a bipolar world, which meant that a gain for one side always involved a loss for the other, only contributed to the general instability of the times. Since there was no agreement on what constituted a legitimate international order, and since the great-power relations were inherently unstable, Kissinger asked whether the two great powers might not be willing to accept military solutions that involved something other than all-out war. He was fairly optimistic on this point; since both powers understood the likely consequences of all-out war, there was a good prospect that leaders would be pushed to consider other possibilities.

Kissinger insisted that limited war not be seen as "a cheaper substitute for massive retaliation." The strategy was particularly suited to contingencies where the threat of all-out war would not be credible. Thus, for example, he believed that it was "the only means for preventing the Soviet bloc, at an acceptable cost, from overrunning the peripheral areas of Eurasia." Kissinger, recognizing the sense of impotence that prevailed in the West, saw the necessity of instructing the West in a very simple maxim; in his words: "The Soviet bloc, behind its façade of monolithic power, also shrinks from certain consequences." If the Soviet Union was confronted with various forms of credible resistance, he wrote, it would be less likely to imagine that its actions, however aggressive, would go unnoticed. There were other reasons also why he favored the limited war option.

In an almost offhand manner, he wrote: "The Sino-Soviet bloc can be turned back short of general war in one of two ways: by a voluntary withdrawal or by an internal split. The former is unlikely and depends on many factors beyond our control, but the latter deserves careful study." Kissinger did not guarantee that a limited war strategy would create tensions within the Communist world; he believed, however, that it could compel one or other of the major Communist powers to hold back on a complete support of one of its allies. The all-out war strategy, in his view, never achieved that objective. Had the Chinese army been defeated in Korea in 1951, Kissinger wrote, the Soviets would have been compelled to face the problem either of coming to China's help, thereby risking an expansion of the war, or of reneging on its promises to China, making China question the advantage of being so closely tied to the USSR. Kissinger did not pretend that one such American success would have caused a rift to open up between the two Communist states, but he did believe that it would have helped the United States in its relations with its allies and with neutrals. Kissinger saw possibilities in all this only if the United States learned how to orchestrate its diplomatic offensive with its military offensive. Thus, for example, had the Chinese been defeated, only "a conciliatory political proposal to Peiping" would have made sense. No other policy, Kissinger wrote, would have achieved the results he intended.

The limited war strategy appealed to Kissinger precisely because he thought it would permit the United States "to fight local actions on our own terms and to shift to the other side the risk of initiating all-out war." That posture, in his view, was one that the United States had every interest in adopting. The country gained nothing from being represented by friend and foe alike as a great power that had constantly to be bridled, lest in a moment of anger or frustration it use its atomic weapons.

Kissinger knew all the arguments that would be advanced to decry an American reliance on a limited war strategy. He expected to hear the familiar stories about the Soviet bloc's geographic advantages; because of its interior lines of communication, it was supposed to be able to attack at many points on the periphery. Kissinger did not pretend that a limited war capability would allow the United States to defend every point. Still, he thought Americans were rather naïve in the way they imagined a Communist attack would be launched; he found unrealistic the "vision of hordes of Chinese or Soviet soldiers streaming into what has come to be known as the 'Grey Areas,' stretching from Turkey to Malaya." It was time that the United States realized that the Communist bloc's resources were not unlimited; they were not in a position to move wherever they wished.

Limited war, in Kissinger's view, permitted the United States to exploit a unique resource—its industrial potential. A limited war would not exhaust or ruin the country, and the Soviets did not have comparable advantages in preparing for such a war. Yet the United States did nothing to press its advantage. According to Kissinger, the greatest gap in the American defense establishment was "the lack of units capable of fighting local actions and specifically designed for this purpose." The Strategic Air Command, with its commitment to an all-out war strategy, would be useless in a limited war operation. Nowhere in American military planning did he find a readiness to experiment with either limited war forces or a limited war doctrine. Only the intervention of a strong president could change that; it was essentially a political problem, calling for great subtlety. In a limited war, Kissinger wrote, "the psychological equation will be of crucial importance not only with respect to the decision to enter the war but throughout the course of military operations."

A limited war, Kissinger suggested, could have only one of three outcomes—a limited victory, a limited defeat, a stalemate. The belligerents had to remain convinced that any one of these outcomes was preferable to what they would secure through an all-out war effort. Limited war would never bring a final solution, but it would also never lead to overwhelming catastrophe; it presupposed a flexible military policy, a subtle diplomacy, and a courageous and vigorous political leadership. Unless the United States adopted a military policy that permitted a wide range of possible actions, limited war was inconceivable. The role of diplomacy would be to guarantee that the enemy had the correct information, so that it understood what was going on. Even if the enemy understood perfectly American intentions, there was always some chance of miscalculation, but Kissinger hoped that this danger could be kept to a minimum. The political problem, in his view, would probably prove to be the most difficult one. Leaders in the United States would have to understand that absolute victory was no longer a real possibility; the public, in turn, would have to be educated to stop insisting on such an outcome.

Having developed all the political, diplomatic, and military reasons for supplementing traditional deterrence concepts with a limited war strategy, Kissinger plunged deeper and raised the sensitive question of the role that nuclear weapons should play in limited war. To advocate any use of nuclear weapons invariably raised controversy, and Kissinger realized that his arguments would be carefully and critically scrutinized. He suggested, in effect, that if nuclear weapons were by definition "horror weapons," useful only for total destruction, then all efforts to create more sophisticated, lower-yield weapons made no sense at all. He believed that situations might well arise where the Soviets or the Chinese accepted "the onus of atomic aggression," and used atomic weapons in something other than an all-out fashion. Thus, for example, he could imagine nuclear weapons being used against American forces in the Middle East or in Southeast Asia without the automatic response being an all-out atomic war. Kissinger wrote: "It is difficult to believe that we would rush into the cataclysm of a thermonuclear war to prevent the defeat of a few conventional divisions, particularly if the Soviet leaders showed their usual skills in presenting their challenge ambiguously." In such circumstances, a limited nuclear war capability could provide an option that no other strategy would offer.

However, such a strategy could not be improvised at the last moment. It would be immensely difficult for proper intelligence to operate in the midst of an atomic battle; the temptation to panic would be overwhelming. The tactics used with conventional arms would not serve also with atomic arms. In conventional war, a front line existed, and each side controlled the territory behind that line; the disruption of supplies, through the bombings of cities, communication centers, and industrial plants, was almost essential in a limited conventional war. Limited nuclear war, Kissinger explained, would not have the same characteristics; tactics for such a war would depend on "small, highly mobile, self-contained units," which would rely principally "on air transport even within the combat zone." Kissinger wrote: "The proper analogy to limited nuclear war is not traditional land warfare, but naval strategy, in which self-contained units with great firepower gradually gain the upper hand by destroying their enemy counterparts without physically occupying territory or establishing a front line." Kissinger insisted that such tactics would necessitate "a radical break with our traditional notions of warfare and military organization."

While public opinion expected that all nuclear war would be highly destructive, and never stopped to distinguish between all-out nuclear war and limited nuclear war, Kissinger argued the importance of making such a distinction. He was determined to make a case for a limited nuclear war strategic option. If a state was prepared to desist from using *all* the weapons at its disposal—including nuclear arms—when it faced defeat in a limited conventional war, Kissinger could see no reason why it should not show a similar restraint in a limited nuclear war. The interest to avoid all-out atomic war would be the same in both instances.

Kissinger did not say that every limited war should be fought as a limited nuclear war; only that the capacity to choose that option should exist. He emphasized always the advantage of being prepared for many very different contingencies. Kissinger insisted on distinguishing between "advantageous" and "desirable" strategies; as he explained, "the nuclear age permits only a choice among evils." When Kissinger spoke of an "advantageous strategy," he meant a strategy that maximized the American relative superiority over that of the enemy, avoided general war, was least costly, and had the greatest potentialities for deterring aggression. The important thing was to make the enemy aware that the United States had many options—that it was not reduced to having to choose between fighting in one way or not fighting at all.

Limited nuclear war was not a substitute for all-out war but a strategy suited to issues where the provocation was clearly not one that called for an all-out response. The risks and frustrations of limited atomic war were real; they could not, however, be avoided. They were the penalties, Kissinger wrote, of our having "permitted our atomic monoply to be broken without having first achieved a workable system of international control." Kissinger summed up his strategic recommendations under five heads:

1. "Thermonuclear war must be avoided, except as a last resort."

2. "A power possessing thermonuclear weapons is not likely to accept unconditional surrender without employing them, and no nation is likely to risk thermonuclear destruction except to the extent that it believes its survival to be directly threatened."

3. "It is the task of our diplomacy to make clear that we do not aim for unconditional surrender, to create a framework within which the question of national survival is not involved in every issue. But equally, we must leave no doubt about our determination to achieve intermediary objectives and to resist by force any Soviet military move."

4. "Since diplomacy which is not related to a plausible employment of force is sterile, it must be the task of our military policy to develop a doctrine and a capability for the graduated employment of force."

5. "Since a policy of limited war cannot be implemented except behind the shield of a capability for all-out war, we must retain a retaliatory force sufficiently powerful and well protected so that by no calculation can an aggressor discern any benefit in resorting to all-out war."

For Kissinger, military strategy had a necessary and essential link with diplomacy. Military planning before World War II depended on secrecy; the enemy had to be kept in the dark about what one intended to do. In the atomic age, safety resided in the enemy's knowing and understanding the meaning of all significant military moves. Kissinger was insistent on this point: "Limited nuclear war is impossible unless our diplomacy succeeds in giving an indication of our intentions to the other side. It may even have to make up for any lack of imagination on the part of the Soviet leaders by conveying to them our understanding of the nature and the limits of nuclear war. To be sure, such a program will not deter an opponent determined on a final showdown. No diplomatic program can be a substitute for an adequate retaliatory power. But to the extent that it is possible to prevent a war from becoming all-out because of miscalculation of our intentions or because of a misunderstanding of the nature of nuclear warfare, our diplomacy should seek to bring about a better comprehension of the range of strategic options of the nuclear period."

Kissinger, in stressing the role of diplomacy, anticipated positions that he was to take also with respect to disarmament and arms control. For, in Kissinger's mind, if the atomic age required the United States to prepare for war, doing so in such a way as to maximize its military and political options, there was a no less urgent necessity: to be prepared to negotiate on arms limitation. Kissinger had no illusions about the difficulty of the enterprise; he also knew why it was essential that it be undertaken. Arms control, in his view, was no less crucial than arms build-up.

He started with a simple proposition: "negotiations can be successful," he wrote, "only if all parties accept some common standard transcending their disputes." While disagreements among the major powers had rarely been so intense, it was also true that they felt inhibited about using force to resolve differences. Kissinger took heart from their inhibitions. While each side was still hoping to gain a technological advantage over the other—the arms race was the inevitable consequence—there was also a growing hope that diplomacy might provide the security that arms did not offer. Kissinger did not expect diplomacy to achieve the objectives that certain of its more ardent advocates hoped for. He saw no possibility of a major diplomatic breakthrough. Still, certain things were possible. Diplomacy could, in Kissinger's view, provide a forum for the settlement of disputes that had become unprofitable for both sides. It could also help tremendously to keep open channels of information; each side needed to keep the other informed of its intentions.

Kissinger recognized three conditions that could jeopardize the fragile stalemate that kept the two great powers at peace. The Soviet Union, for one reason or other, might conclude that it had sufficient strength to attack the United States with impunity. Alternatively, the Soviet bloc, believing that the United States would not respond to an act of local aggression, might be confronted with a quite violent American reaction, produced largely by the fear that the Soviet thrust presaged a more serious Soviet aggression. Finally, the Soviets might misconstrue American intentions, assuming, for example, that the American use of nuclear weapons in a local engagement heralded the beginning of an all-out war, when, in fact, such was not the United States intention at all. To prevent the first contingency, the United States could rely only on an effective and invulnerable deterrent force; to prevent either of the other contingencies, diplomacy was the only resource. If diplomacy failed where the interests of the two sides were so close—and did not avoid the terror of all-out war—then there was no hope that diplomacy could cope with more complex and difficult issues, such as those that related to ideological conflict and revolutionary upheaval.

Just as military policy had been too greatly preoccupied with absolutes—to prevent all-out war—so, Kissinger argued, diplomacy had become equally absolutist. Its only stated objective was to secure absolute peace. Kissinger deplored the concentration on "total remedies." While he understood why certain arms control advocates imagined that their principal concern should be with banning all atomic weapons, he wondered whether they realized that they were attacking the most intractable of all the problems. Was there no advantage in making an effort to cope with a somewhat less difficult issue? Specifically, Kissinger proposed negotiations to mitigate the consequences of the use of atomic weapons; in his view, this would prevent any war that did break out from becoming an all-out war.

He had no faith in the simple expedient of reducing arms stockpiles. They were not the cause of war; they generated fear because they suggested that the state which had constructed such a vast armament was prepared to run substantial risks. The problem, then, was to reduce the tension that made states willing to expend such vast sums in arms buildup.

Any disarmament plan that gave an advantage to one side over the other would never gain acceptance. In the past, Kissinger wrote, disarmament plans were generally based on the assumption of a reasonably stable weapons technology. That assumption made little sense in the atomic age. A laboratory breakthrough of some importance was always a distinct possibility; this only served to increase the general reluctance to reduce forces. Nothing, Kissinger wrote, would induce the Soviets "to accept a level of armaments which reduces its ability to control the satellites or to play a major role in contiguous areas such as the Middle East."

Given the difficulties of achieving agreement on the reduction of forces—and given the instability of such an agreement even if concluded—Kissinger could understand why the great powers had come to concentrate their disarmament efforts on the problems of inspection and control. Yet these efforts generally foundered, in Kissinger's view, and not only because of Soviet unwillingness to permit the kind of foreign intrusion that any responsible inspection scheme made necessary. Where the possibilities of cheating were so large, particularly where sophisticated weapons systems were involved, there was a great incentive to violation; concealment was always a threat, and this made both sides uneasy. Also, it was by no means certain that even workable control and inspection schemes would prevent new weapons development; the prospect of such development only increased the hesitations of the great powers. Because weapons generally labeled "defensive" might also be used in "offensive" operations, both sides hesitated when suggestions were made for the banning of only offensive weapons. In short, most proposals for inspection and control failed to make much headway because of suspicion on both sides of the other's intentions.

Disarmament negotiations, having failed to reduce existing stockpiles and having failed to prevent the development of new and more powerful weapons, had become increasingly preoccupied with a third problem— the prevention of surprise attack. In this area, as in the others, the success had been minimal, mostly, Kissinger argued, because too many of the arms control advocates argued for absolute programs, for what he called "final solutions." The urgent need was for more modest proposals.

Kissinger proposed an approach to arms control that would "have the advantage of focusing thinking on things to accomplish rather than on those which should not be done." From his point of view, war limitation negotiations provided the opportunity for each side to gain a better sense of the other's intentions, thereby minimizing the danger of war by miscalculation. He thought it imperative that the Soviets be instructed in the possibilities of limited nuclear war. He wrote: "Insofar as the repeated Soviet denials of the possibility of limited nuclear war represent a real conviction and not simply a form of psychological warfare, an energetic diplomacy addressed to the problem of war limitation can serve as a substitute for lack of imagination on the part of the Soviet General Staff." Before that could happen, however, the Americans needed themselves to understand the nature of such a strategy, and he was not at all certain that such understanding existed in either American military or political circles.

In limited war, Kissinger wrote, "it will be necessary to give up the notion that direct diplomatic contact ceases when military operations begin. Rather, direct contact is never more necessary to ensure that both sides possess the correct information about the consequences of expanding a war and to be able to present formulas for a political settlement." Kissinger recognized the paradox of the situation; secrecy had to disappear in the nuclear age; battles would approach "the stylized contests of the feudal period which served as much as a test of will as a trial of strength." If, Kissinger wrote, American military leaders understood what was implied by a doctrine of limited war, negotiations could start to guarantee that limited war remained limited. Agreement on limitations with respect to targets and the size of weapons might be explored. The elimination of certain targets—cities, for example—would serve to place an upper limit on the size of weapons that it would be profitable to use. Efforts might be made to reach agreement that "all weapons above 500-kiloton explosive power should be 'clean' bombs." These agreements would have to be made before the outbreak of hostilities. The United States would do well, Kissinger wrote, to "shift the emphasis of disarmament negotiations from the technically almost impossible problem of preventing surprise attack to an effort to mitigate the horror of war."

Believing that there was no prospect for the early realization of any of the existing plans for arms control, Kissinger advocated negotiations that would communicate two principal messages. First, the Soviet Union had to be made aware that the United States was no longer committed to its all-out war strategy, to the exclusion of all others; it was time that the Soviets knew that other options were being considered, and that military planning was proceeding to make such options real. Second, the Soviet Union needed to habituate itself to the fact that a whole range of military actions were possible for the United States, and that these ought not to be seen as a prelude to all-out war. Kissinger recognized that other objectives might also be realized through negotiations; he regarded them as a necessary first step in a process that was certain to be long and tedious. Kissinger wrote *Nuclear Weapons and Foreign Policy* immediately after Suez and Budapest, at a time when many were outraged by Soviet truculence and aggression. He showed an almost studied indifference to many of the preferred solutions for dealing with the Soviet Union. He favored negotiations—for purposes that he thought important—but he insisted that they deal with an agenda in great part determined by the United States. Diplomacy that proceeded along such lines, Kissinger wrote, would produce beneficial results, not only for the United States but for the international community more generally.

Having given the broad outlines of a new policy to govern American relations with the Soviet Union, Kissinger turned next to a consideration of the relations of the United States with its allies. Since the end of World War II, the United States had entered into "a vast and complicated system of alliances" that involved some forty-four sovereign states. In looking at this alliance network, Kissinger found many incongruities. With certain of its allies, the United States appeared to share no common purpose at all; with others, the alliance appeared to add little to the effective strength of the United States. So long as the United States relied on a military doctrine that made all-out war a plausible response to any major crisis, many of its allies could be expected to press for a policy of minimum risk; they had no reason to wish to become involved in what they conceived to be America's quarrels; to jeopardize their own national survival for such ends seemed utterly insane.

The doctrine of massive retaliation, Kissinger wrote, removed every incentive for the Allies to make substantial military contributions of their own. They saw no need to do so, and were quite prepared to imagine that they had done their duty by offering bases or facilities for American forces. Worse still, the strategy compelled them to act as a permanent pressure group, urging America to be cautious, avoiding all unnecessary risks. Kissinger, looking at the American and allied disposition of forces, spoke of "half measures and mutual pretenses," all generated by a faulty military doctrine. In Europe, where there were substantial ground forces, American strategic doctrine specifically discounted the possibility of limited war. The argument had always been made that if the Soviets moved in Europe, the United States would use its all-out nuclear capability. If so, what were the ground forces preventing or deterring? While Kissinger was prepared to support a policy that allowed for a local defense of Europe, he insisted that this would require a commitment of forces and a strategic doctrine quite different from any that existed at that moment.

Kissinger went to the heart of the matter when he wrote: "What if the Red Army attacks in Europe explicitly to disarm West Germany and offers to the United States and the United Kingdom immunity from strategic bombing and a withdrawal to the Oder after achieving its limited objective? Is it clear that France would fight under such circumstances? Or that the United Kingdom would initiate an all-out war which, however it ended, would mean the end of British civilization? Or that an American President would trade fifty American cities for Western Europe? And, even if he should be prepared to do so, it would still be the task of our strategy to develop less fearful options than national catastrophe or surrender." Many Europeans, scrutinizing the hazards of the nuclear age, much preferred a neutralist policy. Kissinger argued that neither neutralism nor surrender would serve Europe's interest; like the United States, Europe wanted to avoid an all-out nuclear war. Were Europe to become neutralist, the United States would be confined to the Western Hemisphere, and, in the event of a crisis, Kissinger wrote, the United States would have no option but to fight an all-out war. Such a war, he insisted, would be fatal to the belligerent states, and probably also to those that remained neutral. There would be no victors after an all-out atomic exchange.

"The acid test of an alliance," he said, was its "ability to achieve agreement on two related problems: whether a given challenge represents aggression and, if so, what form resistance should take." A limited aggression would necessarily affect the interests of different states differently. The United States' alliances were all explicitly regional; their purpose was to make possible regional military cooperation, and, in time, one hoped, other forms of cooperation as well. It simply did not make sense to pretend that Pakistan would be seriously disturbed by events in Hungary, or that Belgium would become anxious over Korean developments. Nothing was gained from pretending that America's allies were ready to involve themselves actively in areas outside their primary concern. Even Great Britain, the one ally that might under certain circumstances be expected to do so, would not, in Kissinger's view, be tempted to act as a major power. A major power in the nuclear age, for him, was one that could "afford a retaliatory capability sufficient to destroy any possible opponent." Only the United States and the Soviet Union possessed that capability; only they could be exptected to do certain kinds of things. None of America's allies could engage in a war with the Soviet Union without the promise of American assistance. None of them could embark on a limited war against a smaller power without America's protection or the acquiescence of the Soviet Union. The lesson of Suez, according to Kissinger, "was that none of our allies can fight a limited war and keep it limited by its own effort." This, for Kissinger, was a demonstration of a certain kind of "impotence," and it was futile to deny or conceal it.

The success of America's alliances, in Kissinger's view, depended on a recognition of the fact that the interests of the United States and those of its allies could not in all instances coincide; the disparity in power and responsibility was simply too great. Cooperation, however, was possible—indeed, mandatory—on purely regional questions. On the world balance of power—a legitimate American interest—Kissinger recognized that agreement would not always exist. He wrote: "Provided our military doctrine does not threaten to transform every war into all-out war, our allies must, therefore, be prepared to let us act alone or with a different grouping of powers outside the area of regional cooperation. We, in turn, should show understanding and compassion for the problems of states whose margin of survival—military, political and economic—is far smaller than ours. Any other course will make for paralysis: it will cause our allies to hamstring us *outside* the area of mutual concern, and it will cause us to frustrate our allies *within* it."

Kissinger wrote all this at the height of the Dulles era, when there was much insistence on the "obligations" of allies, who were expected to keep in step with American policy. Kissinger's injunction, in effect, was to urge a relaxation of all such pressures; it was unnecessary for every American move to be supported by every American ally. As for the uncommitted states—the so-called neutrals—who caused such grief for Dulles and others who thought like him, the injunction was much the same. Kissinger asked American leaders to take a much less grave view of the neutralist stance of the uncommitted. While the United States interest lay in identifying itself with the "hopes and aspirations" of the new states, and with trying "to prevent an alignment of the white against the colored races of the world," this did not oblige American leaders to become uncritical admirers of the newly created states.

The leaders of these new states, in Kissinger's view, were the children of colonialism; they had imbibed along with the foreign rule they detested much of their political and social philosophy. When they emerged as leaders of independence movements, they thought it necessary to emphasize the distance that separated them from their colonial masters; they had to insist on their moral and spiritual superiority. Once independence was achieved, many of these same leaders, Kissinger said, realized that their way of thinking was closer to that of their former colonial rulers than it was to the populations which they governed. Rather than admit this, they became all the more passionate in their anti-colonial bias; it was as if they needed their anti-colonialism to make secure their personal identity. Neutralism and anti-colonialism, when viewed from this perspective, appeared almost as a spiritual necessity; it was only incidentally a calculated political policy. Kissinger urged the United States to accept the situation, and not to be confused or troubled by it. There was nothing to be achieved in trying to court the newly independent states. "A too ardent embrace," Kissinger wrote, "might only lead them toward the Soviet bloc." This did not mean, obviously, that they ought to be ignored. Specific and limited objectives could be sought; it made no sense, however, for a general effort to be made to compel them to abandon their neutralism.

With a bluntness no less great than that revealed in his appraisals of

Great Britain and the other Western European states, Kissinger wrote of "the unfamiliarity of many of the leaders of the newly independent nations with the elements of international stability and with the nature of modern power relationships." Many of these men had achieved prominence largely through their opposition to the colonial powers; that training, Kissinger wrote, was not particularly suited to coping with international problems. Nor was it at all obvious that being schooled in the traditional liberal orthodoxies of the nineteenth century was an advantage. Neither experience prepared men for the problems of international relations in the atomic age. In the new societies, rhetoric almost always played a too important role. Kissinger cautioned lest there be "an overestimation of what can be accomplished by words alone." He noted how vulnerable the new states were to Soviet "peace offensives," and explained the Communist success largely in terms of the attractiveness of moral precepts to such societies. The Communists knew how to couch their activity in words calculated to appeal to newly independent states. Also, because Chinese or Soviet power was very visible, often taking the form of armies massed along frontiers, this made a deep impression on the new states. American power, by comparison, seemed abstract and ephemeral.

Because domestic problems were often intractable in the underdeveloped world, Kissinger believed that there was a great temptation for leaders to ignore these problems and to seek to make a reputation for themselves in international affairs. Kissinger did not criticize the leaders of new states for doing this; he did, however, ask whether it did not lead them to assume roles for which they were unprepared. He knew that such an argument would seem condescending, but he felt obliged to make it. Kissinger believed that policy could no more be founded on moral precept alone than it could be founded on power alone.

Kissinger urged the United States to find "a twentieth-century equivalent of 'showing the flag,' an ability and a readiness to make our power felt quickly and decisively, not only to deter Soviet aggression but also to impress the uncommitted with our capacity for decisive action." He emphasized the need to alter the mistaken reliance on purely military associations with the new states; the United States, in Kissinger's view, emphasized far too much "a military grouping of powers." The new states desperately needed peace; their economic development and security depended on it. It was entirely understandable that they were suspicious of American military alliances, involving other former colonial areas. Since these alliances offered such dubious military advantages, Kissinger wondered why they were persisted in. A more rational American policy would be to help establish regional groupings with sufficient economic power to be able to defend themselves. Kissinger wanted the United States to "develop not only a greater compassion but also a greater majesty." He deplored the constant scurrying about of high American officials who lived with the illusion that it was their business to be concerned with every crisis. The United States, Kissinger wrote, would do well to worry less about offending the uncommitted and do more to maintain a posture that made sense to the new states and that they would be able to react to. Kissinger's familiarity with the emerging nations was too limited for him to elaborate an appropriate diplomatic or military strategy. Instead, he cited the few general principles that ought to guide American policy in those parts of the world.

With Europe, where he was on more solid ground, it was possible for him to be much more specific. He thought the arguments generally advanced for America's alliances, particularly for NATO, were inadequate. Arguing in much the way he did in his studies of Metternich and Castlereagh, he saw the United States as the "island power" of the twentieth century, whose "survival" depended "on preventing the opposite land mass from falling under hostile control." The key to Eurasia, Kissinger wrote, was Western Europe. If Europe were lost, the Middle East and Africa would also go, and the strategic advantage in an all-out war would shift to the Soviet Union. If that ever happened, the United States "would be forced into a military effort incompatible with what is now considered the American way of life." That, however, in Kissinger's view, was not the most pessimistic assessment that could be made of the likely consequences of a "loss" of Europe. "At worst," he wrote, "we would cease to be masters of our policy."

None of this had to happen. The industrial and manpower resources available to the NATO countries exceeded by a very considerable margin those available to the Soviet Union. The problem, according to Kissinger, was that NATO had never organized its power effectively; it still lacked a military force capable of offering a meaningful defense. NATO, on a larger scale, was experiencing the same kinds of difficulties that were afflicting the United States. NATO lacked a clear sense of the type of war it might be compelled to fight, or the type of forces that would be necessary for such a war. While new force levels were periodically announced, they were never realized; no one pretended that NATO had a military defense system capable of withstanding a Soviet assault.

Kissinger saw many reasons for this failure; it stemmed from America's unwillingness to share its atomic information, but also from the reluctance of America's European allies to make any of the economic sacrifices that a credible defense system required. Some states clearly preferred not to face the realities of Soviet power. So long as the United States persisted in its policies of making the defense of Europe depend on American willingness to conduct an all-out war, Kissinger wrote, there would be no incentive for the European members of NATO to make a meaningful contribution to their own defense. They would continue to provide facilities (bases and the like), contributing to the "trip wire" that theoretically deterred the Soviets, but such policies, in his view, did not constitute a major defense effort. As Kissinger explained, "a trip-wire is not to hold a line but to define a cause of war." America's NATO allies, to the extent that they made any military contribution, simply duplicated what the United States was itself doing.

Until NATO could resolve two questions—what the purpose of a military establishment on the Continent should be, and what the implications of nuclear weapons were for allied strategy—there was no possibility of a coherent NATO deployment of forces. Kissinger saw a proliferation of military establishments on the Continent, "too strong to serve as a trip-wire, too weak to resist a Soviet onslaught, and in any case, not really designed for that purpose." Kissinger wrote: "NATO has evolved in a never-never land, where our strategic doctrine has undermined the European incentive to make a substantial military effort, while the Europeans have been reluctant to make their hesitations explicit lest we withdraw the guarantee of their frontiers which, in terms of an all-out strategy, has been NATO's only really meaningful function." It was imperative that NATO define its task precisely. Kissinger asked: "Is it a device to serve warning on the Soviet bloc that an attack on Western Europe will inevitably unleash an all-out war? Or is it designed to assure the integrity of Europe against attack?" If the first was its purpose, then the policy of maintaining substantial British, Canadian, and American contingents on the Continent made no sense at all; if the second was intended, then there was a need for radical changes in strategic doctrine.

In the final analysis, no military policy could be effective that did not lead the United States and its allies to estimate correctly the nature of the Soviet challenge. That challenge, in Kissinger's mind, was contained in what he called their "strategy of ambiguity." Though the Soviet Union and Communist China frequently announced their revolutionary intentions, which were nothing less than to destroy the existing social and political order, many refused to take their declarations seriously. What had been true in the nineteenth century with Napoleon and in the twentieth century with Hitler was still true; non-revolutionary states imagined that a demonstration of "good faith" and a "willingness to come to an agreement" would make the revolutionary states less intractable. Repeating almost verbatim from *A World Restored*, Kissinger suggested that "against a revolutionary power, tactics of conciliation are self-defeating." "Safety," he insisted, "can be found only in a precautionary policy which stakes an assessment of future menace against current protestations of innocence."

Soviet strength, Kissinger believed, derived from its "combination of revolutionary righteousness and psychological adeptness." The Soviet leaders knew how to expand their power "into the center of Europe and along the fringes of Asia by coupling each act of expansion with protestations of peace, democracy and freedom." Kissinger thought that the strength of the Communists derived not so much from Marxist doctrine as from their being acquainted with the liberal doctrine of the West, and knowing how to exploit it for their own purposes. Every major Soviet policy shift, Kissinger wrote, could be attributed to a specific assessment of what were thought to be the tactical requirements of the moment. Soviet peace offensives alternated with threats of war because each served different Soviet purposes at different times. When the Communists launched a peace offensive, they appeared to have no interest in exporting their revolution; when they became belligerent, they insisted it was because the capitalist powers were encircling them. Both refrains became dull through repetition, but neither failed to gain a sympathetic audience; Kissinger claimed that "each new Soviet move has been taken at face value and has produced infinite arguments over whether the Soviet Government was preparing for a 'showdown' or ushering in a period of peace." This was a total misconception of the way in which the Soviet Union conducted its affairs.

The Soviets, Kissinger wrote, did not believe in negotiation as a bargaining process; for them, negotiation simply served to "ratify" an "objective situation." They were generally cautious; they almost never made bold moves; their policies were understood only after the fact. Thus, for example, no one in 1954 thought that the Soviet objective was to become a power in the Middle East. The Czech sale of arms to Egypt did not prepare the West for the threats that the Soviets delivered at the time of Suez. Kissinger believed that the Soviet "strategy of ambiguity" was one that the West had great difficulties coping with. The challenge posed by Soviet power, Kissinger said, was more moral than physical, and the question was whether the West would recognize a danger early enough, and do something about it before it knew absolutely that the threat was real, by which time it was generally too late to act. Kissinger attributed many of the Soviet successes to a "greater moral toughness," and to a greater willingness to run moral and physical risks. He thought that Communist theory was morally bankrupt, but this did not deter the Soviets; they had greater resolve and greater self-confidence than those who opposed them.

In their diplomacy, Kissinger wrote, Leninist doctrine remained crucial. Lenin, he said, had seen negotiation as "one tool among many others in the conduct of the international class struggle, to be judged by its utility in advancing Soviet objectives, but without any inherent moral value in itself." Americans placed a much greater value on negotiation; at times, it seemed almost an end in itself. Kissinger attributed this in part to the dominant position of lawyers among those responsible for the conduct of American foreign policy. Law and business were the two principal training grounds for American diplomacy. In Kissinger's view, the legal approach was particularly unsuited to negotiations with a revolutionary power. As he explained: "Law is a legitimization of the *status quo* and the change it permits presupposes the assent of two parties. A revolutionary party, on the contrary, is revolutionary precisely because it rejects the *status quo*. It accepts a 'legal' framework only as a device for subverting the existing order." Ordinary diplomatic methods, Kissinger wrote, cannot serve in dealings with a revolutionary power. In a legitimate international order, the purpose of negotiation was to reach agreement; in a revolutionary order, Kissinger explained, "the protagonists at the conference address not so much one another as the world at large." Kissinger believed that the major weakness of American diplomacy was its failure to heed this "symbolic aspect of foreign policy."

By so totally ignoring the psychological dimension, the United States gave its adversaries an enormous advantage. According to Kissinger, the international debate was "carried on almost entirely in the categories and at the pace established by the Soviets." While everyone concentrated on "the horror of nuclear weapons," no one thought to worry about "the danger of Soviet aggression which would unleash them." The Soviets were remarkably tranquil; they negotiated when they wished to, broke off negotiations when they saw no advantage in continuing, and never expected to pay a penalty for doing so. The Soviets almost always chose to discuss subjects calculated to give the greatest pain to the United States. Since their purpose was never to lessen tensions, let alone to reach agreement, they saw no reason to change their tactics. Kissinger characterized such diplomacy as "political warfare"; it had little to do with the objectives that normally governed diplomatic dealings. He understood why Clausewitz's famous epigram about war's being a continuation of politics by other means could be so easily converted into the Soviet maxim that "peace is a continuation of struggle, only by other means."

In reflecting on Communist military doctrine, Kissinger gave his highest accolade to the Chinese Communists, particularly to Mao. Two of Mao's essays, written in the 1930s, were said to be "remarkable for their sense of proportion and their skill in adapting the Leninist orthodoxy to Chinese conditions." Maoist theory, Kissinger wrote, combined "a high order of analytical ability with rare psychological insight and complete ruthlessness." The basic Chinese military strategy was "protracted limited war." Kissinger emphasized Mao's insistence on the importance of psychological advantage; that, for Mao, was quite as important as any physical advantage. Mao believed that in any war a psychological advantage accrued to the side that was not determined to make peace; the side that desperately wanted peace, even when it enjoyed a military advantage, was seriously handicapped. In any war with Communist powers, Kissinger wrote, the first and most important prerequisite was to know precisely the objectives of the war. In one of his very exceptional uses of italics, Kissinger wrote: *"And no conditions should be sought for which one is not willing to fight indefinitely and no advance made except to a point at which one is willing to wait indefinitely. The side which is willing to outwait its opponent—which is less eager for a settlement—can tip the psychological balance, whatever the outcome of the physical battle."*

Kissinger asked whether there was any indication that the Soviet leaders sincerely wanted peace, and that they were honest in their protestations of peaceful intentions. He thought that the evidence suggested the contrary. This did not mean, he hastened to explain, that the Soviets would continue to be revolutionary for all time to come. History showed many instances where a revolutionary movement "lost its Messianic élan," but this generally happened "only when a Messianic movement came to be opposed with equal fervor or when it reached the limit of its military strength." Kissinger disparaged those theories that emphasized the "embourgeoisement" of the Soviet Union, and that waited patiently for a new "middle class" to come forward to change Soviet doctrine. Being skeptical, he warned against false hopes being raised. The United States, he thought, needed to do everything in its power to reassure the Soviet bloc, and to bring it to more reasonable policies. However, if the Soviets insisted on total security—something unattainable in any international system of sovereign states—there would be no way to reassure them. So long as they persisted in their search for total security, the only safe course for the United States was to expect the revolutionary struggle to continue, though in quite new forms. This, Kissinger explained, did not imply that he expected an imminent showdown with the Soviet Union, or that the United States needed to prepare for all-out war. "An all-out attack," Kissinger wrote, "is the least likely form of Soviet strategy, either politically or militarily."

The United States, Kissinger implied, needed to develop both greater flexibility and greater self-assurance. It might begin by taking somewhat more seriously the Soviet Union's endemic threat to "bury" capitalist America; there was no advantage to be gained from arguing that such statements were simply rhetorical. Kissinger criticized the American habit of talking about the conflict with the Soviet bloc as a temporary aberration, likely to be terminated by some great breakthrough. "History demonstrates," Kissinger wrote, "that revolutionary powers have never been brought to a halt until their opponents stopped pretending that the revolutionaries were really misunderstood legitimists." The United States, he explained, would do well to study Soviet psychology as closely as the

Russians studied the American character. There were no purely political *or* military solutions, Kissinger insisted. The object of American policy ought to be to create a strategy in which political, psychological, economic, and military components meshed. Neither China nor the Soviet Union, he explained, was prepared to risk everything for any objective other than its own national survival.

Kissinger reflected on what the Soviet leaders must have felt at the end of World War II. Having made a herculean effort to defeat Nazi Germany, and having suffered during the previous twenty years from internal turmoil, deprivation, and repression, they must have been dismayed to emerge from all this and find the United States in possession of a weapon that put the Soviet Union in greater peril than it had ever been. But their years of revolutionary militancy prepared them admirably for their newest adversity. They began by denying that the atom bomb in any way altered Leninist theory; the new weapon, far from delaying the inevitable decline of capitalism, they said, would only hasten it. Kissinger was impressed by their cool and calculated response; he wrote: "The result was a *tour de force*, masterful in its comprehension of psychological factors, brutal in its consistency, and ruthless in its sense of direction." The Soviets systematically developed three related themes and then used diplomacy and propaganda to disseminate them. First, they argued that the United States exaggerated the power of atomic weapons; this, Kissinger explained, was intended to prove that in the "essential categories of power" the Soviet Union remained preponderant. Second, they argued that though atomic arms were not so powerful as the Americans pretended, they were more horrible than the Americans admitted, and should therefore be banned. Finally, they insisted that the only legitimate use of the atom was for peaceful purposes, and that in this area they were themselves prepared to take the lead. A more ingenious political, diplomatic, and propaganda response to the atom bomb could scarcely have been made. Kissinger was impressed with Soviet resourcefulness, not only during the period when the American nuclear monopoly was complete and the Russians concentrated on their "ban the bomb" propaganda, but also later, when they alternated threats of nuclear retaliation with suggestions that the bombs be eliminated entirely. As Kissinger explained, the Soviets knew how to exploit both American inhibitions and fears.

Throughout Stalin's lifetime, every effort was made to play down the importance of the bomb; any suggestion that it had altered the course of history was dismissed as laughable. Soviet news media gave no attention to Western nuclear achievements; in fact, Kissinger noted, they gave no news of their own first atomic explosion—the world learned of it through an American announcement. Kissinger interpreted the reticence as reflecting a Soviet fear that the Americans might launch a preventive attack on the Soviet Union to destroy the Russian atomic capability before it became too highly developed. Another reason for the reticence, Kissinger believed, was that Soviet doctrine had no place for nuclear weapons. The Soviets could not think of modifying their doctrine, certainly not when their atomic capability was clearly inferior to that of the United States. Until 1953, Kissinger wrote, Soviet strategy was based largely on military lessons learned during World War II. The Soviet belief in the efficacy of mass infantry attacks was undiminished; victory would be achieved, they imagined, through the undermining of the enemy's morale. If war came, the Soviets expected it to be not too unlike the war they had known in World War II. Kissinger, in contrast to those who imagined that the Soviets generally concealed their intentions, believed that they generally did what they said they were going to do.

The principal Communist objective, during the years of the American atomic monopoly, was to prevent the United States from using its bomb against the Soviet Union. According to Kissinger, the peace movement was an immensely effective campaign "to enlist the hopes and fears of many eminent men, appalled by the prospect of nuclear war, who would have nothing to do with overt Communist efforts." The Soviet Union was exceedingly resourceful in everything that it did at that time; as Kissinger explained, while it sought to paralyze its opponents' will to resist, by constantly emphasizing the horrors of atomic war, it did not propose itself to be inhibited by the same dangers. The idea that atomic war might produce a stalemate, thereby delaying the long predicted demise of capitalism, was not even entertained by Soviet theoreticians. After 1949, Kissinger said, the coming struggle between socialism and capitalism was constantly emphasized. Soviet propaganda refused to admit that this might mean the end of civilization; as Malenkov pointed out, it would only mean the end of capitalism. Kissinger wrote: "The Soviet leadership did not propose to inhibit its freedom of action by any doctrine of the horrors of nuclear war, however useful such ideas might be to paralyze the resistance of the non-Soviet world."

Kissinger called this a "*tour de force.*" "The Soviet Union," he wrote, "had retained its militancy despite the United States atomic monopoly; indeed, it had transformed its relative weakness into an asset and solidified a position in the center of Europe denied the Tsars in centuries of striving." While the Soviets pretended to be uninterested in the development of atomic arms—constantly prating about the necessity to use atomic power only for peaceful purposes—they made persistent efforts to perfect their nuclear weapons. Their true achievement, in Kissinger's eyes, was not their technological breakthrough, or even the skill they showed in using espionage to gain access to certain information, but their *sang-froid* and their inventiveness in knowing how to render the United States impotent. In reflecting on this success, he wrote: "It thereby demonstrated that in the relation among states, strength of will may be more important than power."

When the Soviets became a nuclear power, they took up other themes. They made the United States appear an irresponsible, power-hungry state that would not hesitate to produce a nuclear holocaust if its leaders imagined that American purposes would be served; at the same time, Kissinger wrote, they thought it perfectly proper to ignore their own propaganda on the hazards of nuclear war and to threaten countries, including France and Great Britain, with rocket attacks if they persisted in their illegal Suez operations. The same threat, periodically issued, involved other countries as well, particularly those who were prepared to accept American military atomic support units. Kissinger admired the Soviets for their daring; he knew what a heavy price the West paid for being unwilling to resist their threats.

The Soviet Union, according to Kissinger, was particularly anxious to deny the possibility of limited nuclear war. Soviet propaganda always insisted that any use of nuclear weapons could only bring about all-out atomic war. The object of the propaganda, Kissinger said, was to paralyze any potential opponent. It never led the Soviets to desist from issuing their own threats. Kissinger assumed, therefore, that the Russians thought themselves inferior in this particular military sphere, and were determined to prevent the United States from developing a capability that might embarrass them. Kissinger saw no reason for the United States to fall in with Soviet strategic plans. Believing that a limited war strategy was particularly suited to the United States, precisely because it would make use of its economic, psychological, and moral strengths, Kissinger rejected all Soviet arguments suggesting that the end result of such a strategy would be all-out atomic war. Kissinger wrote: "Just as during our atomic monopoly the Kremlin obscured its weakness by a show of bravado, it may now be seeking to inhibit our most effective strategy by declaring it impossible."

Whether Kissinger was examining military strategy, inter-allied relations, or relations with the Soviet bloc, he returned always to a single theme—the United States lacked a doctrine adequate to the needs of the nuclear age. Kissinger compared society's need for a doctrine with the individual's need for an education. By "explaining the significance of events *in advance* of their occurrence," Kissinger wrote, it "enables society to deal with most problems as a matter of routine and reserves creative thought for unusual or unexpected situations." A doctrine, Kissinger said, made it unnecessary to think everything out *de novo*; that was no small advantage when governmental decision-making machinery was greatly overloaded. Also, he explained, the existence of a doctrine guaranteed the United States against being perpetually surprised by the turn of events in the world. Kissinger wrote: "Our doctrine must be clear about the nature of our strategic interest in the world. It must understand the mode of Soviet behavior and not make the mistake of ascribing to the Soviet leaders a pattern of action in terms of our own standards of rationality. Since our policy is so explicitly based on deterrence, our doctrine must pay particular attention to determining how the other side calculates its risks."

Kissinger criticized the decision-making processes of both the Joint Chiefs of Staff and the National Security Council. Both, in his view, aimed principally at developing a consensus that powerful departments would accept. This, he said, was not the same thing as providing "a sense of direction." Inter-service rivalries only exacerbated the situation; it was becoming increasingly difficult, he wrote, to ascribe any primary mission to any of the military services. The service chiefs had no incentive to develop an over-all strategic doctrine, and budgetary considerations served only to complicate the problem. The budgetary process gave priority to cost; it subordinated doctrine to technology, reinforcing "the inherent conservatism of the military," and, in Kissinger's view, encouraging "a subtle form of waste." To relinquish a weapons system, for example, simply meant giving up the appropriations that went along with it; there was a powerful incentive to avoid such actions; and the result, inevitably, was that obsolete weapons systems were maintained. Both short-term civilian officials who headed individual departments and members of Congress sometimes tried to intervene; they almost always failed; they had neither the knowledge nor the organization to succeed.

Kissinger appreciated why it was so difficult to formulate a strategic doctrine; "no previous generation," he wrote, "has had to master so many revolutions occurring simultaneously, in ideology, in emerging new nations, in the existence of an irreconcilably hostile bloc of powers and in the rapidly changing weapons technology." The difficulties were substantial; they did not, however, wholly explain the poor performance. "The basic challenge of any society," Kissinger wrote, "is how it can bring its leadership to think naturally and spontaneously about the problems of greatest over-all concern." The solution was not to make every higher official spend some part of his day thinking about over-all strategy. The need, Kissinger wrote, was for higher officials to become habituated to thinking about such problems before they reached positions of the greatest importance.

The United States prided itself on its empiricism; yet, according to Kissinger, that empiricism created many of America's most serious problems. For the United States, nothing was "true" unless it was "objective"; the search for objectivity led also to a search for certainty. "Policy,"

Kissinger wrote, "is the art of weighing probabilities; mastery of it lies in grasping the nuances of possibilities." To believe that policy was a science, and to act on that belief, was to invite rigidity. For Kissinger, only risks were *certain;* opportunities were always *conjectural.* He wrote: "One cannot be 'sure' about the implications of events until they have happened and when they have occurred it is too late to do anything about them." Kissinger argued that "empiricism in foreign policy leads to a penchant for *ad hoc* solutions." American leaders, in search of certainty, refused to commit themselves until all the facts were in. By the time that happened, Kissinger wrote, "a crisis has usually developed or an opportunity has passed." He saw American policy as "geared to dealing with emergencies." There was no equivalent attention given to developing the kinds of long-range programs that would avert crises. Because of what Kissinger called America's "cult of specialization," government departments tended to negotiate policy. There was no one to scrutinize these efforts except an overburdened president who was generally not in a position to do so. The most serious charge made by Kissinger was that the United States was "trying to cope with political problems by administrative means."

These situations served only to increase America's vulnerability to Soviet pressure. There was a constant incentive for every Soviet change of policy to be taken at face value, since it was impossible to know when the Soviets really meant what they said. Soviet "blandishments" and Soviet "intransigence" posed equally serious problems for the United States government, which was trying always to react to what the Soviets were doing. Even when it tried to get on with the Soviets, the United States government was generally characterized as "rigid, unimaginative and even somewhat cynical." In Kissinger's view, the "absence of a tradition of foreign policy" only tended to exaggerate the bias inherent in American empiricism. Measures were almost always badly timed; the naïve assumption that a good policy was good at any time seemed to dominate American thinking.

American policy, according to Kissinger, had no "feeling for nuance"; it was generally so rigid that any reappraisal of fundamental positions became an agonizing affair. The United States, because of its history—which Kissinger thought to be uniquely lacking in tragic dimensions—found great difficulty in coping with the concept of an impending disaster. The country was unprepared, emotionally and psychologically, for any outcome that might be disastrous. Inevitably, there was great difficulty in generating a sense of urgency; the idea that a mistake might be irrevocable was alien to most Americans. Also, there was a genuine reluctance to think in terms of power; power was thought to be corrupt, a thing to be avoided. Kissinger wrote: "As a nation, we have used power almost shamefacedly, as if it were inherently wicked. We have wanted to be liked for our own sakes, and we have wished to succeed because of the persuasiveness of our principles rather than through our strength. Our feeling of guilt with respect to power has caused us to transform all wars into crusades, and then to apply our power in the most absolute terms. We have rarely found intermediary ways to use our power and in those cases we have done so reluctantly."

Kissinger scored the tendency that led Americans to believe that peace was the "normal" pattern of relations between states, and that everything else was an aberration. "No idea," he wrote, "could be more dangerous." Repeating an argument first made in *A World Restored*, Kissinger explained why peace could never be made the goal of foreign policy, and why it needed to be seen as a bonus that flowed from a well-conceived policy. Survival, Kissinger insisted, depended on a willingness to run risks on the basis of partial knowledge, and to accept a less than perfect realization of one's principles. "The insistence on absolutes either in assessing the provocation or in evaluating possible remedies," he wrote, "is a prescription for inaction." In calling for a "more dynamic conception of world affairs," he defined his goal as being "ready to profit from opportunities in the Soviet orbit as the Soviet bloc feels free to exploit all the difficulties of the non-Soviet world."

Kissinger believed that leadership—defined as a capacity "to transcend a framework which has come to be taken for granted"—was the only hope for the atomic era. While he accepted that "a society must be able to assimilate and utilize mediocrity," leadership depended on "the refusal to confine action to average performance." Leaders had to be willing "to define purposes perhaps only vaguely apprehended by the multitude." Kissinger said: "A society learns only from experience; it 'knows' only when it is too late to act. But a statesman must act as if his inspirations were already experience, as if his aspiration were 'truth.' He must bridge the gap between a society's experience and his vision, between its tradition and its future."

Kissinger saw the statesman restrained always by bureaucracy; there was an inevitable tension between the two. In a series of observations on bureaucracy that closely paralleled what he had written in *A World Restored*, Kissinger argued that "the basic motivation of a bureaucracy is its quest for safety." A bureaucracy, he wrote, "tends to exaggerate the technical complexities of its problems and to seek to reduce questions of judgment to a minimum." Bureaucracies, inclined to be hostile to great ideas, dismissed them as "unsound" and "risky." The viability of a society, Kissinger explained, depended on its capacity "to strike a balance between the requirement of organization and the need for inspiration." To achieve such a balance was never easy, particularly in the modern world, where much stress was placed on expertness. The need for creative thinking had never been greater, but the sheer complexity of problems caused attention to be riveted on purely technical solutions. Politics, in his mind, was superior to administration. The latter demanded purely "manipulative" talents: "the ability to adapt to prevailing standards and to improve efficiency within a framework which is given." Leadership called for creative abilities; it needed to establish the framework within which administration would operate. Bureaucracy, in short, depended on specialized skill; leadership depended on vision.

In the United States, Kissinger wrote, the leadership groups were formed at a time when the society was predominantly concerned with domestic problems. Politics "was considered a necessary evil and the primary function of the state was the exercise of police powers. Neither training nor incentives impelled our leadership groups to think in political or strategic terms. This emphasis was compounded by our empiricism with its cult of the expert and its premium on specialization." Industry and law generally provided the talent for many of the higher positions in government. Industry—particularly large-scale industry—Kissinger said, rewarded men principally for administrative competence. Law, on the other hand, trained its practitioners to "deal with a succession of discrete individual cases," and this produced a bias in favor of "*ad hoc* decisions and a resistance to the 'hypothetical cases' inherent in long-range planning." Both law and business, Kissinger believed, trained people more to deal with technical than with conceptual problems; it was not surprising that men trained in this manner preferred to deal with economic rather than political issues.

Given the type of leadership that existed in the United States, Kissinger was not surprised by the magnitude of the Soviet successes. He believed that Communist training, overwhelmingly political and conceptual, was better suited to the problems of leadership than any provided by legal or business experience. Against men who thought in large categories, combining every kind of interest, America "pitted leaders overwhelmed with departmental duties and trained to think that the cardinal sin is to transgress on another's field of specialization." Kissinger thought the Soviet leaders better prepared for the contest they were required to compete in.

The virtues of American society—its ease, good manners, and absence of dogmatism—did not, in Kissinger's view, help to produce effective leadership groups. There was "a preference for decisions by committee," he wrote, "because the process of conversation permits disagreements to be discovered and adjustments made before positions have hardened." Kissinger did not suggest that America would do well to imitate Soviet dogmatism. He asked, however, whether it ought not to "leaven" its "empiricism with a sense of urgency." It had to learn to run risks, and not always look for a guarantee of success. It was on this note that he closed his book.

While *Nuclear Weapons and Foreign Policy* was not intended to be a popular text, and while few of the officers in the Council on Foreign Relations expected large sales of a book that many reviewers were certain to find difficult, it did, in fact, sell extremely well. Why the general—indeed, overwhelming—success of the book? Several explanations are possible. The book was obviously controversial. At a time when few dared think about—let alone write about—"the unthinkable," Kissinger raised questions about national survival and set down his views in terms that were unmistakable. Kissinger did not believe that an all-out Soviet attack was imminent; on the contrary, he believed such an attack to be one of the least likely possibilities. He drew attention, however, to an equally insidious, though less mortal danger: the United States had neither the military strategy nor the diplomacy adequate for coping with the aggressive political and military operations that the Soviet Union might choose to undertake in various parts of the world.

Although some who read the book thought its originality lay almost wholly in the sections devoted to the concept of limited war—indeed, the most severe criticism came over Kissinger's insistence on making atomic limited war a strategic option—the book, in fact, dealt with many other subjects as well. Kissinger's purpose had not been to write a manual for experts on limited war, atomic limited war, arms control, or civilian defense; he knew that others would do this even if he did not. His object had been considerably more ambitious. He believed that those responsible for American foreign policy were operating with concepts totally inappropriate to the atomic age. Since they did not even know what the right questions were, it was impossible for them to discover the correct answers. *Nuclear Weapons and Foreign Policy* was, in certain respects, an arrogant work. It showed immense independence, not simply in striking out at so many prominent persons who were accustomed to being treated more deferentially, but in offering a rather unconventional analysis of the first atomic decade. Kissinger had written the first "revisionist" history of the Truman and Eisenhower administrations.

Though the book might be thought difficult—it was so described by a number of commentators—it was not technical. Any layman who wished to, could read and understand it. This was what Kissinger intended. He had written it not for himself or for a small coterie of friends and experts who would have a special reason for being interested in the subject. Kissinger had taken a theme that was only beginning to be defined—the political, diplomatic, and military implications of thermonuclear weapons—and had written a book that any conscientious lay reader could master if he made the effort to do so.

Kissinger's Council on Foreign Relations study group did not provide him with his general ideas; he had already developed many of these in his doctoral dissertation on Metternich and Castlereagh. Nor did the group provide him with the specific theoretical approaches that he used in considering the problems of atomic war; insofar as these were not original with him, they came from a very small body of fellow scholars. The Council members did, however, serve two absolutely crucial functions: first, if many of them lacked a theoretical understanding of diplomacy and military policy in any sense comparable to Kissinger's, they could claim other experience that he was in a position to draw on. Whether they used a half hour's casual conversation to illuminate an issue that might otherwise have remained obscure, or helped to explain a scientific or military matter on which Kissinger needed information, he learned from being with these men. Had the study group served no other purpose, that would have been reason enough for Kissinger to be grateful to it. In fact, it served an infinitely more important function, but one that was neither recognized nor acknowledged.

The group was made up of famous men, who had a certain reputation in the United States. Some were born rich, and had managed, despite the hazards of wealth, to be active in ways that suggested that they were not only privileged but also talented. Others, who started more humbly, had managed to reach positions of considerable eminence, often in law or business, in New York or Washington. A number had held high governmental posts; others had served in various public capacities while pursuing their professions. A few were prominent scholars—men whose names would be familiar to colleagues in their several disciplines. There were also a number of high-ranking military officers, publicists, journalists, and foundation officers. The greatest number of these men were informed, articulate, and self-confident. Almost every member of the study group had a record of performance that contrasted markedly with that of Kissinger. They were prominent men; he was a young scholar, unknown, not given to consorting regularly with military officers, bankers, lawyers, journalists, scientists, and governmental officials. His position was a somewhat anomalous one. While many in the group knew each other intimately, having served on such committees previously, and having, in addition, the inestimable advantage of acknowledged accomplishment, Kissinger had no such experience or record. Before successful men of this sort, someone else in Kissinger's position might have held back, showing the deference that many in the group were accustomed to receiving. There is no evidence that Kissinger showed himself either retiring or deferential. He was courteous and tactful, but from a very early moment in his relations with the group, he, in effect, used them as a professor might use his students. The major contribution the Council made to Kissinger's education was that it assigned him a class, but a class quite different from any that he could expect to find at Harvard or in any other university.

Kissinger, like any good professor, listened intently. He heard things he had not previously known. What interested him were not isolated facts, which he might have learned from reading or private conversations, but the words and arguments that were used. What kinds of evidence did such men introduce to support their conclusions? When did they resist certain recommendations? What explanations did they find persuasive? When Kissinger spoke—and he often did—he was curious, as any teacher would be, to determine the reactions of those who heard him. Which of his arguments failed to persuade? Which found ready acceptance? Should he make an additional effort to explain what seemed incomprehensible or unacceptable?

While the study group (and the book) became the most important thing in Kissinger's life, for many of the distinguished men who joined him this was simply one more obligation at the end of a busy day. The book took shape, then, not because there was a study group advising Kissinger but because Kissinger was prepared to spend twelve or more hours each day writing, revising, and discussing. He knew how much he owed the Council, not because he found ardent supporters there for every point that he wished to make, but because he found an audience. If he could persuade such a group—and Kissinger never doubted its importance —to take his ideas seriously, or at least be willing to discuss them, there was reason to believe that he could make others outside the Council, who were not so different from these men, read his work and respond to it.

Nuclear Weapons and Foreign Policy was written to be read, not least by those who held responsible positions in the United States government or who might be expected one day to hold such positions. The work lacked the personal qualities of the Metternich and Castlereagh studies; its language was more restrained; there were fewer rhetorical flourishes; the prose was more measured. Kissinger clearly intended the work for an American audience. The constant use of "we," referring to "we Americans," was almost disconcerting. He ranged over many quite different subjects, treating matters that he sometimes knew only superficially. He expected that many who read his book would disagree with individual points, but his concern was not with any single detail, but with a set of larger propositions that he was trying to establish.

On one level, Kissinger appeared to accept all the traditional arguments about the nature of Soviet power—he seemed almost a classical "cold warrior"—but a closer examination of his text reveals substantial differences with what others were saying. While he acknowledged Soviet aggressiveness, his interpretation of what the Soviets had accomplished and why they had been able to do so much was not at all commonplace.

The Soviets were not "supermen," at least not to Kissinger, nor were they "misunderstood pacific types" who simply wanted American expansionism to end. Kissinger discarded all the traditional explanations of Soviet behavior; he suggested, in effect, that American policies had facilitated Soviet aggression. If the United States wanted a stable international order, it would do well to adopt military and diplomatic strategies that made such an order possible.

Within the framework of an essentially optimistic analysis, which told America's leaders that the problems of the United States, while difficult, were not insolvable, Kissinger argued for greater political intelligence at the highest levels of government. His remedies were calculated to appeal to men like those who gathered at the Council on Foreign Relations. The book described complex problems, suggested that they would not be settled by technological or "manipulative" breakthroughs, and implied that they required the intellectual rigor and the personal fortitude of men who were prepared to take risks. While Kissinger expressed reservations about the abilities of men trained in law and business to cope with difficult political issues in foreign policy, he had no suggestions for an alternative professional pool to recruit from. He was telling his Council colleagues, in effect, that they could do better than those who were then managing the country's affairs if they agreed to "return to school" to learn what the atomic age was really all about. Henry Kissinger was more than ready to serve as their principal teacher.

That this is not a farfetched interpretation of what Kissinger hoped to accomplish with his book is evident from another important association that he formed during this crucial period of his life. In 1956, under the chairmanship of Nelson Rockefeller, the Rockefeller Brothers Fund established a Special Studies Project; its purpose was to consider where the United States ought to be moving in the next decade. Henry Kissinger, appointed director of the Project, served from the time of its formation until June 1958, when he resigned, remaining, however, as consultant to the group and a member of its Planning Committee. Nelson Rockefeller, at approximately the same time, gave up the chairmanship to seek election as Governor of New York. The work of the group was largely done; the reports of its various panels began to be published in 1958, and emerged in a single volume in 1961. Laurance Rockefeller, who had succeeded his brother as chairman, explained that the Project had three principal objectives; in his words: "To define the major problems and opportunities that will challenge the United States over the next ten to fifteen years; to clarify the national purposes and objectives that must inspire and direct the meeting of such great challenges; and to develop a framework of concepts and principles on which national policies and decisions can be soundly based." Kissinger played a major role in the study, in his capacity as

Director of Special Studies, but also as principal author of the paper published by Panel II on "International Security: The Military Aspect," which appeared in January 1958; it was, in effect, an abbreviated version of *Nuclear Weapons and Foreign Policy*.

The Special Studies Project would have been inconceivable in almost any country other than the United States. It is difficult, for example, to imagine such a group being established in France, the United Kingdom, Germany, or Italy. In the context of the United States in the mid-1950s, there seemed to be nothing incongruous about the enterprise. A small Planning Committee was set up, together with a highly efficient staff. A distinguished group of American men and women were named to an over-all panel. As always with such groups, there was some effort to achieve representation: there were a number of women, a black, a recognizable Catholic, and two prominent trade unionists. The greatest number, however, were simply famous—businessmen, lawyers, publishers, professors, politicians, college presidents, foundation officials, and the like. At least a few of those on the over-all panel had also served on Kissinger's Council on Foreign Relations study group. Members of the over-all panel included, in addition to the chairman, Adolf Berle, Jr., professor of corporation law at Columbia University, former Assistant Secretary of State and ambassador to Brazil; Chester Bowles, Governor of Connecticut, former ambassador to India, Price Administrator during World War II; Arthur F. Burns, chairman of President Eisenhower's Council of Economic Advisers; General Lucius Clay, postwar commander in chief of American forces in Germany, chairman of the Continental Can Company; John Cowles, publisher of the Minneapolis *Star & Tribune;* Justin Dart, drug-company executive; John Dickey, president of Dartmouth College, assistant to the Coordinator of Inter-American Affairs; John Gardner, president of the Carnegie Corporation, later Secretary of the Department of Health, Education, and Welfare; Lester Granger, executive director of the National Urban League; Caryl Haskins; Theodore Hesburgh, president of the University of Notre Dame; Margaret Hickey, public affairs editor of the *Ladies' Home Journal;* Oveta Culp Hobby, newspaper publisher, first director of the Women's Army Corps, later Secretary of the Department of Health, Education, and Welfare; Devereux Josephs, investment banker and insurance executive; Milton Katz, professor of law at Harvard University; James Killian, Jr., president of the Massachusetts Institute of Technology, Special Assistant to the President for Science and Technology; Henry Luce, of *Time, Life,* and *Fortune;* Thomas McCabe, formerly chairman of the board of governors of the Federal Reserve System; General James McCormack, Jr.; Richard McKeon, professor of philosophy and Greek at the University of Chicago; Lee Minton, labor-union executive; Charles Percy, president of Bell &

Howell, later United States senator from Illinois; David Sarnoff, director of the Radio Corporation of America and the National Broadcasting Company; Charles Spofford, lawyer, active in the North Atlantic Council; Edward Teller, physicist, former assistant director of the Los Alamos Scientific Laboratories, later director of the Lawrence Radiation Laboratory of the University of California; Frazar Wilde, insurance executive; and, for a time, Robert Anderson, former Secretary of the Navy, Deputy Secretary of Defense, later Secretary of the Treasury; and Gordon Dean. These over-all panel members served also on one or other of the six individual panels, together with others only scarcely less well known.

Kissinger, because of his association with the Project, extended his acquaintanceship with some of the more prominent Americans who enjoyed a national reputation for public service. These were all exceedingly busy people, and it fell to the staff and a hundred or so others who served as consultants to provide the raw material from which the panels eventually developed their reports. They were uneven in quality and express admirably the limitations of all such collaborative research projects. Kissinger, however, had no reason to regret what he had done for the Project. He had found an additional forum for his ideas. More important, however, it provided him with an opportunity to come to know Nelson Rockefeller. Their relations were extremely close; the two managed the Project together. Rockefeller became Kissinger's friend.

The Special Studies Project would have been inconceivable without Nelson Rockefeller. He inspired the effort, and it was his personality that led otherwise busy men and women to accept his invitation to serve. When he invited them in 1956, his greatest asset was his name; not so obvious, perhaps, was his political promise. Although Nelson Rockefeller had never held a major elective political post, many both inside and outside the Republican Party in 1956 hoped that he would one day contend for high office, perhaps for the presidency itself. Rockefeller's immense fortune, wedded to what was generally conceded to be his highly marketable political personality, made that a not entirely outlandish possibility. Having some governmental experience, but no knowledge of politics greater than that of any number of others who wandered in and out of the federal bureaucracy on an appointive basis, and who made their principal professional commitments elsewhere, Rockefeller desperately needed instruction in the rudiments of public policy. His name, fame, and age militated against his doing this by starting at the bottom of the political ladder. In the American system, it made sense for him to aspire to a higher place.

Many who joined the over-all panel of the Special Studies Project were aware that they were in the presence of someone who might be president of the United States in the 1960s or 1970s. Their decision to join the group was not unaffected by that awareness, though most accepted the invitation because they believed that the study had promise, and that they would learn something from it. They were flattered to be asked, and enjoyed the attentions paid them by a man who believed absolutely in the crucial importance of the enterprise. His hospitality delighted them, and his energy and enthusiasm were infectious. There was every reason for the operation to succeed. Nelson Rockefeller proved to be a vigorous and active chairman; he took his responsibilities seriously, and the meetings of the over-all panel, whether in the offices of the Rockefeller Brothers Fund or, more rarely, in Nelson Rockefeller's home, were lively and spirited occasions. This, at least, is how they are remembered.

While the Special Studies Project prided itself on its political objectivity, making almost a fetish of involving both Democrats and Republicans, its mere existence was a reproof to the Eisenhower administration. Four years after the Republicans had returned to power in Washington, a prominent New York Republican thought it necessary to create a study group that would establish guidelines for future public policy. A vigorous Republican administration, which had engaged the sympathy and support of its most ardent party members, would not have offered an excuse for the creation of such a body. Although Rockefeller refrained from criticizing the President or any of the others who governed in Washington, the recommendation of alternative policies implied at least some dissatisfaction with the way things were going. The Eisenhower "team" clearly did not include a number of younger men and women who believed that the Republicans were in a position to do better than they were doing.

The Special Studies Project did not even think to question the proposition that a consensus could be reached on major issues of national and international policy. In 1956, it seemed entirely reasonable to assemble Democrats and Republicans, mix them with a number of Independents, and then wait for agreement to follow. There were difficult moments, of course—Adolf Berle and Edward Teller did not always see eye to eye, and others disagreed—but no one expected the group to break apart; no one intended that it should. Agreement was expected; indeed, it was planned for. Such a procedure would not have worked nearly so well during the Depression; nor would it have been conceivable in the last years of Lyndon Johnson's presidency. It seemed entirely right in the context of 1956; no one raised questions about the "representativeness" of the group; no one resigned in outrage over any of the recommendations. The national consensus seemed real, and though many of the reports found fault with specific governmental policies, there was nothing shrill or wounding in what was said.

It was a good time for learning; Nelson Rockefeller proved an avid student. The Special Studies Project, more than any other single experience, gave Rockefeller the basic education in public policy that he lacked. His principal teacher was Henry Kissinger, who served as coordinator of studies and accepted the assignment of keeping the chairman informed. Kissinger interpreted the work of the various groups; he met frequently with Rockefeller, sometimes in the company of one or other of the large staff of personal associates that a man in Rockefeller's position commanded. Kissinger was teacher both to an individual and to his entourage; he soon won respect from both, though this did not mean that all his suggestions were enthusiastically accepted. Rockefeller was a valuable "property" in several senses of the term; those who protected him, or imagined they needed to, jealously guarded a reputation that they did not wish to see compromised. It was important to them that Rockefeller's name not be associated with policies that might raise adverse criticism. They were not as anxious for their chief to take "risks" as Kissinger, living with a very different philosophy, seemed to be. They recognized the warm relations that existed between the two men, and did nothing to impede them, but they never forgot the importance of being politically prudent. As a consequence, inevitably, the reports were somewhat more tepid and less controversial than they might otherwise have been. Also, inevitably, a great effort was made to guarantee that the reports received the support of all members of the over-all panel.

Rockefeller's legal and business associates operated pretty much as such men did when they or their colleagues became part of the federal bureaucracy. Kissinger's views on the attitudes of American lawyers and businessmen were in great part confirmed by his experience in New York. Kissinger went to New York knowing very little about any profession other than his own; he returned to Cambridge with extensive knowledge about what certain of the principal American practitioners of other professions believed and said. More than that, he had established relations with a number of people whose friendship he valued; he maintained close associations with these men till the heavy responsibilities of the White House pushed him in quite other directions.

Nelson Rockefeller became a trusted friend. Rockefeller liked Kissinger, admired him for his intelligence and wit, and enjoyed his company. He received a good part of his education on national security and foreign policy from conversations with Kissinger. Building on his substantial knowledge of the problems of Latin America, Rockefeller had a better sense of how the introduction of nuclear arms had altered the American position in the world. Because he learned best through personal encounters, Rockefeller spent a great deal of time with Kissinger. Kissinger enjoyed the association, not least because he admired Rockefeller's loyalty and enthusiasm. He knew how much Rockefeller esteemed him, and it was impossible for him not to be moved by that knowledge.

Among the many others Kissinger met while in New York, two men particularly influenced him—Caryl Haskins and John Gardner. Haskins, president of the Carnegie Institution of Washington, was the first prominent scientist whom Kissinger came to know well. He helped with both the Council on Foreign Relations study and the Rockefeller Brothers Fund reports. Kissinger became devoted to him. He immensely appreciated Haskins's critical abilities and submitted almost everything that he wrote to him in manuscript form. Kissinger, knowing how difficult it was to write well, admired the grace of Haskins's prose, evident in the annual reports he published as president of the Carnegie Institution, but also in his correspondence, which greatly impressed Kissinger. He felt grateful to the Council for having brought him together with Haskins, a man of exceptional generosity and gentleness.

Through the Special Studies Project, Kissinger came to know John Gardner, the president of the Carnegie Corporation. Again, a close relationship developed, which was cemented by many hours of talk. Gardner, preoccupied with the problems of "excellence," combined the scholar's appreciation of the difficulties of achieving high levels of competence in a democracy with the public servant's determination to do something to effect that purpose. An intellectual who prized action, he wanted very much to communicate his ideas to a larger audience. He and Kissinger became good friends; Gardner's report for the Rockefeller Brothers Fund Project drew heavily on conversations that extended over many months in New York. Kissinger had reason to be grateful for such associates.

New York was where Henry Kissinger started his American life. Just as he had needed to get away from Washington Heights to learn something of what America was about, so he needed to leave Cambridge for a while to appreciate more keenly the variety of American intellectual and political experience. In his association with Rockefeller, no less than in his association with the Council on Foreign Relations, the teacher became also the student. Kissinger, who always knew how to listen, profited immensely from being required to do this in the company of men whose experience of life was considerably greater than his own.

4

The Eisenhower Years
A Radical Critique

The two years that Henry Kissinger spent in New York were absolutely crucial for his career. He lived in the midst of a bustling city, sometimes in great isolation, choosing to see almost no one for days on end. The small apartment on East 73rd Street where he and his wife spent a great part of their time was almost monastic in character; it was as if a vow of silence had been imposed. An unremitting work schedule permitted Kissinger to write, revise, and publish *Nuclear Weapons and Foreign Policy* in something less than two years. Only the most extraordinary self-discipline made it possible for such a schedule to be maintained. It was as creative a time for Kissinger as he had ever known; he looked back on the experience with some nostalgia, not so much for what he had been able to accomplish as for the support he had received. He had never been treated more considerately; he had never been made to feel that so much depended on what he was doing.

Kissinger had maintained his ties with Cambridge even when he lived in New York; because he remained responsible for the International Seminar and continued to edit *Confluence,* he visited Cambridge regularly and spent his summers there. In the fall of 1957 he left New York permanently, though he did not sever his relations with the Rockefeller Special Studies Project. He expected that he would be required to spend several days in New York each month till the greater number of the panel reports were completed. Appointed a Lecturer in Government at Harvard, he went to Cambridge to resume his academic career. No one—least of all his senior colleagues in the Government Department—took much notice of his return. He came not as a famous man but as a still fairly anonymous younger member of the Harvard faculty. He was no more lionized in 1957 than he had been in 1950; men and women who barely knew him did not delight to talk of their chance encounter with "Henry"; he was just another member of the Harvard junior faculty.

Yet something had changed, and Kissinger was soon made aware of the gap that separated him from what he had been at the beginning of the decade, a recently graduated Harvard senior. The Council on Foreign Relations had put him into touch with dozens of people whom he might not otherwise have met; the Special Studies Project had established a close bond with Nelson Rockefeller. In all these instances, the relation was not social; it was based on a shared interest in foreign policy issues. Not everyone in Cambridge ignored the importance of such associations for someone who clearly aspired to influence public policy. Also, some, at least, wondered what Kissinger's influence would be in the rapidly developing field of international relations at Harvard. When Kissinger had been an undergraduate, that field had been largely untended. There were a scattering of courses in several departments, but no major centers. Now a Center for International Affairs was being organized, and Kissinger had been appointed Associate Director. What form would the Center take? Would it resemble the Russian Research Center, organized in 1948, and concentrate on supporting basic research, or would it aim for a more activist role? These were all unanswered questions when Kissinger returned to Cambridge in 1957. When he had left in 1955, he had held the rank of Instructor; he was now awarded the rank of Lecturer. While the rank was an anomalous one at Harvard, and could signify almost anything, in the case of Kissinger it seemed to imply departmental confidence; there was a good prospect of his being promoted to a permanent position on the faculty at an early date. McGeorge Bundy, the Dean of the Faculty of Arts and Sciences, had held the same rank for two years in the Government Department before being named an Associate Professor. Would the same thing happen to Kissinger? It was difficult to know, but by being appointed Lecturer, he had almost certainly avoided the longer route to academic tenure that generally required an individual to spend three years as an instructor and five years as an assistant professor.

Kissinger, before he left Harvard in 1955, had some teaching experience; it made no very lasting impression on him. Serving as a teaching fellow in the early 1950s in one of the most popular undergraduate courses in the university, Kissinger almost never spoke of Social Sciences 2, where he conducted discussion-group sessions that touched on a broad range of philosophical and historical questions. The course, Western Thought and Institutions, brilliantly presided over by one of the university's great lecturers, Samuel Beer, had already become something of a Harvard institution, but Kissinger seemed almost oblivious to its fame. It was not that he disliked the course or that he regretted having taught in it; it was simply that the experience of teaching undergraduates gave him no particular pleasure. He learned remarkably little from doing it. Nor, if the truth were told, did he learn very much from offering tutorial. Recalling his indebtedness to his own undergraduate tutor, Kissinger was pleased to take on tutorial obligations, but he recognized that he was only partially successful in fulfilling them.

Tutorial, of all the forms of instruction at Harvard, was far and away the most demanding. For a conscientious teacher, it meant weekly sessions with individual students, with the instructor being frequently required to read or reread texts he had assigned; memory would rarely suffice in a prolonged discussion with an able undergraduate who commanded a specific text. Such encounters were at least interesting; many others were dull. The obligation to read badly written and badly conceived student essays, and to correct them for stylistic shortcomings, for faults in logic, reasoning, and fact was never entirely satisfying. While no one of Kissinger's senior tutees presented him with a 377-page thesis, as he himself had done, the supervision of theses of even a hundred pages often imposed obligations of a kind that he would willingly have forgone. While Kissinger tried hard to keep his tutorial appointments, he frequently fell behind schedule in all his daily engagements. His tutees found him affable and interested, but it was impossible for them to ignore the increasingly frenetic character of his life. He rarely had as much time for them as Elliott had had for him.

When he returned in 1957, new teaching and administrative chores fell to him. In his first year as Lecturer, he collaborated with others in giving several courses; the preparation of these became a major concern. Again, Kissinger did as well as he could, but he never found the time to prepare to his own satisfaction. It was not until some years later that he gained the reputation for being an outstanding teacher. When he achieved that distinction—in part, because of very serious efforts he made to improve his teaching—his classes grew large, and he became well known among students in the university generally. In the 1950s, Kissinger enjoyed no such renown; he did not figure among the more distinguished teachers of the university, or even among the best in his own department. He began by offering two courses: a lecture course entitled Principles of International Politics, which he gave jointly with Daniel Cheever, and a seminar on Administrative and Policy Problems of the United States in the Field of Diplomacy, which he shared with his former teacher, William Y. Elliott.

Though Kissinger had great energy and resilience, and enjoyed excellent health, he was obviously overextended, too heavily involved in too

many disparate activities. His official duties at Harvard and his continuing obligations in New York would have been more than enough to keep
him fully occupied. They represented only a small fraction of his total
activities. Kissinger guarded his time less well than he ought to have
done. The publication of *Nuclear Weapons and Foreign Policy* brought
him considerable public acclaim; there were now many more invitations
to speak, lecture, and write; also, numerous private and governmental organizations turned to him, asking for his services as consultant or adviser.
Kissinger did not always refuse them. Those who knew him slightly or
cared little for him commented on what they regarded as the increasingly
disorganized character of his life; he seemed always to be running, always
late, and constantly harassed. Those who knew him better—and this included a number who both liked and admired him—were surprised less
by his occasional lapses than by his continuing accomplishments. Despite
all sorts of distractions, Kissinger continued to write, to attend conferences and committee meetings, and to do all the other things that became
commonplace for prominent academics in the 1950s.

At Harvard, in addition to course teaching, tutorials, and work in the
International Seminar, there were obligations that attached to his position
as Associate Director of the Center for International Affairs. The post
was one that he never came to enjoy. His relations with the Director,
Robert Bowie, were never close, and Kissinger concluded at an early date
that there was not much he could do to influence the shape the Center
would take. He accepted his responsibilities there, particularly to the
Fellows—higher civil servants or military officers, American and
foreign—who came for a year on leave from their official duties. Occasionally, one of the Fellows became a friend; more often, they consulted
Kissinger as they would any other member of the Harvard faculty. Kissinger participated in a number of the Center seminars and study groups,
and gradually extended his knowledge of Harvard's social science faculty.
Two Center colleagues, Edward Mason and Thomas Schelling, both
economists, were particularly important for him. Mason's insights into developing countries were valued in many quarters, and Kissinger came to
share the general admiration for him. So, also, he came to have great respect for Thomas Schelling, whose elegant theories had large implications
for strategic thinking. Kissinger used the Center as a base of operations; it
provided him with office facilities, secretarial and library services, and a
convenient place for small meetings. He never felt great enthusiasm for
the Center, and never thought it contributed to his own intellectual development in the way he hoped it might.

This did not prevent him, however, from acknowledging the help that
it did give. Thus, for example, he felt indebted to the Center for its arms
control seminar, which brought together MIT and Harvard professors

from various disciplines, together with a few others from outside, who then engaged in a continuing discussion of a whole range of problems that were then still very little understood. The Center's arms control group was small; it included Robert Bowie, Saville Davis, Max Millikan, Thomas Schelling, Arthur Schlesinger, Jr., Marshall Shulman, Jerome Wiesner, and Jerrold Zacharias. While it would be wrong to select out from the group any single individual whose influence on Kissinger was paramount, several, including Jerome Wiesner, certainly exercised considerable authority. Wiesner's distinction as a scientist derived from work he had done on radio-wave propagation and on communication techniques and systems. His interest for Kissinger lay in his sensitive appreciation of the complexities of the problems of arms limitation. Before his return to Harvard in 1957, Kissinger's acquaintance with scientists was exceedingly limited. Neither the International Seminar nor *Confluence* had done much to make him familiar with the large and powerful scientific community. When he went to the Council on Foreign Relations he met a number of scientists, but with the exception of Caryl Haskins, none of them became his close friends. It was through the arms control seminar, and particularly through some of the men to whom Kissinger was introduced by Wiesner and others, that he began to have a more precise notion of the kinds of contributions scientists might make in the arms control area. Through the Rockefeller Brothers Fund Project, Kissinger had come to know Edward Teller, one of the few prominent American scientists who persistently expressed skepticism about most arms control proposals. It was useful for Kissinger to hear from scientists who held quite opposite views on many of the issues that he had first discussed with Teller. Kissinger had written about arms control in *Nuclear Weapons and Foreign Policy;* he was now meeting regularly with others who were producing pioneer studies in that newly developed field.

Because natural scientists formed a truly international community of scholars, Kissinger profited from becoming acquainted with Americans who were in a position to introduce him to their colleagues abroad. He owed several of his initial meetings with Soviet scientists to introductions effected by his American scientific friends. Also, he soon became involved, though never in an important way, with the Pugwash movement, which traced its beginnings to a manifesto issued by Bertrand Russell in 1957. Russell had called for closer cooperation between Western and Soviet scientists concerned with the dangers of thermonuclear war. Plans were made for a small initial international gathering at Pugwash, Nova Scotia; the auspices were entirely private; Cyrus Eaton, the wealthy American philanthropist, provided the initial financial support. From these very simple beginnings, procedures were developed for larger international meetings. At a time when the opportunities for exchange were very limited, the chance for Soviet, European, and American scientists to meet periodically, in fairly informal circumstances, to discuss issues of mutual concern to them, was highly valued. Arms control issues figured prominently in all the Pugwash discussions, whether held in Moscow or Stowe, Vermont. Kissinger was not a "charter" member of the American Pugwash group; he did not attend the Moscow meetings in 1960. He did, however, know many of those who went, and took a very considerable interest in what they discussed. Given that interest, he was soon invited to attend other of the Pugwash conferences.

In 1958, he added substantially to his teaching obligations at Harvard. He organized and became the Director of the Defense Studies Program. Those who were most critical of Kissinger—and the number never approached zero—were inclined to disparage the seminar he introduced under the Program. The course, Government 259, Defense Policy and Administration, brought high-ranking military and civilian officials from Washington (and elsewhere) to Cambridge for weekly two-hour sessions throughout the academic year. Kissinger presided; those who had little sympathy for the course suggested that it too often degenerated into a dialogue between Kissinger and his guest, to which the students were privileged auditors. For those who believed that Kissinger's principal pleasure in life was to surround himself with famous men, the seminar appeared to have no other rationale. Others, more sympathetic to Kissinger's effort, realized that he was introducing a new and important subject into the Harvard curriculum, and that he had organized the course in such a way as to make possible the kind of discourse in which he excelled. He enjoyed the weekly discussions; his carefully recruited staff instructed students in small group meetings more effectively than he would ever have been able to do. Kissinger knew that there was no adequate system of instruction in the field of strategic studies, and he was pleased to do something to help create the discipline. More than that, he was delighted to be able to do this at Harvard, where a very substantial number of able and interested students might be expected to enroll. Kissinger expected that the field would probably soon become highly specialized, and that this would exclude the kind of thinking that he deemed most important. Without disparaging technical research, Kissinger wanted to assert the importance of another kind—of the kind he himself was doing. He saw the possibility of achieving some of these purposes through the Defense Policy seminar.

Kissinger insisted that the seminar be open not only to students in the Faculty of Arts and Sciences but to students in all the graduate and professional schools. In the late 1950s, such freedom of cross-registration was not common at Harvard. Kissinger's concern was as much to "subvert" the lawyer, and make him rethink his professional goals—whether or not he entered a Wall Street law firm—as it was to instruct the student who would eventually go on to teach the subject in a university or enter government service. Though the seminar was technically open only to graduate students, qualified undergraduates were welcome. A number of undergraduates enrolled, and some were "converted" to the field largely as a consequence of their experience in the seminar. The course was always popular; enrollments were always high.

In July 1959, Kissinger received his appointment as Associate Professor of Government at Harvard. He was pleased. How could he fail to be? While he had come to have increasingly serious reservations about the academic profession—wondering about the absence of generosity that he so often observed—he had no doubt that the profession afforded an incomparable privilege: the right to think and publish without hindrance. He spoke frequently of the insecurity and narrow-mindedness of professors, not only those whom he met in Cambridge but those whom he met around the country. In his view, they struggled too hard for prizes that were too small; their greatest pleasure seemed to be to compel others to scramble as they themselves had once been required to do. They lived with visions of power—their own and that of their colleagues—which Kissinger found comic. He much preferred many of the people he met in New York and Washington. They seemed more complete as human beings, more modest, and, surprisingly, more gentle. Yet he had no desire to exchange his profession for theirs. He wanted to be a professor —not because he was born in Germany and had a residual respect for the distinction that attached to the professorial role, but because a professorship carried the promise of an independence that he craved. Kissinger's travels through the country taught him that many of Harvard's shortcomings were common in universities everywhere; they seemed almost endemic in the American academic system. As for Harvard's strengths, they were not always present. It made very good sense for him to remain in Cambridge.

Yet as he moved up in his profession and men talked more casually to him, with less concern about what they were revealing about themselves, he found the experience genuinely disconcerting. Many of those who prided themselves on their political liberalism seemed incapable of making the slightest human gesture. Kissinger, while pleased to be a permanent member of the Harvard faculty, never entirely liked Harvard; he distrusted the reactions and values of too many of his academic colleagues. While he immensely treasured the freedom that his Harvard appointment gave him and was proud of his position, he felt himself to be somewhat marginal in Cambridge. He did not "belong" as certain others did. He claimed to be unaffected by this, or by the reports that reached him of unflattering comments made by colleagues, some of whom he scarcely knew. He was generally characterized as ambitious and power hungry. Many saw him as a schemer, who chose his patrons with a deliberation worthy of a greater objective. Very few were aware of either the range or the variety of Kissinger's associations. If he stood to gain from knowing Nelson Rockefeller, it was less obvious what he hoped to secure from spending endless hours with foreign students every summer. One part of Kissinger's life was public; that part aroused envy. Other parts were largely unknown. If he consorted with famous men in New York and Washington, he also kept in close touch with many of no great reputation or position; it was by no means certain that he gained more from the first than from the second. In the end, however, Kissinger knew that all such associations were incidental to his larger purpose, which was to develop a coherent critique of existing foreign policy and to offer viable alternatives. Conversation, however excellent, was never a substitute for writing. The need to go off alone—to think and to write—was a need that Kissinger indulged; it permitted him to produce the books and articles that gave him his reputation.

Kissinger, without ever proclaiming his purpose, became the principal American critic of United States foreign policy. Had he been differently motivated—had he wished to make Eisenhower or Dulles the villains of his piece—had he chosen to use irony and insult as his principal literary instruments, he might have been recognized as one of America's prime detractors of the Republican administration. That, however, was not his intention. He did not see Eisenhower and Dulles as the sole authors of many of the mistaken policies that were being pursued. There had not been much greater wisdom under Truman, though the opportunities from 1945 to 1952 had been enormous. Nor was it a foregone conclusion that there would be a more effective handling of foreign policy under a new Democratic administration. Kissinger was quite impartial in his criticism; party labels had no importance for him.

Kissinger owed a debt to the Council on Foreign Relations for what it had done to help him with *Nuclear Weapons and Foreign Policy*. He discharged that debt—in part, certainly—by what he wrote for *Foreign Affairs* in the years that followed. He had already written in *Foreign Affairs* before the publication of his book; it now became the principal vehicle for his writings and remained so until the advent of the Kennedy administration, when it came to share that place with *The Reporter*, edited by Max Ascoli, who became a close friend. During the Eisenhower years, however, it was *Foreign Affairs* that enjoyed almost "exclusive rights" to Kissinger's articles. What use, then, did Kissinger make of that forum? What ideas, other than those implicit or explicit in *Nuclear Weapons and Foreign Policy*, did he seek to develop?

In October 1956, on the eve of the presidential election, Kissinger wrote an article in *Foreign Affairs* entitled "Reflections on American Diplomacy." He began by saying: "There can be little doubt that the foreign policy of the United States has reached an impasse. For several years we have been groping for a concept to deal with the transformation of the cold war from an effort to build defensive barriers into a contest for the allegiance of humanity. But the new Soviet tactics, coupled with the equally unassimilated increase in the destructive potentialities of the new weapons technology, have led to a crisis in our system of alliances and to substantial Soviet gains among the uncommitted peoples of the world." Anyone reading that statement and choosing to stop there would assume that Kissinger's purpose was to make a deliberate assault on the Eisenhower administration. Kissinger, in fact, intended a more sweeping indictment; as he explained, "It would be a mistake . . . to ascribe our difficulties to this or that error of policy or to a particular administration, although the present Administration has not helped matters by its pretense of 'normalcy.' " Kissinger was not simply finding fault with the Republicans. Yet, in arguing his case, he constantly chose examples from recent American experience. In a very calculated criticism of Eisenhower's way of doing things, Kissinger wrote: "We consider policy-making concluded when the National Security Council has come to a decision. In fact, the process of coming to a decision is so arduous and a reappraisal so 'agonizing' that we are reluctant to re-examine policies after they have outlived their usefulness." He went on to say: "We lack tragic experience. Though we have known hardship, we have not known disaster. Men like Secretaries Humphrey and Wilson cannot believe that in the nuclear age the penalty for miscalculation may be national catastrophe. They know it in their heads but not in their hearts; we cannot go the way of Rome . . ." Kissinger's judgments were harsh; he criticized the American habit of making the Soviets seem respectable; he saw no reason for Eisenhower's having given Bulganin a "certificate of good conduct" by suggesting that he believed in the "peaceful intentions" of the Soviet leader. The American policy vis-à-vis the Soviet Union, in Kissinger's mind, lacked subtlety. He gave the administration almost no credit for what it had accomplished. To read the article was to be aware mostly of failures.

The same note was sounded by articles that Kissinger wrote for *Foreign Affairs* in 1958 and 1959. In these, there was not even the pretense of evenhandedness. The administration was old and tired; it seemed incapable of purposeful action. Writing on "Missiles and the Western Alliance" in April 1958, Kissinger commented on the debate that the launching of the Soviet earth satellite had generated throughout the Western world. Even after the United States lost its atomic monopoly, Kissinger wrote, the West continued to speak as if every Soviet threat would be countered with an all-out American atomic response. That kind of naïveté was no longer possible; however, Kissinger found the new attitude equally disconcerting. Men now argued as if the United States had suddenly become totally vulnerable, incapable of doing anything before Soviet technological power. In Europe, some insisted that the United States was more dependent than ever on its NATO allies, and that the only reasonable course —the only safe course—was to deny America the use of European missile bases; failure to do this would only increase Europe's vulnerability to attack. Others suggested that it was questionable whether the United States should be permitted to remain in Europe at all. There was new talk of "disengagement" and of the need for a "neutral belt" in Europe. Many of these arguments, Kissinger wrote, showed massive confusion; they implied that NATO bases existed in Europe solely for the advantage of the Americans. Few who spoke in this vein were able to distinguish between a strategy for deterrence and a strategy for the conduct of war should deterrence fail. Worse still, they confused vulnerability with strategic inferiority, and misinterpreted the likely consequences of a temporary strategic inferiority.

Both the advocates and the opponents of missile installations in Europe were mistaken, Kissinger wrote; each was misled by an absolutist approach. The advocates made the mistake of believing that the same deterrent was useful for every kind of challenge. The opponents were mistaken in believing that they could become immune to risk by simply rejecting the missiles. Because all countries would suffer severely in the event of a nuclear war between the United States and the USSR, the Allies could have only one interest: to prevent such a war entirely. Kissinger asked whether a decision to opt out, which was really what Europe's neutralists were recommending, would not weaken the credibility of the American deterrent and encourage the very aggression it was designed to prevent. The growing Soviet missile capability undoubtedly increased Europe's vulnerability, but Europe had been vulnerable for many years, exposed, as it was, to the threat of Soviet short- and medium-range bombers. So, also, the United States had been vulnerable before Sputnik; it was wrong to believe that it was the new Soviet missile capacity that had suddenly made the country vulnerable. Nor was there any advantage in failing to recognize that such vulnerability was certain to grow. This, however, did not mean that the United States had to accept the position of being strategically inferior to the Soviet Union. That would happen, Kissinger wrote, only if the Soviet Union developed missiles capable of destroying America's retaliatory force, or if it developed an air defense of such power as to reduce any potential American retaliatory response to levels that the Soviet Union would find tolerable. There was no great likelihood of either of these things happening in the near future. Whether they in fact ever happened depended largely on what the United States chose to do. There was no point in making the American strategic inferiority seem greater than it was by comparing future Soviet capabilities with existing American strength.

The Soviet Union, Kissinger explained, did not possess at that moment operational intercontinental missiles in any very great quantity. Nor was there any reason for such a gap to develop if the United States acted energetically. By the time that the Soviets did have accurate intercontinental missiles in quantity, the United States could also have a well-developed missile force, which it could supplement with the still powerful bomber force of the Strategic Air Command. Both sides, in time, Kissinger wrote, would certainly have "well-dispersed missiles in a high state of readiness." Even were the Soviet Union to forge ahead at some point, as it might well do, there was no great hazard in this. Kissinger continued to believe that American strength, particularly in its manned bombers, virtually precluded the possibility of an all-out Soviet surprise attack on the United States. The Soviets, he explained, would be foolish to risk their survival in such an attack. He did not say that it could not happen; only that it was extremely unlikely.

Looking ahead to what he called "the approaching missile age," Kissinger suggested that the results would be "precisely opposite to what some of our critics allege." Once the United States had a sufficient number of intercontinental missiles, the Allies would be dispensable in a purely military sense. Even under existing conditions, given the American strength in its Strategic Air Force, the United States did not rely on European help. If the United States favored the installation of missiles in Europe, the reason was not that the defense of the United States required such bases but that the defense of Europe required them. Kissinger wrote: "They [the missiles] are essential for the very reason that Europeans are reluctant to accept them; with the increasing speed and destructiveness of weapons *every* country will be reluctant to risk its existence for anything except the most direct challenge to its survival. If Europe is reluctant to participate in an all-out war for the defense of the United States—the only meaningful rationale for rejecting missile bases—so will the United States be reluctant to risk total destruction for the defense of Europe. Our NATO allies should have every incentive to develop a strategy which does not force the United States to choose between all-out war and inaction in the defense of Europe."

In Kissinger's view, the American offer of missiles to Europe provided the only means for Europe to gain some degree of influence over its own future. Should Europe refuse America's offer of missiles, Kissinger wrote, that would not increase Europe's security; it would simply make Europe even more dependent on the United States. As the United States itself became more vulnerable, Kissinger wrote, "fewer and fewer objectives will seem 'worth' an all-out war." Europe itself, in time, might not seem important enough, particularly if the Soviet threats against Europe were limited and ambiguous. Europe could not hope to influence its own destiny if it did not possess a capability—in part, based on its own resources—for resisting Soviet aggression. Kissinger did not believe that the threat of the Soviet Union's overrunning the whole of Europe was very great; he looked for local encroachments, which would demonstrate the impotence of NATO, and, in the process, limit NATO's diplomatic effectiveness. "The greater the disparity in strength between Europe and the U.S.S.R. and the greater the vulnerability of the United States," Kissinger wrote, "the bolder Soviet policy towards our allies is likely to become."

Local forces, Kissinger explained, "would perform a vital function even if they could not withstand *every* scale of Soviet attack." He cited the examples of Sweden and Switzerland; those countries maintained armies not because they imagined that their forces were capable of defeating a major power but because they wanted it known that any power that attacked them would have to pay a price for its action. "A substantial military establishment on the continent," Kissinger wrote, "will do much to deter Soviet adventures." If it did not achieve that purpose, he said, it would at least force the Soviets "into a scale of military effort that would remove any ambiguity" about their intentions.

Kissinger found it easy to understand and sympathize with the motives that led certain Europeans to favor disengagement. Their mistake, however, was to believe that such a policy would lead the Soviet Union to withdraw its armies from the satellite countries. The idea that the Soviet Union needed to be reassured concerning the sincerity of the West's desire for peace did not much appeal to him. Such arguments, he wrote, ran counter to the whole postwar experience; he said: "Where forces exist, there has been no Soviet penetration. Where they are absent, the Soviets have often moved." Kissinger wondered whether the Soviets might not be more interested in negotiating about disengagement than in actually achieving disengagement. The so-called Rapacki Plan, which was intended to create a nuclear-free zone in Central Europe, did not, in his view, resolve any of the major problems; nor did it create any advantages for the West. Western Europe, under such a plan, would still be vulnerable to a nuclear attack from missiles stationed in the USSR. The West would gain no additional security; it would simply lead to the withdrawal of all American forces from Central Europe. In time, Kissinger wrote, it would put pressure on the United States to remove all its nuclear weapons from Europe, including those stationed in the United Kingdom. Since it was impossible to defend Europe at that moment without nuclear weapons, such a plan would simply serve to create a vacuum, which the Soviets could be expected to fill. The result, in Kissinger's mind, would be a NATO "so weakened that the withdrawal of the American military establishment from Europe would be almost certain."

Nor did Kissinger see great merit in the proposal for a simultaneous withdrawal of Soviet and American forces from Central Europe and the creation of a so-called neutral belt. In his view, such a plan, far from improving the situation, might only cause it to deteriorate further. Were revolutions to break out in the satellite states, for example, Kissinger expected the Soviet armies would return in even greater force. While Kissinger did not exclude the possibility that the United States might one day withdraw its forces from the center of the Continent, he insisted that the time for such a withdrawal would be when the Allies were strong and chose such a policy out of confidence. So long as NATO lacked an effective deterrent to Soviet aggression in Western Europe, the possibility of successful negotiation on such issues seemed remote.

The argument that there was evidence of increasing Soviet good will did not much impress Kissinger. He saw few signs of a diminished interest in the Soviet Union in challenging the West. Believing that Soviet attitudes would be affected by what the West did, he wrote: "Our failure to engage in an adequate defense effort may well be the deciding factor in the Soviet decision to launch a blow." Kissinger believed that the West could more easily affect Soviet attitudes by the "restraint and moderation with which it uses its strength than by seeking to purchase Soviet forbearance by impotence." The whole posture of the West vis-à-vis the Soviet Union worried Kissinger. Too many were urging negotiations on the basis of what they believed Soviet intentions to be. To argue about Soviet intentions made no sense whatever; there was no way to discover them, and those who spoke most confidently about them knew much less than they pretended. Kissinger was not much concerned with Soviet intentions; there was not a great deal that could be known, and the absence of knowledge, in his view, gave no excuse for refusing to negotiate with the Soviets. He was not being ironical when he wrote that negotiations were "especially necessary if Soviet intentions have *not* changed." Kissinger wrote: "The more intransigent the U.S.S.R. is the more important it is for us to put forward proposals that show we are ready to settle, but that also define the issues for which we are prepared to contend." Kissinger made his position very clear when he said: "We should make no proposal we are not willing to see accepted but by the same token we should not refrain from making proposals simply because we believe they may not be accepted. We are under no obligation to frame proposals we are sure the U.S.S.R. will accept. We *are* under an obligation to make responsible proposals which are not designed to undermine legitimate Soviet interests." Negotiations, in Kissinger's mind, needed always to deal with concrete issues.

In October 1958, shortly after President Eisenhower announced his intention to suspend all nuclear tests for a year and to seek a permanent test ban through negotiations with the Soviet Union, Kissinger wrote a major article for *Foreign Affairs*, entitled "Nuclear Testing and the Problem of Peace." While the article showed some departure from what many who were interested in arms control thought to be the rigidities of his earlier position, as expressed in *Nuclear Weapons and Foreign Policy*, Kissinger remained skeptical about certain of the proposals being made. He reviewed the arguments of those who advocated a test ban and noted that while many emphasized the dangers of fall-out, others insisted that a ban would be the first step to larger disarmament measures, contributing perhaps to the solution of "the nth country problem." There was a great deal of concern with those states that still lacked atomic weapons but were expected, for one reason or other, to try to develop them. Kissinger refrained from commenting on the validity of any of these arguments, but pointed out that Soviet propaganda had always insisted on the unconditional prohibition of tests and the outlawing of all nuclear weapons. Kissinger asked whether a complete cessation of tests was desirable, irrespective of the possibilities of inspection. He clearly believed that a complete test ban did not make sense. He worried less about whether the United States would be able to detect Soviet violations of a test ban agreement, and more about what it would in fact be able to do if it did detect such violations. A violation of the ban, for example, was clearly not an excuse for war; there was some uncertainty whether it would even justify the injured party's starting to test again. Kissinger worried that if nuclear tests were once banned, even extreme provocation would not lead to a resumption of testing. Even if the will to test existed, the machinery would not be in place. Testing apparatus would have to be reassembled; new staffs would need to be recruited; all this would require a certain amount of time. Some argued that public opinion would be so outraged by a violation that it would demand an immediate resumption of testing. Kissinger was not at all sure that this would happen. The violation would almost certainly not be open; charges and counter-charges would fill the air, and it would be hard to know where the truth lay. Also, he wondered whether the test ban would not give the Soviets a very real technological advantage. They could keep their staffs intact; also, because, in his view, they were less dependent on experimental proofs than were the Americans, they could do without testing more easily. Kissinger kept hearing the test ban referred to as a "first step"; he asked what it was intended to be a "first step" toward.

Kissinger worried that the Soviets would use the test ban as a "first step" in demanding the total abolition of nuclear weapons. He could already hear the argument: if nuclear weapons were too dangerous to test, they were obviously too dangerous to use. Kissinger believed, given the state of the West's defenses, that an "outlawing of nuclear weapons would be tantamount to unilateral disarmament." If the West had a true conventional defense capability, a test ban would not be so dangerous. Because the West lacked such a defense, Kissinger thought the ban was "a real threat."

What, then, did he propose? Additional conventional forces; a wider spectrum of nuclear weapons. "We must stop pretending," Kissinger wrote, "that we can buy security on the cheap." Because the offense necessarily enjoyed an advantage over the defense—and because Kissinger expected the West to remain on the defense—the West had to have the most advanced technological systems, capable of defending all likely targets against any weapons systems that the Soviets might employ. In Kissinger's view, the West needed "weapons of finer discrimination, less destructive power and greatly reduced fall-out." He did not think it impossible that one of the reasons the Soviets insisted on a complete and unconditional test ban was that they were aware of "the paralysis" that such a ban would produce in the West.

Kissinger had long maintained that one of America's principal difficulties in negotiating with the USSR stemmed from the fact that, in his words, "we know more what we are opposed to than what we stand for." The Soviet Union was always the initiating power; the United States generally reacted to Soviet moves. This, in his mind, was happening again with the nuclear testing issue; he wrote: "Our diplomacy has concentrated on questions of inspection or of belittling dangers of fall-out. We ought not to negotiate only on issues that the Soviet Union says are soluble." Kissinger's own recommendations for the negotiations that were about to begin were simple: since there was universal concern about the fall-out issue, that question needed to be confronted at once. A more complete test ban, he thought, could wait on a more comprehensive disarmament agreement. Kissinger recommended that each side be given a fall-out quota that would be reduced within two years to zero. After that date, failing an agreement, the nuclear powers would be free to test only so long as there was no fall-out. "Such measures," Kissinger wrote, "would impede the arms race, but not stop weapons development altogether. It would not put the United States in the position of keeping its allies from getting weapons that the U.S.S.R. already has in quantity." If the Soviet Union refused such an agreement, Kissinger wrote, then the United States would do well to impose such a prohibition on itself unilaterally. Were the United States to do so, he was confident that world pressure would begin to build up on the Soviet Union and that she would probably be forced to follow suit.

To those who believed passionately in the importance of an immediate test ban, such a proposal would seem scarcely adequate. Clearly, Kissinger did not belong to that segment of the academic community that saw a complete test ban as the necessary first step toward meaningful arms control. He took issue not only with the Eisenhower administration, but with what many of his academic friends and colleagues thought was a rational move toward an eventual understanding with the Soviet Union. It took some courage for him to be so skeptical about developments that were so universally applauded in the academic circles that he frequented.

He argued his position in the arms control seminar but did not write again on the subject until the summer of 1960, when an article on "Arms Control, Inspection and Surprise Attack" appeared in *Foreign Affairs*. In the autumn of the same year, he contributed to a special *Daedalus* issue, *Arms Control*, with an article entitled "Limited War: Conventional or Nuclear?—A Reappraisal." The second article created something of a stir among Kissinger's academic friends and colleagues, if only because he appeared to be backing away from his earlier espousal of the theory of limited nuclear war. Both articles were republished in virtually their original form a few months later in Kissinger's *Necessity for Choice;* they are perhaps best examined in the context of that larger work.

Meanwhile, Kissinger turned to a more careful consideration of the German problem, on which he felt a very special competence. His interest in the subject was long-standing, but he had written relatively little about the matter. In July 1959, in an article entitled "The Search for Stability," Kissinger gave vent to his feelings. The West had offered the Soviet Union a "package," linking German unification to certain larger questions of European security. That link had been rejected by the Soviet Union; the Russians insisted that the problem of unification was one for the two German states to decide; the Foreign Ministers ought to concern themselves only with those issues that the Soviets defined as "soluble." Kissinger thought that the Western response to Soviet tactics of this kind had been "tentative and irresolute." "We have worried," he wrote, "more about what to concede than what our goals ought to be."

Many who pretended to know Soviet intentions argued as if the Russians were simply interested in gaining Western acceptance for the status quo in Eastern Europe; they generally urged the West "to yield to facts that we are powerless to change." Kissinger asked whether "the only reasonable response to facts is to adjust to them." He was not very certain about what was meant when the recognition of the status quo was argued for. The Soviet Union's problems in Eastern Europe, according to Kissinger, derived from the fact that the Communist leaders there were unable to win the support of their populations. If the West really wanted to help the Communist leaders of these countries, it could do so by "renouncing the *principle* of self-determination." Kissinger could not believe that the

West would gain very much by "collaborating" with the Soviets in that way. As for the East German problem, it had to be distinguished from that of the other East European Communist states. East Germany suffered not simply from the hostility of its own population but from a West German example that mocked its much vaunted accomplishments. Kissinger believed that the Federal Republic would suffer a possibly irreparable blow if the Allies agreed to accept its existing frontiers as final. If the Federal Republic concluded that it could not gain reunification through its ties to the West, there would be a powerful incentive to "seek to achieve its aims through separate dealings with the East." Also, Kissinger feared that there would be "a resurgence of virulent nationalism." Germany's continued membership in the Atlantic community, he wrote, was important not only for the future of Germany but for the peace of the world.

Kissinger doubted that the Soviet Union simply wanted to perpetuate the status quo. He believed that the Soviets intended to consolidate East Germany as a first step toward destroying the cohesion of the West; the ultimate Soviet purpose, he thought, was the "Communization" of Germany. The Soviet insistence that unification could only be carried out by the two Germanys was, in his view, a cynical ruse. If the Soviets really wanted unification, they could achieve their purpose by free elections. Confederation would never work; it would give the East Germans a voice in West German affairs, while the West Germans did not secure equivalent rights in East Germany. The Communist police-state apparatus, Kissinger explained, made East Germany relatively immune to popular pressure. Kissinger recommended that the Allies insist on free elections at some reasonable time in the near future. In the meantime, it was most important that the Allies support the Federal Republic in its demands for unification. He wrote: "It is said by some that nobody really *wants* German unification. But surely it is within our control to set our own goals. If the West understands its interests, it *must* advocate German unification, despite the experience of two world wars and despite the understandable fear of a revival of German truculence. The West may have to acquiesce in the division of Germany but it cannot condone it. Any other course will in the end bring on what we should fear most: a militant, dissatisfied power in the center of the Continent. To strive for German unification is not a bargaining device but the condition of European stability."

Kissinger believed that the Soviets would oppose German unification on any terms that did not convert Germany into a Soviet satellite. There was no reason for the United States to accept Soviet proposals. American interests could only be served by insisting on the principle of self-determination. Kissinger wrote: "During Suez we insisted that we would uphold our principles *even* against our allies. Are we to leave the impression now that we will uphold them *only* against our allies?" The American obligation, he explained, was to make "responsible proposals" that would take into account the legitimate security concerns of all parties. What should those proposals be? According to Kissinger, the Soviet Union had a right to be protected against the dangers of a resurgent Germany; it ought to be protected also against an attack from NATO territory. The West, in turn, needed to be protected against the Soviet Union. Absolute security for either side was impossible; each had to be satisfied with relative security. Believing that the Soviets intended to "wreck NATO" through making a local defense of Europe impossible, Kissinger asked whether there might not be an advantage in conceiving "of two military establishments on the Continent capable of defensive action but deprived through appropriate control measures of offensive power." Kissinger believed that a comprehensive European security system along the frontiers of a unified Germany was possible. Through a system of mutual withdrawals, involving American, Soviet, British, French, Polish, and Czech forces, and through the control of weapons, there would be a separation of Soviet and Western military forces and a measure of arms control in a specific zone. If such measures served to produce a "climate of confidence," further agreements might follow. For any of this to happen, however, it was essential, Kissinger wrote, for the "weaknesses and irresolution" of the Western alliance to be overcome. If the Soviet Union rejected a reasonable program for the reunification of Germany, as was very probable, there would be new pressures to introduce arms control in the border areas that separated Eastern and Western Europe. Proposals for a troop freeze or a thinning out of forces were commonly made. Neither of these solutions, Kissinger thought, really came to grips with the security problem in Central Europe. These measures did not reduce the dangers of political upheaval in Germany; they might, indeed, serve only to increase the possibilities of revolutionary outbreaks. Nor did they reduce either the Soviet or the American capacity to launch an all-out attack. They simply made the task of establishing a purely local defense even more difficult. Kissinger believed that a troop freeze would only perpetuate the existing Soviet superiority.

Three and a half years elapsed between the publication of *Nuclear Weapons and Foreign Policy* and the end of the second Eisenhower administration. In January 1961, on the eve of John Kennedy's inauguration, Kissinger published a book entitled *The Necessity for Choice: Prospects of American Foreign Policy*. Those who had been reading Kissinger's published articles recognized certain segments of the book, which had been published previously, as he indicated in his Preface, in slightly different form in *Foreign Affairs*, *The Reporter*, *Harper's*, and *Daedalus*. What made the book interesting—particularly for those who knew Kissinger's earlier work—was the extent to which he built on foundations that had been laid many years before. The book showed a continuing fidelity to ideas that Kissinger first developed when he was a graduate student at Harvard.

The reviews were almost uniformly favorable, but not one noted a fact that ought to have been immediately apparent: the work was a sustained and radical critique of policies pursued by the Eisenhower administration. Kissinger never intended that his book should be read simply as an indictment of American foreign policy over the preceding eight years, but his disillusion was evident on every page. The reviewers were possibly misled by the opening paragraphs, where Kissinger's indictment seemed to be a more general one. He appeared to be saying farewell to a whole generation of American leaders, and, by implication, to be saying also "good riddance." Kissinger could not have been more forceful; he wrote: "We have come to the end of the policies and of the men that dominated the immediate post-war period. Whatever aspect of American foreign policy we consider, the need for new departures is apparent. The issues which have gone unresolved for a decade no longer permit delay." At another place, he was even more emphatic, extending his criticisms to the beginning of the Truman period; he said: "The United States cannot afford another decline like that which has characterized the past decade and a half. Fifteen years more of a deterioration of our position in the world such as we have experienced since World War II would find us reduced to Fortress America in a world in which we had become largely irrelevant." A reviewer might have thought this mere rhetoric, particularly when Kissinger chose to follow this blast with what seemed to be a partial retraction. He wrote: "It is futile now to debate the causes of this state of affairs. Many of the misconceptions of the immediate post-war period were no doubt inevitable. Without them, we could not have endured psychologically the pressures and tensions of the Cold War. We would never have known whether a more trusting policy might not have succeeded. Nor has the period under discussion been without great achievements. The Marshall Plan, NATO, Point Four, the decision to enter the Korean war, were major acts of statesmanship. Measured against our historical experience, we can even be said to have done rather well."

Had Kissinger withdrawn all his charges? Not at all. He continued with an even more absolute criticism of American policy; he said: "Relative achievements are small comfort in the present world. Our period offers no prizes for having done rather well. Nothing is more difficult for Americans to understand than the possibility of tragedy. And yet nothing should concern us more. For all the good will, for all the effort, we can go the way of other nations which to their citizens probably seemed just as invulnerable and eternal." Kissinger believed that the "margin of survival" had "narrowed dangerously," but that there was still time for choice. In the very questions that Americans were asking, Kissinger wrote, there was evidence of the deterioration of America's position: "Is there or is there not a missile gap? Is Communism gaining ground in the underdeveloped nations? Is there any hope for democracy in the new nations? Is NATO still meaningful a decade after its inception?"

An insufficiently attentive reader, perusing these passages, might dismiss them as a too sweeping condemnation of everything that had taken place in American foreign policy since the war. Was there no difference, then, between what was accomplished under Truman and what was done under Eisenhower? In Kissinger's mind, such a difference did exist. Whatever the faults of the Truman administration, there had been a number of substantial accomplishments. By comparison, the Eisenhower record was barren. Kissinger could point to no action or decision that he thought was worthy of the country. While praise for the creation of NATO and the economic rehabilitation of Europe through the Marshall Plan formed a perpetual theme in his works—a near-litany—there was no comparable praise for any action taken after 1952. Indeed, some of the things for which others chose to praise Eisenhower—his decision to condemn the Anglo-French intervention at Suez in 1956 and his willingness to land Marines in Lebanon in 1958 when civil war threatened in that country, to take only two examples—Kissinger dismissed as mistaken or badly conceived policies. Eisenhower, in Kissinger's mind, showed little understanding of the foreign policy imperatives of his day. Kissinger regretted the fact that so few had been able to challenge him openly and to do so in a way that had effect. Kissinger wrote: "Over the decade of the 1950s one looks in vain for any fundamental criticism of the main trends in American policy. No Churchill or de Gaulle has hurled warnings or offered alternatives. It is difficult to remember even what some of the so-called great debates were about. Such criticism as has been offered was frequently tactical or *ex post facto*. The fatuous diplomacy which preceded the abortive summit meeting of 1960 in Paris went largely unchallenged until its failure became apparent. But the test of statesmanship is the adequacy of its evaluation *before* the event. A democracy, to be vital, requires leaders willing to stand alone."

Kissinger's indictment of the foreign policy of a whole decade, then, was not simply the criticism of a small group of men who held high office, but of the many others who ought to have formed the opposition, and who failed in their task. In the name of bipartisanship, the "sacred cow" of that epoch, inferior doctrine had been accepted, and actions were approved of that were quite inadequate to the situations they were intended to serve. These were serious charges, only slightly less serious than those leveled by Kissinger at the men actually responsible for enacting policy. Too many of them lacked the "yardsticks" that might have permitted them to judge the adequacy of their policies. Kissinger, surveying the arms control policies of the Eisenhower administration, wrote scathingly of them; he said: "Because we lack a strategic doctrine and a coherent military policy, it is inevitable that our proposals on arms control are fitful. We are in no position to know whether a given plan enhances security, detracts from it, or is simply irrelevant. As a consequence, proposals are developed as a compromise between competing groups and without an over-all sense of purpose. Instead of urging disarmament conferences because we wish to advance a scheme in which we have confidence, we have reversed the process: typically we have been forced to assemble a set of hasty proposals because we have agreed to go to a conference under the pressure of world opinion or Soviet diplomacy. The confusion is demonstrated by the fact that, though our military establishment is built around nuclear weapons, our arms control negotiations have stigmatized the strategy on which we have been relying. To conduct both policies simultaneously is clearly disastrous."

There was no need to name the President when Kissinger wrote: "NATO, the cornerstone of our foreign policy, has not been adapted to changed strategic and political relationships. The role of the military forces in Europe, the future of Germany, the nature of Atlantic relationships, have all gone largely undefined. Formal declarations of unity cannot obscure the confusion within the alliance." The American response to the anti-colonial upheaval, Kissinger wrote, was just as inadequate. Despite vast expenditures for military and economic assistance, there was little basic understanding of the problems of the emerging nations. Kissinger said that "much of our foreign aid program has been characterized by a kind of nostalgia for the Marshall Plan and the New Deal." Anyone who read only the introductory chapter to *The Necessity for Choice* might have concluded that Kissinger was seeking to ingratiate himself with the Kennedy entourage. A reading of the whole text, however, and a realization that the principal themes simply repeated what Kissinger had said elsewhere, suggested a quite different possibility. Kissinger came of age as a student of strategy and foreign policy during the Eisenhower years; while he eschewed commentary that could be mistaken for journalism, he felt very deeply the obligation to criticize.

Inevitably, he repeated arguments that he had first developed in *Nuclear Weapons and Foreign Policy*. Strangely enough, he showed that he had not forgotten, either, what he had written in *A World Restored*. He knew that in the nuclear age victory had lost its traditional significance. The outbreak of war, he realized, was the ultimate catastrophe. In such a situation, the "capacity of the military to keep the peace," and to do so effectively, was "the ultimate test of the efficacy of any military establishment." All the conventional rules of war had changed; the object was no longer to win a war but to avoid it. How could such a purpose be achieved? Kissinger returned to his old remedy—psychological insight. The "state of mind of the potential aggressor" was the all-important variable. If a state *seemed* weak, thereby inviting attack, the fact that it was not *actually* weak did not matter. If an attack occurred, then the deterrent had failed. Kissinger wrote: "A gesture intended as a bluff but taken seriously is more useful as a deterrent than a bona fide threat interpreted as a bluff." Deterrence depended on the possession of military power, but also on the willingness to use it, and on the assessment that a potential aggressor made of both these factors.

If the United States had been psychologically deterred from using its nuclear weapons when it enjoyed a monopoly of these arms, Kissinger wrote, it was not likely to use them now that it was vulnerable to atomic attack. There was no way to achieve invulnerability again; that had been lost forever. However, that did not mean that the United States could not have an "invulnerable retaliatory force," which could serve as a credible deterrent. Kissinger, like so many others, accepted the fact that a "missile gap" had developed. The existence of the "gap," however, did not mean that the Soviets would soon attack. The Eisenhower administration had not believed that it would do so, and there was no reason to alter that judgment. The new administration, he wrote, needed to give high priority to making the existing retaliatory force less vulnerable. That, however, could not be the whole of its policy, since an invulnerable retaliatory force would only, in Kissinger's words, "bring us face to face with the issue we have avoided for nearly a decade: the relation between deterrence and strategy should deterrence fail."

Kissinger distinguished between four types of relationships that might exist between the retaliatory forces of the United States and those of the Soviet Union. He could conceive a situation where both were vulnerable; alternatively, where the American force was invulnerable and the Soviet force vulnerable (that situation, he explained, had existed when the United States had its atomic monopoly); alternatively, where the United States force was vulnerable and the Soviet force invulnerable (some thought the missile gap had given the Soviets that kind of advantage); finally, where both retaliatory forces were invulnerable. Where there was mutual vulnerability, Kissinger explained, each side could win by striking the first blow and would lose by striking the second. In this situation, the gap between a first-strike and a second-strike capability was total. That, in his mind, was the most unstable relation; the incentives to forestall a danger by striking first would be enormous. As he explained: "When two vulnerable retaliatory forces confront each other, the offense is not the best, it is the *only* defense." Any crisis could set off a holocaust; the object had always to be to prevent the enemy from striking first.

Where one side's retaliatory force was vulnerable and the other side's was not, a quite different situation prevailed. It then made a great deal of difference whether the side with the invulnerable force was the potential aggressor or the potential defender. Kissinger never doubted that the Soviet Union belonged to the first category and the United States to the second. Where the defender was invulnerable and the aggressor vulnerable, stability would be enhanced; Kissinger explained: "A *status quo* power, by definition, will not take advantage of its superiority to attack and the aggressor will be deterred by his vulnerability from pressing military moves too far." If the potential aggressor was invulnerable and the defender vulnerable, the aggressor's position would be "overwhelming"; as Kissinger explained: "He will be able to choose between blackmail and military action." In either case, the intended victim would operate under a great disadvantage. He would not wish to test the aggressor's bluff; he would not dare to threaten all-out war, knowing what the likely consequences would be. Kissinger wondered whether the early 1960s might not be a "time of mortal danger" precisely because of the missile gap.

Where both retaliatory forces were invulnerable, stalemate would generally result. As Kissinger explained: "With no advantage to be gained by striking first and no disadvantage to be suffered by striking second, there will be no motive for either surprise or pre-emptive attack." The risks of all-out war would be minimal where such dual invulnerability existed. Limited war, however, would still be possible. The United States, whatever its preferences, Kissinger wrote, ought to prepare for the day when there was mutual invulnerability.

His argument reiterated points made many times in his earlier writings: the United States simply could not fulfill its treaty obligations if it was prepared to fight only one kind of war—a war that was increasingly unlikely. The threat of massive retaliation was no longer credible; it had never been entirely credible. Where Kissinger differed with many of his contemporaries, however, was in his minimizing the importance of the "missile gap." While accepting the existence of the "gap," and admitting that it might have a certain significance in the short run, he was already looking ahead to the time when the gap would not exist, and when the two great powers had invulnerable deterrents. What would happen then? Kissinger was concerned above all other things with the political implications of mutual invulnerability.

The threat of all-out war would no longer be credible. It had in fact not been credible for some time, but American theorists, according to Kissinger, had concealed their misgivings by suggesting that if American retaliation was not certain, the deterrent still operated because the Soviets could not be absolutely sure that the United States would not retaliate. Kissinger believed that the Soviet Union, in a "war of nerves," enjoyed a substantial psychological advantage over the United States. Offering a hypothetical example, he asked what the United States' "rational response" would be to a limited Soviet operation in West Germany that aimed at disarming the Federal Republic. The Soviet attack would certainly not be blatant; Kissinger could imagine a situation where the move was "coupled with a guarantee of immunity of our territory and that of our allies," together with an offer to begin peace negotiations at once. Kissinger was certain neither of what the American response would be nor of what the Russians would expect it to be. He wrote: "We could, of course, devastate the Soviet Union, but only at the price of suffering catastrophic damage in return. What would the Chairman of the Joint Chiefs of Staff advise the President regarding the purpose of a war that could have no victory and could only guarantee mutual suicide?"

These were not abstract issues for Kissinger; they were the kind that he believed the United States needed to be militarily prepared for. Kissinger created another scenario where the United States lost 50 percent of its retaliatory force in a surprise attack, but maintained the rest and suffered only insignificant casualties. The Soviets proceeded next to present an ultimatum; if the United States retaliated with attacks on Soviet cities, American cities would be destroyed, with enormous casualties resulting from the Soviet attacks. Kissinger asked whether the United States, with half its retaliatory force destroyed, was likely to respond massively, knowing the probable consequences of such an action. Kissinger wrote: "Considered purely rationally, there would be little sense in American retaliation." Kissinger did not say that the United States would not retaliate; only that it would serve no rational purpose for the United States to do so.

Kissinger recalled that Eisenhower had once said with reference to Berlin: "Only a madman would start a nuclear war." Those brave words were intended to warn the Soviet leaders; they had not, in Kissinger's view, achieved that purpose. As he explained, the Soviets had no need to start a nuclear war to threaten Berlin; the United States, however, because of its all-out war strategy, could not defend Berlin except by threatening a nuclear holocaust. Kissinger wrote: "We, not the Soviets, would have to be ready to act like madmen." It was unthinkable that the United States would maintain so foolish a posture. The American bluff would be called; public opinion would never support it; America's allies were certain to be hostile. Such a policy was not one that could be maintained over any period of time.

Khrushchev had shown how easy it was to counter such a meaningless American threat. His "irresponsibility"—his rantings and ravings— were possibly a pose, but there was no way of knowing, and no way of reacting to it. A peaceful status quo country like the United States would never be able to persuade a country like the Soviet Union that it would "prefer to strike an all-out blow rather than acquiesce in a Soviet gain, however small." Only if the Soviet Union launched a pre-emptive attack against the United States was there any risk of a massive American response. The Soviets would never be so irrational as to plan such a move.

The development of Soviet nuclear capability and the growth of its missile force led Kissinger to make even more emphatic the warnings he had first issued in 1957 in *Nuclear Weapons and Foreign Policy*. He continued to believe that a limited war capability was central to any meaningful military strategy. Deterrence, Kissinger wrote, depended not only on the extent of retaliation to overt aggression but on the likelihood of such a response. Because the idea of massive retaliation had lost much of its credibility, not to speak of its utility, Kissinger detected a growing support for a limited war capability. Those who supported the strategy, Kissinger said, often emphasized its sureness. A state that had such a capability might in fact choose to use it if provoked. It was not simply an empty threat. Also, many were beginning to recognize that limited war would not necessarily escalate; its purpose was not the obliteration of the enemy—it simply prevented him from securing what he hoped to gain by aggression. Kissinger wrote: "The worst that could happen if we resisted aggression by means of limited war is what is *certain* to happen if we continue to rely on the strategy of the past decade." Persuaded that a strategy based on a limited war capability enhanced the possibilities of deterrence, Kissinger knew that many violently opposed the concept, imagining that a willingness to prepare for a limited war reflected a desire to bring about such a war. Kissinger, exasperated with what he felt was the irrationality and dishonesty of that position, wrote: "No responsible person advocates *initiating* limited war. The problem of limited war will arise only in case of Communist aggression or blackmail. . . . And it does not make sense to ridicule the notion of limited war because it *might* lead to general war and then to rely on a general policy which gives us no other choice but all-out war." Limited war was not preferable to peace, Kissinger said; it was preferable to surrender or to all-out war. He did not underestimate the difficulties of the strategy; it presupposed, in his words, "a blend of psychological, political and military skill."

Kissinger believed that a strategy of local defense would substantially increase the flexibility of Western diplomacy, but it inevitably raised the question of whether nuclear weapons should be employed. Kissinger's own position on this matter had been fully given in *Nuclear Weapons and Foreign Policy*. Was he still prepared to argue that a nuclear strategy offered "the best prospect of offsetting Sino-Soviet manpower and of using our superior industrial capacity to best advantage"? Kissinger indicated that he no longer held to the views he had first expressed in 1957. He had shifted his opinion because of many circumstances. First, he noted the continued disagreement within the American military establishment and within the alliance itself about the nature of limited nuclear war; this, he said, raised doubts as to whether the United States would know how to limit nuclear war. Second, he remarked on the growth of the Soviet nuclear stockpile and the increased importance of long-range missiles, which altered the strategic significance of nuclear war. Finally, he noted the impact of arms control negotiations, which necessarily influenced the framework in which any strategy would be carried out. Kissinger continued to believe in the possibility of designing "a theoretical model for limited nuclear war," but knew that fifteen years after the beginning of the nuclear age, it was "next to impossible to obtain a coherent description of what is understood by 'limited nuclear war' from our military establishment." The disagreements within the American military services were only replicated within the alliance. Kissinger wondered whether the West had either "the knowledge or the daring to impose limitations." Given the changes brought about "by the advent of nuclear plenty and of the long-range missile," and the fact that the Soviet Union was now plentifully supplied with nuclear arms, any advantage that Kissinger had once seen no longer existed. Nuclear weapons, used tactically, could not substitute for numerical conventional inferiority. Finally, Kissinger noted that nuclear weapons continued to be placed in a category apart; many believed that they ought to be banned totally. In these circumstances, serious inhibitions would always militate against their use. Whatever the other consequences of a nuclear test ban, Kissinger wrote, it would certainly "reinforce the already strong reluctance to use nuclear weapons in limited war."

Kissinger's continuing discussions with colleagues and others had persuaded him that even if nuclear weapons were used in a limited way, this would stimulate certain of the non-nuclear countries to acquire nuclear weapons of their own. Nuclear proliferation would become an even more serious hazard. Also, a world outcry denouncing the use of nuclear weapons was certainly to be expected. For all these reasons, Kissinger revised his earlier recommendations. Even if military opinion were suddenly to support a limited nuclear war option, and all sorts of other difficulties were overcome, the international political resistance would remain. That, for Kissinger, was reason enough to consider other possibilities.

The most rational option, in his mind, was to increase the West's conventional forces. If the Allied forces were strong enough to halt Soviet conventional attacks, which they could be equipped and trained to do in Europe, the onus and risk of initiating nuclear war would fall on the Soviets. Kissinger had no sympathy for those who claimed that a conventional defense of Europe was impossible. Both in available manpower and in industrial potential the West was superior to the Soviet Union. Also, in conventional warfare, Kissinger pointed out, the defense had a certain advantage. Conventional war, however, offered no panacea. While it was preferable to limited nuclear war, just as limited nuclear war was preferable to all-out nuclear war, it would have its maximum impact only if the enemy knew that it was one of several Allied capabilities. Kissinger could imagine a situation developing where the Soviet Union overran Europe or Japan with conventional forces and then offered peace, threatening to use nuclear weapons if an effort was made to restore the *status quo ante*. Would the United States acquiesce in the Soviet victory or would it use its nuclear forces? It was impossible to say, Kissinger wrote. Of one thing he was certain: it would "be extremely risky to create the impression that we would acquiesce in a conventional defeat in vital areas." Kissinger was suggesting, in effect, that despite American promises not to use nuclear weapons, if a defeat occurred in a "vital area," it might feel compelled to do so. Certain limited conventional war defeats simply could not be accepted by the United States. Conventional weapons would not serve to protect every Allied interest; it was folly, however, to pretend that they would not serve to protect *any* interest.

If the United States was serious about building up its conventional forces, Kissinger wrote, it would do well to stop pretending that those forces could be "equipped and trained as dual-purpose units capable of fighting both nuclear and conventional war." If nuclear weapons became a part of the equipment of every unit, it would be "next to impossible to keep a war conventional regardless of the intentions of both sides." Kissinger wanted the two forces to be separated as much as possible; it should not be left to a company commander to determine whether to use nuclear or conventional weapons.

Arms control, Kissinger emphasized, was not "a *substitute* for an effort in the conventional field." Kissinger insisted that the two efforts proceed in tandem: that new conventional strength be built up while efforts were made to negotiate arms control. Kissinger warned of the danger of slighting either enterprise. To create a conventional force of sufficient strength would require a major effort to be made. No serious disarmament could take place, in his view, until there was a much "better balance" in America's military establishment.

Kissinger knew how unpopular such a recommendation would be. Public opinion, both in the United States and abroad, was irrevocably opposed to any significant increases in military spending. The fact that a number of American divisions were under strength and in some instances less well equipped than their Soviet counterparts seemed to cause no one great concern. "Recent budgetary levels," Kissinger wrote, "have caused *every* mission to be neglected." It was idle to pretend that existing levels of expenditure would be sufficient if only Pentagon waste was eliminated.

Kissinger wrote: "The times are too serious for such evasions. To be sure, waste should be eliminated. But the basic requirement is a dedication to a major national effort."

Kissinger, without mentioning Eisenhower by name, criticized his sanguine and inaccurate representations of American strength; he said: "One of the symptoms of our difficulties is the self-delusion to which we have become subject. It is maintained that we have never been stronger." To prove their case, administration supporters drew attention to what the United States had been able to do in Lebanon with quite limited forces. Kissinger found the arguments specious. Lebanon, he wrote, if it proved anything, proved America's weakness. "In order to intervene in the Middle East," he said, "we were forced to pull two divisions out of Germany and tie up most of our strategic airlift. In other words, we weakened the most sensitive area, Europe, at the precise moment when international tensions were highest and the threat to it was therefore potentially greatest. And we had to reduce the mobility of our Strategic Air Command while it was most needed to perform its deterrent function."

Kissinger complained of those who equated a concern with military security with an interest in perpetuating the cold war. He refused to accept the proposition that any debate about military preparedness inevitably deflected attention from the search for peace. Nor was he much impressed by those who claimed that there was no military problem and that the United States would do well to worry about economic competition and the improvement of its own society rather than nonexistent military threats. Some of the most virulent attacks on the concept of limited war came from those who advocated *universal* or *unilateral* disarmament; Kissinger had no very high opinion of either of those remedies. They would never serve to reduce tensions; they would, in his view, only increase Soviet intransigence. Kissinger, taking aim at a great variety of critics, wrote: "A responsible leader does not have the right to stake the survival of his society merely on the assessment that a country which has subjugated tens of millions of people in a decade is not concerned with military expansion." It was wrong to believe, he said, "that we must be motivated by either fear or euphoria, that we cannot be both strong and conciliatory."

While arguing for arms control, Kissinger advocated negotiating tactics and military preparedness of a kind that many of his academic colleagues considered unnecessary and dangerous. Nor were they very pleased by what he had to say about NATO, which he wished to see revivified. Eisenhower's policies in Europe were bankrupt; Kissinger wrote: "Since the creation of the Marshall Plan and of NATO, we have been in effect barren of ideas, evading difficult choices, drawing on capital." He sounded a note of deep gloom: "Unless the North Atlantic group of nations devel-

ops a clearer purpose it will be doomed." There was no common strategy; during the first decade of its existence, NATO had relied wholly on
a retaliatory strategy; the American nuclear deterrent was everything.
The Continent refused to make larger defense contributions, partly because of economic difficulties, but largely because it was feared that this
might lead the Americans and the British to reduce their forces and their
commitment to the defense of Europe. Kissinger found the whole NATO
deployment in Europe faulty. In his view, it was "too strong for a trip
wire, too weak to resist a major advance." It was, according to Kissinger,
an "uneasy compromise which tempts Soviet blackmail and must lead to
irresolution in the face of pressure." If American forces, for example,
were in Europe principally for symbolic reasons—to demonstrate
America's commitment to defend Europe—there was no need for an
army of the size that existed. Smaller—indeed, token—contingents
would suffice. If the United States seriously wished to have European
contributions, it would have to guarantee that such a buildup would not
simply "substitute" for the American presence. Kissinger believed that it
would be "disastrous" to leave the defense of Europe in the hands of the
Europeans. Whether or not Americans cared to know it, the United
States' presence in Europe was what in fact deterred the Soviet Union.

Kissinger believed that NATO's reliance on a retaliatory strategy had
produced two unfortunate results: either America's allies considered
themselves protected by the United States deterrent and saw no need to
make a military effort of their own, or, not being entirely confident about
what the United States might do in a crisis, they sought to create their
own deterrent, duplicating strength that already existed. Kissinger equated
the first response with unilateral disarmament, tacit or avowed; the second, a search for an independent retaliatory capability, was equally shortsighted. Both attitudes, he argued, were disastrous for NATO. Europe
gained nothing from these policies; its capacity for local defense was in
no way increased. As for the retaliatory forces created, they were virtually defenseless. The nuclear forces of Great Britain and France might
inflict great damage in an offensive war, but it was extremely unlikely
that they would be used for such a purpose; in the event of a surprise attack, they were almost certain to be destroyed.

Kissinger believed that the growth of individual retaliatory systems
could only serve to weaken the alliance. The decision to build such systems showed either a lack of confidence in American understanding of
the interests that tied the United States to Europe or a fear that the
United States would not run certain risks in the defense of Europe. By
building their own deterrent, the British and French, in effect, were seeking to protect themselves, forgetting that this was quite impossible. Kissinger interpreted these moves as early warning signals, pointing to the

disintegration of NATO. He found the situation parlous. The United States government was doing nothing to alleviate it. There was no point in the Americans being self-righteous and finding fault with France and Great Britain for what they were doing. They were right to be suspicious. Europe, knowing how common it was for allies to be abandoned, was seeking a form of reinsurance.

While the logical solution to NATO's strategic problems might have been for the United States to concentrate on nuclear armament while her European allies concentrated on conventional arms, Kissinger knew that this was politically impossible. Europe would interpret any such move as evidence of America's intention to abandon the Continent. Also, Europe would never choose to use its conventional forces unless it knew that the United States would follow through with nuclear retaliation. The United States, recognizing the extreme delicacy of the situation, had tried to do something, but Kissinger cared little for the hasty improvisations of the Eisenhower administration. The stationing of intermediate-range missiles in Europe and the stockpiling of nuclear weapons, to be used under the so-called double-veto system, requiring the consent of the host country before they were fired, were termed "panic measures," brought about by a wish to do something quickly to meet the threat produced by the Soviet Union's successful firing of Sputnik. The 1,500-mile missiles, Kissinger wrote, were too vulnerable; besides, it was never made clear whether they were intended to be defensive or offensive weapons. In any case, the really important issue was that the USSR would soon have the capability to attack the United States and Europe simultaneously. Insofar as the IRBMs had any utility, it was for local defense, and even that was achievable only if they were moved around constantly. As for the double-veto system, it seemed both awkward and unworkable to Kissinger. America's allies had the power to prevent United States retaliation, but they were unable to compel retaliation. The prospect of having to secure two permissions to fire in what might prove to be a lead time of less than ten minutes seemed quite unfeasible. The Allies were perfectly aware of this, Kissinger wrote; these were some of the reasons for their restlessness.

Clearly, new measures were needed. In Kissinger's view, a drastic reform of NATO was called for. He recommended the creation of a North Atlantic Confederation, and outlined the responsibilities that such a body might have. He would have had the nuclear stockpile available to NATO fixed periodically by agreement among the NATO powers. The United States would not be permitted to withdraw from that stockpile except by a two-thirds majority vote. The NATO countries would in turn determine the conditions under which nuclear weapons were to be released to SHAPE (the military command). The United States would earmark part of SAC for NATO and place those forces under NATO command. The

French and British retaliatory forces, except for certain token units, would also be placed under NATO command. Finally, the Allies would proceed to build up their conventional forces to agreed-upon levels and not reduce those forces except by a two-thirds majority vote. Kissinger's object, quite obviously, was to halt what he felt to be the disintegration of NATO; more than that, he wished to repudiate theories like those of General Pierre Gallois, in France, who was making what to him seemed totally outlandish claims for France's independent nuclear deterrent. No country, Kissinger implied, was in a position to go it alone; any policies or theories that weakened NATO and made nuclear independence seem a realizable defense goal were a delusion.

Kissinger believed that Germany remained *the* critical problem for the Western alliance. The ideal situation, he knew, would be one which saw Germany strong enough to defend itself but not so strong as to be able to attack. Achieving that kind of balance was not going to be easy. Kissinger knew all the arguments for accepting Soviet rule in Eastern Europe; there were many who insisted that if the Russians were secure in that area—if certain facts were finally accepted—the Soviet Union would become a "satisfied" power. Kissinger doubted this; he questioned the constant demand for "adjusting to facts." While entertaining no illusions about the possibilities for achieving German unity, he continued to believe that it mattered very much whether or not the Western Allies supported Bonn in its call for unification.

The draft treaty recommended by the Soviet Union in January 1959, according to Kissinger, had two major purposes: to demoralize the Federal Republic and to separate it from its allies. Not only did the treaty provide for the immediate recognition of East Germany, but it required the Federal Republic to give up all ties with the West, including economic links. Certain clauses, Kissinger said, would have permitted the Soviet Union to interfere in West German affairs, ostensibly to protect the "democratic" character of the Federal Republic. Unification would, in theory, have been settled through negotiations between the two regimes. Kissinger saw the treaty as the "beginning, not the end of a process," and he expressed grave concern that the end would be an unfortunate one for the Federal Republic.

Kissinger opposed any recognition of the East German regime. Such a policy, he believed, would cause severe disillusionment in the Federal Republic; also, it would probably lead the Communists to "attempt to cajole or threaten West Germany into a 'neutralist' course." He could imagine a situation developing where the Communist states withdrew their recognition of the Federal Republic because of its alleged "fascism," and then proceeded to deal with the East German regime as the representative of all Germany. Kissinger feared that the Communists would repeat a tactic they had used with such success in Eastern Europe and in China: first demoralizing the intended victim, then isolating, and finally destroying him. Kissinger knew, of course, that there was no prospect for immediate unity between the two Germanys. He was determined, however, that the West should so comport itself that the onus for the continued division of Germany should fall entirely on the Soviet Union. In his view, the Soviets were alone responsible for rejecting every scheme that accepted the principle of free popular choice. The West ought to adhere to that principle; it was one that conformed to its interests. Kissinger believed that one of the great mistakes of the years 1953–1957—when, following the death of Stalin, the Communists were in considerable disarray—was the failure to negotiate the German issue. The West was continuing to pay a very heavy price for having neglected that opportunity.

In any negotiations on the future of Germany, Kissinger explained, there were two principal dangers: first, that the West would accept the division of Germany; second, that in bargaining for unification, solutions would be accepted that would one day make possible a Soviet domination of all Germany. The issue of free elections could not, in his view, be set aside. The West had to support German unification, whatever its misgivings, if it did not wish to see the establishment of "a militant, dissatisfied power in the center of the Continent." The West might be compelled to acquiesce in the continued division of Germany, but it ought not to agree to it, and it certainly ought not to advocate it. All these issues, Kissinger explained, had great importance for the future of Berlin. The Berlin question did not have to do with whether that city was "worth" a war. The symbolic importance of the place had to be acknowledged. If Berlin's situation deteriorated, the Federal Republic would become demoralized, and questions would be raised as to whether its Western-oriented policies had not been a great mistake. The "folly" of resisting Communist pressure would then be understood by everyone in Europe. Western impotence, revealed through a failure to maintain Berlin as a free city, would have wide repercussions. Kissinger did not think it impossible that it would affect adversely relations between Israel and the Arab states, possibly jeopardizing peace in that corner of the world. Kissinger, shocked by the indifference with which the West accepted a threat to the freedom of two million Berlin citizens, asked whether the West's capacity for moral indignation was not now "confined to the free world's shortcomings."

Kissinger did not believe that the danger to Berlin was primarily military. He expected "a slow whittling away of the Western position" through a whole series of actions, no one of which seemed sufficiently serious in itself, but which in the aggregate did matter. Also, he anticipated a pattern of negotiations that made the West agree to a series of respites that in the end jeopardized the safety of the city. Kissinger spoke of every

Western offer's being "banked" by the Soviet Union, which, in effect, used the offer as the basis for its next demands. Kissinger wrote: "The only thing to be determined by negotiation in these conditions is the extent of the defeat." The Soviets had totally confused the issue of what in fact was being negotiated. Some thought the question had to do with access rights to Berlin in general. That was not the issue at all; as Kissinger explained, it was the right of access to supply the Western garrison of 10,000 men stationed in Berlin that was being contested.

How had the West responded to the Soviet challenge? Not at all correctly, in Kissinger's view. It proposed to accept a limitation on the size of its military garrison in Berlin in return for a five-year guarantee of the right of military access. Also, the West offered to forgo stationing nuclear weapons in the city and agreed to have no "intelligence" or "subversive" activities conducted from there. These were not acceptable terms in Kissinger's mind. Nor did he think at all well of the proposals to recognize East Germany as a *quid pro quo* for Soviet recognition of Berlin's status. A proposal that would have made Berlin a ward of the United Nations had no greater appeal. As Kissinger explained, while there was nothing the West could do to prevent the Soviets from turning over the control of military traffic to the East Germans, the correct Allied position would be to treat the East German guards as Soviet agents who, in effect, were carrying out rights previously granted the Soviet Union. If they comported themselves as the Soviet guards did, there would be no problem; if, however, they harassed shipments to Berlin, a threat would exist, and a response would have to be made. Kissinger wrote: "The West should have no illusions. The end of the freedom of Berlin would be the beginning of the end of the freedom of Europe."

Turning to the German problem in its larger manifestations, Kissinger saw that Poland's misgivings in respect to the Federal Republic would persist as long as the Oder-Neisse boundary was not recognized. He urged the West Germans to accept it as final. This, however, did not also mean that the Soviet Union's constant requests for "reassurance" had to be heeded. Using almost the same words he had first used in writing about the Napoleonic era, Kissinger spoke of the impossibility of "reassuring" a state that was determined to feel "threatened." The West needed to be aware of this problem also in its arms control negotiations with the Soviet Union. Those negotiations, Kissinger wrote, ought not to serve as a cover behind which the Soviet Union planned the disintegration of NATO. No proposal was acceptable that weakened NATO; in the absence of NATO, no European defense was possible. The Soviets, on the other hand, were perfectly right to insist that there be no danger of attack from any of the NATO countries.

Kissinger found the talk of "disengagement" far too vague. The term could mean almost anything—the withdrawal of troops (Soviet and American) from Europe; a troop freeze; a demilitarized zone in Central Europe. Some suggested that "disengagement" would speed unification; others insisted that it would occur simultaneously with unification; still others expected that it would simply serve to relax tensions between the United States and the Soviet Union. The idea of "nuclear free zones" in Europe did not have much appeal for Kissinger. Such zones, he believed, would only create further "psychological and political imbalance" between the United States and the Soviet Union. Kissinger did not say that a denuclearized zone in Central Europe ought never to be considered; simply that such experiments should not be tried so long as there was so little unity in the Western alliance.

Kissinger's own recommendations were very comprehensive. He hoped that the eastern frontiers of a united Germany might serve as the dividing line for a European arms control system. He proposed a fairly complex system of troop withdrawals, involving German, Polish, Czech, Soviet, American, British, and French forces. NATO would agree not to station weapons of more than 700-mile range on German territory, and an inspection system would be established. The virtue of the system, according to Kissinger, was that it would make offensive ground operations on the Continent much more difficult; also, Soviet and Western forces would be separated. There would, however, be a sufficient Western force on the Continent (and in Germany) to discourage any would-be aggressor. The unification of Germany would, in his view, remove the principal source of political tension in Europe. Kissinger argued that the creation of a zone of arms control would encourage bolder experiments, looking to larger arms control measures. Kissinger expected that his scheme would not commend itself to the Soviets. The Soviet leaders, he said, "in their present state of mind . . . are interested only in those agreements in Europe that contribute to instability."

Kissinger referred to the increasing talk of the need for "neutralization." That term, like so many others, was immensely ambiguous; it could mean almost anything. The most persuasive scheme, Kissinger wrote, had probably been the original Gaitskell Plan, which would have coupled the neutralization of Germany with that of Poland, Czechoslovakia, and Hungary. While Western security would have been "diminished" by this plan—largely because of the neutralization of Germany—it would have had the great political advantage of ending the division of Germany. Its success, in Kissinger's view, would have depended on the ability of NATO "to maintain a substantial military establishment in Western Europe to back up Germany." Unless substantial local defense forces were stationed in France and the Low Countries, the defense of the Continent would have rested entirely on American retaliatory power.

The chief purpose of the Atlantic alliance, Kissinger insisted, had to be the creation of a new North Atlantic community. National self-sufficiency was breaking down in every area. It was impossible to devise a national system of defense. The kind of diplomacy that had preceded the abortive summit conference of 1960 ought to be avoided. Such diplomacy implied the possibility that individual members of the alliance might reach separate settlements with the Soviet Union. It was becoming fashionable for politicians in many Allied states to seek election on the pretense that they enjoyed special access to the Soviet leaders, and that they were in a position to bring peace. The myth of "partnership" was not likely to survive the practice of independent action. Kissinger thought that the time was ripe for a new effort to be made to strengthen North Atlantic community ties. He proposed a conference of heads of state or of Foreign Ministers to recast North Atlantic plans for mutual defense, define ten-year political and economic goals, and develop plans for assisting the new nations. "Nothing is more crucial than for the West to develop policies which make of it a true community," Kissinger wrote.

His views on the subject were closely linked to his views on negotiations more generally. Some who found fault with American diplomacy deplored what they felt was a too great unwillingness to negotiate. The charge was not justified, Kissinger thought, except for the years when John Foster Dulles served as Secretary of State. Otherwise, Kissinger said, the opportunities to meet had been numerous; he spoke of six Foreign Ministers' conferences and three summit meetings. Looking at the most recent abortive summit encounter—that of 1960—Kissinger implied that any student of diplomacy might have come away persuaded that tensions were as often increased by the manner in which diplomacy was conducted as by the refusal to negotiate. "The Cold War," he wrote, "has been perpetuated not only by the abdication of diplomacy but also by its emptiness and sterility." Why had the conduct of diplomacy become so difficult? Why did tensions persist whether or not negotiations proceeded? Kissinger pointed to the destructiveness of nuclear weapons, the polarization of power, the nature of international conflict, and a whole set of national attitudes peculiar to the West, particularly to the United States.

The destructiveness of modern weapons made for many problems, Kissinger said. Negotiations, he explained, had rarely depended exclusively on the persuasiveness of arguments. A country was generally able to penalize another country for refusing to agree; an abortive conference rarely returned matters to the original starting point. When diplomacy failed, other pressures were brought into play. The threat of force or the use of force had immense utility in pushing negotiations along. Given the power of modern weapons, the threat of war, or the actual decision to go to war, was now excluded in all but very exceptional circumstances.

"So long as the international system was made up of many states of roughly equal strength," Kissinger wrote, "subtlety of maneuver could to some extent substitute for physical strength." In such a world, it was impossible for any one nation to eliminate all the others. When, however, the number of key states declined and nationalism became predominant, some of the "play" went out of foreign policy. Security was now looked for in physical strength. Kissinger believed that the armaments race preceding World War I was as much the result as the cause of an inflexible diplomacy. Power had come to substitute for diplomatic dexterity. In the period immediately before World War I, there had been a substantial increase in the size of standing armies. World War I and World War II served only to accelerate the polarization of power. Yet, as Kissinger explained, a two-power world could only be unstable. The weakening of one automatically meant the strengthening of the other. In such a situation, diplomacy had to be rigid; every issue was necessarily thought of in terms of survival.

When, in addition to such destabilizing factors, there was a clash of ideologies, normal diplomatic procedures were virtually excluded. In traditional diplomacy, Kissinger wrote, there had always been an incentive to persuade the other party. In modern negotiations, where the adversary's point of view was discounted from the beginning, and generally treated as propaganda, bargaining became exceedingly difficult.

The United States, a status quo power, found it particularly difficult, in Kissinger's view, to come to grips with the problems posed by a revolutionary age. He sounded a now familiar note from his previous writings. America's historical experience was too much at variance with the world in which twentieth-century Americans were obliged to live. Having wanted to be left alone, having no experience of foreign attack and giving no thought to the possibility of such attack, Americans found it easy to imagine that the United States was invulnerable. Kissinger believed that the United States would not have risked a war for Belgium in 1914 or for Poland in 1939. He thought that American notions of war and peace were too "mechanical and absolutist." The country could not get over the feeling that peace was "normal" and that diplomacy was essentially a device for settling disputes during times of peace. In the American imagination, diplomacy resembled business dealings; a disproportionate emphasis was given to bargaining technique. Since the advantages of peace were obvious and self-evident, it seemed entirely reasonable to believe that war was caused by the machinations of wicked men. American military actions, by this standard, were largely inspired by a concern to punish aggressors. It was easy to make an American crusade of every war. Once the aggressors were punished, it was assumed that the normal pattern of international relations would re-establish itself, and that the United States could return to its proper business. Americans were so satisfied with the international system that they never recognized the necessity for examining it with any care.

Because war and peace were seen as distinct and successive phases of national experience, a policy like that of containment was entirely congenial to Americans. The idea that the United States needed to help the West rebuild itself, so as to make possible meaningful negotiations with the Soviet Union, seemed very reasonable to most American leaders. Acheson clearly believed in the policy; in the context of 1951, he was not greatly mistaken. How the force of American power would communicate itself to the Soviets, or how the country would go about negotiating once its strength had been demonstrated—these were questions that no one really asked. It was taken for granted that Stalinist Communism was inherently expansionist, and that if the United States succeeded in thwarting the Soviet Union, the Soviets would have no option but to change. When that happened, negotiations would become possible. Kissinger understood how such an opinion could commend itself to a world weary of war, worried that the hopes born of war were not being realized. Under Dulles, Kissinger wrote, "what had originally been considered the condition of policy—security against aggression—seemed to become its only goal." He explained: "The Baghdad Pact, SEATO, the Eisenhower Doctrine marked steps of a policy which seemed unable to articulate any purpose save that of preventing an expansion of the Soviet sphere."

Kissinger believed that the United States played its cards badly; the Soviet Union, by comparison, made relatively few mistakes. As Soviet maneuvers gained in subtlety, it became increasingly difficult to rally the West against them. Also, the longer that negotiations with the Soviets were deferred, the more the West gained the reputation for being intransigent. Kissinger wrote: "The closer we approached the theoretical point at which, according to the containment theory, fruitful negotiations should have been possible, the more elusive they seemed." Because of a too literal view taken of containment, the United States was "mesmerized by the vast Soviet ground strength," though, in fact, the Russians were militarily inferior to the United States until at least 1956. This did not mean that the Russians were not in a position to overrun the Continent; it did mean, however, that America's "relative military position would never be better than it was at the very beginning of the containment policy." Kissinger wrote: "We were so aware of the vulnerability of our allies that we underestimated the bargaining power inherent in our industrial potential and our nuclear superiority. By deferring negotiations until we had mobilized more of our military potential, we in fact gave the Soviet Union time—the most precious commodity considering its losses in World War II, its inferiority in the nuclear field, and its need to consolidate its conquests."

Winston Churchill was the Western statesman who understood the situation best. Kissinger wrote: "His repeated calls for a diplomatic confrontation in 1948 and 1949 were based on the realization that a failure to negotiate would mortgage the future." Churchill, as early as 1948, in what Kissinger called a "major, much-neglected speech," began to urge the West to reflect on what the Soviet Union would be like when she had developed the atom bomb. Churchill had said at that time: "You can judge yourselves what will happen then by what is happening now. If these things are done in the green wood, what will be done in the dry? If they can continue month after month disturbing and tormenting the world, trusting to our Christian and altruistic inhibitions against using this strange new power against them, what will they do when they themselves have large quantities of atomic bombs? . . . No one in his senses can believe that we have a limitless period of time before us. We ought to bring matters to a head and make a final settlement. We ought not to go jogging along improvident, incompetent, waiting for something to turn up, by which I mean waiting for something bad for us to turn up. The Western Nations will be far more likely to reach a lasting settlement, without bloodshed, if they formulate their just demands while they have the atomic power and before the Russian Communists have got it too."

Kissinger shared that point of view entirely. The West ought to have been negotiating in the late 1940s. It missed its opportunity; even more serious, it missed the opportunity offered by Stalin's death. This, in Kissinger's mind, was a particularly tragic failure; at the very moment that the Soviet leaders, in order to consolidate their new power, might have made a dramatic break with Stalinist policies, the West did nothing. Though the name of Eisenhower was never mentioned, there could be no doubt that an extraordinary opportunity had presented itself during the first years of his administration and that both he and Dulles had failed utterly. Kissinger wrote: "The longer we deferred negotiations, the more committed the new Soviet leadership became to the empire it had inherited and the more it was tempted into adventures by the upheavals associated with the rise of the new nations. The more uncertain our performance, the more confident the successors of Stalin became."

The complete collapse of the containment policy occurred during this period. The concept of deterrence—on which American military strategy was based—could not operate alongside the idea of containment. Deterrence was most successful when nothing happened. How, Kissinger asked, was it possible to demonstrate strength when there was no evi-

dence of it? Inevitably, Dulles's idea of negotiating once strength had
demonstrated itself came to nothing. Being unwilling to assume the diplomatic initiative, Dulles simply produced a stalemate, and the situation deteriorated even further when the Soviet nuclear arsenal began to grow. In
response to this development, a new argument—a wholly preposterous
one, in Kissinger's view—took hold; it was now thought that "since the
quest for strength had produced a stalemate, weakness, by reassuring the
Soviet Union, might lead to a settlement." Some argued as if the mere
possession of power might be detrimental to negotiation.

A great deal of hope was placed in the possibilities of a summit meeting.
When the Paris summit of 1960 collapsed, Kissinger wrote, the formula
proclaimed for years "as the magic solvent for all tensions" came to be regarded "as a parody of diplomacy." The personal diplomacy once
thought to be a way of ending the cold war was now seen to be responsible for perpetuating it. Khrushchev's "frown" became as much a matter
of concern to the West as his "smile" had once been a major encouragement. Kissinger found it surprising that no one had pointed out the hazards of "summitry" long before the Paris debacle. So much attention had
been given to the fact that a meeting was to take place that no one asked
what its purpose or agenda would be. Had the U-2 incident never occurred, Kissinger wrote, the summit of 1960 would not have accomplished very much.

The idea that tensions were caused by shortsightedness or misunder-
standings, and that they could be removed by a change of heart on the
part of certain leaders, seemed to Kissinger to be a parody of diplomacy.
Eisenhower's concept of what a diplomatic conference could accomplish
was simplistic; the press was no better informed. Kissinger recalled that
within two years of taking office, despite all the Republican charges about
the Democrats' being "soft on Communism," Eisenhower rushed off to a
summit meeting. The press was ecstatic; since it assumed that the cold
war was caused largely by personal distrust, it believed also that personal
diplomacy would inaugurate an era of peace. "Diplomacy was seen as a
public debate between us and the Soviet Union," Kissinger wrote, "with
other nations occupying the moderator's chair and awarding the winner's
prize." Kissinger quoted from the New York *Times*, the *Herald Tribune*,
and *Life* magazine to suggest the quality of the press comment on the Geneva meetings. The most moving, but also the most "fatuous statement of
the philosophy of personal diplomacy," according to Kissinger, was probably made by Harold Macmillan, Britain's Foreign Secretary, who spoke
of the "thrill of hope and expectation round the world" caused by the
meeting of the heads of two powerful coalitions who "met and talked and
joked together like ordinary mortals." Macmillan saw Geneva as "a return to normal human relations." Kissinger wondered "whether the de-

mocracies' notion of normality is not their Achilles' heel." Clearly, an atmosphere of confidence and cordiality were helpful, but Kissinger asked
"whether the free countries render themselves or the cause of peace a service by making a settlement seem so simple and by evading all difficult
issues."

Kissinger noted that one year after the Hungarian uprising of 1956,
men in the West were again calling for a summit; every attempt to fix an
agenda beforehand was dismissed "as transparent attempts to sabotage a
conference." Kissinger asked whether "it was not a misconception to believe that after a decade of Soviet intransigence it was *our* task to reassure
the Communist leaders." In his view, the failure of the United States to
insist on a concrete program probably convinced the Soviets that a
détente was achievable without any of the problems that had caused the
tensions being resolved. The demand was always for a relaxation of tensions, a removal of distrust, and the establishment of good will, but no
one explained how any of these objectives could be achieved. Then,
when the summit conference of 1960 collapsed even before it started, "a
shudder of apprehension went through the world." Many claimed that a
chance for peace had been lost; Kissinger doubted this. In his view, "what
imperiled peace was our self-righteousness and evasion of responsibility."
The prelude to the Paris summit had never given any reason for confidence. Reviewing the events leading up to the meeting, Kissinger wrote:
"By insisting on 'progress' at a lower level before he would agree to a
conference of heads of state, President Eisenhower only brought about
the preposterous situation where he finally claimed that Mr. Khrushchev's
ambiguous postponement of an unprovoked threat and his willingness to
go to the summit were in themselves an indication of progress. These vac-
illations were hardly calculated to motivate the Soviet leaders to approach
the summit conference with responsibility."

Kissinger suggested that "many of the arguments advanced on behalf of
summit diplomacy were fatuous in the extreme." The proposition that
only heads of state could settle intractable disputes was not borne out by
experience. Kissinger believed that problems of great complexity which
had divided the world for a decade and a half were not likely to be resolved in a few days "by harassed men meeting in the full light of publicity." He was not even certain that the interests of the democracies were
served by such a premium being placed on the authority of a few leaders.
Kissinger ridiculed the idea that the prospect of meeting the leaders of the
West could mean so much to Khrushchev as to make him forgo specific
demands. Summits, Kissinger insisted, were risky affairs. Contrary to what
people believed, the imminence of a summit meeting did not necessarily
place a constraint on intransigence. Both sides, in fact, in the period immediately before a summit meeting, were generally pushed to state their

positions most extremely. Kissinger thought that such maneuvers were inherent in the nature of personal diplomacy; he said: "When heads of state are the principal negotiators, their most effective bargaining device—in some circumstances the only available one—is to stake their prestige in a manner which makes any concession appear as an intolerable loss of face." It was the "evasion of concreteness, the reliance on personalities, the implication that all problems can be settled with one grand gesture" that led the Soviets to favor such diplomacy; they could use it to demoralize the West, suggesting that failure was caused simply by a clash of personalities.

Kissinger insisted on the importance of distinguishing form from substance. While summit meetings had certain advantages, they also entailed certain risks. Kissinger listed their principal assets: the participants generally had the authority to settle disputes; they were in a position to raise new questions, indicate new directions, and move rather rapidly. The great liability was that decisions made at a summit could not easily be repudiated. It was not clear to Kissinger why the men who might one day be required to make the final decision on the use of thermonuclear weapons should also be the ones to negotiate about their use. If a summit meeting carried the promise of new agreements, it also carried the risk of new schisms. Kissinger worried that the bargaining process could come so to preoccupy heads of state that they were left little time for formulating policy. During his final two years in office, Eisenhower, for example, according to Kissinger, spent much of his time at conferences; when he was not actually engaged in meetings, he was preparing for or recuperating from them. Such a diplomacy, Kissinger wrote, might be suited to a dictatorship; it was not suited to a democracy. Also, he wondered whether it was a method conducive to developing constructive long-range policies. It might be a useful device for buying time, but Kissinger asked whether the time was not being purchased at too high a price, and whether, in the end, it was being advantageously used.

Summit diplomacy, in Kissinger's view, made the reaching of an agreement the all-important thing. Leaders wanted to believe that their role was to create a climate of "confidence," and that this served to improve the general situation. According to Kissinger, "more ingenuity is expended in finding things to agree on, no matter how trivial, than in coming to grips with the issues that have caused the tensions." Inconsequential matters were settled; grave issues were put aside. There was an immense incentive to show that substantial "progress" had been made. Such meetings, Kissinger wrote, did almost nothing to end the cold war; in fact, they served only to perpetuate it. The agenda for the Eisenhower-Khrushchev Paris meeting, Kissinger said, showed all the flaws of the summit method; it included as major items: discussion of exchange visits, nuclear testing, arms control, and Berlin. Of these several items, Kissinger wrote: "These are either so unimportant that they can be solved fairly easily, but would hardly require the attention of heads of state, or they are so complicated that a summit conference can at best serve as a means of deferring a decision." Kissinger thought that the question of the exchange of persons was of no great consequence; such matters did not need to preoccupy heads of state. He thought that cultural exchange as a method for reducing political tensions was greatly overrated. The nuclear test ban negotiations depended on technical considerations; heads of state were not likely to make important contributions in that area. Arms control was so complex a subject that no summit meeting could do more than issue a general statement that promised a more detailed examination. As for Berlin, Kissinger thought that "the Soviet Union could have made a greater contribution to peace by never provoking the Berlin crisis than by insisting on holding a summit meeting about it."

The question of whether or not to hold a summit meeting, Kissinger argued, was a practical and not a moral issue. He was particularly wary of summit meetings whose primary purpose appeared to be the establishing of good will; such meetings ought to be avoided—they only concealed the fact that there was no agreed-upon policy. Kissinger wrote: "The constant international travels of heads of government without a clear program or purpose may be less an expression of statesmanship than a symptom of panic." On the most recent Paris summit, Kissinger was particularly severe; he wrote: "The real indictment of the diplomacy culminating in the fiasco at Paris, then, is the attitude of trying to get something for nothing, the effort to negotiate without goal or conception." Kissinger went on to say: "We can negotiate with confidence if we know what we consider a just settlement. If we lack a sense of direction, diplomacy at any level will be doomed."

Kissinger believed that the reverse side of the "reliance on personalities" had been the "tendency to relate diplomacy to assumptions regarding Soviet domestic developments." There was a will to believe that peace, which was the "natural" order of things, would be achieved when a "change of heart" on the part of the Soviet leaders occurred, when there was a fundamental transformation of Soviet society, or when both took place simultaneously. Too much ingenuity had been expended in the West in trying to prove that the Soviet Union had indeed changed, and that Khrushchev himself was the "apostle" of this new course. Many believed that other leaders in the Kremlin were less reasonable, and that a failure to treat with Khrushchev would only bring them to power. Neo-Stalinism was said to be the threat; Khrushchev was represented as the safeguard; the West would be foolish to ignore him. The habits of World War II survived; it was Stalin who had been depicted as the man of peace by Americans who wished to justify closer relations with him. The same kinds of things, Kissinger wrote, were now being said about Khrushchev. Because the Communists were thought to be "reasonable," it was only a matter of time before they turned from old-fashioned aggressive expansionism and took up the more modern tasks of economic development.

The Soviets exploited the situation to their own advantage. They alternated between bellicose statements and others that sounded a more pacific note; in Kissinger's words, they gained "a reputation for being conciliatory by retreating to a position still considerably in advance of their starting point." Kissinger, while willing to grant that there might be an element in Soviet society interested in a more peaceful course, wondered whether the eagerness with which every small Soviet gesture was seized upon would not in the end do more harm than good. The West's almost craven posture before Khrushchev, for example, did not, in his view, serve to reduce Soviet intransigence. Kissinger wrote: "No Communist leader can afford to make a settlement on a personal basis. No member of the Soviet hierarchy—whatever his convictions—can advocate a program to his colleagues with the argument that he is promoting good will in the abstract. The more we speculate about the liberal nature of individual Soviet leaders, the more we may force them into actions designed to demonstrate their ideological purity to their colleagues as well as to their allies."

Kissinger expressed doubts also concerning those who imagined that the United States might use its diplomacy principally to promote a rift between the USSR and China. While he accepted the fact that the United States ought to take advantage of such a rift, were it to occur, that was a far cry from suggesting that something should be done to promote it. The *real* intentions of Communist leaders ought not to be America's concern. Rather, it ought to spend its time defining its own purposes. Kissinger wrote: "If the Soviet Union really wants a settlement, negotiations will reveal this. If Soviet overtures to end the Cold War are a tactical maneuver, a purposeful diplomacy should be able to make Soviet bad faith evident."

Americans were told that it was their duty to make "acceptable" proposals. Diplomatic deadlocks, it was said, had to be broken with new offers. A "willingness to compromise" was represented as the *summum bonum* in diplomacy. Kissinger suggested that such arguments were credible only because the whole of America's experience with negotiations had been in the commercial field. There was no reason to believe that business experience was at all useful in international diplomacy. Kissinger argued against those who recommended always the acceptance of the agenda that the other side found reasonable. He wanted the United States to be conciliatory, but this did not require it to have no ideas of its own.

It was not the duty of the United States to come up constantly with new offers. Nor ought the United States to indicate that if an initial offer was rejected, another one would be forthcoming. Negotiations conducted on that basis would never be serious; there would be no incentive for the Soviets to treat specific proposals with care; they would always be waiting for the American fall-back positions. Kissinger also opposed the idea that a compromise should generally be sought somewhere between the two initial positions; this gave an incentive to each side to start with impossible propositions, knowing that they would be cut down. For a democracy to offer extreme proposals was particularly difficult, Kissinger wrote; the general public would rarely support them. If flexibility was sought, it made sense to start with "maximum" demands and then offer concessions. If, however, proposals were to correspond with what the country wanted, it was impossible for them to be changed every year. This, Kissinger saw, was a real dilemma for the West. If it started with a program, however reasonable, and continued to propagate it year after year, it would be accused of inflexibility. If it started with a program that it expected to be whittled away, it would be accused of being hard and intransigent.

Kissinger said that the confusion of bargaining technique with purpose caused the "diplomatic debate to be confined to issues of maximum embarrassment to the West, issues, that is, which the Soviet Union has raised and on which the West feels obliged to negotiate because, as the saying goes, no avenue of settlement must be neglected and because the mere readiness of the Soviet Union to talk about *anything* is considered 'encouraging.' Conversely, the West is prevented from raising issues of possible embarrassment to the Soviet Union because, it is said, we must not destroy the climate of confidence by making 'unacceptable' proposals." In these circumstances, Kissinger wrote, diplomacy became a form of "Soviet political warfare." So long as the Soviets determined what was discussable, the attention of the world would be focused on the symptoms of the international malaise and not on its causes. The negotiations would be about NATO and not about the Soviet hostility that brought NATO into being; about the Congo or Cuba and not about Hungary, Tibet, or East Germany. Such diplomacy simply fostered the illusion, Kissinger wrote, that the cold war could be ended by a generous proclamation.

Kissinger wondered whether "the real obstacle to a flexible and purposeful Western diplomacy [was] not the absence of moral assurance." He worried about the unwillingness to make moral distinctions and to see Khrushchev for what he really was; the willingness of some people in the West to confuse the Russian leader with Adenauer, and to act as if both were difficult men, was the kind of fundamental mistake that Kissinger found inexcusable. He commented unfavorably on those who imagined that conviction was incompatible with negotiation. Such people were generally too hard in their judgments of the West and too lenient in their judgments of the Soviet Union. This had become almost a traditional stance with them. Kissinger wrote: "The tendency to equate our moral shortcomings with those of the Soviet bloc deprives the West of the inward assurance to negotiate effectively. It leads to a policy of the guilty conscience."

Kissinger believed that a lasting settlement was possible only if the Soviet leaders became convinced "that they will not be able to use the West's desire for peace to demoralize it." Were they to seek a settlement seriously, they had a right to expect to find the West "flexible" and "conciliatory." Kissinger wanted the West to abandon its guessing game about whether or not the Soviets had *really* changed; it was far more important for the West to define its purposes and do so in such a way as neither imperiled Western security nor contradicted Western values. If that were achieved, Kissinger wrote, the West would be in an advantageous position for negotiating.

Arms control seemed to Kissinger to be an "obvious subject" for serious negotiations with the Communist states. Kissinger saw four major areas where agreements were needed: surprise attack; local aggression; the nth country problem; nuclear testing. He said that if "the two sides cannot give expression to this community of interests by proposing concrete, serious programs, little hope exists for negotiations on other subjects." He did not, however, see such agreement as a substitute for dealing with the political causes of the cold war. Arms control measures, Kissinger explained, could "ameliorate" but not dispel the prevailing climate of distrust. Such negotiations would be lengthy; they would depend on detailed, careful, and objective study. They were desperately needed, but the West ought never to imagine that everything depended on them. Kissinger wrote: "Much as arms control may be desired, it must not be approached with the attitude that without it all is lost."

Kissinger began with a consideration of the problem of "surprise attack," which, after five years of intermittent negotiations, had not, in his view, been adequately defined. He saw control schemes as falling into three large categories: measures which sought to reduce the incentives for deliberate attack; measures to reduce the incentive for pre-emptive attack; measures to reduce the likelihood of pre-emptive attack on the basis of misinformation. The last referred, quite obviously, to the problem of "accidental war." Kissinger believed that deliberate surprise attack could be inhibited by two kinds of measures: a reduction in the physical capability to win through such an attack; a reduction of the possibility of achieving surprise, generally by an inspection system. In Kissinger's view, proposals for the total elimination of stockpiles and retaliatory forces would have a built-in incentive for evasion. Under complete nuclear disarmament, for example, even fifty hidden weapons could give an overwhelming advantage to the state that had violated the agreement. Nor did he think very highly of proposals to ban all delivery systems. Under such a system, all missiles, including those that were ostensibly defensive, would have to be banned; as Kissinger explained, there was no way of telling the range of a rocket by simply inspecting it. Also, as solid-fuel missiles developed and the weight of nuclear warheads diminished, many missiles now considered defensive or short-range could come to be used for offensive purposes. The same could be true of airplanes. Under conditions of total disarmament of certain delivery vehicles, Kissinger could foresee the use of ordinary civilian transport planes or even Piper Cubs to carry thermonuclear devices. As he explained: "After a decade and a half of the growth of nuclear stockpiles and nearly a decade of the development of missiles, simple remedies can no longer work."

Kissinger saw two objectives that any control system against surprise attack needed to have: the aggressor had to realize that his chances of success were minimal, and the defender had to be as invulnerable as possible. Unilateral actions taken to reduce vulnerability could, according to Kissinger, be misinterpreted, and be thought threatening by the opponent. Hence, whenever a choice existed, only defensive measures of a kind that could not be misconstrued ought to be adopted. "If the goal is stability," Kissinger wrote, "negotiated arms control schemes must therefore accompany unilateral efforts to enhance invulnerability." The objective of such schemes, he said, "should be to define a stable equilibrium between the opposing retaliatory forces and then to devise a control system which protects both sides against violations."

One of the ironies of warfare in the atomic age was that a very small and vulnerable retaliatory force might increase the dangers of war more than a large, well-protected force. A small force might encourage the opponent to risk surprise attack. The primary goal of any arms control scheme, Kissinger explained, was to remove the incentive for deliberate attack. This was most likely to be achieved when both sides had developed invulnerable retaliatory forces. Although "invulnerability" was a relative term, the object ought to be to do as well as was possible both in securing one's own force and in complicating the calculations of the would-be aggressor. Vulnerable forces were a standing invitation to attack.

Kissinger considered the choices that a state might have when it believed an attack on itself to be imminent. The choices, he thought, were four: The country could await the blow, and gear its retaliation to the scale of the attack. That option, Kissinger explained, was open only when the retaliatory force was invulnerable. Alternatively, it could increase the readiness of its own retaliatory force so that the aggressor, losing the advantage of surprise, would desist from the attack. Third, it could issue an ultimatum, insisting that the preparations end. Finally, it could launch a pre-emptive attack. Kissinger thought that the first option was the safest and that the third was the most hazardous.

If Kissinger had grave doubts about the utility of inspection for staving off surprise attack, he had no doubts concerning its utility for stabilizing the size of opposing retaliatory forces. The question, however, was how an inspection system could operate to reveal the size of a weapons system that was mobile, and how it could be reconciled with the measures that he had advocated for unilateral efforts at increasing weapons invulnerability. Kissinger saw that these were highly complex issues; there was no way to minimize their difficulty. Kissinger proposed a scheme which would have each country with nuclear weapons agree to station no retaliatory weapons in certain areas and to concentrate all these weapons, in specified numbers, in specific areas. The areas that were free of nuclear weapons might be inspected at any time; in the others, periodic inspections (perhaps twice a year) would be permitted. Such a system, Kissinger suggested, "could be effective in preserving the equilibrium or at least in keeping evasions within limits that prevent either side from obtaining a decisive advantage."

Kissinger believed that his scheme would also give the maximum protection to the civilian population should deterrence fail by accident or miscalculation. Since the first objective of a surprise attack had to be the enemy's retaliatory force, an attack that began by concentrating on cities, leaving the retaliatory force intact, would be a form of madness. "For blackmail purposes," Kissinger wrote, "the opponent's civilian population is more useful alive than dead. Thus surprise attack against centers of population is likely only if they are thought to shelter retaliatory weapons." This did not mean that all population areas should be placed in the disarmed area. Were that to happen, there would be no possibility of land-based mobility, since cities served as major road and rail-network hubs. Also, to put all cities in the category of areas open to inspection would be to guarantee Soviet rejection of the proposal. Some cities would have to be vulnerable; they would be the "fortified towns" of the atomic age.

Kissinger wrote also of the need for "positive evidence inspection," designed to provide evidence "not of what each side may want to hide but what it is eager for its opponent to know." Both sides might desperately wish the other to understand that it was not preparing an attack. Particularly in times of crisis, Kissinger wrote, it was important that both sides should have the means to exchange and verify information. All-out war should not be stumbled into; every effort should be made to "reassure the opponent clearly and convincingly." Kissinger spoke of joint Western-Soviet offices that needed to be established in Washington and Moscow, with their own special communications equipment; he described various special mobile surveillance teams, under Western-Soviet or United Nations auspices, that could be trained to move quickly to trouble spots to verify information that one side wanted the other to have. Kissinger insisted that the new technology could be mastered "only by political innovations as dramatic as those in the field of science."

If there were no simple solutions to the problem of coping with surprise attack, so there were none for dealing with local aggression. The idea that total disarmament would guarantee universal peace was, for Kissinger, one of several panaceas that had been skillfully exploited by Soviet propaganda and diplomacy. A control system for total disarmament would have to allow for such a complex form of inspection that, for the United States alone, some 30,000 highly trained specialists would be required. Kissinger suggested that the stationing of so many inspectors in foreign countries and the surrender of control over what had been traditionally considered key attributes of sovereignty would in itself pose problems of a kind that had not been much reflected on.

The problem of dealing with evasions, or even defining evasions, would be formidable. Kissinger wondered whether one of the unintended consequences of disarmament—even if it were inspected—might not be the militarization of society. "Under conditions of total disarmament and in the face of the threat of evasion by the opponent," Kissinger wrote, "security could best be maintained by the militarization of what has been traditionally considered the civilian aspects of national life." If it became difficult to distinguish civilian from military aspects of life, inspection would become hopelessly complicated or meaningless. Kissinger wondered how one would determine the legitimate size of the domestic force. Might countries not exaggerate their domestic instability so as to justify a higher level of military force? Kissinger could see all sorts of difficulties arising. How could one know that a specific product was intended for a civilian rather than a military use? Would all products having potential military applications be proscribed? Kissinger argued that total disarmament had all the difficulties of a deterrent equation stabilized at very low levels. A relatively minor violation could confer a substantial, perhaps decisive, advantage.

The problem of reducing the dangers of local aggression remained. Kissinger thought that the principles he had developed for dealing with surprise attack might be used in this instance also. "The equilibrium of forces suitable for local conflict should be stabilized at a level," Kissinger wrote, "where the demands made on the inspection system are not so severe as to magnify insecurity. The evasion required to upset the equilibrium should be sufficiently large so that it could not fail to be detected. And even then a violation should not confer a decisive superiority." The inspection of the size of a standing army or of stores of conventional weapons posed quite substantial problems. Since the Western conventional forces were markedly inferior to those of the Communists, no control scheme would work that did not involve a reduction in Communist strength, a buildup of forces in the West, and provision for the inspection of agreed-upon manpower ceilings. There had to be provision also for inspection of the size of specific forces and limitations of a zonal character. Kissinger favored unlimited rights of inspection in areas adjoining troubled or disputed territories. In other zones he would settle for inventory inspection. Any such plan presupposed Soviet consent; otherwise, inspection would be meaningless.

In considering the nth country problem, Kissinger noted that a recent report of a committee of the American Academy of Arts and Sciences had indicated that eleven countries were in a position to produce nuclear weapons within five years of their deciding to do so, and that eight others were not far behind. Six of the nineteen were NATO members; four were Warsaw Pact countries. Atomic secrets no longer existed; the only obstacle to the production of nuclear weapons was technical—engineering capacity. Given a certain level of industrial development, any country could produce nuclear weapons. Kissinger agreed that an unchecked dispersion of such weapons would profoundly alter the structure of international relations. Why, then, did nth countries appear to want nuclear weapons? Because they were afraid of one of the larger powers; because they wanted to be independent of the established nuclear powers; because they were rivals of other nth countries or feared them; because they were seeking national prestige. While nuclear weapons would give the nth country a greatly increased capacity to inflict damage, Kissinger doubted that they would improve the strategic position of the minor vis-à-vis the major powers. No nth country, with the exception of China, Kissinger wrote, could withstand a pre-emptive attack by a major power. Also, with the exception of China, no one of them could initiate an attack on a major nuclear power without being obliterated. An nth country that lacked allies would be hopelessly vulnerable; even with allies, it could not be certain of support under all circumstances.

The great danger of the proliferation of nuclear weapons, in Kissinger's view, was not that a small power would attack a large power but that one nth country would attack another. This was particularly true where tension already existed, as between the Arab states and Israel. If one country had such weapons and the other did not, there would be a powerful incentive to use them. The advantage would be seen to be temporary, and there would be a great temptation to exploit it. How, then, could the diffusion of nuclear weapons be stopped? Kissinger thought there were three principal approaches. The present non-nuclear countries might agree not to produce or acquire nuclear weapons, and they might accept an inspection system to guarantee that they not do so; the major nuclear powers, particularly the United States and the USSR, could agree to abstain from supplying nth countries from their own stockpiles, or from assisting nth countries technologically; again, suitable controls would be mandatory. Finally, there might be a combination of these two factors.

The simplest solution was the idea of a non-nuclear club, first proposed by the British Labour Party in June 1958. While the idea appeared superficially simple, it was, in fact, exceedingly complex. As Kissinger explained, it would require, among other things, a complicated inspection system that would keep an inventory of all fissionable materials, whether produced locally or brought in from the outside. With countries like Britain and France, which would be joining the club after they had already developed nuclear weapons, secreted fissionable materials would have to be searched for. The most intensive searches would have to be made also in all nth countries. As Kissinger explained, "the hiding of a few nuclear weapons in an Arab country may be a matter of life and death for Israel; it is of much less significance for, say, France." Also, all the non-nuclear countries combined could not force China to join the club, or guarantee that she would abide by the agreements reached. Finally, if one of the established nuclear powers gave or bootlegged weapons to one of its client states, there would be no effective system of sanctions that could be used against those who had violated the agreement. The major powers, Kissinger wrote, would not gain enough additional security from such an arrangement to justify its immensely complex inspection machinery.

If the United States and the Soviet Union were serious in their protestations of concern about nuclear proliferation, Kissinger wrote, then they ought to consider measures that would cut off nuclear production and reduce nuclear stockpiles. The first could be accomplished only if there was a proper inspection system. An inspected cutoff, Kissinger wrote, would freeze stockpiles and provide an additional restraint against giving nuclear weapons to nth countries. It would also complicate the problem of creating new weapons which would upset the deterrent equation. If both sides went a step further and turned over substantial amounts of fissionable material to the International Atomic Energy Agency for peaceful uses, this would be immensely helpful. To maintain a nuclear equilibrium, the inspection system would have to be nearly foolproof. An inspection system that failed to detect continued production on one side could be fatal to the other. Kissinger explained: "For the side continuing production could overwhelm its opponent not only by numbers but by refinements in technology." Everything would depend on "the ability to devise an airtight system to monitor a cut-off on nuclear production." The inspection system would have to be far better, Kissinger explained, than the one devised for the nuclear test ban. Unless access could be gained to Soviet territory for periodic inspections, it would not work.

In considering the problems associated with a ban on nuclear testing, Kissinger remarked on the emotional character of the debate. Adlai Stevenson's proposal for such a ban in 1956 had been ridiculed by the Eisenhower administration on the ground that it would jeopardize national security. Two years later, Eisenhower decided, on the basis of a single experiment—the so-called Mount Rainier underground shot—that the test ban could be tried. An East-West conference of scientists was called to determine the feasibility of the monitoring system. Though the conference was supposed to furnish the technical data for a subsequent political decision, the United States felt impelled to announce a moratorium on all testing—including underground testing—even before the political conference met. The moratorium had been in effect for two years. "In the interval," Kissinger wrote, "most of the conclusions of the technical conference have been proved either overoptimistic or simply wrong." He went on to say: "Yet the basic positions have been oddly unaffected by the new knowledge. Different arguments to defend well-entrenched positions have emerged to replace the old." As Kissinger explained, the fact that an inspection system existed was considered more important than whether it was adequate or not. The gains to be achieved by evasion were said to be so marginal that the running of a "calculated risk" seemed to be no risk at all.

In any case, many argued that the Soviet Union had no intention of cheating. They never explained why they were so certain. Kissinger noted that many well-intentioned people had concluded that if the United States and the Soviet Union did not agree on a test ban, all hope for effective arms control was at an end. The attitude toward nuclear testing had become a "test of sincerity," and the test ban was represented as a necessary first step, on which all others depended. Such a ban, its proponents said, could only serve to strengthen "the more responsible elements in the Kremlin who may be seriously trying to bring about a relaxation of tensions." When anyone suggested that a prohibition on testing would militate against the development of "clean" bombs, this was dismissed as a negligible loss. Nuclear war, by definition, had to be horrible, and any attempt to mitigate its horror was simply illusory. There could be no "clean" nuclear war, test ban proponents said; that illusion ought to be set aside. As for a so-called anti-ballistic missile system, which might be developed through testing, the test ban advocates doubted its feasibility. They had no interest in refining tactical nuclear weapons; since "limited" nuclear war, in their view, would probably become all-out war, it was best that the maximum number of inhibitions against any war be instituted. If the test ban advocates were to be believed, Kissinger wrote, the nth country problem would be solved through the ban, and cooperation with the Soviet Union on an inspection system would help produce a climate of optimism. Kissinger was obviously dubious; he wrote: "The desire to make a start on arms control is understandable. Yet the idea that a nuclear test ban can be a model for other agreements cuts both ways. It is not clear why an inadequate control scheme should be a model for anything except another inadequate control scheme. Precisely because it is so important to make a start towards arresting or slowing down the arms race, we should be doubly careful about the direction in which such a start will take us. And there is serious reason for concern about both the efficacy of the inspection system and the political implications of a test ban."

Kissinger reviewed the principal difficulties in monitoring nuclear explosions; he concluded that ordinary underground explosions below one kiloton could not be detected; "undecoupled" explosions above one kiloton would resemble hundreds of other natural explosions, and there was need for a system of a fixed number of "free" inspections; decoupling could make possible evasions up to perhaps 150 kilotons without detection; other methods of evasion existed, including high-altitude testing and testing in the oceans. Kissinger spoke of the constant "haggling over an inspection system known to be incapable of discovering many of the evasions it is supposed to monitor." While the inadequacies of the system had been admitted, Kissinger wrote, there had been an unwillingness to admit failure. The United States was afraid that it would leave itself open to the charge of sabotaging the negotiations. Kissinger believed that once a control system was installed, there would be little incentive for the Soviet Union to change it. He did not pretend to know Soviet purposes, but he felt that the moratorium came very close to being a permanent ban. Kissinger wrote: "Once a treaty is signed, the political and psychological pressures against the resumption of testing will be enormous."

Kissinger accepted the fact that there could be no foolproof control system. It was impossible to devise an inspection system that would protect against all violations. But even imagining that the Soviet Union was caught evading the ban, and that Soviet propaganda did not confuse the situation by suggesting that the United States was doing the same, what could the United States do about it? Kissinger's implied response: very little. Contrary to those who thought that the United States would then resume testing itself, Kissinger dwelt on the difficulties of doing so. The testing staffs would have been dispersed; it would not be easy to reassemble them. Obviously, the possibility always existed that the Soviets would not evade the agreement. If they complied, Kissinger said, it would not be because the control system offered a significant obstacle to them, but only because no strategic advantage would be gained by further testing.

Kissinger did not suggest that the test ban negotiations had been without good effect. They had compelled the United States to give serious attention to the problems of arms control. The relations between strategic doctrine and arms control had come to be better understood, and Kissinger saw these as very substantial gains. However, because a complete test ban had become such a symbolic goal—theoretically, a warranty of a sincere interest in peace—it had been forgotten that the original choice had not been between a complete ban or no agreement at all but for an accord that was expected to be much more limited. Had the United States understood the problem from the beginning, Kissinger wrote, it would have split the negotiations into two parts. The United States ought to have offered an immediate ban on tests that were inspectable. The remaining part of the test ban should have been made conditional on wider arms control agreements, including a cutoff of nuclear production, a reduction of stockpiles, and, if possible, inspection schemes to cover the contingency of surprise attack. Had agreement not been reached on these matters, then the United States ought to have insisted on inspection systems of greater reliability than those promised by existing methods of detection. In addition, the United States ought unilaterally to have renounced any future testing capable of producing fall-out.

All these would have been excellent first steps; none of them had been taken. What, then, ought a new administration to do? First, it ought to put a limit on how long negotiations were permitted to drag on. If there was no terminal date, Kissinger wrote, "the practical consequence will be the same as an uninspected moratorium on *all* testing." The United States had two options: to sign the Geneva accords, with all their inadequacies, or seek other arrangements, along lines similar to those suggested by Kissinger. While he clearly preferred the second course, he recognized the heavy political price that it involved, at least in the short run. The Soviet Union, Kissinger wrote, would certainly mobilize world opinion against the United States; it would only be in the long run that the wisdom of the American action would become apparent. Kissinger expected the United States not to press for alternative schemes. When the Geneva accords were agreed to, Kissinger wrote, efforts should be continued to improve methods of detection. Kissinger said also: "If we do not make progress in improving the detection apparatus or if startling breakthroughs in the nuclear field appear possible, the proposed moratorium should be ended at its expiration." There must also, he said, be a substantial buildup in America's conventional forces. Since the test ban would create increased psychological inhibitions against the use of nuclear weapons in resisting local aggression, and since everyone would argue against any move that might jeopardize the test ban, it became all the more important that alternative forces be available that were capable of coping with local aggression. Kissinger spoke of the necessity of quickly defining the next step in arms control negotiations. Everything depended on the American capacity to take additional steps with "confidence, precision and responsibility."

Kissinger believed that arms control had received far too little serious study, and that such investigation was an imperative need. "Before there can be successful negotiation on arms control," Kissinger wrote, "we must get our intellectual house in order." Arms control schemes were as subject to rapid obsolescence as military strategies. Technological change made new schemes constantly necessary. An arms control arrangement that might be effective when four powers had nuclear arms would not be equally useful when a greater number of states had such capability. New weapons needed to be controlled in the very early stages of their development; after that period, it became immensely difficult to do very much.

Arms control, Kissinger said, had been more often the subject of passion than of objective understanding. The idea that a country could increase its security more effectively by sharing information with a potential enemy than by withholding it—which was a central doctrine in many arms control schemes—was difficult for men to accept who had spent their lifetime believing that secrecy was a military necessity. Nor was it easy for them to believe that not every technological advance increased a society's safety. That a certain equilibrium of destructive ability might prove more conducive to the prospects of peace than an unchecked arms race was another doctrine that needed to be learned. Kissinger believed that the necessary preliminary to any effective arms control would be agreement within the American military establishment and within the Western alliance concerning the elements of military security. An agreed-upon strategic doctrine was a first requirement.

If, Kissinger wrote, on one extreme of the political spectrum were congregated all those who equated safety with physical power, the other extreme was no less absolutist. Those who pretended that arms control was an alternative to America's security effort—and not simply a complement to it—made a tragic mistake. The debate between the two extremes, in Kissinger's view, had paralyzed understanding. There were too few considered judgments in the arms control field. When the United States came under pressure to produce a proposal before an approaching conference, it generally came up with something tailored for the occasion. The proposals for the negotiations on surprise attack of November 1958 and for the disarmament meetings of March 1960 were prepared by *ad hoc* committees assembled when the conference was imminent. No *ad hoc* committee could do justice in six months to problems of such complexity, particularly where opinion was so divided. Policies were improvised; those who presented them felt no confidence in them. The Soviets, Kissinger wrote, seemed to have no better understanding of the problems, but their ignorance provided no excuse for America's confusion. In any case, one could never be certain what they did understand; it was always possible that they intended to demoralize the West, disarm it unilaterally, and achieve their purposes in that way. The United States' concern needed to be the devising of serious and specific schemes that would increase *both* American and Soviet security—that, Kissinger insisted, was the essence of any responsible program—and there ought to be absolute confidence that if such terms were rejected, it was because the Soviet Union had no real interest in reaching an agreement.

Until the United States knew what it wanted to get out of arms control negotiations, there would always be confusion. Some favored arms control because they imagined it would liberate both countries to do what was really important—engage in economic competition. Others thought that arms control would reduce taxes; still others expected that it would hasten the evolution of the Soviet system. Kissinger found all such arguments irrelevant. Nor did he believe that arms control depended on whether the United States could safely trust the Soviet leaders. If they could be trusted, there would not be so desperate a need for control. The economic advantages were not, in Kissinger's mind, likely to be substantial. Inspection would be expensive. Economic development did not depend on arms control; economic programs could be supported even if substantial defense needs persisted. To argue for arms control as a way to save money, Kissinger implied, was to be attracted to the wrong schemes for the wrong reasons. The purpose of arms control was to enhance the security of all parties. Any attempt to achieve a unilateral advantage would doom arms control. The test of any agreement was whether it added to or subtracted from security, whether it made war more or less likely. Kissinger disdained the sentimentality that he found so prominent in the arms control area. Simple remedies, he said, were always dangerous. It was time to stop arguing that a failure in arms control would doom humanity. Such an approach, Kissinger wrote, only increased the pressures for unilateral disarmament and made the Soviets less interested in real issues. If the Soviets became convinced, Kissinger wrote, that the United States was so afraid of war that it would do anything to avoid it, this would only encourage the Soviets to move in ways calculated to demoralize the country further. A Soviet power unafraid of the United States would never take arms control seriously. "Paradoxical as it may seem," Kissinger wrote, "a measure of instability in the arms race is required to provide an impetus for arms control."

Arms control was *one* road to peace; it was not the only one. Kissinger opposed the idea of calling the new body to oversee arms control the National Peace Agency. In the nuclear age, he explained, all national policies—diplomacy, military preparedness, arms control—were related to peace. "If we are to make progress in the field of arms control," Kissinger wrote, "the military establishment must come to understand that in the present state of technology an arms race is the most unstable of all forms of security, and that properly conceived arms control must increase the security of *all* countries. And many enthusiasts for arms control must realize that ardor is no substitute for precision. A great deal depends on the ability to be concrete. In the next few years we may have perhaps our last opportunity to stabilize the arms race by means of negotiation. Perhaps Communist obduracy will foil our most earnest efforts. But it would be unforgivable if we failed because we refused to face either the importance or the complexity of the challenge."

Kissinger, as in *Nuclear Weapons and Foreign Policy*, returned always to the need for doctrine—for correct understanding. America's perception of the outside world was skewed. America wanted to believe that both the Communist states and the new nations were evolving, and that in the end they would become less ideological and more concerned with material comforts. Industrialization was supposed to require complex technical skills; education was said to foster a questioning spirit. It was easy to believe that evolution was certain, and that America might even assist the world in its evolutionary process. Kissinger found an implicit Marxism in all such analysis; he suggested that it was "a purer version of Marxism than that practiced in Communist countries." Americans who believed in such inevitable evolution believed also that economic factors were determining in all political change. It was not the export of American ideas that was expected to change the world, according to such theories, but the influence of a changing economy. If Marxists insisted that industrialization necessitated the dictatorship of the proletariat, America's "evolutionary theories" posited the end of the historical process as the universal triumph of liberal institutions. Communism used its philosophy to "spur" effort; "too many in the West," Kissinger wrote, "rely on history as a 'substitute' for effort." Survival seemed to become a primary goal; "All will end well if we live to see it." Kissinger called this "an attitude of resignation, destructive of purpose and values." There was nothing heroic in the Western stance; waiting for the Soviets to become "bourgeois" was, in his view, a fairly pathetic policy.

Kissinger felt only contempt for the "evolutionary theories," and was not at all persuaded of their truth. History did not seem to demonstrate that economic development brought democracy in its train. He was unable to discover any country where democracy followed on the heels of industrialization, or where it appeared to have been a product of economic development. In Germany and Japan, democracy—insofar as it existed—came as the result of a catastrophic war. In the more traditional democracies, it preceded the industrial revolution; in the United States and Great Britain, democratic institutions developed in a largely agricultural society. In the nineteenth century, Kissinger noted, men believed that political freedom produced economic development, and not the other way around.

Industry, Kissinger wrote, "depends on predictability, efficiency, productivity." While these occasionally called for "constitutionalism," they did not require democratic government, at least not as that term was commonly used in the West. The managerial group in industrial society was not very politically active. Industrial enterprise, he wrote, involved "manipulation, specialization, direction." Its test was efficiency. Managers, with a great deal to lose in the event of a social upheaval, were not likely to rebel against the existing system. Kissinger saw the managerial class as made up of men interested in concrete technical matters and not in abstractions. Their pragmatism generally made them willing to accept any regime that did not become unduly arbitrary. They had no great interest in political ideas; revolution was not likely to attract them. Where, as in the West, they were democratic, it was not because the economic system made them so but only that a social environment had helped to form them in this tradition.

"The irony of Communism," Kissinger wrote, "is that most of the evils it ascribed to capitalism—many of which were real enough—have become magnified and have grown more intractable under the Communist system." The emphasis of industrialism—efficiency and productivity —was as much present in Communist as in capitalist countries. Because there was no true separation between political and economic legitimacy in the Communist world, Kissinger called Communism "the feudalism of the industrial epoch." Kissinger wrote: "Its [Communism's] managers, like the feudal lords, combine political and economic power and their authority is as difficult to assail by those below them." Where "liberal" Communist regimes existed—as in Poland at the moment —the pressure for liberalization generally came from traditional elements: the church, intellectuals, peasants, nationalists. Nor did Kissinger expect universal education to produce "liberalization" through the development of a "critical spirit." Kissinger believed that freedom could be won only through persuasion or through violence. It was rare for freedom to be achieved without some measure of violence. "Whether the emphasis is on persuasion or on struggle," Kissinger wrote, "it is not the questioning spirit as such but the affirmation of some absolute value that transforms societies." Education did not by itself produce a critical attitude that led inevitably to political action. "From the ideological point of view," Kissinger wrote, "the Communist regime resembles a monastic society much more closely than it does the modern democratic state. A priesthood—the Communist party—controls a doctrine of considerable complexity. It relies on a special liturgy with its own vocabulary. Those not part of this monastic order have no right to an opinion. Those within the Communist hierarchy conduct their disputes as a struggle over doctrine. Opposition, when it takes place, expresses itself as a reinterpretation of the existing orthodoxy. Almost invariably it is confined to the circle of those who are authorized to make a political judgment." Schisms, Kissinger explained, when they developed, were most likely to occur within the Party, which, in recruiting the ablest people, protected itself against certain kinds of criticism. This was, Kissinger wrote, a "caricature" of democracy, though the Party had good reason to believe that it enjoyed the support of the majority of the population, whether that support was gained through propaganda, a rigging of incentives, or a suppression of all alternatives. When upheaval occurred, it rarely came from below; it usually resulted from the weakness inherent in any doctrinaire orthodoxy, where there was no way to settle disputes except to treat opponents as heretics.

Kissinger did not argue that evolution in Communist societies was impossible. However, evolution appeared inevitable only to posterity. In fact, the process depended on three factors: the starting point, the values that animated the participant, and the pressures of the environment. The prospects of political evolution, Kissinger believed, were different in the new countries from those that existed in the Soviet Union. It was foolish to imagine that they would all end up in the same place.

If the West was naïve in its expectations of what would inevitably come to pass in the Soviet Union, it was no less simple in its thinking about the new nations. "To rely on economic development to bring about enlightened political institutions," Kissinger wrote, "is to reverse the real priorities." He wrote: "Whatever political system brings about industrialization may well be confirmed by it." The West was loath to impose its political institutions, believing them not to be useful until a certain stage of economic development had been reached. Kissinger thought this to be a mistake. He wrote: "Unless we are able to make the concepts of freedom and respect for human dignity meaningful to the new nations, the much-vaunted economic competition between us and Communism in the uncommitted areas will be without meaning."

Kissinger had no doubts about the difficulty of the challenge. The new nations had gained unity through resentment of a colonial power. They were now obliged to seek more positive goals. Many of them lacked a common history, culture, or language; many, in fact, lacked an identity.

Where social cohesiveness was so insubstantial, the struggle for the control of authority could become quite intense. Opposition was generally equated with treason in these countries, and many were perpetually on the verge of civil war. Their difficulties were only exacerbated by the modest educational attainments of most of their people and the low productivity of their economies. Kissinger saw psychological pressures also; he wrote: "The leaders of independence movements have sustained themselves through years of deprivation by visions of the transformations to be wrought after victory was achieved. To surrender power or to admit even the possibility of giving it up in their hour of triumph seems to many of them a negation of all their struggles."

Kissinger had the greatest doubts whether the United States understood what it needed to give the new countries. He wrote: "One of the difficulties we face in contributing to the political modernization of other countries is that we have not fully grasped the implications of our own modernization." Kissinger was convinced that the underdeveloped world was watching the United States, and that an "aura of confidence" and a "sense of purpose" would communicate itself were it to be sincerely felt. He did not, however, suggest that the United States act simply out of such considerations; as he said: "We are not putting on a play for the benefit of a foreign audience." If America sought a resolution of its racial problem, for example, it would not be because it wished to influence Africa but because the solution would favorably affect the mind and values of America, and give the country new confidence. Kissinger emphasized the need for economic aid, "on a substantially larger scale than in the past decade." Economic aid, despite its technical complexity, Kissinger thought, would be the simplest of America's problems in the underdeveloped world. The real problem was to support the development of democratic institutions. America ought to show preferences, and ought to show an interest in the political structures of the countries it helped. Kissinger believed that revolutionary leaders filled a spiritual void. The United States had to compete with its own values and beliefs. To fail to do so was to doom to sterility any policy of economic assistance to the new states.

This did not imply that a great effort should be made to compel the underdeveloped nations to join the United States as its allies. On most issues, it was doubtful whether the United States would ever win the support of the uncommitted nations. Where the new nations wanted to remain aloof from world affairs, their wish ought to be respected. The uncommitted, Kissinger explained, would take "a stand against dangers which seem to them to affect their vital interests. They will not take a stand on problems which seem to them far away, or, if they do, it may make the situation worse rather than better." Many leaders of new states wanted the best of two worlds: to be neutral and to judge all disputes.

Kissinger spoke of their being flattered by the rewards that fell to them through the competition of the great powers. Playing a role on the international stage was easier and more gratifying than attending to domestic problems. While they were willing to declaim on major issues, this did not mean that they were ready to assume major responsibilities. To encourage them in the role of being arbitrators would in the end only have a demoralizing effect on international relations. If the uncommitted were permitted to determine what the real problems were, many basic questions would be evaded and major issues would be falsified. Kissinger feared that abstract declarations would substitute for concrete negotiations and that diplomacy would be reduced to slogans. He wrote: "World opinion is not something abstract which our diplomats must seek to discover and to which we then have to adjust. We have a duty not only to discover but to shape it." Though it was natural for the United States to wish to be popular, it could not gear its policies to an attempt to win favor with the new nations.

If *A World Restored* was Kissinger's intellectual autobiography and *Nuclear Weapons and Foreign Policy* was an attempt to teach all sorts of Americans certain basic facts about diplomacy and military policy in the atomic age, what function did *The Necessity for Choice* have? As suggested, on one level it could be read as a basic critique of the eight Eisenhower White House years. Would such a book not have great appeal for the Kennedy administration that was about to take over? In fact, it did not. The book appeared after the electoral campaign; even if it had appeared six months earlier, it is doubtful that it would have been greatly consulted, though it would probably have sold more widely. Kissinger's grievances were not those of the men who surrounded Kennedy, and his solutions did not commend themselves to a group like the one that descended on Washington in early 1961. Neither in his views on the need for conventional forces nor in his opinions on summit meetings or arms control negotiations did Kissinger sound notes that the Kennedy entourage wanted to hear. The book had a modest success, but the attention of Washington (and New York and Cambridge) was too much riveted on the brilliant young men gathering in Washington to pay much heed to one who had stayed behind in Cambridge.

5

The Kennedy-Johnson
Years
A More Moderate Critique

January 1961 was a heady time in Cambridge, Massachusetts. A new American president was about to be inaugurated—one of Harvard's own alumni—and he was reaching out to select several of his principal aides from men of his own generation, many of whom he scarcely knew, but who were themselves well known in and around Harvard Square. There was no precedent for what Kennedy did in recruiting so extensively from the Harvard (and MIT) professoriate. While there had been an insignificant recruitment of academics in 1933 when Roosevelt formed his first administration, his so-called brain trust was never Cambridge-based. Harry Truman, when he began to replace the men he inherited from Roosevelt, chose overwhelmingly from those he knew as a senator in Washington. Dwight Eisenhower clearly preferred businessmen to professors, and even when he selected James B. Conant as High Commissioner for Germany, no one took this to be a precedent for other appointments. American presidents were not in the habit of choosing professors as their principal aides; even Kennedy, if the truth were told, did so only sparingly.

This, however, was not how the situation appeared to academics in Cambridge, or to the mass media who reported on his first appointments. Harvard professors moved from their classrooms to large embassies in

Tokyo and New Delhi; others, from both Harvard and MIT, received major posts in the State Department, the Department of Defense, and elsewhere in the administration; the White House itself, and not only its basement, came to be populated by men well known in Cambridge. These appointments only served to confirm the impression that this was indeed a new administration, animated by new kinds of concerns, interests, and people.

Cambridge professors were not entirely strangers to Washington; some had held important military or civilian positions during World War II, and a number had maintained connections of one kind or another throughout the postwar period. Whether they were consulting or advising, serving for longer or shorter periods, being used for their technical capabilities or their more general knowledge, they almost never figured at the highest levels of government. Until 1961, no one of them enjoyed a daily, continuing relation with the President of the United States; very few achieved the kinds of responsibility in government that regularly fell to men who came to Washington from business or law. Presidential politics—indeed, federal administration more generally, insofar as it did not depend on those who made the whole of their careers in Washington—recruited overwhelmingly from professions other than the academic.

So much was happening for the first time in 1961—so much that seemed to refute what certain academics thought were the less savory aspects of American political life—that it was easy to believe that a new generation had indeed taken over. The mass media were not alone in propagating the view that new winds were blowing in Washington, and that novel and exciting possibilities lay in store for the nation. Those who joined the administration did so with high hopes; January 20, 1961, was not just another inauguration day for them. The symbolism of the occasion, though traditional, had certain innovative features that were intended to suggest a break with the past. This was not simply the inauguration of the first Roman Catholic president of the United States; it was the arrival of a man very different from the one he was replacing, who recognized the importance of emphasizing those differences in a code that had particular meaning for those who wished to decipher it. The decision to invite Robert Frost to read a poem especially written for the event was symptomatic of the occasion. A gesture, perhaps, but to many in the country a highly significant one. Everything seemed to be falling into place; America at long last had an "intellectual" president; the proof was everywhere, most conspicuously, perhaps, in the men Kennedy chose as his principal aides.

For those who lived in or near universities, Kennedy's first appointments seemed immensely promising. Even where there was no personal knowledge of the men involved, the feeling was generated that their own kind of people were being selected, the kind that other presidents had generally excluded or ignored. Even when Kennedy chose a business executive to be his Secretary of Defense, it was not just another "faceless" corporate leader, but a man said to be "cerebral" and "intellectual," a man like the President himself. Robert McNamara, president of the Ford Motor Company, had once taught at the Harvard Business School. Dean Rusk, most recently with the Rockefeller Foundation, came with other credentials. As a former Rhodes scholar, he started with a certification that seemed very meaningful to those who looked closely at academic qualifications. These were characteristic Kennedy appointees. There were dozens of others like them.

The administration clearly had "tone"—that amalgam of intelligence and taste, fueled by money, that made certain Anglophilic Americans imagine that what they had long admired in London had finally arrived on the Potomac. There was a good deal of talk about "style," another virtue said to inhere in the President, which was discovered also in many whom he had chosen. The "style" involved verbal facility, a positive flair for language that many were to remark on; more than that, it involved a craving for action—a derring-do quality that seemed natively and appropriately American. The new administration presented itself as youthful, vigorous, and industrious; there was no need to compare its energy with what had recently passed for energy in the Eisenhower administration. The old World War II soldier seemed almost senile when compared with those who now appeared in Washington.

Why should any of this have had any importance for Henry Kissinger? First, and most obviously, because he was not one of those called to Washington by the President. Along with 99 percent of his Harvard colleagues, he was left to "watch the shop" along the Charles. Had he expected to be offered a post? Almost certainly not. Kissinger's political affiliations, insofar as they existed, were with the Republican Governor of New York and with certain of Nelson Rockefeller's colleagues. His views, while extremely critical of policies pursued by the Eisenhower administration, were not especially congenial to many who advised John Kennedy. He was almost certainly unknown to a number of those who were particularly influential with the President in making recommendations for appointments. In 1960, Henry Kissinger belonged to a company of a dozen or so who were engaged in serious study of foreign policy. There was no greater reason to choose him for an appointment than there was to choose any one of several others. Kissinger started with no special claims for consideration. He scarcely knew the President, and had never contributed ideas to his campaign; his political allegiances, insofar as they were known, appeared to be Republican, or, more accurately, Rockefeller

Republican. While he was personally acquainted, through his Cambridge and New York friends, with many who now joined the Kennedy administration, no one of them imagined that it was imperative that Kissinger be made a member of the team. The accident that made Dean Rusk Secretary of State and Robert McNamara Secretary of Defense, or that might just as easily have left them out of consideration entirely, was a commonplace in American politics. Kissinger had no reason to expect anything; it was not surprising that he received nothing.

There was, however, one circumstance that did favor him, making it possible that he would one day be used in some capacity or other. Two of Kissinger's closest Harvard colleagues, McGeorge Bundy and Arthur Schlesinger, Jr., were both in the White House—Bundy as the President's National Security Adviser, Schlesinger as a Special Assistant to the President. Kissinger's friendship with both men went back to the early 1950s; each was sufficiently close to Kissinger to have served on the original editorial board of *Confluence*. Both were familiar with Kissinger's views on foreign policy, and were aware of the kinds of criticisms he had made of the Eisenhower administrations.

If friendship had depended on a sharing of political opinions, Kissinger and Schlesinger would never have become friends. Arthur Schlesinger, Jr., was not the radical intellectual that certain of the more antediluvian of his reactionary critics imagined him to be; his opinions were in most respects conventionally liberal. Living in the shadow of the New Deal, and writing its history, he expressed in a very spirited prose ideas that showed him to be both anti-Soviet and pro-civil rights, a pragmatist who admired the idealism of Adlai Stevenson, but chose to support Kennedy in 1960. He was fiercely partisan, and had an appetite for political combat that was never entirely appreciated in academic Cambridge. As the son of one of Harvard's most distinguished historians, chosen at a very early age to be Associate Professor of History, "young Arthur" carried the distinction lightly. He was not overly impressed with academic Cambridge, and the feeling was sometimes reciprocated. Schlesinger befriended Kissinger when Kissinger was an obscure graduate student; impressed by Kissinger's intelligence, he was one of the few in Cambridge to recognize and delight in his wit. He was a considerate friend, who felt a great obligation to bring Kissinger into touch with men he might not otherwise meet, whom he imagined Kissinger ought to know. Schlesinger's home in Cambridge was something of a "liberal salon," in which Kissinger was a welcome guest.

However unwittingly, Schlesinger helped instruct Kissinger in the classic intellectual orthodoxy of mid-twentieth-century America; he made Kissinger aware of the nature of American liberalism. It would not have been possible for Kissinger to have learned so much from other sources.

While he never shared Schlesinger's opinions on many subjects, he respected his views and knew how representative they were of political opinion in academic and intellectual circles. The two men were philosophically very distant; their easy relation belied their commitments to quite different sets of values. If Kissinger enjoyed seeing Schlesinger, and even profited from knowing him, Schlesinger felt equal pleasure in his friendship with Kissinger. It was an intellectual relationship on one level, a social relationship on another. Schlesinger's interests were America-centered and almost wholly political; his attention was fixed on Washington; Kissinger's interests were always more global. Both lived in Cambridge as if Harvard scarcely existed for them.

With McGeorge Bundy, Kissinger's relations were very different. Technically speaking, the two men were departmental colleagues, though separated for much of the 1950s by the deepest gulf that exists in a university—the one that separates tenured faculty from those who hold term appointments. Bundy was "safe home" when Kissinger had scarcely begun to run the base paths. It is a comment on both that this did not affect their relationship in any significant way. Nor is there evidence to suggest that Kissinger found Bundy's elevation to the deanship of the Faculty of Arts and Sciences anything of a problem. Kissinger realized, after 1954, that his future in the Government Department would depend largely on how his colleagues esteemed his work; he knew that the Dean's intervention in his behalf could facilitate an early appointment to a permanent position. Neither factor affected the relation; Kissinger was not dependent on Bundy, and Bundy had no interest in making him feel that he was dependent.

Their relations were cordial and easy, perhaps helped by the fact that neither could conceive of the other as a potential rival. Though they were technically in the same discipline—both were teaching courses in foreign policy—no one thought to compare their work or judge between them. In the 1950s, Bundy occupied a somewhat unique position at Harvard. His intellectual powers were universally acknowledged; while it was uncommon for stories to circulate about how well other professors had done at school or college, Bundy's records at Groton and Yale were open secrets, only slightly exaggerated in the telling. Bundy had been the brightest boy from the beginning; his years as a Junior Fellow at Harvard simply confirmed what many had long known: Bundy would achieve great distinction early, and there was no way of knowing where it would eventually lead him. When he became Dean of the Faculty of Arts and Sciences, it only confirmed expectations that had long existed. When he performed brilliantly in the role, delighting his colleagues by his urbanity, wit, and competence, no one was surprised. Bundy was in a class apart; in the Cambridge of the 1950s, he had no peer.

Bundy was a central figure at Harvard when Kissinger was scarcely known. It would have been ludicrous for Kissinger to compare himself with Bundy. It would have been a comparison not of unequal men but of men so different in character and opportunity—so different in what life had provided them—that no one would have known what to make of the comparison. Bundy, who could be generous to a fault with those whom he liked, clearly esteemed Kissinger. He read Kissinger's manuscripts, contributed to his journal, supported his appointments, and showed every evidence of being pleased to have Kissinger as a colleague and friend.

With both Bundy and Schlesinger in the White House, and with many other friends and acquaintances scattered throughout various departments of the government, Kissinger enjoyed unofficial access to kinds of information that had not been so readily available during the Eisenhower years. He knew how worried the administration was about Khrushchev's repeated threats to sign a separate peace with East Germany, thereby effectively abrogating all the wartime agreements that legitimated the four-power presence in Berlin. In the late spring, with the situation steadily deteriorating, Bundy invited Kissinger to become a part-time consultant to the National Security Council, to advise on German policy. Kissinger continued his teaching at Harvard, and there was no immediate change in his life except for the fact that he gained access to papers he would not otherwise have seen. A massive safe installed by the government in his Divinity Avenue offices was the only external evidence of his new role.

In the summer of 1961, both before and after the building of the Berlin Wall, Kissinger worked steadily in Washington. For the rest of the year, he commuted, spending a few days each week in Washington and the rest of the time at Harvard. The arrangement was never very satisfactory; Kissinger was not in a position to impose his ideas on his White House colleagues, and few of them saw any reason to pay particular heed to his recommendations. In Washington, Bundy was "boss"; Kissinger made the grave mistake of believing that something like the collegial relations that obtained in Cambridge could be maintained at the National Security Council. Also, he never fully appreciated the difficulties of working in a clearly subordinate position where he was required to compete with many others who imagined that they had more reason to be consulted than he did. Their commitment to the administration, after all, was total; they had pulled up stakes and gone to Washington "for the duration." Kissinger was a part-time consultant, coming in occasionally from Cambridge. He could never hope to influence policy in the way that they did.

Yet the experience was invaluable for him; he learned a great deal about the federal bureaucracy—and about the National Security Council—and increased his knowledge of the Berlin situation. Impressions that he had gained from being a student of the American policy-making process were both confirmed and corrected. Kissinger, looking back on the experience, recognized that it introduced him to policy-making at a level he had not known previously. He realized more than ever how difficult it was to be an active consultant in Washington while pursuing a professorial career. Between Kennedy's inauguration and the summer of 1962, Kissinger wrote almost nothing. So long as he served in two places, with so many various demands on his time, it was quite impossible for him to write for publication. Also, serving in the government, even on the *ad hoc* basis that was arranged for him in 1961, restricted him in other ways. He was not *of* the administration, but he could not pretend to be *outside* it.

But beginning in early 1962, he was free of these restraints; in theory, at least, he should have been able to return to the kind of writing he had been doing during the Eisenhower years. Articles did begin to appear again, very conspicuously in *The Reporter*, but also in *Foreign Affairs*. However, an attentive reader of these articles, who knew Kissinger's earlier work, might have noticed certain subtle differences. While it would be wrong to exaggerate the change, Kissinger's criticisms of the Kennedy administration seemed somewhat more muted than those he had made of the Eisenhower administration. Two explanations were possible: that Kissinger thought the new administration was doing significantly better than the old one, or that he felt himself somewhat restrained in criticizing the Kennedy administration because of his personal acquaintance with so many of those who were making policy. Kissinger knew how able many of these men were. He also knew something of their energy and dedication. There was every reason to believe that these men—"a new generation," in the President's words—would be in or near Washington for the rest of their professional lives. It was difficult for him to be too cavalier in the way that he wrote about them, even when he disagreed with them. He knew how strongly many of them felt about the President. Whether rightly or wrongly, they took for granted that Kennedy was a very remarkable President; it seemed inconceivable to them that the administration would not achieve extraordinary things. The ardor was infectious; even when the accomplishments were negligible, publicity and public relations made them seem impressive. Not since Franklin Roosevelt had there been a more charismatic leader. Vast programs were on the drawing boards. The Peace Corps and the Alliance for Progress, like the much advertised presidential interest in Africa, while constantly mentioned, were scarcely daring initiatives toward resolving the difficult international dilemmas that Eisenhower had left untended.

Kissinger knew this, but chose to speak guardedly. To become an outspoken critic of the Kennedy administration was to run very serious risks.

The Kennedy administration included men who read, who would be certain to read almost anything that he wrote. There would be little appreciation of his criticism; it would be treated as the sniping of someone who had not been asked to stay, who was unable to control his resentments. Kissinger was in a difficult position; to be openly critical of the administration was not only to jeopardize friendships but to risk being ostracized from a community that he wished to belong to. Kissinger experienced after 1961 all sorts of internal pressures that made him see the wisdom of holding his tongue. The frustration came from his being unable to criticize in the way that had once been so easy. In the 1950s, while he had generally avoided dwelling on individual failures, he had been totally candid in pointing to larger intellectual and institutional rigidities. For those who read him with any care, there was never any question as to where he stood. After 1961, he was more circumspect. The difference was not blatant. For those who had no knowledge of his earlier works, he would appear as a very articulate and forceful critic. For those who knew those works, he would appear more guarded.

Kissinger, after his service with the National Security Council, resumed his Cambridge life without any obvious difficulties. The transition may have been made somewhat easier by visits to Israel, India, and Pakistan. In India, he was the guest of the American Ambassador, John Kenneth Galbraith. In Israel, he met all the major political leaders, and pursued the exhaustive schedule that had become almost "classical" for visiting foreign dignitaries. In Pakistan, there were meetings with political leaders, higher civil servants, and Americans involved in various economic assistance programs. Kissinger knew the great advantages that were to be derived from all such encounters. He was never a tourist, but worked hard at securing the kinds of information that were not so easily obtained at home.

Between January 1961 and July 1962, Kissinger wrote only a single article; it appeared in *The Reporter* on February 2, 1961, and was entitled "For an Atlantic Confederacy." Intended as a charge to the new administration, it outlined the elements of a new European policy that the Democrats were asked to pursue. There was no softening of earlier strictures on the Eisenhower policies; the alliance, Kissinger wrote, could not survive the kind of diplomacy that had preceded the abortive summit meeting of 1960. Kissinger said that the new administration faced no problem more crucial than the restoration of the Atlantic alliance. In every crisis, Kissinger wrote, the West was divided or uncertain. European statesmen had got into the habit of running off to Moscow, Kissinger complained, to hold "conversations" with Khrushchev. Heads of state, he said, do not normally converse; all "conversations" on such a level raised the possibility of bilateral agreements, and these would not benefit the alliance. Kissinger resented the antics of European leaders who wanted to enhance their local political reputations by appearing to be interested in bridling the more belligerent members of the alliance. So long as NATO appeared as a barrier to a settlement with the Soviet Union, its value and utility would be compromised. Repeating arguments he had made at other times, he called for an Atlantic confederacy—in his words, "a true commonwealth."

Kissinger believed that the Marshall Plan had been the great achievement of the first postwar decade. He argued that the creation of a political framework capable of transcending traditional nationalism was the imperative need of the moment. The Western Allies had to be made to realize that the advantages of partnership could not be sustained if independent action was insisted on. Western unity was a prerequisite to meaningful negotiations with the Soviet Union, including arms control negotiations. There were real possibilities of going forward to new negotiations, but these depended on Allied unity and initiatives.

In the summer of 1962, Kissinger wrote an article for *Foreign Affairs* entitled "The Unsolved Problems of European Defense." This was Kissinger's first published estimate of the administration's accomplishments in the defense field. He had some good things to say for what it had done, but his disappointment was obvious. The NATO Defense and Foreign Ministers had recently met in Athens, where, according to Kissinger, some effort had been made to undertake a fundamental reassessment of NATO strategy. The Kennedy administration was credited with providing at least some of the impetus for this long overdue development. The administration, soon after it took office in 1961, had called for a strengthening of NATO's conventional forces; specifically, for an increase in strength to the thirty divisions agreed to in 1957, but never implemented. When the United States insisted that this target be acknowledged and realized, the allies inquired whether this implied a reduced American reliance on nuclear weapons, and whether this did not reflect the reduced credibility of the American nuclear deterrent. The administration's response was firm: the deterrent remained America's principal weapon; in fact, it was explained, every effort was being made to expand the strategic striking force, to make it even more invulnerable. As for the recommended non-nuclear buildup, far from diminishing the credibility of the United States nuclear power, the Americans insisted that it would only enhance it. Kissinger referred to this as a "curious dialogue"; while its ostensible purpose was to reassure America's allies, it served only to increase the general uneasiness. Everyone knew that as Soviet missile strength developed, and as Soviet missiles were dispersed and hardened, the task of preparing a counterforce strike would be made much more complicated. Unless the American deterrent became highly mobile, with part of it stationed at sea, there was no possibility of its being adequate to the tasks ahead. The problem, quite obviously, was to define a proper role for the conventional forces, and, given the new Soviet strength, for the deterrent.

Kissinger saw no point in minimizing the differences between the United States and its allies on military policy in Europe. The allies kept their own military contributions on a level sufficiently high to guarantee that the United States maintained its forces on the Continent; they were careful, however, not to maintain forces so large that they might be considered an alternative to the ultimate strategic weapon, the nuclear deterrent. When Kennedy came into office, official doctrine insisted that any war that brought American forces into collision with either Soviet or Chinese Communist forces would necessarily be a general war. The Kennedy administration recognized the unreasonableness of that doctrine, and began to take steps to alter it.

In theory, the administration was seeking what it called a more "flexible response," one that permitted the United States and its allies to meet a Soviet challenge at whatever level it presented itself. Kissinger implied that the administration had not faced "squarely" the kind of flexibility it was aiming for. The United States argued that a conventional force buildup would provide "a capability for a last warning *before* implementing a counterforce strategy." Kissinger did not believe that the creation of three or four additional divisions in the United States would in any significant way enhance the credibility of the nuclear deterrent in defense of an area like Southeast Asia. In Europe, on the other hand, where the United States was already physically committed, the stationing of even a few additional divisions might make a substantial difference. However, even in Europe it was important to clarify what the divisions would be used for. Frequent American assertions that an increase in the "shield forces" would make a counterforce strategy more likely were not generally believed. Many in Europe thought that argument a thinly veiled subterfuge for America's growing reluctance to use its nuclear deterrent.

Kissinger sympathized with the skepticism of the Europeans. If the United States adopted a strategy based on the idea of "flexible response," it was impossible to justify it by saying that it made a counterforce strategy all the more likely; on the contrary, it needed to be presented as a departure—the old reliance on immediate all-out war had clearly become outmoded. Until this was admitted, Kissinger wrote, it made no sense to argue that thirty divisions stationed in Europe provided a security that was unattainable with twenty-two divisions. If "the implications of the impending invulnerability of retaliatory forces" were squarely faced, Kissinger wrote, then there would be some point in considering what a conventional arms buildup would provide in the way of additional security.

The strategy that Kennedy and Lauris Norstad, the Supreme Commander of SHAPE, had propounded, Kissinger wrote, implied that the shield forces—presumably the conventional forces—needed to be strong enough to enforce a "pause" in any offensive Soviet military operations. The "pause," in theory, would permit the Soviets "to appreciate the wider risks involved." Kissinger found it difficult to follow their reasoning. Why, he asked, would the American bargaining position be better at the end of thirty days, when presumably the Allied conventional forces would have been decimated, than it was at the beginning? Also, what would the response be if the Soviets agreed to negotiate once they had gained their prime objectives? What would the Allied response be? If nuclear war was too hazardous to undertake at the start of a Soviet operation, Kissinger wrote, he could not see why it would not be even more risky once the local issue had been decided against the West.

Kissinger found difficulties also with the administration's concept of a "threshold." Roswell Gilpatric, Deputy Secretary of Defense, had said that if NATO forces were about to be overwhelmed by non-nuclear arms, NATO should make use of nuclear weapons. Kissinger wanted to know who would determine whether the Allied forces were about to be overwhelmed. Assuming that such a determination was made, how were the nuclear weapons to be used? Kissinger thought that the use of such weapons after a Soviet breakthrough might well favor the aggressor, whose units could be dispersed; the Allies would be obliged to move their units into predictable areas. If nuclear weapons were to be used tactically, Kissinger wrote, the optimum—perhaps the only—time to use them would be early, when the shield forces were reasonably intact and the Soviet reserve forces had not yet appeared on the battlefield.

Kissinger found analogous difficulties with the concept of "forward strategy," the capacity to maintain a defense along the Iron Curtain, particularly to protect cities close to the dividing line. Those who argued for the necessity of thirty divisions to achieve these purposes were, in Kissinger's view, insufficiently precise about what they imagined these divisions would accomplish. If the purpose was "to prevent a limited *coup de main*," such a force might be adequate; if, however, the purpose was to hold the central line to resist a major assault, it was an extremely dangerous strategy. Any attempt to hold a line along the Iron Curtain with thirty divisions, Kissinger wrote, would only repeat the mistakes the Allies made in 1940 when they were surrounded in the Low Countries. Kissinger could imagine a thirty-division army helping a country like Greece or Turkey defend itself against a Communist satellite attack; it would be useful also to countries like Austria or Yugoslavia, should they suffer a Communist onslaught. On the central front, however, a force of that size could resist minor incursions only, perhaps permitting a somewhat longer resistance to full-scale attack, but having no other decisive importance.

NATO, Kissinger believed, had two options. The first was to

strengthen the shield forces and the ready reserves so that they could hold not only for thirty days but for as long as it took for the West's superior military potential to make itself felt. The second was for NATO to rely more heavily on tactical nuclear weapons. If NATO embraced the first option, it would need to build up its conventional forces to a point where they could achieve a local stalemate equivalent to the stalemate that obtained in the strategic nuclear field. That would require a force far greater than thirty divisions, trained in nuclear warfare and supported by a nuclear arsenal to guard against the threat of the Soviets' suddenly introducing nuclear weapons.

Kissinger believed the NATO powers capable of making such an effort; Europe's manpower and material resources were certainly equal to the task. He knew, however, that it would require sacrifices of a kind that many Europeans were disinclined to make. Also, the policy carried certain risks, but Kissinger insisted that the alternatives were even more hazardous. If the West lacked a military capability adequate to its needs except for the nuclear deterrent, the Soviets might well conclude that they could move in certain ways in Europe without running an unacceptable risk. There was no point in modifying NATO's military doctrine, Kissinger wrote, if forces were not created capable of sustaining the new doctrine.

There was another option, of course: to rely more heavily on tactical nuclear weapons. This strategy required conventional forces strong enough to halt the Soviet forces in Germany and Eastern Europe from a rapid breakthrough. To counter these Allied units, the Soviets would be obliged to create very substantial forces of their own, which would be vulnerable to nuclear weapons. The deterrence would be achieved by the USSR's being confronted with the prospect of a conflict with incalculable consequences. There would be no resort to a counterforce strike; nuclear weapons would be used at once, and not after a pause; they would be used primarily in the battle area.

Kissinger was aware of the stigma that attached to the use of nuclear weapons. It was exceedingly dangerous to start on the nuclear path, given the state of opinion in many Allied countries. Gilpatric was himself on record as having said, "I, for one, have never believed in a so-called limited nuclear war. I just don't know how you build a limit into it once you start using any kind of nuclear bang." McNamara seemed to share that opinion. If limited nuclear war was impossible, Kissinger wrote, then what was the point of having nuclear arms stocked on the Continent? If any war that involved the use of nuclear weapons was bound to escalate, then why run the risk of having this happen, particularly when the intended targets were already covered by America's strategic forces? The atomic arms stored in Europe were simply redundant.

Clearly, Kissinger did not believe this. He was telling the administration to clarify its doctrine. He agreed with the President's argument that some alternative was needed between total surrender and general nuclear war. In Kissinger's mind, such an alternative existed in tactical nuclear operations. In his view, the most effective way to use nuclear weapons was to use them tactically—to stop a battle and prevent a break-through. If a standstill could be achieved, Kissinger wrote, then the major purpose of the defense would be realized.

Kissinger never underestimated the opposition to any such proposed strategy. Having himself originally proposed it in *Nuclear Weapons and Foreign Policy*, he had abandoned it three years later. Why, then, was he returning to it? Because he saw only one other option—the building of very substantial conventional forces—and he could not believe that Europe or the United States would in fact choose this alternative. If NATO developed a concept and a capability for tactical nuclear war—described now as control of the battlefield—it would still require larger conventional forces, but not of the order that would be necessary if there was no tactical nuclear option. Two years earlier, Kissinger had indicated that the unwillingness of the military to conceive and plan such limited nuclear operations suggested a degree of resistance that was not likely to be overcome. Now he was saying that the resistance *had* to be overcome. Tactical nuclear weapons were the only kinds of weapons that could be used in certain contingencies. While accepting all the hazards of their use, Kissinger insisted that the worst that could happen was certain to happen if a counterforce strategy was employed.

Kissinger had returned to his idea of limited nuclear war; he had, however, related his concept to a change within the NATO alliance. Why had he been led back to the theory? Because he continued to believe that the threat of all-out war was not credible, and that the new independent nuclear forces only underscored Europe's restiveness. France, pursuing a policy initiated by Great Britain, was creating its own retaliatory force; no longer confident of American support, given the new Soviet capability, France imagined that she could develop her own defenses. Germany was no less agitated, asking for guarantees that the nuclear weapon stockpiles on the Continent would not be withdrawn without the consent of NATO; also, that there be, in Kissinger's words, "a degree of unspecified joint control over weapons fired from German soil." Other NATO allies had expressed similar misgivings. Kissinger understood and sympathized with their feelings; it was "against all reason" to expect America's European allies to integrate their conventional forces in a joint command and accept an increased reliance on a conventional defense, while the United States retained "a monopoly on the means of responding to the Soviet nuclear threat," enjoying complete freedom to determine whether or when to employ nuclear weapons.

The American government, openly hostile to the French effort to build an independent nuclear retaliatory force, insisted that national nuclear forces in Europe were useless; they could not possibly survive a determined Soviet surprise attack. Nor were they useful as offensive weapons; to use them independently against the Soviet Union would be an act of national suicide. Kissinger admitted the validity of both arguments, but stressed that neither Great Britain nor France showed any interest in using its forces separately. As for the Soviet Union's conducting a surprise attack against the strategic forces of either, Kissinger asked whether this would not require the Russians to run the unacceptable risk of a counterblow from the United States or from the European ally temporarily spared. He asked also whether it was a foregone conclusion that the United States would do nothing if one of its allies attacked the Soviet Union. While that was a possibility, it was by no means certain.

If the United States was totally candid, Kissinger wrote, it would have to admit that one of its principal objections to the spread of national nuclear forces within NATO was its fear that such a capability might create circumstances that would permit an ally to pressure the United States into nuclear war. The fear was not at all unreasonable. The solution, however, was not to condemn such forces but to coordinate policies so that the United States and its principal allies agreed both about objectives and about strategic options. Kissinger knew that some tentative efforts had been made to achieve greater unity and to reduce duplication and waste. Thus, for example, in May 1961, President Kennedy offered to commit five Polaris submarines to NATO, subject to agreed-upon NATO guidelines for their control and use. Kennedy indicated that he intended for this to be the first of several such transfers. In Athens, McNamara made good on the presidential promise. Kennedy had also expressed a willingness to consider a NATO sea-borne force, truly multilateral in ownership and control, and Dean Rusk had gone out of his way to indicate a willingness to receive precise suggestions from America's allies.

Kissinger, without disparaging these words or gestures, indicated that the transfer of Polaris submarines to NATO was more symbolic of an American commitment than an actual device for joint control. In the absence of joint plans for the total nuclear forces of the alliance, including the Strategic Air Command and the British Bomber Command, setting guidelines for a handful of submarines was not a very substantial action. But even the guidelines seemed ambiguous to Kissinger. How were they to be interpreted? The submarines were to remain under exclusive United States command, subject to joint guidelines. What did this mean? Were there to be contingency plans for the use of nuclear weapons provided that the governments, when approached, agreed? Or was NATO committed to use nuclear weapons in certain specified conditions, with the NATO commander being given authority in advance?

Kissinger did not believe that NATO could be made into a "fourth nuclear power," able to plan jointly and provide a substitute for the national nuclear establishments. In theory, four forces would exist: the American, which would be the largest; two smaller national forces (controlled by Great Britain and France); finally, a medium-sized NATO force to which all would presumably contribute. Kissinger argued that the "plethora of forces would present formidable problems of command and control." Also, he worried that the Soviets would misinterpret the purpose of these several forces, believing that they reflected varying degrees of American commitment to the defense of Europe. To create such a force without a clear purpose, Kissinger wrote, would only be to provide an incentive for discovering a purpose. In his view, Europe's concern about the American nuclear predominance would be unaffected by such an innovation. Even if such a force existed, the United States would retain its veto; American consent, along with the consent of all the others, would be mandatory. As for SAC, it would remain under exclusive American control. What did the Europeans stand to gain? They might prevent the use of the NATO force, but they could not compel its use. As for the larger force —represented by SAC—which remained in the exclusive control of the United States, the Europeans were as impotent as they had ever been. If, Kissinger wrote, the United States was prepared to give up its veto in the NATO force, that would be a true concession. But there was no possibility of its happening; a constitutional crisis in the United States would almost certainly follow from any decision that permitted foreign powers to commit the United States to military action without its explicit consent.

Kissinger believed that the only separate multilateral force within NATO that would make any sense at all would be a European Atomic Force that merged the British and French nuclear forces. If the United States supported the creation of a European Atomic Force, that would lay to rest rumors that represented the United States as trying to keep Europe in a state of dependence on nuclear matters. Such a force, he wrote, would symbolize the new European thrust toward integration; it would do a great deal to hasten further integration.

He was under no illusions, however, about the difficulties of securing such a force. Neither the United States, France, nor Great Britain seemed particularly interested in such a possibility. Because he believed it imperative that NATO reconsider its strategy, even if it did not at once accept so bold a recommendation, he advised the United States to be more temperate in its criticisms of France. Even if the Americans were essentially correct in their negative assessment of the independent French nuclear force, there was nothing to be gained from disparaging their effort. That, for Kissinger, was not the crucial strategic issue. He was less worried about the spread of nuclear weapons than he was about the issue of local defense. Believing that no local defense of Europe was possible without French cooperation, he stated his own position very succinctly when he said: "Our present policy cannot work. It would not prevent the spread of nuclear weapons, not even to France; it would make impossible the local defense of Europe." Kissinger added: "If we want our primary objective, we must be prepared—painful though it be—to reassess our attitudes toward France's nuclear ambitions."

Kissinger recommended that the United States help France in its nuclear program, even if it did nothing more than assist in the development of delivery vehicles. If the United States did this, he wrote, France might then be asked to use resources she was saving to strengthen the conventional shield of NATO. He did not think it impossible that supporting a modest French force might be the best way to bring about a European force. Such a strategy, he believed, would show American good will; if France refused to cooperate on such a basis, it would be obvious, in his words, that she placed "notions of grandeur above the common interests of the alliance and ultimately above her own best interests."

This was Kissinger's first systematic analysis of the defense policies of the Kennedy administration. While it would have been easy to applaud the efforts the administration had made, particularly in seeking to build up conventional forces, Kissinger showed himself singularly unimpressed. In his view, neither McNamara nor Gilpatric understood the full implications of a switch from a counterforce strategy to a strategy of local defense. He refused to agree with them in their continued rejection of the idea of tactical nuclear defense. Most important, however, he took issue with the administration's growing antipathy to de Gaulle and the French effort to create an independent nuclear capability. Kissinger, as if to dissociate himself further from the administration, showed a mild skepticism about some of the more extravagant claims made for the Polaris offer to NATO.

Why so negative a verdict on an administration that had been so active in the defense field, and that appeared so receptive to certain ideas that Kissinger favored? Kennedy, as early as 1958, had spoken of the mistaken reliance on massive retaliation, using the same Maginot Line analogy that Kissinger favored in his *Nuclear Weapons and Foreign Policy*. A president who had spoken against "a dependence upon a strategy which may collapse or may never be used, but which meanwhile prevents the consideration of any alternative," might be thought to hold defense views very congenial to someone like Kissinger. While the Kennedy administration clearly understood a great deal that had eluded the Eisenhower administration, and was prepared to act on its knowledge, Kissinger believed it had failed to develop a coherent military doctrine, and that its policies toward France were fraught with danger for the alliance. Kissinger, return-

ing to a theme he elaborated very early in his career, insisted that
NATO's problem was not military but political. He called for a "fundamental reassessment" of the political problem on both sides of the Atlantic. If de Gaulle needed to rethink what he was doing, so did Kennedy;
neither performance, in Kissinger's mind, was at all adequate. If he was
right in believing that there were new possibilities of turning NATO into
a true Atlantic community, the Kennedy administration had the obligation to move toward that objective. Kissinger's criticism was not hostile,
but there was no fawning over the remarkable achievements of a new defense team led by Robert McNamara. Kissinger, while moderately
friendly, had clearly not been swept off his feet. This was the stance that
he maintained throughout the Kennedy-Johnson years. It contrasted
markedly with what others, perhaps more intimately involved, were saying about themselves or their friends.

In October 1962, the Kennedy administration passed through its most
serious crisis, touched off by the Soviet decision to install missiles in
Cuba. For thirteen days, according to Robert Kennedy, there was the risk
of a "confrontation between the two giant atomic nations," and this
"brought the world to the abyss of nuclear destruction and the end of
mankind." Robert Kennedy's memoir is a tale of a crisis safely passed; it is
a proud statement, which ends, appropriately enough, with the recollec-
tion that the President took no "credit for himself or for the Administration for what had occurred."

Robert Kennedy's memoir ought to be read in conjunction with an article that appeared in *The Reporter*, and that Kissinger wrote shortly
after the crisis. While Kissinger made no effort to minimize Kennedy's
success—in fact, went out of his way to underline it—there were
substantial differences between what he said and what others wrote, particularly those who regarded this as Kennedy's greatest foreign policy accomplishment. The difference may be expressed quite simply: Kennedy's
admirers dwelt mostly on his fortitude, intelligence, and moderation; Kissinger was struck mostly by Khrushchev's ineptness and stupidity.

What had tempted the Russians into so rash and foolhardy an adventure? How could they have believed that they could get away with establishing missiles on an island ninety miles from the United States?
Kissinger thought that part of the answer lay in a fault common to dicta-
torships: the Soviets had begun to take their own propaganda too seriously; having so frequently spoken of their ability to protect "national
liberation movements," they had overlooked the difference between supporting guerrilla forces in Southeast Asia and establishing missile bases in
the Western Hemisphere. Communist operations in Asia were always ambiguous; they posed very real problems for the United States; there was
no comparable problem with Cuba. Was it possible, Kissinger asked, that

the Soviets believed that a limited number of missiles in Cuba would seem insignificant to the United States, entirely acceptable, and certainly not worth running the risk of nuclear war? Given the vulnerability of Cuban bases to American attack, Kissinger could not conceive of any military purpose that the missiles could have served. The Soviets, he wrote, were obviously not so much concerned with a military gain as with a political gain. The operation was comprehensible only if the Soviets intended to use it to give an overwhelming proof of their own power and of American impotence. Had they succeeded, Kissinger wrote, extremist elements throughout Latin America would have been "emboldened" and America's allies would have been "disheartened." It seemed inconceivable to him that a Soviet success in Cuba would not have been followed by a showdown on Berlin.

The question that he constantly reverted to was how the Soviets could have been so misled as to believe that they could get away with installing missiles in Cuba. Had the Soviets learned all the wrong lessons from their experiences in the previous decade? Did they remember Suez as a time when the United States collaborated with the Soviets to "humiliate" Britain and France, America's closest allies? What about Lebanon? Why had the American intervention there not prevented the displacement of the only Middle Eastern government that had accepted the Eisenhower doctrine? What about the Bay of Pigs? How had the Soviets looked on America's gamble, and on its willingness to accept failure when the American operation miscarried? Was it possible that the American acceptance of the Berlin Wall suggested to Khrushchev that the United States would accept any *fait accompli?* If so, they probably expected no resistance in Cuba. It was not impossible, Kissinger wrote, that the Soviets believed that the United States "would accept any face-saving formula and retreat rather than face a head-on confrontation." Also, the first American reaction to the Soviet arms buildup possibly misled the Soviets. While Kennedy made very clear in his news conference that the United States would take a grave view of the introduction of offensive weapons, the distinction was perhaps not clear enough; in any case, the statement was made in the context of explaining why the Americans were not intervening at once. Also, Kissinger wrote, administration spokesmen, in commenting on the matter, tended to emphasize the risks inherent in a blockade or an invasion. When Senator Keating warned that offensive weapons were being installed, the allegation was denied. It was possible that the Soviets believed, Kissinger said, that the United States knew of their preparations and had decided to acquiesce in them by denying that there was any threat.

Khrushchev had clearly misunderstood the character of the President and the mood of the country. For a man to be elected president of the

United States, Kissinger wrote, meant, among other things, that he had a will to prevail. Certainly, in the case of Kennedy, obliged to overcome several major handicaps, including age and religion, Khrushchev ought to have reckoned with a man who would not sit idly by and tolerate so flagrant an aggression. Even had Kennedy wished to do so, Kissinger doubted that the general public would have acquiesced. If Soviet intelligence and diplomacy did not alert Khrushchev to that fundamental fact, it was proof that the disease of dictatorship had already ravaged the Soviet state, and that its leaders were being told only what they cared to hear. In Kissinger's view, the Soviet action was militarily confused; it hardly merited the risks taken; politically, it was naïve and simple. There was no possibility of the United States' agreeing to settle issues outside the Western Hemisphere in return for a Soviet pledge to withdraw the missiles from Cuba. It was unthinkable that the Americans would trade away the vital interests of allies in order to protect their own interests. Had the United States done so, in Kissinger's words, it would have mortgaged its "claim to leadership in the West."

The Soviets could have anticipated Allied indecision—even Allied pressure on the United States to avoid a confrontation—but Kennedy's decisiveness prevented even that from happening. As Kissinger explained, after the President's speech there was only one way for others to have influence on the United States, and that was to support her. The Soviet leaders were not much more effective when it came to estimating how the uncommitted states would react. While many of them were only too ready to play one of the great powers off against the other, they were themselves not prepared to run large risks. It was safe to support "national liberation movements"; it was quite another thing to support the Soviet Union's decision to construct missile bases in Cuba. The latter action threatened war, and the uncommitted had no interest in that possibility.

The Soviets had learned all the wrong lessons from their earlier successes. In expanding in Eurasia, Kissinger wrote, they had been able to choose both the battlefield and the issue. By confronting the United States with ambiguous challenges, where the threat to American security was never obvious, a quick American reaction was virtually precluded. Also, because such areas were geographically close to the Communist world, gradual escalation of Soviet involvement was relatively easy. In most instances, the only possible American response was the threat of nuclear war—a very unlikely response. In such circumstances, it was comparatively easy for the USSR to achieve its objectives. These conditions did not obtain in the Cuban venture, where the threat was direct and brutal. In the Cuban crisis, Kissinger wrote, the Soviets found themselves in the position that was generally occupied by the United States.

The Americans were able to increase the pressure gradually; the only possible Soviet response was the threat of nuclear war. In Kissinger's words, the Soviets "threw away their traditional advantages in a gamble that left them no recourse if it failed."

Kissinger credited McNamara and Gilpatric with having estimated correctly the nature of America's military power. In his view, the crisis would not have ended so rapidly had the United States not been in a position to win if it struck first, and able to inflict intolerable damage even if it was itself the victim of a surprise attack. Kissinger, without withdrawing any of his reservations about the efficacy of the counterforce strategy, admitted its usefulness in the Cuban crisis. The Soviet leaders dared not invoke the threat of nuclear war against the American blockade, and did not choose to create crises in places like Berlin and Turkey, where they enjoyed local superiority. The credibility of the American deterrent was greater than the credibility of the Soviet deterrent; the Soviets had no choice but to retreat.

Kissinger wondered what the United States would do next. He was certain that the successful negotiating of the crisis provided the country with a unique opportunity, if it knew how to use the occasion correctly. America's European allies felt more certain about the United States than they had for some years; new possibilities existed for making American influence felt in Latin America; in Kissinger's view, the United States had improved its position also among the uncommitted. The "overweening self-confidence" of the Soviets had suffered a serious blow. Kissinger wrote: "We should now be able to confront the Soviets with confidence and moderation. Henceforth, moderation will appear an act of policy, for it is a virtue only in those who are thought to have a choice." He warned, however, against those who chose not to understand what had happened; rumors were already circulating, suggesting that Khrushchev had "faced down militant generals in a dramatic confrontation." Some were saying that Khrushchev needed to be saved from hard-line Stalinists. Kissinger's reaction to this was one of unconcealed impatience; he wrote: "Surely the time has come to declare a moratorium on such trivial speculations. Our capacity to play domestic politics in the Kremlin is extremely limited. There is no evidence of 'peaceful' Khrushchev facing down hard-line Stalinists. If Khrushchev planned the Cuban adventure, it is difficult to see how much more reckless hard-line Stalinists could have been. If the Cuban policy was imposed on Khrushchev, he does not need any further assistance to prove that such tactics are bound to be disastrous."

Kissinger thought that the crisis provided the administration with an opportunity to review the events of the preceding two years, to see what influence, in Kissinger's words, "the confusion of a conciliatory tone with a conciliatory policy by so many self-appointed emissaries to the

Kremlin—and by some official ones as well—had on Khrushchev's expectation that his gamble in the Caribbean would succeed." Kissinger hoped that the crisis would demonstrate the limited utility of terms like "tough" and "soft," which "served as substitutes for thought," and had no place in serious foreign policy discussion. There was no point in constantly arguing for keeping negotiations open, but never explaining what propositions one intended to advance. Kissinger worried about the American penchant for "new ideas," which made any set of proposals discussable, but also expendable. He deplored the American readiness to invite Soviet demands—to offer a shopping list—from which a few items might be chosen in the mistaken belief that this served to improve relations. Negotiating tactics of this kind were anathema to him.

He urged the Kennedy administration to fix its proposals, and to do so before a crisis developed. The missile crisis "victory" ought to be used, Kissinger wrote, to press for a solution to serious international problems, including, most obviously, the problem of Berlin. America's allies were more favorably disposed than they had been for many years; it was a good time to press for closer Atlantic relations. The Alliance for Progress might also be pushed with greater urgency, and a new approach to the uncommitted nations was in order. The meaning of Cuba had not been lost on them, nor had the Chinese invasion across the Indian frontier gone unnoticed. America's relations with the new nations could be freed "from the inhibitions of a dialogue between opportunism and sentimentality." Kissinger was not at all certain that the administration would seize its opportunities; it all depended on whether there was a disposition to run certain risks. Repeating what he had said many years earlier, Kissinger wrote: "The dilemma of any statesman is that he can never be certain about the probable course of events. In reaching a decision, he must inevitably act on the basis of an intuition that is inherently unprovable. If he insists on certainty, he runs the danger of becoming a prisoner of events. His resolution must reside not in 'facts' as commonly conceived but in his vision of the future."

Kissinger praised the administration for its "skill, daring, and decisiveness in dealing with a problem once it was recognized." He wondered, however, why the problem was not recognized earlier, and suggested that the fault lay not with the intelligence services but with the unwillingness to accept ambiguity and uncertainty. "The challenge," he wrote, "is to couple the prudence, calculation, and skill of a government of experts with an act of imagination that encompasses the opportunities before us." Kissinger had no doubt that opportunities existed.

Two months later, in writing about "The Skybolt Affair," he indicated how these opportunities had been used. The story was disheartening. Reviewing the sequence of events that had led to the Nassau meeting between Kennedy and Macmillan, he dwelt on the policies pursued by Britain in the 1950s in its effort to maintain an independent nuclear capability. In February 1960, Britain had agreed to accept the Skybolt missile, which was then being built in the United States. After Kennedy's inauguration, however, Harold Wilson, the leader of the Labour Party, visited Washington and returned to London with the report that high administration officials doubted the necessity of the British nuclear deterrent, and would be pleased if Britain chose to direct its defense efforts to other weapons. Harold Macmillan promptly denied this, but when challenged to produce evidence to support his contention that the Americans favored the British nuclear effort, he was unable to do so. He referred instead to an agreement that Britain had with the United States which guaranteed that the Americans would supply Skybolt. Neither Eisenhower nor Kennedy denied the existence of such an agreement. When, therefore, a week before a scheduled NATO meeting in 1962, the United States announced its intention to cancel Skybolt, there was an uproar in Britain. The Nassau conference, originally scheduled to permit a wide-ranging survey of the world situation after Cuba, turned into a discussion of nuclear strategy; out of those meetings, in Kissinger's words, came an agreement "of extraordinary ambiguity." The United States undertook to furnish Polaris missiles of an unspecified type to Great Britain, which was charged with supplying the warheads and the submarines. The British Polaris forces were to be committed to NATO, "targeted in accordance with NATO plans," and made part of a multilateral NATO force. France was to be invited to join the force on the same basis. There were, according to Kissinger, many unanswered questions: What would Britain be able to do if it determined that its supreme national interests were involved in a particular crisis? Could it use its missiles independently? Who, in fact, determined the deployment of the submarines assigned to NATO? How was this to be decided? The Nassau communiqué, reversing traditional NATO doctrine, spoke of nuclear weapons as the "shield" and conventional weapons as the "sword." Did this mean, Kissinger asked, that the United States would resist massive Soviet attack with conventional forces only? If that was the implication, Kissinger wrote, then none of America's continental European allies agreed with the strategy. Because the atmosphere created by Nassau was so confused, there was no possibility of questions of this sort being discussed. But the Americans seemed oblivious to all this. They went around congratulating themselves on the scrapping of Skybolt and the offer of Polaris. Although the President imagined that he was dealing with a technical problem, Kissinger insisted that it could be correctly understood only if its political implications were recognized.

He doubted whether France would accept any of the arrangements proposed. If the United States could be so brutal with its special friend, Great Britain, de Gaulle would expect no greater understanding of the needs of the Continent. Whatever the merits of the Polaris offer, Kissinger suggested that the American proposals to NATO had now changed so frequently that no one knew any longer what the United States wanted or believed. America had become, according to Kissinger, a very "mercurial" ally. He worried also that every aspect of America's changing military policy seemed geared to technological necessity. Attention was never given to the psychological or political dimensions of a problem. Unless many of the ambiguities were cleared up, Kissinger wrote, and unless the United States approached its allies "in a less hectoring spirit," the possibilities of a further deterioration in the alliance were very real.

Kissinger's article on Skybolt was written in response to a specific crisis. In an article entitled "Strains on the Alliance," which appeared in *Foreign Affairs* that same month (January 1963), Kissinger reflected more generally about the state of the alliance. Despite the presidential call for a partnership between the United States and Europe, Kissinger spoke of growing divisions, with skepticism rampant in many European circles. Kissinger did not expect that all members of the alliance would agree on all issues; he wondered, however, whether the alliance could take a position that violated the deepest feelings of one or more of its partners. The Berlin question worried him. In Britain, particularly, influential opinion was beginning to support the proposition that a divided Germany should be accepted in return for agreement about new access arrangements. Kissinger believed that any such solution would seriously upset the domestic equilibrium of Germany; he wrote: "If the West tacitly or explicitly abandoned the principle of national unity, the Germans would consider it a sacrifice of their basic interests." It was for this reason that the Wall so shocked German public opinion, and why Germany so resented what it interpreted as the West's rather tepid reaction to an act that seemed to symbolize the end of any hope for unification. Alliance with the West had always been presented in the Federal Republic as a device for hastening unification; it seemed suddenly quite irrelevant to that purpose, and one of the consequences was a growing rift between Bonn and Washington, which France took advantage of. The French were not disinterested; de Gaulle believed that France's position in Europe depended on its having close relations with the Federal Republic. Kissinger wrote: "President de Gaulle has grasped the fact that if Germany feels itself an outcast it cannot remain a willing partner of the West. He has realized that an irredentist, dissatisfied Germany would be a menace to the security of all of Europe. He has therefore deliberately flattered German self-esteem. In his view, devising negotiating formulas on Berlin is less important than making the Germans feel that when under stress they do not stand alone. He has seen that there is no permanent solution to the Berlin problem so long as it is considered in isolation. To accuse the French of cynicism is irrelevant. They have pursued the policy appropriate for their objective." Kissinger believed that the French position sometimes reflected German feelings more faithfully than what the Germans were themselves able to say publicly.

American discussions with the Soviet Union on Berlin, in the absence of France, which refused to participate, and in the absence of the Federal Republic, whose misgivings were known, put the United States in an impossible negotiating position. According to Kissinger, the Soviets treated American offers as "fishing expeditions," and engaged in a few of their own. American negotiators, instead of worrying about the future of Germany and security in Central Europe, permitted themselves to be drawn into discussions of the status of Berlin. Kissinger thought the Soviet tactic masterly, making it appear that all that separated the world from lasting peace were a few specific issues that they were themselves raising. Kissinger wrote: "This set up a pattern of negotiations in which, in return for Western concessions, the Soviets would withdraw the threat which they themselves had initiated."

Inevitably, relations between Washington and Bonn deteriorated. The mere existence of bilateral negotiations raised the fear of an American-Soviet agreement at the expense of Western Europe. American diplomacy thereby encouraged the Franco-German entente. France would have aimed for this in any case, but American policy simply made it easier. By focusing negotiations on access rights and modalities with respect to Berlin, Kissinger said, the possibilities for disagreement within the alliance were maximized. Instead of trying to get the Soviets to agree to a specific formula for Berlin, every effort ought to have been made to compel the Soviets to make concrete proposals for a comprehensive settlement in Central Europe. That, however, depended on the West's knowing itself what it wanted. No such agreement existed.

Kissinger believed that the best hope of keeping "a latent nihilism in Germany from again menacing the West is to give the Federal Republic a stake in something larger than itself." The West, recognizing the psychological and political dilemmas of a divided country, needed to bend all its energies toward making the Federal Republic part of a larger community. The Federal Republic, in turn, would do well to stop talking about theoretical issues that involved self-determination, and start settling concrete matters such, for example, as its frontier with Poland. It was imperative that Germany's Atlantic orientation be safeguarded. If Adenauer could, however, be induced to be more flexible, that would be a gain. The West, Kissinger wrote, ought never to push too hard, realizing how much it gained from having a reliable and staunch advocate of Western orientation in Adenauer.

Turning next to de Gaulle, Kissinger said that "a sense of outrage is not a good guide to policy." Nothing was gained by fuming and fretting about the French President. Acknowledging that he could not be easily pressured or persuaded, Kissinger asked whether American tactics did not play into his hands, strengthening him particularly with his own bureaucracy. He was certain that the United States, however unintentionally, helped to increase de Gaulle's stature in Europe. It was clearly time to stop dwelling on de Gaulle's difficult personality, Kissinger wrote, and start reflecting on the strength of his character and the quality of his vision. The dispute with France centered on defense issues. McNamara's great weakness was his political and psychological obtuseness; his presentations at NATO meetings, while invariably brilliant, only served to increase Europe's restiveness. Kissinger wrote: "This is because our approach was generally to demonstrate a military capacity, which was not primarily in question, while ignoring or brushing aside the political or psychological considerations which were the real core of the uneasiness."

Kissinger could not understand why American officials were so outraged when Europeans expressed doubts about American constancy. He himself found ambiguities in the American position, and suggested that these had been "obscured by the fact that those most responsible for developing it belong to a single school of thought and through years of association have come to take for granted some assumptions which are not really as self-evident as they have tried to make them appear." The administration had claimed too much for what an increase in strength from twenty-two to thirty divisions would produce; it had been inept in its handling of the nuclear issue; its attitude toward France was churlish. France had responded with equal intransigence, banning American nuclear weapons from French soil, standing aloof from the Berlin negotiations, and blocking British entry into the Common Market. Kissinger made no defense of what the French had done, but suggested that if the Americans had the better technical arguments, the French were closer to certain psychological realities in Europe. Kissinger wrote: "It was simply not in the cards for us to maintain a special relationship with Great Britain on nuclear matters without arousing the resentment of France." American proposals for multilateral NATO forces were never persuasive; the continued American concern with preventing the development of national nuclear forces in Europe seemed, to Kissinger, to focus too much on a peripheral issue. The United States refused to understand why the Europeans wanted national forces; their aim, he explained, was to gain some slight influence over American planning. Kissinger believed that the growth of European nuclear power could have only one of two results, and he was not greatly worried by either. If Europe became strong enough to defend itself, the United States would have reason to be pleased. The more likely outcome was that Europe would learn through hard experience that the security of the Atlantic area was indeed indivisible. Why, then, all the excitement over France's transgressions, particularly when there was so little that the United States could do to prevent her from developing a nuclear capability?

Kissinger accepted the reasonableness of the American preference for a European nuclear force over purely national forces; he even understood why America tried so hard to secure that objective. He asked, however, whether attention should not be given to determining that force's assignments, and developing plans for its coordination with the American force. Its internal characteristics seemed a very secondary matter; the American insistence on "mixed crews" (crews of various nationalities) Kissinger dismissed as a concern with "technical safeguards," almost irrelevant to the political problems which he thought were primary. His concern, as always, was with "over-all strategy" rather than with the "internal mechanics of particular solutions."

What the situation called for was the restoration of confidence on both sides of the Atlantic. Kissinger did not believe that the difficulties of the alliance would disappear when two old men—de Gaulle and Adenauer—left the political stage, nor did he believe that "historical evolution" would settle the problem for the United States. Kissinger wrote: "A policy which sees in two great national leaders an obstacle rather than an opportunity runs the risk of making us prisoners of events. The time for creative action is at a moment when old patterns are disintegrating, not some time in a future which is problematical and when the challenges may prove quite different."

Kissinger had been circumspect in his criticisms; he had tried to avoid naming individual Kennedy appointees with whom he disagreed. Nor did he point his finger at the President himself. Yet there was an implied criticism of the whole administration. Its military policies were creating havoc in NATO; on Berlin, its diplomacy was inadequate; it did not know how to deal with de Gaulle. The charges were muted; they could not, however, be misinterpreted, particularly by those who read them in the White House, the State Department, or the Department of Defense. Kissinger gave little pleasure to the more ardent of the administration's supporters in or out of Washington.

While he generally avoided criticism of individual members of the Kennedy administration, he wrote in March 1963 in the greatest detail about McNamara's failings. United States strategy for NATO, Kissinger explained, was based on four major elements: the doctrine of "flexible response; antagonism to national nuclear forces; hostility to tactical nuclear weapons; a theory of conventional defense." On "flexible response," McNamara had changed his mind several times, and Kissinger outlined a few of the principal changes. There was somewhat greater consistency in the administration's hostility to independent nuclear forces, though the administration tended to show less hostility to the British capability than to any other. On tactical nuclear weapons, the administration opposed their use, claiming that they posed a grave risk of escalation; this being the case, Kissinger could not understand why they were still being stored on the Continent. McNamara wanted Europe's conventional forces to be adequate for dealing with many kinds of Soviet attacks, yet he constantly altered his estimate of what was indeed adequate. Kissinger wondered that the administration was surprised at Europeans' finding such a rapid change of doctrine unsettling.

McNamara, in a major speech at Ann Arbor in June 1962, had argued that the principal military objectives in a general nuclear war ought to be the enemy's military forces and not its civilian population. Kissinger explained that McNamara believed that "all nuclear weapons of the Alliance had to be under tight control, indeed under a single command, which in effect meant U.S. command." These ideas formed the basis of what came to be known as the McNamara doctrine. Kissinger noted many ambiguities in the doctrine; it was not clear, for example, whether the more important objective was to spare cities or destroy the enemy's retaliatory force. This, Kissinger pointed out, could be very important if many of the Soviet strategic bases were located near cities. Kissinger assumed that the destruction of the enemy's retaliatory force remained the prime objective, even when this involved a major hazard to the enemy's cities. Since the enemy's retaliatory forces would certainly grow and become more diversified, hardened, and dispersed, Kissinger expected it would become increasingly difficult to coordinate an attack against those forces. There would be fragmentary intelligence at best, and Kissinger appreciated the difficulties of fighting a war with a weapons system with which one had so little experience. The McNamara doctrine could not but make America's European allies restive. Did the United States actually have the superiority it claimed? If it had that superiority, why did it not live with the traditional doctrine which made the conventional forces the "shield" and the nuclear forces the "sword"? If the United States insisted on reversing the two, did it not suggest an unwillingness to use the nuclear forces even in the event of a Soviet attack on Europe?

Confusion, Kissinger said, had become widespread in NATO. McNamara, in trying to reformulate his theory, suggested that general nuclear war would certainly produce millions of civilian casualties; all hardened Soviet sites could not be destroyed, and there would always be a Soviet submarine-launching capability. This being the case, Europeans asked, what purpose would retaliation serve? They noted also that McNamara spoke always of a full-scale attack against the United States. What would follow a full-scale attack on Europe? McNamara advocated a United States strategic force capable of absorbing a surprise Soviet attack, then striking back at Soviet bomber bases, missile sites, and other military installations associated with their long-range forces (which would be capable of a second attack), this to be followed, if necessary, by selective strikes at Soviet urban and industrial targets. McNamara insisted that the Soviets would never attack the United States if such a capacity existed, particularly if the American deterrent was hardened, with part of it permanently at sea in Polaris submarines. Kissinger asked whether the United States would in fact find all the Soviet targets; even more, he worried—as many Europeans did—about the implications of the McNamara doctrine for civilian casualties. In theory, the Americans would spare the Soviet cities, and this would give the Russians an incentive to do the same with respect to American cities. If the Russians attacked America's cities, the United States promised to respond in kind. All this made good sense to the Europeans; they wondered, however, why they should not have the same capability. Kissinger wrote: "In short, what started out as a quest for maximum flexibility has produced a new form of rigidity. We have polarized options between conventional war and a kind of general war that with every passing year will acquire the very characteristics of uncontrollable massiveness we have tried to avoid."

Kissinger understood the Europeans' concern, though he did not imply that all of it was reasonable or justified. He spoke of the French "pressing their own arguments with a kind of Cartesian rationalism that sometimes threatens to turn valid arguments into parodies." Still, he understood that Europeans should "want to have a share in determining their fate if the Soviets do not follow the strategy preferred by the United States." Europeans, Kissinger pointed out, would almost certainly view a Soviet attack on themselves differently from the way their American allies regarded the operation. Thus, for example, to a European ally on whose territory a war was being fought, a Soviet penetration of even a hundred miles might well spell national disaster. It was not at all surprising that countries having such concerns should place a higher value on deterrence than on defense; they were interested more in magnifying the risks to the aggressor than in reducing the losses of the defenders.

George Ball, Under-Secretary of State, in trying to persuade Europeans that the Cuban crisis had proved the importance of superiority in conventional weapons, used arguments that were not very convincing. Europeans, in looking at the missile crisis, drew two lessons from the affair: "that they were faced with nuclear war without being consulted and that a settlement was made by the two nuclear powers without the participation of Cuba—the country which was most concerned but which possessed conventional weapons only." Europeans of an uncertain number, who were concerned with their bargaining position, believed that a small nuclear force might be more useful for bargaining purposes than a conventional force of somewhat increased size and power. Also, many hesitated to entrust their security for all time to an American president. They might be willing to do so with a specific individual; this did not mean that they were willing to give up their ability to defend themselves for the indefinite future.

Kissinger wrote: "Europeans, living on a continent covered with ruins testifying to the fallibility of human foresight, feel in their bones that history is more complicated than systems analysis. They have had too much experience with the nuances of interpretation that are possible with all formal commitments." He wanted very much to explain the European position to his American friends; a certain bluntness was required. He said: "Our frequently expressed outrage with the seeming European doubt about the reliability of our nuclear guarantee has blinded us to the fact that we have in effect accused our allies of being too irresponsible to be entrusted with the ultimate means for their protection. The asymmetry—to use a favorite word of the new strategic analysis—between the two kinds of distrust is pronounced. For if the Europeans are wrong, the chief penalty is a certain duplication of effort; while if they are right, our policy would seal their fate." Kissinger believed that the Americans exaggerated the uselessness of independent national European nuclear capabilities. Even a few hundred British and a few score French delivery vehicles would probably have some effect on Soviet calculations. The real fear of the Americans—despite all concealments—was not that the weapons would be useless but that they might pull the United States into a war it did not wish to enter. Kissinger saw no reason to believe that France or Great Britain would be more reckless than the United States; they would almost certainly be more careful. Also, their concern to develop their own nuclear programs, Kissinger wrote, showed no lack of interest in the alliance; as he explained: "Taking out fire insurance does not indicate a liking for fires. On the contrary, it may prevent a remote contingency from turning into an obsession and thus free energies for more constructive tasks."

Kissinger expected most Europeans in time to see the advantages of the American nuclear arsenal. Trying to bludgeon France into submission made no sense; the effort would almost certainly fail, and it would only advertise the extent of the United States' lack of confidence in an ally. The United States would do well to realize that not every loyal ally was necessarily easy or congenial. He contrasted de Gaulle's behavior at the time of the Cuban crisis with that of Fanfani in Italy; the implication was clear; de Gaulle, while infinitely more difficult, proved himself to be the more reliable ally. Kissinger acknowledged the crudeness of French strategic doctrine; they would learn in time. The real issue, however, was not what they did but whether the United States was ready to accept a certain measure of European independence in nuclear matters. If so, then European purposes could be related to those of the United States. Americans, Kissinger said, showed too great a preference for hegemony; de Gaulle's charge was not unjustified. Terms like "multilateralism" and "interdependence" generally concealed efforts to maintain United States control. The Europeans had probably overreacted, but the crisis within the Atlantic alliance could be resolved through American restraint.

The key element in the administration's nuclear policy was the idea of a NATO multilateral force composed of mixed crews. Kissinger reviewed the arguments advanced for a multilateral force and found them all wanting. It was said that this would prevent atomic weapons from falling into German hands. Kissinger questioned this; he wrote: "The multilateral force as now conceived may wind up by frustrating every member. If West Germany is seriously interested in acquiring strategic weapons, the multilateral force is apt to prove only an interim step and may turn out to be the easiest way of getting Germany into the nuclear business." Also, he expected that the expenses would be very heavy. He doubted if many European countries would be willing to contribute to such a force and also build up their conventional forces. The two policies, in his mind, were antithetical.

The principal reasons for his opposition, however, were political. He expected the cohesion of the alliance to be seriously weakened by the pressures the United States was imposing on Germany and others. France would probably be isolated as a result, but, in Kissinger's view, at much too great a price. The United States would increase the influence of the temporarily pliable states of Europe, but many of these were highly unstable. He feared that if Germany's power in the nuclear force grew too large, it would only push other states, including Britain and the Low Countries, toward neutralism. A policy that made Germany increasingly suspect to its NATO allies, in Kissinger's view, simply served Soviet purposes. It was not in Germany's interest to be put in the kind of position that the United States was preparing for her. If Germany was to make a greater contribution to the alliance, it ought not to be through her becoming the largest European contributor to a multilateral nuclear force.

Kissinger worried mostly about America's reputation for constancy and reliability. He wrote: "How can the most well-disposed governments follow our lead when our proposals are in a constant state of flux, moving from indifference to eager advocacy of a NATO force and from submarines to merchant ships all within two months?" He knew how difficult it was to reverse course, but he asked for the effort to be made. It was time for the United States to allow Europe a certain identity in the nuclear field. Kissinger wrote: "We have had two choices with respect to Europe's nuclear future. We could accept the British and French national efforts and encourage first a common Franco-British and ultimately a European program. Or else we could group the non-nuclear countries into a multilateral force more responsive to our notions of a single chain of command and an indivisible target system." He went on to say: "We have chosen the second course. The first is preferable by far." Kissinger could not conceive of a Europe that did not include France and Great Britain. He wrote: "Thus, instead of being hostile to the French nuclear program and, at best, indifferent to the British effort, we should use our influence to place them in the service of a European conception. This would also be the most reliable road to Atlantic partnership."

Kissinger saw the need also for greater political cohesion in the alliance. The alliance was endangered by bilateralism in diplomacy; it desperately required a political organism to define common objectives and to devise means to achieve them. Unless NATO could agree on such questions as Berlin, disarmament, and the test ban—and develop common negotiating positions—it would be impossible to devise a common military strategy. These problems needed to be seen in their proper perspective. The threat to the alliance, in Kissinger's view, came not from the outside—from Soviet pressure—but from internal differences representing different perspectives on a common problem.

Kissinger did not write again during Kennedy's lifetime. There is no record of what he thought of the test ban treaty, which was signed in the summer of 1963, and no published comment on what the administration was doing in Vietnam during the last autumn of Kennedy's life. Kissinger's Harvard life continued in its somewhat frenetic manner till that tragic November day in 1963 when his secretary rushed into his office to tell him that the President had been shot, and, a few moments later, that he had died. Kissinger mourned an unlucky man who had been cruelly treated by fate; he did not believe that a remarkable and gifted leader had been lost to the nation. Try as he would, Kissinger was never able to make Kennedy his hero. Many of Kennedy's friends and associates sensed the reserve that Kissinger felt about the President. By the standards that he used, Kennedy did not measure up to what he believed might properly be expected of someone said to be one of the great leaders of the twentieth century. An assassin's bullet did not lead him to change his verdict. It was not so much a negative judgment as a neutral one; he was simply unimpressed. He admired the energy and the *brio;* he doubted the substance of many of the accomplishments. He was genuinely curious as to how well Johnson would do; after a few weeks it became apparent that in the foreign affairs field—the only one that preoccupied Kissinger—Johnson was doing about as well as Kennedy had done. Kissinger was not surprised; the administration was too close to the 1964 elections to chart a new course.

When, in March 1964, Kissinger was asked by the Council on Foreign Relations to deliver a series of lectures in its Atlantic Policy Studies series, he chose to dwell on America's deteriorating relations with its European allies. Parts of the lectures appeared as an article in *Foreign Affairs* in July 1964, entitled "Coalition Diplomacy in a Nuclear Age." In April 1965, the lectures, in an expanded form, appeared as a book, *The Troubled Partnership*. It was, as its subtitle indicated, a reappraisal of the Atlantic alliance. Kissinger made no distinctions between policies pursued by Kennedy and those that had been initiated since his death. Most of Kennedy's foreign affairs and defense appointees had retained their places, and were continuing with policies that Kissinger found in varying degrees disappointing. The alliance, in his mind at least, had fallen into a very sorry state.

Kissinger opened his book with praise for those "far-sighted and bold measures starting with the Greek-Turkish aid program and the Marshall Plan," which had enabled Europe to recover from the devastations of six years of war. Every administration since that time had promoted European recovery, Atlantic cooperation, and joint defense. In recent years, however, the promise of greater cooperation had been marred by increasingly sharp disputes, and there was no longer substantial agreement on major issues. While some disagreement was to be expected, the existing differences seemed fundamental; Europeans were asking embarrassing questions about the validity of American conceptions. Americans who had helped rebuild Europe were now compelled to deal with a rebellious Continent. It was not altogether agreeable for them to have America's pre-eminence challenged. They had been accustomed to another kind of relation, and some were finding it difficult to adjust. European economic recovery and European integration, decolonization and the Cuban missile crisis had all contributed to the greater European restiveness and independence. As the threat from the Soviet Union had receded, it became increasingly difficult for the United States to maintain influence over its European allies. The difficulties were not caused by individuals, though they were often exploited by willful men. Rhetoric on both sides was excessive; there was a tendency to emphasize form over substance.

The great paradox of the nuclear age, according to Kissinger, was that power had never been greater, but also that it had never been less useful. War had supposedly become unthinkable, and diplomacy was asked to take over. The tasks of diplomacy, Kissinger said, had never been more difficult. Where there was no penalty for non-compliance, the incentives to reach agreement were minimal. The problem was made even more acute by the nature of modern weapons. Since their principal purpose was deterrence—making the would-be aggressor believe that there was no profit in going to war—if deterrence succeeded, there was no way to prove its success. Also, there was no way to give warning. As Kissinger wrote: "How does one threaten with solid-fuel missiles? As these are always in an extreme state of readiness, how does one demonstrate an increase in preparedness which has historically served as a warning?"

Allied relationships had suffered, Kissinger said, from the sheer complexity of the problems of the nuclear age. He wrote: "It is unlikely that even the most conscientious Allied leader can devote as many hours to a given problem as the American experts have had months to study it. And few of our Allies have the technical possibility to develop expertise of their own." While Europe had developed economically and politically, it remained militarily backward. Inevitably, the United States, with its monopoly of power and expertise, was resented, and the Americans did nothing to improve matters by treating all psychological and political problems as if they were purely technical. The United States made matters worse by choosing to treat the Atlantic world as a unit, ignoring its existence as a collection of separate sovereign states who did not all see political and military issues from the same perspective. By refusing to admit the possibility of many points of view, the United States only generated hostility.

France, for example, was not just like any other country. An understanding of France, Kissinger explained, had to start with an appreciation of her tragic experiences during the twentieth century. She lived with a nightmare—that she would again be obliged to stand alone. That, in Kissinger's view, went deeper than the personal feelings of any individual French leader. The same was true for Germany. In Germany, Kissinger explained, there is a "need to belong to something, to rescue some predictability out of chaos." The United States, by constantly changing its policies, created insuperable problems for such societies. Also, unilateral action on the part of the United States was deeply unsettling to states that did not need to be or care to be reminded of their impotence. France, Kissinger wrote, exaggerated her differences with the United States. Other countries concealed theirs, but they existed. Only a close association of all the nations in the Atlantic community could create the kind of stability that the international system required.

Europeans were themselves divided on both the necessity and the utility of supranational institutions. The smaller countries, together with Germany and Italy, seemed receptive to the idea of supranational institutions; France and Great Britain, with their long traditions of independence, were less interested. Kissinger, recognizing that European economic recovery had diminished Europe's interest in the American political experience, knew also that the end of empire had reduced its interest in playing a world role. Within a purely European frame, the nation-state seemed to be a more than adequate institutional form. Also, the idea that economic unity would necessarily lead to political unity had simply not been confirmed by experience.

Kissinger questioned the unexamined American assumption that a united Europe would generally agree with the United States on most basic issues. There was no historical precedent for such agreement. Kissinger wrote: "A separate identity has usually been established by opposition to a dominant power: the European sense of identity is unlikely to be an exception to this general rule—its motive could well be to insist on a specifically European view of the world." He thought that this would be particularly true when a European sense of identity could "no longer be nourished by fear of the U.S.S.R." The United States would be wise to prepare itself for European challenges to its hegemony, which might well prove to be the price the United States paid for European unity. Most Americans, Kissinger wrote, acted as if there would be no price to pay; European unity would come as a free gift.

Americans sometimes gave the impression that they had resigned themselves to waiting for de Gaulle to withdraw from the political arena; Kissinger called that not a policy but an evasion. De Gaulle was, for Kissinger, an "illusionist," concerned principally with making France believe it was strong. That was not, in his view, a mean aspiration. A country that had been on the verge of civil war three times between 1958 and 1962 might easily have been dismissed by others. Why should such a society be taken seriously? France's collapse in 1940 was not so much military as moral. The country knew, though it did not always say so, that it had come through World War II largely because of the efforts of others. The two decades of frustrating colonial war that followed had done nothing to improve the national morale; a feeling of self-confidence was not generated by such experience. Kissinger wrote: "Though de Gaulle often acts as if opposition to United States policy were a goal in itself, his deeper objective is pedagogical: to teach his people and perhaps his continent attitudes of independence and self-reliance." There was no point in ignoring the substantial differences between de Gaulle's vision of the world and that of most American leaders. Kissinger said: "Where United States spokesmen stress the concept of partnership, de Gaulle tends to emphasize the idea of equilibrium. Many United States officials assert that all disputes can be settled by talking things over in a 'community spirit.' To de Gaulle, sound relationships depend less on a personal attitude than on a balance of pressures and the understanding of the relation of forces. If these are correctly calculated, negotiations can be successful. If not, goodwill cannot serve as a substitute."

Kissinger believed that de Gaulle was bound to clash with Americans because he operated "in a different time-frame." The United States, as leader of the alliance, was always concerned with solving immediate problems; de Gaulle was considerably more interested in events that might occur in ten or fifteen years. Being confident about American protection in the immediate future, he looked ahead to the time when another generation of American leaders would govern and when their first concern might not be Europe. He did not pretend to know the future as so many Americans did. Kissinger recalled that Churchill had once acted very much as de Gaulle did, trying to introduce safeguards for the future; American leaders had dismissed Churchill as a shortsighted nationalist. Because of the more intimate ties that bound the United States to Britain, the differences never came into the open; they existed. De Gaulle, by insisting that European unity be achieved through a confederation of states rather than through supranational institutions, made many Americans believe that this was a transparent design for establishing French hegemony in Europe. Kissinger admitted that it was difficult to know what de Gaulle's real designs were, but if hegemony was de Gaulle's aim, Kissinger wrote, he had taken a strange road to achieve it. A Europe composed of sovereign states could be dominated—if, indeed, that was at all possible—through moral leadership only. The other European states, Kissinger explained, were "not likely to be so blind to their interests or so unsure of themselves as to refrain from casting their veto" if they disagreed with French policy.

The United States preference for supranationality reflected its own greater familiarity with federal institutions; also, Kissinger added, it probably reflected American ambivalence about European unity. While the United States favored European unity, it guarded rather jealously its special relations with several European states, and had no wish to see its dominance challenged, least of all in the defense field. De Gaulle deeply resented such limitations on Europe's independence. His purpose was to have Europe articulate its own defense policy, and then treat with the United States as a powerful and independent entity. The Nassau agreement offended him precisely because he saw it as another American device for imposing its will on European allies. He did not welcome the assigning of specific military tasks to France; that, in his mind, placed the security of France in the hands of others. Integration, in his view, led "to an abdication of responsibility and a sense of impotence." It was more important, he thought, to integrate the French army into French society —given everything that had happened in the preceding several decades —than it was to integrate the French army into NATO.

Americans, incensed with de Gaulle, condemned him for his distrust of the United States, and lectured him on his ignorance of the fundamentals of nuclear strategy. Kissinger took a very different position; he saw certain analogies between de Gaulle's analysis and that of McNamara; only in their solutions did they differ markedly. McNamara, believing that NATO depended on a division of labor, wanted French resources to be spent largely on conventional arms. De Gaulle, interested in France's identity, was not nearly so much concerned with the technical aspects of strategy as he was with the political problem of choice. The Americans, interested principally in a central control over nuclear weapons, believed this to be crucial in the event of general war. De Gaulle cared deeply about the conduct of day-to-day diplomacy. McNamara worried mostly about strategic options; de Gaulle worried mostly about political options. De Gaulle, as late as 1961, proposed a global directorate composed of the United States, Great Britain, and France; when the United States rejected that suggestion, saying it could not choose one European state to speak for all the others, the possibility of a "wider forum" was thrown away. It was only after 1961, Kissinger noted, that the French leader stopped urging this device and began to speak of the importance of a united Europe that would receive a respectful hearing from both the United States and the Soviet Union.

Kissinger did not suggest that the change in de Gaulle's policy resulted simply from a rebuff at the hands of the United States. When de Gaulle proposed the directorate, the dangers of war with the Soviet Union were very real; de Gaulle was trying to assure Europe of American support if war came. After 1961, when the Soviet threat was considerably reduced, de Gaulle began to think of another kind of Europe—of a Europe from the Atlantic to the Urals. He looked forward to the day when Russia ceased to be ideologically Communist and became national. This, in Kissinger's mind, was not so different from what four American postwar administrations had thought to be a prerequisite for resolving outstanding difficulties. Kissinger thought it ironical that the United States and France, for all their insistence on their disagreements, were at one in thinking that the possibilities for meaningful negotiation would be greatly improved when there was a basic transformation within the Soviet Union. Both looked for such a change and confidently expected it. Each wanted to be the principal spokesman for the West when the change came.

Each had very distinctive notions about the nature of a stable international order. The United States, Kissinger wrote, believed that peace and stability were "natural," that crises were caused by personal ill will and not by objective conditions, and that twentieth-century tensions were produced by unreasonable Communist leaders. If a favorable political climate could be created, there would be an atmosphere of trust; excellent personal relations could then be expected to produce the change of heart that would make agreement possible. De Gaulle saw matters very differently; he took a historical view of the problem. Peace, in his mind, was not a final settlement, "but a new, perhaps more stable, balance of forces." Tension was caused not by individual leaders but by the dynamics of the system. He saw internal instability as the distinguishing characteristic of Communist leadership groups; Communists were constantly trying to divert attention by engaging in foreign adventures. Since Russian expansionism grew out of internal instability, and not out of genuine grievances, their aggressions could not be ignored. Since the internal Soviet pressures would persist, providing constant incentives for new demands, a certain instability in the international system had to be looked for. De Gaulle opposed British and American plans for "exploratory" conversations with the Soviets on Berlin principally because he could see no point in these conversations. If the Soviets sincerely wanted peace, they had only to desist from making new threats. He felt much the same way about the continuing disarmament talks in Geneva; they were certain to lead nowhere.

Kissinger saw a significant difference also in the way the United States and France looked on Communist China. Behind the differences in policy, he argued, were fundamental philosophical differences. De Gaulle worried very little about the "intentions" of states. He knew that the Soviet Union was strong while Communist China was weak; it made good sense to build up China as a competitor to the Soviet Union in the Communist world. Also, de Gaulle's attention was generally focused on Europe. There China posed no threat whatever; the Soviet Union was a very real threat. It was reasonable for the French leader to be more indulgent with respect to China.

De Gaulle refused to believe that peace could be achieved through a personal reconciliation of heads of state; there was only one road to peace; it was the establishment of a more stable equilibrium. Believing that France could play a major role in creating such an equilibrium, he criticized the United States for trying to deal directly with the Soviet Union over the heads of France and the rest of Europe. Kissinger found a certain consistency in de Gaulle's views, and refused to see them as cynical or disingenuous. He had no patience with those who insisted that it was impossible to deal with de Gaulle, and that the only reasonable policy was to wait for his withdrawal from the political scene.

Kissinger was also aware of de Gaulle's failings, and made no attempt to conceal his misgivings about the French President's "abrupt tactics" and "imperious style," not to speak of his "excessive rationalism"—an attribute few Americans thought to associate with the French President. Most Americans saw him as a romantic, trying to recapture a lost French dominance. Kissinger saw him as an extreme rationalist, who failed to understand the sensibilities of others. This, in his view, was his greatest weakness. When he claimed to speak for the whole of Europe, he spoke mostly for his French compatriots, and not for all of them. He alienated other Europeans, Kissinger said, by his "excessive rationalism and unilateral tactics."

Kissinger found it ironical that a man who desperately sought European unity allowed himself to be represented abroad as a nationalist who cared only about France. Kissinger wrote: "By evoking so many memories of authoritarian rule, de Gaulle has polarized the discussion within Europe in a manner that makes it next to impossible to come to grips with the substance of his thought. A strong Europe was bound to present a challenge to American leadership. But by couching this challenge so woundingly, de Gaulle has spurred American self-righteousness rather than the objective re-examination of Atlantic relationships which the situation demands." Kissinger believed that history would judge de Gaulle's conceptions—as distinct from his style—superior to those of his critics. This, however, did not alter the fact that he had failed to realize his objectives. His style defeated him, and his ideas were never given a fair hearing. There was not very great likelihood that de Gaulle's concepts would be followed by those who came after him. Kissinger wrote: "Great men build truly only if they remember that their achievement must be maintained by the less gifted individuals who are likely to follow them. A structure which can be preserved only if there is a great man in each generation is inherently fragile. This may be the nemesis of de Gaulle's success."

Kissinger wondered whether de Gaulle had not exaggerated what any state in France's position could do. He had done well to raise France's sights and to insist on France's rights vis-à-vis the United States, but there were limits to assertions of this kind. France was not the equal of the United States in power, and in any contest between them, France was bound to lose. Neither country had an interest in pursuing the quarrel, but leaders on both sides were being pushed to do so. Kissinger wrote: "The irony of the Franco-American rivalry is that de Gaulle has conceptions greater than his strength, while United States power has been greater than its conceptions."

This, for Kissinger, was the true tragedy of the situation. Even with all the talented men who had joined the Kennedy administration in 1961 and who had stayed on with Johnson, the foreign policy conceptions of American leaders were not adequate to the opportunities. Kissinger cared little about de Gaulle's reputation—history would attend to that—but he cared immensely that the alliance was threatened by passion and misunderstanding. De Gaulle bore some of the responsibility for what had happened; Kissinger's chief concern was to instruct Americans who persisted in believing that the French President was the enemy. The casualty of any policy based on that misconception, Kissinger warned, would not be de Gaulle but Atlantic unity. Kissinger wrote: "Either the 'American' or the 'French' concept of Atlantic relationship might have succeeded. Competing as they do—with no comprehension by one side of the real intentions of the other—they may bring on what each side professes to fear most: a divided, suspicious Europe absorbed once again in working out its ancient rivalries." Then, in a characteristic comment, which recalled what he had written as a young graduate student, Kissinger added: "Tragedy, to many Americans at least, is to find oneself thwarted in what is ardently desired. But there is another and perhaps more poignant tragedy, that of fulfilling one's desires and then finding them empty."

Kissinger thought the American-French rivalry symptomatic of a general lack of understanding by prominent Americans of what their true interests in Europe were. France was not the only mysterious country for Americans; Germany seemed equally puzzling. Again, the difficulty originated in an innocence about Germany's twentieth-century experience. Kissinger wrote: "Every German over fifty years of age has lived through three revolutions. He has known four different regimes, each claiming to be morally antithetical to its predecessor. He has seen Germany lose two world wars and has experienced two catastrophic inflations. Every German over thirty-five has witnessed the trauma of the Nazi period, of World War II and of the post-war collapse." Germany became prosperous, Kissinger said, after it lost its national, political, and territorial integrity. The country's leaders lacked assurance; they worried constantly that they would be deserted by their allies. Kissinger believed that Adenauer's great achievement, like de Gaulle's, stemmed from a profound understanding of the psychological needs of the citizens of his country. Understanding Germany's problem, Adenauer tried to give the country a stake in something larger than itself. Kissinger wrote of the man whom his enemies called the Chancellor of the Allies: "He realized that Germany was too exposed geographically and too vulnerable psychologically and politically to be able to sustain a very active policy. He understood that a divided and rootless country, viewed with suspicion and fear, would be excessively tempted by either nationalism or neutralism, or both, if forced to undertake an autonomous foreign policy. The fabric of German political life might not withstand the pressures inherent in such a course."

It was only when United States policy on Berlin threatened what Adenauer conceived to be vital German interests that he "renewed his always strong tendency for close associations with France." The Franco-German Treaty of Collaboration of January 1963, Kissinger explained, was a further stage in Germany's continuing concern to secure "the moral and physical backing of a senior partner." Kissinger treated Adenauer as another European illusionist; he thought that Adenauer's "most notable achievement was to bring about the optical illusion that conditions in the Federal Republic were as firm and stable as his own policy."

Kissinger knew that this was not the case. For twenty years after the war, the country was engaged principally in physical reconstruction. Beginning in 1961, it was shaken by successive crises: Khrushchev's threats and the development of Anglo-American negotiating tactics to meet them; the Berlin Wall; de Gaulle's European policy and the United States reaction to it; American pressure for greater diplomatic flexibility. Many influential people in the United States and Great Britain were prepared in 1961 to accept new rules for access to Berlin in exchange for an acceptance of the permanent division of Germany. They thought this "a small price to pay for a promise of stability." What these people did not recognize, Kissinger explained, was how such an agreement would upset the domestic equilibrium of the Federal Republic. One of the reasons the Soviet Union wanted to secure Western acceptance of the status quo was precisely that it knew what a shock this would give to the Federal Republic.

The Kennedy administration, according to Kissinger, showed no great adeptness in its handling of either France or Germany. Nor, for that matter, did it know how to handle its closest ally, Great Britain. Kissinger believed that Britain, with a unique opportunity to lead Europe immediately after the war, missed its chance entirely. According to Kissinger, "Britain could have had the leadership of Europe for the asking," and did not even know that the opportunity existed. When it finally recognized that there was such a possibility, it agonized over whether it ought to remain faithful to the Commonwealth, maintain its "special relation" with the United States, or embark on a new adventure in Europe. Unwilling to choose, Britain tried to do all three. Kissinger was not much impressed with the performance. He refused to believe that Britain's exclusion from the Continent could be attributed to the decision of an aging French leader who recalled World War II slights. Some said that Britain lacked an identity; Kissinger did not agree. Britain had an identity; it was precisely her identity that prevented her from entering wholeheartedly into Europe. When, after the early success of the Common Market, Britain became interested in Europe, her interest was not in a supranational or integrated Europe but in a Europe similar to the one in which de Gaulle believed. The British opposed supranationalism not so much for ideological as for pragmatic reasons. The Americans were less offended by the British position than by the French; they were pleased by the implied promise that any commitment Britain made to Europe would do nothing to alter its "special relationship" with the United States. The British were more subtle than the French in the way that they handled the United States. Kissinger wrote: "Britain never contests an abstract or theoretical point. It almost never disagrees openly with fundamental American policies. Instead, British policy usually concedes us the liturgy while seeking to shape its implementation through intensive formal and informal consultation. . . . Whatever the 'reality' of the 'special relationship,' Britain has tried hard to give the impression to the outside world that American policy is strongly influenced, if not guided, by London."

While Britain probably exaggerated its influence in Washington, Kissinger wrote, the United States exaggerated Britain's pliability. He did not think it preordained that Britain would be America's spokesman in the Common Market. In fact, he said: "One ironic result of Britain's entry into Europe might well have been that Europe would henceforth have conducted de Gaulle's policies with British methods." That was mere conjecture; for the time being, Britain was barred from the Common Market, and some of the responsibility could be put on the United States. The cancellation of Skybolt, Kissinger wrote, produced an uproar in Great Britain which "had little to do with the technical merits of Skybolt or with the strategic posture of Great Britain." The issue was political; successive British governments had expended ten billion dollars to create an independent nuclear deterrent. The government's life was endangered, and, in such a crisis, the "technical merits of arguments" mattered very little.

There had been endless argument about whether the Nassau agreement did in fact influence de Gaulle's decision on Britain's application to the Common Market. Many said that it was simply de Gaulle's pretext. Kissinger believed it a contributory cause; it demonstrated conclusively that Britain thought first and foremost of its relationship with the United States. It was possible that de Gaulle decided the issue even before Nassau; if, Kissinger wrote, he was still considering the matter at the time, it could only have pushed him toward rejecting Britain's application. Kissinger thought the British had been remarkably maladroit; he wrote: "Britain had received an abrupt rebuff on the Skybolt issue. Yet it never seems seriously to have considered that it might use this opportunity for closer cooperation with its European partners in the military field. Instead, it concluded an agreement with the United States without even consulting France, the other nuclear power, and it developed a nuclear plan for NATO without the participation of its prospective members in the Common Market." The United States, however unwittingly, had contributed to Britain's discomfiture. Its own preferred scheme, envisaging an Atlantic partnership based on friendly relations between a united Europe, including Great Britain, and the United States had to be shelved. Kissinger never said that Skybolt and Nassau created the situation; only that it helped de Gaulle justify, and not to himself alone, what he had done. The United States responded with a whole series of frantic efforts to isolate France. What had started out as a quarrel over the internal structure of Europe and the role of individual European states within the Atlantic alliance risked upsetting elaborate alliance structures that had been painfully constructed. The Americans did not gain what they were looking for: there was no new Atlantic union, only a stalemate. Kissinger did not point a finger at the Kennedy administration, but his meaning was clear enough.

Whatever the ineptness of diplomacy after 1961, it was nothing as compared with the inadequacies of American strategic doctrine. Kissinger was mordant on that point. He showed great vehemence in his denunciation of the Multilateral Force (MLF). Kissinger wondered how it had been possible for the MLF to become the principal United States defense proposal in NATO for almost two years. He knew that but for de Gaulle's veto of British membership in the Common Market it might not have surfaced at all. Once the government became committed to the MLF, it had to find reasons to support it. Some argued as if the issue of nuclear control was the fundamental problem of the alliance. There were said to be only three possible solutions: continued American hegemony, declared to be impossible; nuclear proliferation, said to be politically divisive and strategically dangerous; and the MLF, which would "give the Federal Republic equal status while supplying a new impetus to European integration and strengthening Allied cohesion." Kissinger thought that the MLF emphasized the wrong problem, and was certainly the wrong answer to the real problem.

He believed that there was no military necessity for the MLF; the MLF was introduced to resolve a political problem. It was supposed to prevent nuclear proliferation by providing a framework within which America's nuclear allies could abandon their nuclear programs, while at the same time satisfying Germany's nuclear ambitions. It failed in the first respect: neither France nor Great Britain was at all disposed to give up its nuclear forces. As for Germany, Kissinger saw no nuclear problem there; the United States invented it. Even if Germany had been determined to have nuclear weapons—and there was no evidence to suggest that she was—the United States' solution made no sense. The problem within the alliance had never been strategic; it was political. Kissinger wrote: "There is something incongruous about NATO's absorption in technicalities of mixed-manning while it lacks a common policy toward the Communist world, flounders dividedly in the former colonial areas and has yet to concert a strategic doctrine. To devote so much energy to the problem of who pushes the button in the remote contingency of nuclear war while neglecting the issues which confront the Alliance daily comes close to being escapism."

Kissinger's opposition to the MLF reflected his conviction that political unity had to precede nuclear integration; the great need of the alliance was for a coordinating body that could attend to certain of the unsolved problems, including East-West relations, strategic doctrine, trade policy, arms control, and relations with the emerging nations. A political body to coordinate NATO policy and manage crises was far more urgent than the MLF. If, as some argued, it was impossible for such a body to function effectively, then there was no hope for nuclear multilateralism. Kissinger wrote: "Nations that cannot agree on common negotiating positions are not likely to be able to concert a common strategy for an apocalypse."

Kissinger recognized that opposition to the MLF in Europe had grown so strong that it could never be adopted without major modifications. The question, therefore—for him, at least—was what lessons might be learned from the whole experience. In his view, the most important was that political problems could not be resolved with technical expedients. Confronted with a political and philosophical challenge from de Gaulle, American policy-makers responded "by staking everything on a scheme of nuclear control which they had previously treated with indifference." They wasted two years in negotiating over mechanical details. Why had that happened? According to Kissinger, "because one small group in the government had become so deeply committed to the MLF that it acted as a lobby rather than an organ for calmly weighing alternatives." Because a relatively small group in the State Department pushed very hard, many of the allies imagined that the whole government supported the proposal and that resistance was impossible. Such support had never existed, not even within the United States government.

Kissinger thought that the whole debate had been "more conducive to self-righteousness than to sober thought." It had not achieved the purposes intended, and had only served to make the United States ridiculous in the eyes of many Europeans. The United States had not thought through its position before it moved. In Kissinger's view, the administration committed the prestige of the country before it knew what it wanted to achieve.

Until the Americans understood what the European concern was—and that it had to do with securing a kind of insurance against unforeseeable events—there was no hope of a meaningful dialogue. American strategic doctrine sought to prepare the alliance for a contingency—the outbreak of general nuclear war—which many of the allies considered "tantamount to their end as functioning societies."

Kissinger saw no merit whatever in the MLF. While he recognized a certain merit in the idea of a European nuclear force, he cautioned the United States against lobbying to secure that objective. It was not in the American interest, Kissinger wrote, to influence internal European arrangements; it was quite another matter if it sought to influence Atlantic relationships. This was a none too subtle hint that the United States would be well advised to allow Europeans to develop their unity without constant intervention (or instruction) from the Americans.

Kissinger's recommendations were very precise. In addition to creating within NATO "a political mechanism to plan long-term policy, to manage crises and to control the nuclear policy of the Alliance," which would operate through the establishment of an Executive Committee of the NATO Council, he hoped that the committee would be advised by senior officers from the United States, France, Great Britain, and the Federal Republic. The existing strategic nuclear forces within NATO, including that part of the United States force earmarked for the defense of Europe, needed to be coordinated in such a way as to make possible the creation of an eventual European nuclear force. The important thing was to bring the alliance together again. That, Kissinger insisted, called for French participation and collaboration. While he admitted that the French had done something to create the disarray within the alliance, the problem was to stop the theoretical quarreling and to move forward toward common policies. Kissinger believed that there was sufficient common interest within NATO for significant agreements to be reached.

Because NATO had been so preoccupied with the question of the Multilateral Force, it had neglected other crucial questions, including the role and control of tactical nuclear weapons. Kissinger, having never accepted the Gilpatric thesis that tactical nuclear war would inevitably lead to general nuclear war, believed that the thousands of nuclear weapons on the Continent could be used for two purposes: to force a standstill of an initial onslaught; to inflict sufficient punishment on an aggressor to force him into negotiations. To achieve these ends, the tactical nuclear forces on the Continent needed to have their mission redefined, their vulnerability reduced, and their deployment changed. Since it was highly improbable that NATO would raise sufficient troops for a purely conventional defense of Europe, planning had to take account of that fact. Kissinger knew that no arrangement of military forces would resolve the problems of the alliance, which were essentially political. The challenge to NATO, he insisted, was to see whether it could develop "common purposes" and "devise a political structure that combines community with flexibility."

While the problems of nuclear control were important, they were secondary, in Kissinger's mind, to the problem of the future of Germany. Yet the first, Kissinger said, engaged many influential minds in the government; the second, by comparison, was neglected. Kissinger thought that this was no accident; he wrote: "Nuclear control, for all its complexity, has the advantage of seeming concrete. Solutions permit technical analysis. Absorption in this problem can therefore serve as an escape from issues that are intangible and much less amenable to mechanical remedies."

He believed that the alliance would be severely tested in the decade ahead because of the German problem. He was not sanguine about how well the alliance would do in handling the issue. There was an almost permanent interest in finding excuses for believing that a real "thaw" had taken place in the Soviet Union and that the times were propitious for negotiations.

The question of whether or not the Soviet Union had changed was endlessly debated. Also, a great deal of time was given over to considering how relations with individual Soviet leaders might be improved. Kissinger found all such discussion silly. Clearly, Soviet society was changing, and would continue to change. No one argued against reducing tensions. The problem was how to achieve that objective. He worried about the intransigence that he found in the Communist world and that he attributed to its leadership and its ideology. The hazards of political life in the Soviet Union were well known. Given those hazards, it was not at all surprising that suspicion and conspiracy should be common. A legitimate system of political succession had never developed; power went "to those skillful and ruthless enough to seize and hold it." Kissinger wrote: "Only an enormous desire for power can impel a man to enter such a career. Anyone succeeding in Communist leadership struggles must be single-minded, unemotional, unsentimental and dedicated. Nothing in the experience of Soviet leaders would lead them to prize peace as an end or to accept protestations of personal goodwill at face value. Their own career—indeed their survival—has been advanced by the ability to dissemble. . . . Suspiciousness is therefore inherent in the domestic position of Soviet leaders. It is unlikely that their attitude toward the outside world is more benign. There is no reason for them to treat foreign statesmen more gently than their own colleagues or to expect more consideration from them."

Marxist ideology, in his opinion, while unimportant in determining daily actions, shaped the Communist view of reality. Marxism guaranteed an ultimate victory; it provided legitimacy and made international Communist discipline possible. It stressed "objective" factors—social and economic conditions, the nature of the economic process, the class struggle—above "subjective" factors, including the personal convictions of individual leaders. In negotiations, Communists believed only in making "concessions" to reality, never in making "concessions" to individuals. They had no interest in the give-and-take of the bargaining process, so congenial to Western negotiators. Their attitude toward these negotiators, Kissinger wrote, was not too different from that of "Western psychiatrists toward their patients: no matter what is said, they think that they understand their Western counterpart better than he understands himself." This, Kissinger believed, was one of the reasons why personal diplomacy, even at the highest levels, so rarely succeeded with the Soviets.

Kissinger believed that peaceful coexistence was never advocated for its own sake; it was "justified primarily as a tactical device to overthrow the West at minimum risk." What restraints, then, did the Soviets operate under? First, the power of modern weapons. Soviet leaders knew the hazard of pushing beyond a certain point; Kissinger wrote: "The West would have to behave extraordinarily foolishly before the Soviets risk an overt military challenge." He went on to say: "It is significant that one of the principal arguments advanced by Soviet leaders on behalf of peaceful co-existence is that nuclear war is too dangerous. It is in the West's interest to see to it that it remains so." A second factor that restrained them was the instability of their own leadership group. Where there were no clear lines of succession and no easy ways to resolve internal differences, there were bound to be difficulties. Also, Communist countries found it extremely difficult to deal with each other. In Marxist theory, there ought not to have been any differences between them; in fact, there were many. The result, Kissinger said, was that "Communist leaders try to deal with disputes among Communist states as they conduct their own internal struggles: by seeking first to ostracize and then to destroy their opponents. But among sovereign states, such tactics cause disputes to harden into irremediable schisms. Each schism, in turn, demonstrates that a supposedly universal orthodoxy can be interpreted in various ways. This must, in time, erode confidence in the universality of Communist ideology as well as the discipline of the world Communist movement." De-Stalinization, the Sino-Soviet split, and the ousting of Khrushchev all created immense strains in the Communist world. The revelations concerning Stalin raised embarrassing questions on how a Socialist system could have spawned such a leader. The Sino-Soviet split raised the issue of whether a movement that claimed to represent a universal truth could tolerate two centers of orthodoxy. Kissinger believed that the rift might "be patched up from time to time," but he thought its underlying cause to be "beyond repair." Once Moscow's doctrinal infallibility was challenged by such an adversary, there was no possibility of going back to the old order.

Khrushchev's fall led to greater autonomy in the whole Communist world. Kissinger believed that among the many consequences of two decades of Communist rule in Eastern Europe was an "intensified traditional nationalism." If the Soviets were temporarily more agreeable, it was not, he said, because a few individuals had "overcome the opposition of some unnamed Stalinists, but because conditions require it." Kissinger wondered what the West would try to use the *détente* for. Absolutely persuaded that it could be used, he hoped that the West would learn to conduct its negotiations without illusions. The Soviets might become difficult again at any time, and for any number of reasons. The temptations to bilateralism would be great. Each Western leader, wanting to appear a hero to his own people, would insist that his only concern was peace. Bilateral negotiations, Kissinger wrote, would be "suicidal" for the West; they would only stimulate new suspicions. The alliance had to develop a concrete program; individual members had to be willing to forgo certain short-term advantages. A united West, Kissinger wrote, would have extraordinary strength, given the disarray that existed in the Communist world. "Central to any long-term policy," he explained, was "some conception of the future of Germany."

Any plan for Germany's future, Kissinger wrote, had to respect the German desire for self-determination, the East European concern for security, and the Soviet concern that a united Germany not impair its own security. Kissinger proposed that the Western countries, including the Federal Republic, agree that unification, while remaining the ultimate objective, was not immediately attainable. Therefore, the object should be to have East Germany choose the form of government it preferred, with the Western Allies agreeing to recognize any government that emerged from free elections. A loose confederation would then be established between the two German states, but East Germany would be independent, neutral, and demilitarized. A commission of European neutrals would supervise the elections and would make certain that the demilitarization clauses were observed. After fifteen years, East Germany would hold a plebiscite to determine whether it wished to continue as a separate state in loose confederation with the Federal Republic or whether it preferred unification. Both German states would recognize the Oder-Neisse frontiers. Berlin would become the capital of East Germany and the seat of the organs of the German confederation. Soviet troops would be withdrawn from East Germany, and "foreign troops would retire a distance roughly equal to that between the Elbe and the Oder" in the Federal Republic. The number of West German troops in that area would be limited. The Federal Republic would renounce access to the ownership of nuclear weapons.

Kissinger saw many advantages in the plan. While it would defer unification for at least fifteen years, it would mean an end to the hostility between the two German states. The East European states would have the security of a divided Germany for at least another fifteen years and a permanently demilitarized line along their borders. The Berlin problem would be solved. There would be a "psychological" as well as a juridical solution of the problem of Germany's frontiers. The generation that had been expelled from Eastern Europe would have largely disappeared by the time that Germany was unified, if that indeed came to pass. Also, and of great importance, arms control agreements could be considered in a wholly new atmosphere. Kissinger recognized the price that would have to be paid for such an agreement. The Federal Republic would have to give up hopes of immediate unification. The Soviet Union would have to give up the hope of a Communist Germany. The East European states would have to stop acquiescing in the plans of their senior partner. The Western Allies would have to overcome their inertia and place the problem of Germany high on their agenda.

Kissinger had no illusions about the possibility of such a formula's being accepted. The long-term unity of Germany, he knew, rested in the unity of Europe. As the nation-state came to lose its significance, the nation-state would not be feared in the way that had been common. If a united Western Europe came into being, it would almost certainly, in Kissinger's view, become a magnet for the East European states. For this reason and for others, he deplored the divisions in the West, particularly the differences between the United States and France. The attempt to use Germany as a balance wheel was precarious; it ought to stop at once. The Federal Republic needed to have a stake in something greater than itself. Its future, Kissinger wrote, depended on two related policies of the West: "recognition of the psychological and political dilemmas of a divided country" and "the ability to make the Federal Republic part of a larger community." Kissinger believed these policies to be interdependent.

Coalition diplomacy was always difficult; consultation was not a panacea. It worked best when it was used to implement a consensus rather than to create one. The consultative machinery of the alliance could be improved, but there were distinct limits to what consultation could produce. Many American schemes for strengthening NATO depended on a structure that prevented any ally (except the United States) from acting autonomously. Kissinger saw this as a procedure that tended to convert allies into advisers, helping in America's own decision-making process. He doubted that these policies contributed to the long-term vitality of the alliance. Even in a purely domestic situation, the weight accorded specific advice reflected the competence of those who gave it. This was even more true in an international alliance of sovereign states. It was not enough to provide a forum; the forum needed to be one that stimulated and demanded responsible attitudes. If an ally was to inform itself so that it could make a responsible contribution, it had to feel that its contribution would make a difference. An alliance of sovereign states, Kissinger wrote, was not a debating club where members scored points with the leader.

Kissinger thought that "American policy has not always been sensitive to the psychological prerequisites for effective consultation." He wrote: "It generally holds that influence in the Alliance is apportioned as in a stock company: the partner with the largest number of shares in a common enterprise is supposed to have the greatest influence." Kissinger thought that this was too mechanical a measure. "In an alliance of sovereign states," he wrote, "a country's influence requires that its effort be considered essential and that its partners do not take it for granted." Americans tended to believe that individual European states did not possess the resources for a global policy; they imagined that Europe would have these resources when it became unified. When that happened, the United States and a united Europe would consult as equals. Americans also assumed that a united Europe would look at the world very much as the United States did. Kissinger questioned the assumption that a willingness to assume global responsibilities was in any way tied to available resources. The United States, he pointed out, enjoyed vast resources without assuming global responsibilities for a very long time. Many European states had large resources—larger than they had once had—but this did not lead them to seek a world role. Several had been traumatized by two world wars and decolonization and had no interest in sharing burdens; they were quite prepared for the United States to act alone. Kissinger thought very little of the conventional American distinction between "interest" and "responsibility"; the idea that the United States had "few national interests—in the narrow sense—outside our own territory" but was prepared to sacrifice itself and assume vast world responsibilities did not much impress him. He wrote: "Aside from the fact that our European Allies are likely to consider a 'disinterested' foreign policy as both mercurial and unsteady, the distinction misses the central point. The chief reason for the reluctance of most of our Allies to assume world responsibility is precisely that in the past decade they have been obliged to give up their global interests. Sharing our burdens would give impetus to Atlantic cooperation only if our Allies have the same view as we of what is at stake outside of Europe and if they believe that the United States would curtail its commitments but for their assistance. Neither condition is met today."

European unity, in short, was no cure for Allied disagreements. It might, in fact, only serve to magnify them. It was very probable that the United States would find itself increasingly involved in the Far East, in Southeast Asia, and in Latin America in the decades ahead; there was no reason to expect America's European allies to become interested in those areas or to pretend to have a stake in them. Coalition diplomacy could not proceed on the basis of the United States making all the decisions, which others then ratified. Allied leaders prepared to play such a role, in Kissinger's view, would never be entirely reliable. Some measure of European autonomy in decision-making was a psychological necessity. He wrote: "A decade and a half of hegemony have accustomed us to believing that our views represent the general interest. The difficulty with which decisions are reached in our government produces temptations to turn Allied consultation into an effort to implement essentially American conceptions."

Europe had been "nurtured" and "protected" by the United States since the end of World War II. It was time to make "the transition from tutelage to equality." The United States needed to share responsibilities even more than it needed to share burdens. Some decline in American pre-eminence would occur, but the result might be a healthier relationship. The United States would do well to stop insisting on its "good intentions." No one was contesting those intentions. The controversy was generally over American style and the nature of the American commitment. In its perpetual search for final answers, the United States too often used abstract models in which nations were interchangeable entities. American pragmatism made the country willing to try everything once; the result was an endless search for novelty. Bureaucratic governmental procedures made it easier to be concerned with the immediate than with the long-term. "Reluctant as we may be to admit it," Kissinger wrote, "we could benefit from a counterweight to discipline our occasional impetuosity and to supply historical perspective to our penchant for abstract and 'final' solutions." Kissinger saw such a counterweight in Europe. He hoped that it would be used.

Americans had talked for so long about a real partnership being possible only between equals that Kissinger felt compelled to ask whether this was indeed true. He wondered whether the idealized picture of a United Europe, propagated by integrationists on both sides of the Atlantic, tended to present too idyllic a prospect. These partisan voices took for granted that political integration could be achieved as easily as economic integration; it almost seemed as if the second guaranteed the first. Kissinger thought that they were wrong. As Europe recovered economically, political confidence grew; inevitably, this produced in certain countries a strengthening of the national state. De Gaulle, in Kissinger's view, had confused the debate about the future of Europe in at least two ways: he had made the test over federalism or confederalism seem a judgment on himself; also, because some of the most ardent pro-Britain elements believed in a federal Europe, which was as unacceptable in London as it was in Paris, anti-Gaullism had been used as a way of proposing schemes that they knew he would veto.

The United States wanted to believe that it could have European unity and still have a docile and obedient set of allies. The American aim was a closely integrated Atlantic community under American leadership. This was not attainable; a difference in perspective was inevitable. A wise policy, Kissinger wrote, would be one that tried to mitigate the impact of that difference. British participation in Europe was mandatory; so long as she remained outside, efforts would be made to isolate her or to isolate France. The United States would do well, Kissinger suggested, to "leave the internal evolution of a united Europe to the Europeans and use its ingenuity and influence in devising new forms of *Atlantic* cooperation." Americans had no reason to peddle their federal solutions in Europe. If Europe opted for supranationalism, well and good, but the decision had to be made there. The United States, if it consulted its interests, would get along with any kind of Europe, including one that was confederal. The United States would do well to start talking again with de Gaulle; if it was able to get on with the Soviet Union, there ought to be no difficulty in consulting with a traditional ally. The final goal ought to be an Atlantic commonwealth; it would not come quickly, but it was no less necessary for its being a long-range objective. The challenge to the West, Kissinger wrote, is "whether it can move from the nation-state to a larger community and draw from this effort the strength for another period of innovation."

Kissinger had been very circumspect. He made great efforts to avoid a frontal assault on the Kennedy-Johnson administration. Yet, if one reviews what he said, is it possible to ignore his disappointment with the performance? So much had been tried; so little had been done. Kissinger said all this, *sotto voce*.

6

The Johnson Years
Silence and Reflection

For well over a decade, Henry Kissinger had written prolifically on questions that dealt with strategy and foreign policy—most frequently in their contemporary setting, occasionally in a more historical frame. Then, in 1965, there was what now appears to be a sudden damming up of this productivity. Although *The Troubled Partnership* was published in April 1965, it was completed many months before Johnson defeated Goldwater in 1964. Between the time that Johnson achieved his massive victory in November 1964 and his decision, announced in March 1968, not to seek another term as president, Kissinger wrote less than he had at any time in the preceding decade. During this period, he published only two major new articles. There were no new books. Aside from an edited collection of essays on strategic issues and a few minor pieces, based on previously published materials, written mostly for foreign newspapers and journals, this was the whole of Kissinger's published intellectual output in almost four years.

How is one to account for this falling off in productivity? A biographer, unfamiliar with the situation and approaching it with no preconceived notions, would probably start by searching for the purely personal factors in Kissinger's life that might explain so sudden and precipitous a drop in publication. He would undoubtedly give some attention to the circumstances that led to the breakup of Kissinger's marriage and that made the early 1960s such a troubled time for him. He might even choose to dwell on Kissinger's difficulties in Washington early in the Kennedy administration. He would be puzzled, however, by the fact that neither of these circumstances contributed to an immediate falling off in productivity. As has been suggested, there was no significant decline during the Kennedy years. Kissinger, except for the period when he was most heavily engaged as a consultant to the National Security Council, was as prolific as he had ever been while Kennedy was in office.

How, then, is one to explain his silence during the Johnson years? Did he have new responsibilities at Harvard that consumed his energies? There were none that made a significant difference in his life. In fact, an argument could be made that he enjoyed greater freedom at Harvard during the years 1964–1968 than he did at any time after the early 1950s. In 1965–1966, he was on sabbatical leave; while he remained in Cambridge, spending some of his time preparing a textbook that he had contracted to write, he had no other obligations. For the first time in many years he was free to read whatever he pleased; he found himself returning to philosophical texts, and began to think of doing historical research. He turned to an early draft of a manuscript he had begun a decade earlier on Bismarck's foreign policy, and wondered whether he ought to complete it. He read extensively in diplomatic history. When he completed his duties with the International Seminar in August 1965, he knew that he had no further Harvard obligations for almost a year. He was invited to visit South Vietnam by Henry Cabot Lodge, whom he knew and liked, and who was then serving as the American ambassador in Saigon. Kissinger's knowledge of Vietnam was minuscule; Lodge believed that even a very brief visit would give him some sense of the country, and of America's political and military problems there.

Kissinger remained in Vietnam from October 15 to November 2, 1965. He met with all the principal South Vietnamese leaders, including Generals Thieu and Ky, the generals commanding the First and Second Corps, and the chiefs of Kien Giang and Vinh Long provinces. In addition, he met heads of governmental ministries, religious leaders, both Buddhist and Catholic, and a number of South Vietnamese politicians who had held high office in the past. He visited both Van Hanh University and the University of Hue. The Ambassador introduced him to many of those who were responsible for the vast American military effort in the country. He met with the principal army officers, and also with those responsible for CIA and AID operations. There were numerous briefings, and an opportunity to visit the countryside outside Saigon. Kissinger came away appreciating the meaninglessness of many of the phrases that American officials habitually used. A "secure area" was often secure only during daylight hours; a "pacified region" was sometimes pacified only on the wall map of the American official responsible for the operations. Kissinger reported his "findings" to the Ambassador. He kept his own journal, but never thought to publish or circulate it. Eighteen days in South Vietnam had not made him an "instant Vietnamese expert."

The rest of his sabbatical year passed almost too quickly. In the summer of 1966 he resumed his International Seminar obligations but broke them long enough to make another hurried trip to Saigon, again at Lodge's invitation. His visit in July 1966 lasted less than two weeks; between July 16 and July 29 he saw many of the same people he had met on his first visit. He went again to the provinces he had visited in the autumn and also to two others that he had not previously seen—Bien Hoa and Binh Dinh provinces. He talked with Generals Westmoreland, Lansdale, and Ewbank, and, of course, with many of the South Vietnamese officials whom he knew. His second visit confirmed many of his earlier judgments, but he realized better than ever that he had only scratched the surface of the problem in South Vietnam; he had no intention of writing about it.

In late September, he returned to his teaching at Harvard with new vigor and interest. He thoroughly revised his course, Government 180, Introduction to International Politics, and, for the first time since he began to lecture, felt satisfied with the response that he received from the undergraduates. He revamped his reading list, and introduced certain of the historical themes that had preoccupied him during his sabbatical year. His reputation for being an excellent teacher drew largely on favorable comment that he received during his last years at Harvard. His success in seminars was what it had always been—he excelled in small group discussions. These responsibilities, in no sense onerous, cannot explain the sudden falling off in his scholarly productivity. Nor can the decline be attributed to the time he spent receiving foreign guests, attending conferences both at home and abroad, or accepting public speaking engagements; such activities had never interfered with his writing before.

Could it be linked, then, to his agreeing to undertake secret negotiations—through French intermediaries—with the North Vietnamese? These peace initiatives, originally inspired by Pugwash, soon involved the United States government, particularly the Secretary of Defense, Robert McNamara. Kissinger handled all the negotiations with the two French emissaries who went to Hanoi. The mission failed in its purpose, but it gave Kissinger a new sense of the difficulties of the Vietnam situation. The negotiations occupied him throughout the summer of 1967. They explain his silence during that period; they do not account for his silence over four years.

Kissinger's silence cannot be explained by obligations of this kind or by a reticence he had never previously shown. He did not write for a very simple reason: he had nothing to say. Kissinger wrote so long as there was an American foreign policy to criticize. Whether it was the lame and in-

plomacy permitted a dialogue to take place between sovereign states precisely because these states shared a common concept of what was
permissible and just. Such conditions did not prevail in a revolutionary
age; discourse was made difficult; it was not always possible even to
know what the disagreement was about. As Kissinger explained, in such
periods "what seems most obvious to one side seems most problematic to
the other."

Kissinger believed that a society's perception of its foreign policy problems was intimately linked to its domestic structure and experience; the
mere determining of what "constitutes a problem and what criteria are
relevant in 'solving' it," he wrote, "reflects to a considerable extent the
domestic notions of what is just, the pressures produced by the decision-
making process, and the experience which forms the leaders in their rise
to eminence." Kissinger thought all three factors to be important, but he
placed particular emphasis on the last. Unless one understood the nature
of leadership in societies contending within a particular international
order, there was no possibility of understanding either the problems
posed, the arguments used, or the concessions made.

Repeating an idea he had insisted on much earlier in his scholarly career, Kissinger suggested that the statesman needed always to rely on conjecture in foreign affairs. He wrote: "When the scope for action is greatest, knowledge on which to base such action is small or ambiguous.
When knowledge becomes available, the ability to affect events is usually
at a minimum." To illustrate his point, he chose the example of Hitler; he
wrote: "In 1936, no one could know whether Hitler was a misunderstood
nationalist or a maniac. By the time certainty was achieved, it had to be
paid for with millions of lives." The need for conjecture, according to
Kissinger, was more imperative in a revolutionary period than at any
other time. In such periods, when institutions were disintegrating, a vision
of the future became mandatory. The question that Kissinger asked, implicitly and explicitly, was whether modern bureaucracies were capable
of generating such a vision of the future, or of accepting the necessity of
not interfering with leaders who aspired to do so.

In considering the influence of domestic affairs on foreign policy, Kissinger chose to dwell at length on two factors—administrative structure, which he virtually equated with bureaucracy, and the formative experience of leadership groups. Both were equally important. Kissinger
recognized that the hazards of the nuclear age gave new importance to
the problems of decision-making. Planning was generally recommended,
Kissinger wrote, because it was assumed that it made for greater predictability and therefore for greater objectivity. Both these qualities were
highly prized by bureaucracies, which were admirable instruments for
dealing with routine matters. When they dealt with these efficiently, Kis-

singer wrote, they liberated others to innovate or handle unexpected situations. It was when they did not handle their routine assignments well that problems were created for others. Bureaucracy, Kissinger wrote, "becomes an obstacle when what it defines as routine does not address the most significant range of issues or when its prescribed mode of action proves irrelevant to the problem." When this happened, top executives were required to intervene. The task of making the bureaucracy work could become so time-consuming that there was no opportunity to consider the merits of specific decisions. Also, in the quest for "objectivity," Kissinger wrote, ends and means were frequently confused; "Attention tends to be diverted from the act of choice—which is the ultimate test of statesmanship—to the accumulation of facts." Valuable time was lost, and when the apparatus was finally in a position to act, the opportunity to do something creative had vanished. All bureaucracies, Kissinger explained, were subject to this danger; it was as true of a bureaucracy operating in a highly ideological political climate, like that of the Soviet Union, as it was of a bureaucracy operating in a more pragmatic setting, like the one that existed in the United States. In Kissinger's view, the hazards for bureaucracy in a pragmatic society were particularly great. In the United States, he wrote, "what passes for planning is frequently the projection of the familiar into the future." The more ideologically oriented bureaucracies also had their problems; in the Soviet Union, for example, "doctrine is institutionalized and exegesis takes the place of innovation."

Kissinger saw that the decision-making process might become so complex that achieving an agreement within the bureaucracy might begin to seem more important than the substance of the agreement itself. While many administrators were aware of the problem, and admitted its importance, few were able to do anything about it. Also, because constant lip service was paid to planning, planning staffs proliferated; too often, in Kissinger's view, the work of these planning staffs became "esoteric exercises," accepted only because everyone knew that nothing would follow from their acceptance. Planning staffs desperately wanted to be "useful"; this, Kissinger wrote, made them almost incapable of developing very novel conceptions. As he explained: "It is one thing to assign an individual or a group the task of looking ahead; this is a far cry from providing an environment which encourages an understanding for deeper historical, sociological, and economic trends." He went on to say: "The quest for objectivity creates a temptation to see in the future an updated version of the present. Yet true innovation is bound to run counter to prevailing standards. The dilemma of modern bureaucracy is that while every creative act is lonely, not every lonely act is creative."

Kissinger saw how complex were the problems of decision-making in a

technologically advanced society. He wrote: "Crucial problems may—
and frequently do—go unrecognized for a long time. But once the decision-making apparatus has disgorged a policy, it becomes very difficult
to change it." Kissinger saw that the political survival of leaders, particularly in heavily bureaucratized societies, depended on their being able to
realize their goals in a relatively short time, without regard to how they
were arrived at or whether they were valid. Keeping the bureaucracy
happy—making it feel that it was not being constantly overruled—
became a major political requirement. If the political leader constantly
intervened and overruled the bureaucracy—which was often difficult
because he rarely knew enough to do so with confidence—the morale
of the bureaucracy could be endangered. The political leader generally
knew better than to try to do that. The result, Kissinger wrote, was that
the bureaucracy tended to become increasingly independent; given its
general competence on a purely technical level, it also grew increasingly
contemptuous of executives who could not possibly know what it knew.
Kissinger wrote: "In many fields—strategy being a prime example—
decision-makers may find it difficult to give as many hours to a problem
as the expert has had years to study it. The ultimate decision often depends less on knowledge than on the ability to brief the top
administrator—to present the facts in such a way that they can be absorbed rapidly. The effectiveness of briefing, however, puts a premium on
theatrical qualities. Not everything that sounds plausible is correct, and
many things which are correct may not sound plausible when they are
first presented; and a second hearing is rare. The stage aspect of briefing
may leave the decision-maker with a gnawing feeling of having been
taken—even, and perhaps especially, when he does not know quite
how."

Kissinger knew how complex and abstract were many of the analyses
put forward by research staffs; he thought that too many of the explanations overlooked "the problem of the strain of decision-making in times of
crisis." As Kissinger explained: "What is relevant for policy depends not
only on academic truth but also on what can be implemented under
stress." It was common for pragmatic executives to clash with "the theoretical bent of research or planning staffs." Also, the executive was often
required to act as an arbiter between rival groups in the bureaucracy. Instead of acting as leader, imposing his views, the executive tended to become the prisoner of his advisers. Even when he was aware that he was
being "boxed in" by the bureaucracy, there was not very much that he
could do. He might try to liberate himself by going outside the bureaucracy, but this only made him suspect; he appeared to be making arbitrary decisions. What was true domestically was also true in international
relations; Kissinger wrote: "Decisions are reached so painfully that the

very anguish of decision-making acts as a brake on the give-and-take of traditional diplomacy."

Relations within an alliance, among nations with a number of common objectives, were difficult enough because of the bureaucratic factors; between antagonistic states or blocs, the problems were even more acute. Once a revolution became institutionalized in a state, Kissinger wrote, it created administrative structures with their own vested interests. Ideology often survived in the criteria used for making administrative choices, and ideological orthodoxy contributed to massive rigidities within the various bureaucratic organs. It was generally exceedingly difficult for an ideologically dominated state to negotiate with states dominated by bureaucracies whose preconceptions were significantly different. In the modern world, Kissinger wrote, the technologically advanced countries were generally overadministered while the developing countries often lacked even the most essential rudiments of an effective bureaucracy. That was yet another factor that contributed to international instability.

Kissinger distinguished between three types of leadership, all present in the modern world: bureaucratic-pragmatic; ideological; and revolutionary-charismatic. Leadership groups in the United States were predominantly bureaucratic-pragmatic; they approached policy in an "*ad hoc*, pragmatic, and somewhat mechanical" fashion. Their approach tolerated long delays, since a solution was generally expected to turn up. There was no anxiety that an irretrievable disaster would follow from a dilatory policy-making process. The tendency, Kissinger wrote, was for every problem to be broken into its constituent parts, with each part dealt with by experts who could be said to have special competence in the area. There was almost no interest in how the various parts were interrelated. Technical issues, Kissinger wrote, tended to receive more careful attention and profited from a more sophisticated treatment than purely political issues. Kissinger explained: "The criteria for dealing with trends which are conjectural are less well developed than those for immediate crises." He went on to say: "Pragmatism, at least in its generally accepted form, is more concerned with method than with judgment; or rather it seeks to reduce judgment to methodology and value to knowledge." The fact that law and business predominated in the leadership groups in the United States only reinforced the tendency to deal with actual rather than with hypothetical cases. Planning, however, was by its nature hypothetical, Kissinger wrote, and lawyers were not particularly well suited to thinking in such terms. As a result, the already powerful tendencies in the United States to identify foreign policy with the solution of immediate issues was only reinforced. Issues were handled only as the pressure of events imposed a need for them to be resolved. When the government finally did move, every part of the bureaucracy had the maximum incentive to state its case in its most extreme form. Since the final outcome depended on a bargaining process, no part of the bureaucracy was ready to give up on its own special point of view. Kissinger objected to the procedure on many grounds; he was particularly critical of it because it emphasized short-range rather than long-term advantages. He wrote: "The premium placed on advocacy turns decision-making into a series of adjustments among special interests—a process more suited to domestic than to foreign policy. This procedure neglects the long-range because the future has no administrative constituency and is, therefore, without representation in the adversary proceedings."

Kissinger believed that these tendencies explained many of the peculiar characteristics of American diplomacy. Before a specific negotiation started, and while a problem was not high on the diplomatic agenda, the government was generally reluctant to define its position; just as soon as it became evident that a negotiation was about to start, there was a great scurrying about. The task was to define a position—almost any position. Since it was taken for granted that a negotiation had no purpose other than success, and since failure was thought to reflect on the abilities of the negotiating team, a maximum incentive existed to develop policies that would be acceptable. Americans, Kissinger wrote, acted as if failure was always attributable to personal shortcomings; the idea that a problem might have such intrinsic difficulties that its resolution in an international bargaining session was all but impossible was never admitted. The concern with reaching an agreement could become so overwhelming that all long-term considerations were lost sight of. Negotiators—often men trained in law—saw a particular virtue in acting as mediators; their principal purpose was to secure an accord. Kissinger questioned the suitability of such training for diplomacy, nor was he at all persuaded that the business executive started with a talent for political negotiation. Law and business were the two principal recruiting grounds for diplomacy, and Kissinger had doubts about both. Most business executives, he explained, knew how to coordinate well-defined functions; these capacities, while "relatively effective in the business world, where the executive [could] often substitute decisiveness, long experience, and a wide range of personal acquaintance for reflectiveness," were not suited to international affairs; they were particularly inappropriate to negotiations in a revolutionary age.

Americans, Kissinger wrote, seldom looked at long-range issues. They preferred to deal with "crises," when and as they developed. Decisions were most often reached on the basis of compromise between competing points of view; accidents of personality and individual persuasiveness played a crucial role. The adversary procedure caused most issues to be defined in black-and-white terms. There was almost no feeling for nuance and relatively little understanding of the relationships that existed among seemingly discrete events. Nor was there very great respect or feeling for history. Nations were rarely seen as distinct entities; there was a tendency to stress their similarities and to ignore their differences. Kissinger added: "Since many of our policy-makers first address themselves to an issue when it emerges as their area of responsibility, their approach to it is often highly anecdotal. Great weight is given to what people say and relatively little to the significance of these affirmations in terms of domestic structure or historical background."

Such a pragmatic leadership bore only a very superficial resemblance to the leadership that existed in the Soviet Union; ideological commitment weighed heavily in Communist societies. Marxism furnished a standard of truth, and those who accepted its maxims believed in the utility of its doctrine for policy-making decisions. Communist self-confidence, Kissinger explained, drew on the belief that Marxism made possible a historical understanding that could not be obtained by other methods. Because Marxists acknowledged only "objective" factors, they were little concerned with the good will of individuals; they had no interest in those who came from a different social system. Their persistent demand was for absolute security; they found it difficult to live with situations they were not able to control. Repeating his view that absolute security for one state meant absolute insecurity for all others, Kissinger noted how easily a seemingly defensive foreign policy could become indistinguishable from one that was openly aggressive. Kissinger wrote: "When there is a choice between Western good will or a physical gain, the pressures to choose the latter have been overwhelming." The Communists, confident of their understanding of the historical process, believed that they knew their adversaries better than their adversaries knew themselves. They had no interest in making concessions to individuals; their preoccupation was not to make a specific negotiation succeed. Having achieved power through methods that were dangerous and sometimes brutal—often involving the physical or bureaucratic elimination of all rivals—they were, Kissinger wrote, "single-minded, unemotional, dedicated, and, above all, motivated by an enormous desire for power." Because suspicion governed in all their domestic political relations, they were not likely to regard the outside world as being very friendly. Nor did they expect very much from the outside world; it was best if it was kept at arm's length.

In theory, Kissinger wrote, relations between Communist states were meant to be amicable; since national rivalries could not exist between Socialist states—such rivalries, according to Marxism, being the result of class conflict—Socialist societies were supposed to be fraternal and pacific. When, therefore, disagreements broke out among them, they were treated as internal disputes. The opposition was ostracized and condemned, and every effort was made to destroy it. Disagreements quickly became schisms; the struggle between the Soviet Union and Communist China, for example, was infinitely more severe than any that existed between Communist and capitalist states.

Within the Communist world, Kissinger wrote, there were substantial differences also between countries that had managed to institutionalize their Marxist ideology and those still dominated by revolutionary fervor. In the Soviet Union, for example, where Marxist ideology had become institutionalized, a form of pragmatism existed, but a pragmatism quite different from any that prevailed in the United States. Even when a Communist society became pragmatic, Kissinger said, doctrinal considerations always had great importance; Marxism guaranteed that a certain respect would always be shown for conceptual problems. While bureaucratization and pragmatism might cause a Communist society to lose some of its *élan*, that would never bring Communist societies to resemble those that were not Communist. Disagreeing with those who expected Western and Soviet societies to become increasingly similar, Kissinger argued that they would remain very distinct. Insofar as he looked for any Communist society to change dramatically, he expected such change to occur in the less bureaucratized Communist states; these were more ideologically oriented, and less committed to established procedures. While this might appear to be a paradox, Kissinger said that it simply demonstrated that where an administrative structure was fluid, there were greater possibilities of significant change.

In reflecting on the revolutionary-charismatic type of leadership, which had little use for either the pragmatism of the United States or the ideology of the Soviet Union, Kissinger emphasized the austerity of its principles. Such leaders had no interest in material gains; they did not risk themselves for such paltry ends. Kissinger wrote: "If Castro or Sukarno had been principally interested in economics, their talents would have guaranteed them a brilliant career in the societies they overthrew. What made their sacrifice worthwhile to them was a vision of the future—or a quest for political power. To revolutionaries the significant reality is the world which they are striving to bring about, not the world they are fighting to overcome." Kissinger believed that one reason why Western leaders had such difficulty in communicating with the leaders of developing societies was that their perspective on world affairs was so totally different. He wrote: "The West has a tendency to believe that the tensions in the emerging nations are caused by a low level of economic activity. To the apostles of economic development, raising the gross national product seems the key to political stability. They believe that it should receive the highest priority from the political leaders of new countries and supply their chief motivation." But, he went on to say, ". . . to the charismatic heads of many of the new nations, economic progress, while not unwelcome, offers too limited a scope for their ambitions. It can be achieved only by slow, painful, highly technical measures which contrast with the heroic exertions of the struggle for independence. Results are long-delayed; credit for them cannot be clearly established. If Castro were to act on the advice of theorists of economic development, the best he could hope for would be that after some decades he would lead a small progressive country—perhaps a Switzerland of the Caribbean. Compared to the prospect of leading a revolution throughout Latin America, this goal would appear trivial, boring, perhaps even unreal to him."

Kissinger suggested also that economic progress often only exacerbated domestic political instability and that leaders of new nations were sometimes tempted to use foreign policy as a way to escape from their own intractable domestic problems; it was a device for achieving greater internal unity. Charismatic leaders were not unaware of the advantages that such a policy might produce. There were no great risks involved. The major powers were not likely to use their arms against the new states; generally, they did not even try to take advantage of their major vulnerability—their fragile domestic institutional structures.

An international system that embraced states with such divergent leadership styles could not fail to be unstable. It would be rare for such widely divergent leadership groups to agree even on the diagnosis of a problem. The twentieth century, in Kissinger's mind, was not a time for statesmanship. The incentive to put a premium "on short-term goals," together with "the domestic need to succeed at all times," meant that long-range purposes rarely received the attention they deserved. In the large bureaucratic societies—both pragmatic and ideological—the possibilities of radical change were minimal; in states led by charismatic leaders, where no bureaucracies existed to impede change, Kissinger thought of the leading politicians as "tightrope artists," who would "plunge from their perch" if they made a single false step. Synchronizing the various systems, and securing agreement among them, was not going to be easy.

Yet Kissinger knew that agreement was imperative. Insofar as he saw any reason for hope, it came from the common interest in avoiding a nuclear holocaust. While the nuclear hazard did not restrain all nations equally, it was acknowledged by all, without regard to their domestic structures or the character of their leadership groups. Kissinger believed that the spread of technology and science might in the long run contribute to the emergence of a common culture; this, he imagined, would foster interdependence, but he was in no sense sanguine. Returning to ideas he had first developed over a decade before, Kissinger commented on two major leadership styles: "political" and "revolutionary," represented by two kinds of personalities: the "statesman" and the "prophet."

Kissinger wrote of the statesman, he "manipulates reality; his first goal is survival; he feels responsible not only for the best but also for the worst conceivable outcome. His view of human nature is wary; he is conscious of many great hopes which have failed, of many good intentions that could not be realized, of selfishness and ambition and violence. He is, therefore, inclined to erect hedges against the possibility that even the most brilliant idea might prove abortive and that the most eloquent formulation might hide ulterior motives. He will try to avoid certain experiments, not because he would object to the results if they succeeded, but because he would feel himself responsible for the consequences if they failed. He is suspicious of those who personalize foreign policy, for history teaches him the fragility of structures dependent on individuals. To the statesman, gradualism is the essence of stability; he represents an era of average performance, of gradual change and slow construction."

The prophet was a very different kind of person, Kissinger explained; he is "less concerned with manipulating than with creating reality. What is possible interests him less than what is 'right.' He offers his vision as the test and his good faith as a guarantee. He believes in total solutions; he is less absorbed in methodology than in purpose. He believes in the perfectibility of man. His approach is timeless and not dependent on circumstances. He objects to gradualism as an unnecessary concession to circumstance. He will risk everything because his vision is the primary significant reality to him. Paradoxically, his more optimistic view of human nature makes him more intolerant than the statesman. If truth is both knowable and attainable, only immorality or stupidity can keep man from realizing it. The prophet represents an era of exaltation, of great upheavals, of vast accomplishments, but also of enormous disasters."

Kissinger saw that the encounter between the two types was always "somewhat inconclusive and frustrating." Each type prevailed at different periods of history; the political approach dominated European foreign policy between the end of the wars of religion and the French Revolution and again between the Congress of Vienna and World War I. The prophetic mode dominated during the religious wars, the French Revolution, and in many parts of the world in more recent times. Kissinger believed that both styles had produced great achievements, though he dwelt principally on the greater dislocation and suffering that the prophetic style produced. Each style, however, also had what Kissinger called its "nemesis." He wrote: "The nemesis of the statesman is that equilibrium, though it may be the condition of stability, does not supply its own motivation; that of the prophet is the impossibility of sustaining a mood of exaltation without the risk of submerging man in the vastness of a vision and reducing him to a mere figure to be manipulated."

Kissinger suggested that there might be a deeper philosophical perspective that separated the two styles. In the West, since the Renaissance, there had been a commitment to the idea that the real world was external to the observer, and that knowledge consisted of recording and classifying data. For those cultures that escaped the Newtonian revolution and retained a pre-Newtonian view, the real world was almost entirely "internal" to the observer. Though developing societies might accept technology, almost as a free gift, and though they might accept it in its most advanced form, this did not mean that they accepted also the philosophical commitment that discovering it imposed on the West. Kissinger wrote: "Empirical reality has a much different significance for many of the new countries than for the West because in a certain sense they never went through the process of discovering it." Kissinger saw Russia as occupying an intermediary position. To those who did not belong to the West experientially, the West might "seem cold, supercilious, lacking in compassion." Kissinger did not believe that such differences in style and philosophical perspective were unprecedented. He wrote: "What is novel is the global scale on which they occur and the risks which the failure to overcome them would entail." He saw the need for creating an international order "*before* a crisis imposes it as a necessity."

Kissinger's article "Domestic Structure and Foreign Policy" seemed to sum up what he had been saying about foreign policy for well over a decade. He continued to believe that the character of leadership groups was absolutely decisive. For him, the quality of American leadership was particularly significant. While others complained that the federal government did not recruit the best people for sensitive political positions, Kissinger saw the matter differently. It was the constant search for consensus—the quest for "objectivity"—that seemed so inimical to the policy-making process. Government encouraged neither reflectiveness nor risk-taking. There was too much reliance on committees, and the committee system was "concerned more with co-ordination and adjustment than with purpose." Of committees, Kissinger had said that they were "consumers and sometimes sterilizers of ideas, rarely creators of them."

Kissinger had so little to say about the policies pursued in the Johnson years because they reflected attitudes that were fundamentally alien to him. It was difficult for him to criticize a set of defensive and ill-coordinated reactions to events taking place half a world away, in a country that he knew only very slightly. Lacking any deep understanding of the character of Vietnamese society, and knowing how futile it was for him to continue to write about Europe—de Gaulle seemed increasingly unimportant to Washington—Kissinger returned to earlier interests and took up a manuscript he had begun more than a decade earlier as a graduate student. Kissinger is sometimes depicted as Bismarckian by those who have not read him; he did in fact write a single essay on the subject; it appeared in *Daedalus* in the summer of 1968.

Kissinger saw Bismarck as a "white revolutionary," a characterization he borrowed from a nineteenth-century German liberal. Revolutionaries, Kissinger explained, "always start from a position of inferior physical strength; their victories are primarily triumphs of conception or of will." Institutions, Kissinger believed, were not suited to accommodating men of genius or demoniacal power. Bismarck, while appearing as a conservative, "recast the map of Europe and the pattern of international relations." But none of this came to be institutionalized; it had to be maintained by men less gifted than Bismarck, and they were quite unequal to the task. Kissinger said: "Bismarck's tragedy was that he left a heritage of unassimilated greatness."

Appointed Prussian ambassador to the German Confederation in 1852, Bismarck showed at once his hostility to the old Metternichian system. Whereas that system had been based on the premise that "Prussia's domestic structure was so vulnerable that it could be protected only by rigid adherence to the unity of conservative monarchs," Bismarck insisted on "Prussia's uniqueness and invulnerability." Believing that German unity could be achieved through Prussian power, and that destiny did not intend for Prussia to be absorbed by Germany, but for Germany to be absorbed by Prussia, he astonished almost all Germans who heard him express this bizarre view. Kissinger wrote: "It was not the first time that revolutionaries succeeded because their opponents could not believe in the reality of their objectives." Bismarck's aim, according to Kissinger, was to have Prussia concentrate its major energies on foreign policy; for that to happen, domestic tranquillity was absolutely essential. In many ways, Kissinger said, Bismarck resembled de Gaulle; he, too, emphasized the "pride and integrity of the historic states." There was, however, one major difference; while Europe in de Gaulle's time was composed of several medium-sized states of roughly equal strength, Bismarck's Prussia was by far the strongest German state. Kissinger saw that Bismarck, unlike de Gaulle, "could impose his convictions on the other contenders by force —provided international conditions were favorable." A great deal, Kissinger said, depended on Bismarck's conception of international affairs and what he chose to opt for.

Bismarck, according to Kissinger, believed that "foreign policy had to be based not on sentiment but on an assessment of strength," and that "policy depended on calculation, not emotion." He began by recommending that Prussia separate itself from Austria; within a short time he was arguing that Prussia would do well to evict Austria from Germany. If Bismarck had been asked what justification existed for German unity, he would have replied that Prussia required it; Prussia's interests as a great power made it imperative that a new German state be created. When Bismarck set out to defeat Austria, Kissinger explained, he thought it sufficient to say that the moment was auspicious for a Prussian attack. Nothing, in Kissinger's mind, proved more conclusively Bismarck's revolutionary qualities. Kissinger wrote: "Bismarck proposed to base the Concert of Europe on precise calculations of power; when they conflicted with the existing order, the latter had to give way or be forcibly overthrown." In his view, "Bismarck represented a new age. Equilibrium was seen not as harmony and mechanical balance, but as a statistical balance of forces in flux. Its appropriate philosophy was Darwin's concept of the survival of the fittest. Bismarck marked the change from the rationalist to the empiricist conception of politics." Choice in foreign policy, in the Bismarckian system, depended entirely on considerations of utility. Because Bismarck was a cynic, though many mistook him for an opportunist, his adversaries misunderstood his purposes. In any case, the "charge of opportunism" missed the point. As Kissinger explained: "Anyone wishing to affect events must be opportunist to some extent. The real distinction is between those who adapt their purposes to reality and those who seek to mold reality in the light of their purposes."

Kissinger, seeing Bismarck as a revolutionary, thought that he resembled all other revolutionaries in wanting to shape reality to his specific vision. Kissinger wrote: "Bismarck sought his opportunities in the present; he drew his inspiration from a vision of the future." He achieved what he set out to do; he goaded Austria into declaring war on Prussia and then soundly defeated her. After expelling Austria from the German Confederation and organizing North Germany on the basis of Prussian hegemony, he picked a quarrel with France and defeated Napoleon III in a short war that dumfounded most European statesmen. Having achieved German unity, along the lines he intended, he took Prussia as the model for the new state. Prussia, in fact, created all the circumstances that made the new state possible. The victory, while impressive, was, according to Kissinger, a Pyrrhic victory. As he explained: "The very magnitude of Bismarck's achievement mortgaged the future." Why? Because, according to Kissinger, ". . . the spirits once called forth refused to be banished by a *tour de force*, however great. The manner in which Germany was unified deprived the international system of flexibility." The number of states was drastically reduced. The kinds of marginal adjustments that had once been possible when there were many secondary German states were more difficult to achieve. Also, and most important, the existence of a powerful Germany pushed other states into new alliances.

Germany, being compelled to prepare for a possible two-front war, increased her military strength; the result was that she frightened her neighbors. The thing that Germany most feared came to pass: France became an irreconcilable enemy; Great Britain moved toward isolation. So long as Bismarck governed, he kept Austria and Russia faithful to Germany. But others were unable to maintain what he had built. The international system grew rigid, hostile alliances confronted each other, and the final result was World War I. Bismarck's successors did not know how to manage his system. Kissinger wrote: "The nemesis of power is that, except in the hands of a master, reliance on it is more likely to produce a contest at arms than self-restraint."

While Johnson worried over Vietnam, and while the country became increasingly agitated by a war that seemed both immoral and impolitic, Kissinger fell silent. He busied himself with philosophical and historical study, and only occasionally expressed himself publicly. He had nothing to say about Johnson's policies, and it was not until Nelson Rockefeller decided definitely that he wanted to seek the presidential nomination that Kissinger began to speak again on contemporary foreign policy issues. There were no new articles in *Foreign Affairs* or in other such journals. Instead, Kissinger wrote anonymously for the candidate. Many of his old themes were repeated. There were, however, a number of new ones; clearly, Kissinger had not spent his years of silence too far from the political arena. In a sense, he was more actively involved than he had ever been.

7

Rockefeller's 1968 Campaign

A Political Legacy

During the spring and early summer of 1968, Nelson Rockefeller did what he could to deny Richard Nixon the Republican Party's nomination for the presidency of the United States. The effort failed, but not before the New York Governor and his principal foreign affairs adviser, Henry Kissinger, formulated and broadcast the main outlines of a foreign policy fundamentally different from the one being pursued by the Johnson administration and different also from any proposed by other candidates, Republican or Democratic. Kissinger took his responsibilities seriously; had he been preparing position papers for a new administration or the inaugural address for a newly elected president, he could not have been more deliberate in the way that he did his work. A foreign observer, uninformed about the American electoral system, observing Kissinger during this period, might have been led to believe that the delineation of a viable foreign policy immensely increased a candidate's chances of winning his party's nomination. Kissinger worked for several months as if the fate of Nelson Rockefeller depended on his efforts.

The experience was an immensely exhilarating one for him. After years of writing about foreign policy, hoping always that the effort was having some influence on public officials—and realizing increasingly how difficult it was for someone outside government to have great influence—it was gratifying to have access to someone who might just conceivably be a presidential candidate. Kissinger's relations with Rockefeller were very close; the New York Governor found a sufficient coincidence between his own views and those of his adviser for Kissinger to have virtually a free hand in the foreign policy area. A flood of material—most of it written by Kissinger, whose style was unmistakable—issued from the candidate's headquarters on West 44th Street in New York City. It was rare for a candidate who was simply vying for his party's nomination to trouble himself with making so many statements on so wide a variety of foreign policy questions. Kissinger wrote as if the press, radio, and television were recording each of the Governor's statements, taking note of the nuance contained in every phrase. He clearly did not reckon with the character of the mass media. They gave virtually no attention to what Rockefeller was saying on foreign policy or on other issues; their interest was whether he would win enough support to be able, perhaps with Governor Reagan of California, to stop Nixon at Miami Beach. They scarcely made use of the Governor's press releases; they wanted to know whether large crowds came out to greet him—as they often did—and whether he was having much success in persuading delegates to vote for him. One would never have known from the mass media—television, radio, or newspapers—that Rockefeller was offering an alternative foreign policy. Kissinger felt acutely the frustrations of the situation; he knew, of course, that nothing could be done, but proceeded as if every word, fashioned by him and uttered by Rockefeller, was being recorded and somehow taken in.

In November 1968, when Richard Nixon asked Henry Kissinger to join him as his National Security Affairs adviser, newspaper editors did not think to rummage through their old campaign files to see what Kissinger had written for Rockefeller. Had they done so, they might have been less surprised by events that occurred in 1971 and 1972. Kissinger developed in the spring and early summer of 1968 the principal planks of a foreign policy intended for Rockefeller's use; it became instead the first of Nixon's inheritances. Nixon secured what others had asked for; he was Rockefeller's legatee.

The 1968 campaign compelled Kissinger to review his thinking about foreign policy issues and to make concrete policy proposals. He used ideas he had been developing for over a decade; also, he insisted on placing the Vietnam war in a larger foreign policy framework. He was determined to protect his candidate against the hazards that had mired down so many others in the Vietnam bog. There was an urgent need for a solution to a tragic war; there was an even greater need for a foreign policy suited to the new conditions of international order. The first, Kissinger believed, was not a problem that could be separated from the second.

Kissinger had been silent for almost four years. The electoral campaign forced him to speak out; the words were his own; the voice was that of Nelson Rockefeller. The message would have been familiar to anyone who knew Kissinger's writings; a great deal of what he had already said was repeated, but there were also substantial differences. Kissinger recognized how much had changed in the world since the death of John F. Kennedy. His own views showed the effect of those changes. He was no longer as preoccupied with de Gaulle as he had once been; NATO and the Common Market, while still figuring prominently in his policy recommendations, were now part of a prescription for an international system that depended on understandings being reached with the Soviet Union and Communist China. Rockefeller had a China policy; every detail was worked out by Kissinger. While it was all still very general, its meaning was clear. There had to be an opening to both China and the Soviet Union; it had to be pursued in a particular way, and ought to aim at specific objectives outlined by Kissinger.

Nineteen sixty-eight, a time of violence both at home and abroad, saw Martin Luther King and Robert Kennedy murdered, rioting in American cities, massive student unrest, a mini-revolution in France, a Soviet invasion of Czechoslovakia. These and other like events made many thoughtful Americans believe that their institutions were in imminent danger of collapse. Rhetoric grew increasingly violent as the country itself became more passionately divided over what seemed to be the never-ending war in Vietnam. While all these events preoccupied the public, they were not enough to divert attention from the quadrennial political battles that proceeded according to the fixed American calendar. As late as January 1968, Rockefeller continued to insist that he himself was not a candidate for the presidency, and that his only concern was to see the Republicans choose George Romney, the Governor of Michigan. Rockefeller had maintained that position for over a year; he hoped the Republicans would choose a liberal, and he did not imagine that he himself could be the party's candidate. After the bruising primary and convention battles of 1964, in which Rockefeller did what he could to deny the nomination to Barry Goldwater, Rockefeller knew how hostile many in the party were to him. Some charged him with having wrecked Goldwater's chances; others chastised him for "sitting out" the election; still others blamed him for dividing the party. Given the hostility in so many influential Republican quarters, he did not believe that there was any chance of the party's uniting around him. It seemed to make excellent sense to support someone whose political credentials seemed not too different from his own, and who would bear the Republican banner as a moderate middle-of-the-road candidate. If Rockefeller could not be king himself, he could at least aspire to be a kingmaker. Romney was his first and only choice for the Republican nomination.

By early 1968, every astute political observer knew that George Romney was not going to win the nomination. Rockefeller's private polls in New Hampshire told him that the Michigan Governor would be trounced by Richard Nixon. Two weeks before primary day, it appeared, according to the best available polling data, that Nixon might well emerge with six votes for every vote garnered by Romney. Recognizing the difficulty of his position, Romney decided to withdraw from the race. No longer bound to Romney's candidacy, Rockefeller was expected by many to enter the race; if he did not do so, Nixon would certainly win the nomination. Throughout the country, liberal Republicans who distrusted Nixon, sometimes doubting that a man of his personality could win a national election, united in urging Rockefeller to become a candidate; the pressure brought to bear on him was intense. Rockefeller procrastinated; he knew that his supporters were confident that if he won the nomination he would go on also to win the election. At the same time, he wondered whether he dared take the risk of dividing the party. On March 21, at a press conference, where it was expected that he would respond to the pressure and accept the call to run, to the consternation of many, including some of his most ardent supporters, he announced: "I have decided today to reiterate unequivocally that I am not a candidate campaigning directly or indirectly for the Presidency of the United States."

In a month already filled with political surprises—including Eugene McCarthy's strong showing in New Hampshire and Robert Kennedy's belated decision to seek the Democratic nomination himself—the Rockefeller decision came as one more unexpected development. The surprises, however, were not over yet. On March 31, in a major televised address, Lyndon Johnson announced that bombings north of the twentieth parallel in Vietnam would cease. He hoped that this concession would make possible the opening of peace negotiations. Then, in a short statement, again unanticipated, Johnson announced his intention not to seek re-election. Nothing, he said, ought to interfere with his chief purpose: to make peace. Less than a fortnight after Rockefeller bowed out, virtually handing the Republican nomination to Nixon, the Democratic Party race was wide open. All expectations were confounded, in both parties.

Four days later, the country learned with shock and dismay of the murder of Martin Luther King; within hours, many of America's black ghettos erupted into violence. The country seemed headed for disaster; it was impossible for Rockefeller to act as if the conditions that had obtained on March 21 still existed. Many both inside and outside the Republican Party urged him to reconsider his decision; they insisted that the country needed the type of leadership he alone could provide. At a moment of great moral and political crisis, when so many were insisting that Rockefeller enter the race, it was impossible for him to stand aloof. He consulted with his close advisers. On April 30, he announced that he would indeed seek the nomination; the events of the previous weeks, he said, had persuaded him of the necessity of doing so.

Rockefeller opened his campaign the very next day in Philadelphia with a speech delivered before the World Affairs Council. The subject was foreign affairs; the hand of Kissinger was obvious in every paragraph. Through the next fourteen weeks, while the mass media described and analyzed the growing public support for Rockfeller, which was perhaps particularly evident in the weeks following the assassination of Robert Kennedy, Rockefeller delivered a series of speeches on public policy issues. Those that had to do with foreign policy were the work of Kissinger; he provided the ideas for the speeches, prepared the position papers on which they were based, and gave his own distinctive interpretation of events. Kissinger, through Rockefeller, spoke on all the most pressing foreign policy questions. As the campaign proceeded, the Rockefeller entourage realized that the chances of the New York Governor's actually winning the nomination were indeed very slight; this did not deter them. Not till the early morning of August 8, when the balloting at Miami confirmed what the news media had been reporting for several days, did the Rockefeller camp admit its defeat. Until the very end, there had been some slight hope that Nixon might somehow be stopped.

Kissinger left Miami Beach with the knowledge that he had served Rockefeller well. He had done as much as any man could to outline in a serious way an alternative foreign policy for the nation. If the news media had given scant attention to his handiwork, and if foreign policy proposals had virtually no influence on delegate votes, that was a comment on the party system. He had used every resource at his command: years of active study of foreign policy problems; familiarity with hundreds of distinguished foreign leaders; experience on the fringes of government during the Kennedy administration; extensive foreign travel; negotiations through French intermediaries in 1967 to open Vietnam peace talks. All of this had been used to develop a concept of international order that owed something to studies that dated back to his earliest researches on Metternich and Castlereagh. Kissinger recognized the seriousness of the Vietnam problem. He did not believe that it could be resolved as an isolated problem. His concern was with a stable international order; that became Rockefeller's concern also. Rockefeller spoke in Kissinger's language; even his intellectual categories were Kissinger's. The Vietnam war had to be ended; it was, however, only one problem among many. In Kissinger's mind, as rendered in Rockefeller's speeches, it was also one opportunity among many.

Kissinger's visits to South Vietnam had taught him two things: the war could not be won militarily; negotiations provided the only possible hope for an early peace. Negotiations, Kissinger believed, would certainly be long and difficult. It was a mistake to pretend that there was any prospect of an early peace. Recalling his studies of the events leading up to the end of the Korean war, Kissinger knew how complicated the negotiating process could be. He had no interest in having his candidate make promises that he could not fulfill. His first visit to Vietnam had told him that the American military deployment of forces was wrong. These ideas, first written privately in his reports to Ambassador Lodge, were now developed more fully for Rockefeller; with them came the most specific kinds of suggestions for the negotiations with North Vietnam that ought to accompany the redeployment of forces. Kissinger knew a certain amount about the leaders of South Vietnam; he had no personal knowledge of the leaders of the north. He had tried to instruct himself, and had listened carefully to what others told him. Herbert Marcovich and Raymond Aubrac, when they returned from Hanoi on the mission that they and Kissinger had hoped might lead to a cessation of the bombings and a beginning of negotiations, immensely contributed to his education on the subject.

The more that Kissinger reflected on the problem, the more he accepted the fact that it was made up of many distinct elements. First, and most obviously, there were a whole host of questions having to do with Vietnam, north and south. Both governments had to be treated with, and it was not going to be easy to deal with either. However, Kissinger saw this as only a very small part of the problem. Indochina had importance also for each of the two major Communist states: China and the Soviet Union. They were an inseparable part of the Vietnamese puzzle; American relations with both would intimately affect decisions that were reached at the negotiating table. Kissinger did not mean for American policy toward the Communist giants to be determined only by considerations in Vietnam; he did not, however, underestimate the importance each could have in Vietnamese peace talks. If certain advantages might accrue to the United States through improved relations with the Soviet Union and China, those advantages would not be confined to Vietnam. Kissinger saw the possibility of a whole new set of relations developing in the world. He was persuaded that these could contribute to making for a more stable international order.

Kissinger never doubted his qualifications for the task at hand. He believed that his understanding of the interconnectedness of political, diplomatic, and military factors made him eminently suited to advising a presidential aspirant, particularly at a moment when so many argued as if all that was needed was a magic formula for peace. In the bustle of the campaign, Kissinger rarely saw Rockefeller for more than a few minutes at a time; the Governor's principal concern had to be to show himself to the public and spend time with those who could help him win additional delegate support. There was no great need for closer communications at that moment; twelve years of friendship made each intimately familiar with the other. Rockefeller knew Kissinger well; he valued his loyalty and his friendship. While admiring and respecting his intelligence, he was never overawed by it. Consummate politician that he was, he recognized Kissinger's gifts and made use of them, but never thought to deprecate his own. If Kissinger could think about foreign policy issues as he could never hope to do, this did not mean that he also knew how to relate to others or that he got on easily with those who were not his intellectual peers. Rockefeller's gift was to make others feel comfortable, even while they never entirely forgot that they were in the presence of one of the richest men in the world. The two made an admirable team; each respected the other for what he could do best. Neither imagined himself in the other's position. There was rarely any tension between them.

Kissinger was given a free hand in the foreign policy area. He used it to propagate his own specific foreign policy doctrines. These had already been fully developed by the early 1960s; the years since 1964, however, had been used for further reflection. Also, through his Vietnam visits and his relations with Marcovich and Aubrac, he had learned a certain amount about Vietnam and Southeast Asia more generally. In July 1967, Herbert Marcovich, a young French biochemist, and Raymond Aubrac, a higher French civil servant, attached to the Food and Agriculture Organization in Rome, had gone to Hanoi to determine what conditions would bring the North Vietnamese to the negotiating table. Aubrac, a friend of Ho Chi Minh, was the key figure in this secret mission to Hanoi. Without him, it would never have taken place. However, Kissinger had been just as important in the operation. Neither Aubrac nor Marcovich would have agreed to go to Hanoi if they did not believe that Kissinger was in a position to communicate information they might bring back to the highest quarters in Washington.

What began as a very private initiative took on greater seriousness when Aubrac and Marcovich, after many hours with Pham Van Dong, returned with a formula that seemed highly promising to both them and Kissinger. Returning from Paris to consult with Robert McNamara and Nicholas Katzenbach in Washington, Kissinger expected for a time that something might come of the effort. In the end it led to nothing. Marcovich and Aubrac often reflected on what had gone wrong. Was it the American bombing of the Paul Doumer bridge that had diminished the North Vietnamese interest in immediate peace talks? Had their hopes been sabotaged by powerful forces in the Department of Defense? Or had there been insufficient interest at the presidential level? Kissinger reflected on the same questions, but did not dwell on them for very long. It was impossible to say whether an opportunity had indeed been lost. In his mind, what was important was that another opportunity be created. Kissinger valued the peace initiative for itself, but also for more selfish reasons: he knew that it increased immeasurably his understanding of the complexities of negotiating with the North Vietnamese. He listened with the keenest interest to everything that Aubrac and Marcovich told him; he felt in the autumn of 1967 that he understood the difficulties in arranging for a viable peace better than at any time previously.

When he came to write for Rockefeller's campaign, he used all such evidence and experience to support his general theories. For him, the most urgent task was not the development of a peace plan but the articulation of a new foreign policy. Just as he had once argued that the greatest problem for the United States was to know how to incorporate its atomic capability in new defense and foreign policy postures, so, now, he tried to incorporate the trauma of Vietnam into a policy that did not misconstrue its true importance. In his mind, both the "hawks" and the "doves" were grossly ignorant; they started with false assumptions; their vision was too limited; they made complicated problems seem simple; they looked at the issue as if it involved only two states called Vietnam.

Rockefeller, echoing Kissinger, started his campaign with the bald assertion that American concepts and actions, as then expressed in foreign policy, were quite unsuited to the world of 1968. While some argued as if the American failure could be ascribed to various institutional insufficiencies, Rockefeller claimed that American institutions were more than adequate; the need was not for new institutions but for men who knew how to deal with the problems of international relations in a "revolutionary" age. So far as the Governor was concerned, the Johnson administration was trying to approach the 1970s with the ideas and practices of the 1940s and 1950s. Rockefeller, in a sentence that perfectly expressed Kissinger's own teaching, spoke of the sterility of America's relations with other states, frozen in patterns established when Europe was emerging from the terrors of World War II.

In his first major address as a candidate for the Republican nomination, Rockefeller congratulated Johnson for the initiatives he had taken toward bringing about peace negotiations. The need, he said, was clearly for "new solutions," but these could not be the "slick and simple solutions" of the hawks or the doves. Rockefeller, before the World Affairs Council, said: "The complex affairs of the world of nations leave no place for Aladdin lamps or magic carpets." There was no possibility of returning to the solutions invented in the 1940s to cope with the problems of Europe. A new policy was needed, and it had to start with a proper understanding of the mistakes—military, political, and diplomatic—that had been made. The military effort had been based on a set of false premises.

Policy-makers seemed to think that the control of territory in Vietnam really mattered. That policy, Rockefeller said, had simply led to "open-ended escalation" and to stalemate at ever higher levels of violence. The war had become "Americanized" in both manpower and direction. This was a tragic mistake. There were no military solutions for the war in Vietnam. Negotiations were absolutely essential. However, negotiations were not a good in themselves; they would succeed only if the American government conceived and put into operation practices suited to the Vietnam situation. It was imperative that the populations in South Vietnam be made secure; military escalation in the north added nothing to the security of peasants living in the south. The existing pacification programs were much too complex; the South Vietnamese were quite incapable of satisfactorily performing according to the requirements of the Americans. The object of all such programs needed to be the building and protecting of units of local government. The Americanization of the war had to be ended at once; the Saigon government should be given the principal responsibility for both military and civilian programs. It was most important, Rockefeller said, for the national government to be broadened.

In a statement that would have been more appropriate to a presidential rostrum than to a campaign platform, Rockefeller said: "I am concerned lest the present diplomatic effort—meanwhile—give rise to extremes of either optimism or despondency around the world and in our country. Some of us have imagined the opening of negotiations to be the beginning of peace. Others—especially among some of our Asian allies—fear that negotiations will mark the abandonment of the American effort in South Vietnam. I believe that neither extreme reaction is warranted. We have nothing to fear—and all to gain—from the careful and responsible quest for a negotiated settlement." He told the North Vietnamese that the American interest was to secure a peace that guaranteed the rights of all peoples to determine their own destiny. He warned the Americans not to be overly preoccupied with "technical issues such as cease-fire, status of forces, and supervision." In his view, "the problems and rewards of peace go far beyond Vietnam itself."

Rockefeller spoke of the legitimate interests that both Moscow and Peking had in Southeast Asia; he expressed the hope that they would cooperate to build something stronger than the existing truce. His greatest concern, however, was with what the United States itself was experiencing as the result of the Vietnam war. His great fear, he said, was that the Vietnam war might lead to "the growth of a new American isolationism." This would be a tragedy not only for the United States but for the world at large. He warned that negotiations over Vietnam would be long and complex, and that they would demand great patience and intelligence.

Repeating an idea that Kissinger had often expressed, he spoke of the necessity of the United States going into the conference room "with a predetermined and purposeful negotiating position." The "tactics of expediency and improvisation" were scorned. Rockefeller insisted that the United States neither accept nor try to impose a solution dictated by force. Any solution had to "safeguard the freedom and security of *all* Southeast Asia."

The most important of Kissinger's ideas were reserved for Rockefeller's peroration. Rockefeller spoke of the need for recognizing that a Vietnam settlement had to be achieved in the context of world relations as a whole. Repeating Kissinger's conventional pleas for closer consultations with America's allies, he spoke also of other opportunities that beckoned. There was the possibility of quite new relations with the Communist countries. Turning specifically to Communist China, Rockefeller said that the United States gained nothing by "aiding or encouraging the self-isolation of so great a people." He spoke of the need for "contact and communication"; both the United States and China stood to profit from this. There was need also for closer relations with the Soviet Union. Rockefeller said: "For in a subtle triangle with Communist China and the Soviet Union, we can ultimately improve our relations with *each*—as we test the will for peace of *both*."

In the hectic weeks that followed, Rockefeller reiterated all these themes. Many of his speeches were almost too serious; they read as if they were learned articles. They drew heavily on everything that Kissinger had been saying for a decade or longer. They were Kissinger's work in every sense. Thus, for example, in New York, on June 12, the Governor spoke of the vast transformations that had occurred in the world in the preceding decade. He spoke of "the changed character of nuclear superiority, the decline in our economic pre-eminence, and the splintering of the Communist monolith." There was a need, he said, for a new international order, a new world structure. There was no reason "to fear contact with any people—including those from Communist countries." He repeated the phrases he had already used about closer American-Soviet and American-Chinese relations, and called for a new leadership, willing to accept that the United States no longer act as the world's policeman. Rockefeller said: "America has no obligation to spill its blood in every local conflict on the globe—unless there is a genuine international threat to peace and our own national interest is directly involved." He went on to say: "Before we commit even small forces, all the far-reaching implications of this act must be faced—as they were not faced in Vietnam. We must not find ourselves with a commitment looking for a justification."

On July 13, he announced a four-stage plan for peace in Vietnam. In

Stage I, there would be a mutual pullback of forces, with the North Vietnamese regulars going back to the frontiers while American and allied forces moved back to the populated areas. An international peace-keeping force would be established to act as a buffer between the two. As soon as the North Vietnamese began to move back, the United States, to show its good faith, would withdraw 75,000 troops. In Stage II, there would be further withdrawals, with the United States removing the bulk of its forces. An expanded international force would move into the populated areas to supervise the withdrawal and arrange for local cease-fires. The National Liberation Front, once it renounced the use of force, would be guaranteed participation in the political life of the country. In Stage III, there would be free elections, supervised by observers from the international force. The United States would withdraw its small remaining force, but the international force would remain. In Stage IV, the two parts of Vietnam would decide whether or not to unite. The international force would withdraw entirely.

Rockefeller hoped that Hanoi would accept some version of these terms. If it refused, he recommended the redeployment of American forces, the reducing of "search and destroy" operations, and the concentration of American armies in populated areas. He hoped that the South Vietnamese army would be re-equipped. If the North Vietnamese infiltration into the south did not increase, he recommended that the American army be reduced at the rate of 10,000 men per month. As for the American civilian staff, Rockefeller urged its drastic reduction.

On July 26, Rockefeller addressed himself specifically to the question of American-Soviet relations. He was clearly concerned by the situation that was developing in Czechoslovakia. The Soviet threat to the liberalizing tendencies of that society was becoming increasingly apparent. Rockefeller said: "If the Soviet Union considers itself threatened by even the liberalization of a Communist regime—by a reform movement led by lifelong Communists—what weight can one give to its avowal that it desires peaceful coexistence between different social systems?" Rockefeller, speaking words that clearly expressed Kissinger's view of the situation, said that he detected two contradictory tendencies in the Soviet Union. There were, unquestionably, new, younger, and more pragmatic Communists who desired a relaxation of tensions in the world; there were also, however, the more conservative, bureaucratic, and Party elements that seemed to have a vested interest in perpetuating conflict with the outside world. Rockefeller said that "only wishful thinking can obscure the long Communist record of broken commitments," but he added that he believed that "the imperatives of the modern age impose the necessity for peace."

If the Soviet Union did become pacific, ready to cooperate with others, a period of unprecedented well-being in the world would result. Rockefeller hoped that this would happen. He knew how little any American could do to influence the Soviet system. There was, however, a good deal that the United States could itself do. In his view, American foreign policy had to define itself by what it believed in, and not by what it rejected. The old anti-Communism was antiquated and useless. It was important for the United States to conceive of a world order capable of replacing the one that had been smashed by two terrible wars. Slogans and good will were not enough; the call for "peaceful coexistence" left Rockefeller cold. In the new age, he said, there was a need for a policy based on closer relations with America's allies, a review of American strategic needs, and a major effort to reduce tensions with the Soviet Union. The arms race, in his view, offered great possibilities of joint action with the Soviet Union. There was no reason for such vast military expenditures to continue to be made. Also, Rockefeller said, it ought to be possible for the United States and the Soviet Union to cooperate more closely so that their interests were not always colliding in the third world. He said: "We must make clear to the Soviet leaders that the willful exploitation of local tensions—as in the Middle East in 1967—produces unacceptable risks of conflict." If the Soviets showed self-restraint, Rockefeller said, the United States (under his leadership) would be willing to do at least as well. There was an urgent need for greater East-West trade and for more extensive scientific and cultural exchange. The greatest problem, however, was to create a new world order. In Rockefeller's words: "Our forefathers pioneered a political framework within which this nation developed a continental wilderness. Our generation is called on for no less a pioneering act of political creativity and economic construction—on an international scale." He spoke of new relations with the states of the Western Hemisphere, but also with those of Western Europe. In Asia, he recommended greater cooperation between states that were too frequently divided; joint efforts should receive American support. He said, repeating his earlier promise: "I would begin a dialogue with Communist China. In a subtle triangle of relations with Washington, Peking, and Moscow, we improve the possibilities of accommodations with each as we increase our options toward both." Rockefeller believed that "in such a framework we can talk with Soviet leaders with new purposefulness and hope about a basic settlement."

Rockefeller refused to make Vietnam the whole of his policy. He would not be mesmerized by the problem. Henry Kissinger prepared a whole series of position papers for him. They dealt with every kind of foreign policy issue: the European Economic Community, Berlin, Communist China, relations with the Soviet Union, defense. Each of these repeats almost verbatim points that Kissinger made in his published work.

Thus, for example, in writing about the Common Market, he urged the United States to let the European countries work out their own solutions; it was not in the interest of the United States to interfere constantly. The quality of his recommendations may be given by considering what he suggested Rockefeller's position on Communist China and the Soviet Union should be.

With respect to Communist China, Kissinger suggested that the question of relations was almost invariably badly posed. The argument was generally over recognition and the admission of Communist China to the United Nations. These proposals, Kissinger said, "put the cart before the horse." As many nations had learned, diplomatic relations and recognition did not guarantee good relations with China. His own recommendation was that the United States work for more cultural and business interchange between citizens of the United States and China. As for diplomatic relations, he hoped that the existing bilateral talks in Warsaw would be used as "a point of departure for wider-ranging exploration." Kissinger said: "We should engage in such contacts without illusion: We cannot take over the responsibility for bringing mainland China into a more normal and communicative relationship with the community of nations; she must bring herself out of the isolation which is principally self-imposed. But we can do more to advance the day when China will be able to recognize that it is in her interest to join in rational and constructive relationships with the outside world." On the matter of United Nations membership for Communist China, Kissinger was equally blunt; he wrote: "The United States should re-examine its policy on United Nations membership for mainland China. Our primary long-term aim should be to protect the continued membership of Nationalist China. Other nations of the United Nations who so desire can pursue membership for mainland China. We must be prepared for the time when Communist China is able and willing to accept the responsibilities of membership in the United Nations."

The same matter-of-fact analysis informed Kissinger's recommendations on American relations with the USSR. He argued against trying to settle all differences at once, but urged that mutual restraint be aimed for. He hoped that the two would be able to agree on some "principles of international conduct," so that there was not constant danger of explosion; this seemed as important a recommendation as any of the more explicit proposals he made for dealing with specific differences between the two states. He hoped for an expansion of trade in non-strategic goods; also, for vastly expanded cultural and scientific exchange. It was most important that agreement be reached on the control of offensive and defensive strategic weapons systems. Kissinger prepared a separate paper for Rockefeller on defense, which treated these and other subjects. He hoped that the United States and the Soviet Union might reduce their forces in Central Europe, and asked Rockefeller to look at his NATO recommendations for further details on that point. He believed that as the dangers of a military confrontation in Central Europe receded, there was a good prospect for closer East-West ties. Kissinger, preoccupied always with Soviet interference in countries that had limited resources for warding off such intervention, wrote: "The danger of interference in local situations escalating into great-power confrontation should be stressed to the Soviet Union by the United States. We should try over the long run to encourage, in the mutual interest, the use of Russian influence in such areas as the Middle East and Southeast Asia to further the chances for peace rather than court greater violence." Kissinger was writing for Rockefeller as if he was president-elect rather than one of several contenders for the Republican Party's nomination. This fact was even more obvious when he came to discuss the Sino-Soviet split. Kissinger wrote: "The United States should watch the Sino-Soviet split carefully, and with detachment. We cannot do much to promote it, but we should be in a position to exploit opportunities by keeping open options towards both countries. Relations with both large Communist nations will become feasible to the degree that we make sure that lines of communication are open to each."

Kissinger wrote as if Rockefeller's candidacy depended on him. He knew that such was not the case. The defeat, when it came in August, was not a surprise. Feelers from the Nixon camp to join his staff were not taken very seriously by Kissinger. So far as he was concerned, the campaign was over. He could return to his Harvard teaching obligations— a new term was beginning—and take up his writing again. The spring and summer had been filled with adventure; there was no reason to believe that the academic year opening in September would be any different from any other. Kissinger began to write again for publication. During the late summer and early autumn, he found time to write two articles; the first appeared in a collection published by the Brookings Institution, entitled *Agenda for the Nation*; the second, on the Vietnam negotiations, appeared in *Foreign Affairs*. Both articles repeated, confirmed, and amplified themes Kissinger had developed for Rockefeller; both were attentively read after he entered the White House in January 1969.

Kissinger began his Brookings study, entitled "Central Issues of American Foreign Policy," with the statement: "The twentieth century has known little repose. Since the turn of the century, international crises have been increasing in both frequency and severity. The contemporary unrest, although less apocalyptic than the two world wars which spawned it, is even more profoundly revolutionary in nature. . . . The international system which produced stability for a century collapsed under the impact of two world wars. The age of the superpowers, which temporarily replaced it, is nearing its end." The times were revolutionary, Kissinger said, in three ways: the number of participants in the international system had greatly increased and their character had altered; their technical ability to affect each other had grown vastly; the scope of their purposes had expanded. Technology had contributed to the turmoil; by making available vast new resources for foreign policy, it had "magnified insecurities because it has made survival seem to depend on the accidents of a technological breakthrough."

The change in the domestic structures of states further exacerbated international problems. Kissinger believed that the twentieth century had seen the full realization of a process started by the French Revolution. Governments were legitimate only when they could claim to be based on popular support. Even modern totalitarian regimes, he explained, were aberrations of democratic legitimacy; they depended on popular consensus, and achieved their image through the skillful use of propaganda and power. Among the many unintended consequences of the democratic revolution, Kissinger said, were the incomparable resources awarded to governments, which made a new kind of competition possible. In a predemocratic age, states enjoyed limited power; their leaders, even when they were absolute, could not command the types of resources available to their "democratic" successors. Ideological conflict put further strains on the system. When diplomats had a similar outlook about aims and methods, Kissinger wrote, agreement was immensely facilitated. In the twentieth century, in most negotiations, he said, "more time is spent on defining contending positions than in resolving them. What seems most reasonable to one side will appear most problematical to the other."

Kissinger saw that the world had become militarily bipolar, and that no country or group of countries would be in a position to challenge militarily the physical pre-eminence of the United States or the Soviet Union over the next decade. In fact, he expected the military superiority of the two superpowers to increase rather than diminish in the coming decade. Military bipolarity, in Kissinger's view, created great rigidity in foreign policy. But, he added, "the age of the superpowers is now drawing to an end." Military bipolarity had produced results entirely opposite to what had been intended; instead of preventing political multipolarity, it had contributed to that end. Allies, imagining themselves protected by one or other of the superpowers, felt no necessity to "purchase its support by acquiescence in its policies." As for the new nations, they felt protected by the rivalry of the superpowers; according to Kissinger, their nationalism led them "to ever bolder assertions of self-will." Kissinger did not believe that political multipolarity necessarily guaranteed stability. Yet, that multipolarity was certain to continue. It required the United States to rethink its purposes within the international system.

In an earlier time, a state's power grew as it extended its territorial influence over areas which it had not previously controlled. That was no
longer true. Kissinger wrote: "China gained more in real military power
through the acquisition of nuclear weapons than if it had conquered all of
southeast Asia. If the Soviet Union had occupied Western Europe but
had remained without nuclear weapons, it would be less powerful than it
is now with its existing nuclear arsenal within its present borders. In other
words, the really fundamental changes in the balance of power have all
occurred within the territorial limits of sovereign states."

Kissinger insisted that as power had become more awesome it had also
become more "abstract, intangible, elusive." Deterrence was the dominant
military policy; it depended primarily on psychological criteria. Kissinger
wrote: "A bluff taken seriously is more useful than a serious threat interpreted as a bluff. For political purposes, the meaningful measurement of
military strength is the assessment of it by the other side. Psychological
criteria vie in importance with strategic doctrine." Deterrence was tested
negatively by things which did not happen; it was always difficult to
prove that a danger had been averted. When no attack was made, some
would insist that there had never been any danger. A bogeyman had been
created to frighten the credulous. In the modern state, Kissinger wrote,
national security was likely to be a highly divisive domestic issue; any use
of force was calculated to set up inhibitions against its being used again.
He believed, for example, that whatever the outcome of the war in Vietnam, it was improbable that the United States would ever again resort to
such a form of warfare.

Not only was it difficult to conceive of power in the modern world, or
to give it a precise formulation, Kissinger said, but it was also difficult to
use power diplomatically. With nuclear weapons, always in a state of
readiness, the mere signaling of the fact that an issue was being taken seriously was not an easy thing to do. How, in fact, did one communicate
with an enemy? Kissinger thought the problem was dramatically illus-
trated by the war in Vietnam; he wrote: "A massive breakdown of communication occurred not only within the policy-making machinery in the
United States but also between the United States and Hanoi. Over the
past five years, the U.S. government has found it difficult, if not impossible, to define what it understood by victory. President Johnson extended
an open-ended offer for unconditional negotiations. Yet our troops were
deployed as if this offer had not been made. The deployment was based
on purely military considerations; it did not take into account the possibility that our troops might have to support a negotiation—the timing
of which we had, in effect, left to the opponent. Strategy divorced from
foreign policy proved sterile."

If the world was to be militarily bipolar but politically multipolar, a new look had to be taken at the global alliance system that the United States had built up during the early postwar years when it was taken for granted that such alliances deterred aggression. The alliances outside the Atlantic area had never worked very well. America's allies in these other parts of the world added insignificantly to American strength. NATO, by comparison, had been "a dynamic and creative institution," but it was no longer that. Frequent unilateral changes in policy by the United States were partially responsible for NATO's problems. The greater reason, however, was "the decline in the preeminence of the superpowers and the emergence of political multipolarity." If the other alliances had failed in the 1950s because they neglected to take account of military bipolarity, NATO was in difficulty in the late 1960s because it had failed to adjust to political multipolarity.

Kissinger emphasized how much had changed since the immediate postwar period. In the first years after World War II, Europe needed the United States for "economic assistance, political stability, and military protection." European statesmen, he said, acted more as "lobbyists" than as "diplomats." Their personalities were made to seem all-important; Kissinger wrote: "A form of consultation evolved whereby Europeans sought to influence American actions by giving us a reputation to uphold or—to put it more crudely—by oscillating between flattery and almost plaintive appeals for reassurance." This situation could not have lasted. Europe's economic recovery, Kissinger indicated, led inevitably to a return to more traditional political relations. For a while it appeared that European unity would create a power capable of competing with the American colossus on something like an equal basis. That had not happened. Instead, European unity was stymied, and domestic politics almost everywhere dominated European security policy. Also, as Soviet power grew, the United States' pledge to defend NATO became more open to question. It was hard to believe that the United States would rush quickly into an atomic war if forty to a hundred and twenty million casualties would follow.

Kissinger wrote: "Atlantic relations, for all their seeming normalcy, thus face a profound crisis." Those who were the architects of "Atlantic partnership" went on talking breezily about its fair prospects; such men, Kissinger said, failed "to take into account the realities of political multipolarity." There was no possibility of returning to the kinds of relations that had existed at the time of the Marshall Plan. Any attempt to do so would be grotesque. The need was not for a new military security plan but for a "common political conception" suited to the multipolar political world that now existed. Kissinger did not expect that most European states, in part because of decolonization, were prepared to conduct a global policy; this quite irrespective of their resources. Therefore, cooper-

room than what to do once we arrive there. The dispute over Communist intentions has diverted attention from elaborating our own purposes. In some quarters, the test of dedication to peace has been whether one interprets Soviet intentions in the most favorable manner."

While both Moscow and Washington found the risks of nuclear war equally unacceptable, this did not lead to an automatic acceptance of *détente*. Kissinger pointed to at least five *détentes* that had existed between the Soviet Union and the West since the Russian Revolution of 1917; not one of them had lasted. Each time the renewed intransigence was ascribed to a victory of Soviet hard-liners. Why, Kissinger asked, was it never attributed to the dynamics of the Soviet system? The West wanted to believe in the battle between the "hawks" and the "doves" in the Kremlin. It suited Soviet purposes to make the West believe that there were such tendencies, for such a preoccupation with Soviet intentions deflected the United States from thinking about its own purposes. These ought to be the major concern of Americans.

Kissinger started to write his article just as Soviet troops entered Czechoslovakia. Feelings were strong in many parts of the world; he knew, however, that sooner or later there would be a new Soviet peace offensive. Kissinger hoped that the United States would not continue to confuse a change of tone with a change of heart. There was, in his mind, no contradiction between working for greater allied unity and working for *détente*; the latter, Kissinger insisted, presupposed the former. In his formula for negotiations with the Soviet Union, he concentrated on concrete issues that threatened world peace: interventions in the third world and the arms race. Even after the Soviet actions in Czechoslovakia, Kissinger remained committed to the ideas he had developed for Rockefeller. His concern was with a "creative world order"; that presupposed improved Soviet-American relations.

Kissinger spoke of the power vacuum in Central Europe, the decline in West European power, and the arrival of Communist China on the international scene. These events alone would have created difficulties. The United States would do well to look at itself more candidly and rid itself of its mythologies; there was no point in going on prating about America's "responsibilities" and the like. The country had to ask itself two questions: "What is it in our interest to prevent? What should we seek to accomplish?" Kissinger was not satisfied with those who claimed that it was in America's interest to stop aggression wherever it occurred, peace being indivisible. "This," he said, "leads to an undifferentiated globalism and confusion about our purposes." He went on to say: "The abstract concept of aggression causes us to multiply our commitments. But the denial that our interests are involved diminishes our staying power when we try to carry out these commitments." America was in difficulty partly because it refused to think in terms of power and equilibrium. Principle, however lofty, had at some point to be related to practice. Kissinger insisted that stability always coincided with an equilibrium that made physical domination difficult. He wrote: "Interest is not necessarily amoral; moral consequences can stem from interested acts." He went on to say: "A new American administration confronts the challenge of relating our commitments to our interests and our obligations to our purposes."

The United States, he said, could no longer hope to operate programs globally; where it had once offered remedies, it needed to "contribute to a structure that will foster the initiative of others." New kinds of creativity and patience were called for. The need was for a conception of world order that sought something more than stability, but that made Americans restrain themselves lest they approach the world as if, in their enthusiasm, they could do almost anything. If Kissinger worried about these "fits of enthusiasm," he worried also about the negative and nihilistic attitudes of many of the young. Specifically, he worried about the change of ethic in precisely the more idealistic among America's youth. He saw that "many in the younger generation consider the management of power irrelevant, perhaps even immoral." Kissinger wrote: "While the idea of service retains a potent influence, it does so largely with respect to problems which are clearly not connected with the strategic aspects of American foreign policy; the Peace Corps is a good example. The new ethic of freedom is not 'civic'; it is indifferent or even hostile to systems and notions of order. Management is equated with manipulation. Structural designs are perceived as systems of 'domination'—not of order. The generation which has come of age after the fifties has had Vietnam as its introduction to world politics. It has no memory of occasions when American-supported structural innovations were successful or of the motivations which prompted these enterprises." Kissinger saw the American mood oscillating wildly between being ashamed of power and exaggerating its possibilities. He wrote: "The danger of a rejection of power is that it may result in a nihilistic perfectionism which disdains the gradual and seeks to destroy what does not conform to its notion of utopia. The danger of an overconcern with force is that policy makers may respond to clamor by a series of spasmodic gestures and stylistic maneuvers and then recoil before their implications."

A satisfied, advanced society would put a premium on operating within familiar procedures and concepts. It would seek to manipulate an existing framework. Much of the world, however, found significant reality not in what they saw but in what they wished to bring about. Kissinger wrote: "If we remain nothing but the managers of our physical patrimony, we will grow increasingly irrelevant. And since there can be no stability without us, the prospects of world order will decline." Kissinger called for "a

new burst of creativity," not only for the sake of other countries, but because Americans—particularly the young—needed it. The modern
managerial, consumer-oriented, highly bureaucratized society did not satisfy; it produced "a spiritual void, an almost metaphysical boredom with
a political environment that increasingly emphasizes bureaucratic challenges and is dedicated to no deeper purpose than material comfort."

Kissinger knew that America's problem had no easy remedy, and he
did not pretend that foreign policy could provide a solution. Yet, even in
this area, there was a need for a greater number of nontechnical responses,
which depended on collaboration with others in pursuit of shared purposes. The most immediate need, however, was to ask the right questions.
Kissinger said, in closing, "We will never be able to contribute to building a stable and creative world order until we first form some conception
of it."

In January 1969, just before he assumed his White House responsibilities, the only article Kissinger wrote on Vietnam appeared in *Foreign
Affairs*. The article had been written by Kissinger before Nixon asked
him to serve. Kissinger had debated whether or not to withdraw it, given
the sensitivity of his new position. He decided in the end to permit it to
be published; it repeated in great part points he had developed for Rockefeller. He began by noting that the peace negotiations had been characterized by "the classic Vietnamese syndrome: optimism alternating with
bewilderment; euphoria giving way to frustration." Whatever the merits
of the arguments of each side, Kissinger suggested that a civil war that
had raged for twenty years and that had involved the great powers was
not likely to be settled in a single dramatic stroke. He wrote: "Even if
there were mutual trust—a commodity not in excessive supply—the
complexity of the issues and the difficulty of grasping their interrela-
tionship would make for complicated negotiations."

President Johnson, in his 1968 State of the Union address, Kissinger
said, had emphasized that the pacification program was proceeding
smoothly, and that Saigon's influence was extending ever more deeply
into the countryside. A week later, the Tet offensive began. Kissinger
asked what had gone wrong. The problem, he said, had been conceptual.
The United States insisted on applying traditional maxims of strategy and
"nation-building" in a situation where neither was appropriate. Victory
was supposed to come through the control of territory and the attrition
of the enemy. Since most of the North Vietnamese main-force units were
concentrated in the Central Highlands, the majority of American forces
were concentrated there and along the frontiers of South Vietnam to prevent further infiltration. It was assumed that if both these operations went
well, the guerrilla movement would collapse. The aim was to inflict "un-

acceptable" casualties on Hanoi, forcing the North Vietnamese to negotiate. Kissinger said that the strategy suffered from two flaws: it did not sufficiently take into account the nature of guerrilla warfare; the American notion of "unacceptable" losses was not necessarily shared by Hanoi.

In guerrilla war, Kissinger explained, the object was not to hold territory but to control population. This depended, in part, on psychological factors; unless the population felt safe from terror or reprisal, it would not cooperate. The American strategy put 80 percent of its forces in areas where only 4 percent of the Vietnamese population lived. Even when the United States achieved a military success, it could not transform its victory into a permanent political advantage. American maps classified areas by three types of control: government, contested, and Viet Cong. What they did not show was that most areas were rarely under the exclusive jurisdiction of any one authority. Saigon might control a village during the day, but its cadres almost always withdrew into district or provincial capitals during the night, leaving the villages in Viet Cong control. The guerrillas had one principal aim—to prevent the consolidation of governmental authority. They did not need to control everything; they needed simply to demonstrate from time to time that active cooperation with Saigon was dangerous. Kissinger wrote: "We fought a military war; our opponents fought a political one. We sought physical attrition; our opponents aimed for our psychological exhaustion. In the process, we lost sight of one of the cardinal maxims of guerilla war: the guerilla wins if he does not lose. The North Vietnamese used their main forces the way a bullfighter uses his cape—to keep us lunging in areas of marginal political importance." While the United States pointed proudly to its so-called kill-ratios, which were not always inaccurate, they told nothing about whether Hanoi was prepared to accept such losses.

Kissinger suggested that there was little relationship between America's military strategy and its declared political objectives. American diplomacy and American strategy existed in totally separated compartments. President Johnson announced repeatedly that the United States was prepared to negotiate, unconditionally, at any time, anywhere. This left the timing of the negotiations entirely to the other side. The American military deployment, Kissinger added, was not well designed to support negotiations. It would have been better for negotiating purposes to have 100 percent control of 60 percent of the country than to have 60 percent control of 100 percent of the country.

The American pacification plan was equally flawed. It ought to have afforded security for the population, providing political and institutional links between Saigon and the villages. American strategy gave too low a priority to the protection of the population, and failed to establish a political framework for tying Saigon to the villages. Kissinger noted that the Americans, while professing an idealistic philosophy, relied almost entirely on material factors; the Communists, by contrast, while holding to a materialistic philosophy, owed many of their successes to "their ability to supply an answer to the question of the nature and foundation of political authority."

While Tet was technically an American military victory, by psychological and political standards it was a defeat for both Saigon and the United States. The United States and Saigon had claimed that they could protect the villages; they were unable to do so. The Viet Cong had never made that claim; they simply argued that they had power; given what they were able to do when they held some twenty provincial capitals, they proved that they were right. The Viet Cong wanted to demonstrate that there were no secure areas for Vietnamese civilians. The Tet offensive, Kissinger wrote, convinced the American military leaders that they could not achieve their objectives within the period promised or with the force levels that the American people were prepared to grant them. They changed their strategy and began to protect populated areas. This, Kissinger wrote, "made inevitable an eventual commitment to a political solution and marked the beginning of the quest for a negotiated settlement." President Johnson's March 31 speech set the stage for the negotiations that opened in May.

Kissinger wrote of the public pronouncements on both sides that had served to define the issues, and also of the secret negotiations that had taken place but that had proved abortive or at least had not achieved their intended objectives. He said: "Both the Hanoi Government and the United States are limited in their freedom of action by the state of mind of the population of South Viet Nam which will ultimately determine the outcome of the conflict." Kissinger believed that the *way* the negotiations were carried out was almost as important as *what* was negotiated. He wrote: "The choreography of how one enters negotiations, what is settled first and in what manner is inseparable from the substance of the issues." Wariness was inevitable on all sides. There were no "easy" issues; all were symbolic and in some sense or other prejudged the final settlement. The United States would have to be very conscious of South Vietnam's concerns.

Kissinger believed that the situation in 1968 was not at all like what it had been in 1961 or 1962, when few Americans were involved in Vietnam. The commitment of 500,000 Americans meant that American "credibility" was at stake; others would judge the United States' capacity to keep its promises by how it acted in Vietnam. He was certain that the collapse of the American effort there would only dishearten those who tended to count on American steadiness.

"Hanoi's position," Kissinger said, "is at least as complicated. Its concerns are not global; they are xenophobically Vietnamese (which includes, of course, hegemonial ambitions in Laos and Cambodia). But Hanoi is extraordinarily dependent on the international environment. It could not continue the war without foreign material assistance. It counts almost as heavily on the pressures of world public opinion." Kissinger continued: "Hanoi's margin of survival is so narrow that precise calculation has become a way of life; caution is almost an obsession. Its bargaining position depends on a fine assessment of international factors—especially of the jungle of intra-communist relations. In order to retain its autonomy, Hanoi must manoeuvre skillfully between Peking, Moscow and the NLF. Hanoi has no desire to become completely dependent on one of the communist giants. But since they disagree violently, they reinforce Hanoi's already strong tendency toward obscurantist formulations. In short, Hanoi's freedom of manoeuvre is severely limited."

Kissinger saw that the Soviet Union's problem was not very easy either. Its large-scale aid to Hanoi made it a semi-participant in the war. If Hanoi won outright, then China would appear to be vindicated; China had always argued that the United States would succumb to intransigence. Were Hanoi to be defeated, that would prove the Soviet Union's incapacity to protect "fraternal" Communist countries against the United States. Also, it would weaken a potential barrier to Chinese influence in the whole of Southeast Asia.

With so many conflicting interests, Kissinger expected no quick breakthroughs. As if matters were not complicated enough, he dwelt on the "vast gulf in cultural and bureaucratic style between Hanoi and Washington." He wrote: "It would be difficult to imagine two societies less meant to understand each other than the Vietnamese and the American. History and culture combine to produce almost morbid suspiciousness on the part of the Vietnamese. Because survival has depended on a subtle skill in manipulating physically stronger foreigners, the Vietnamese style of communication is indirect and, by American standards, devious—qualities which avoid a total commitment and an overt test of strength. The fear of being made to look foolish seems to transcend most other considerations. Even if the United States accepted Hanoi's maximum program, the result might well be months of haggling while Hanoi looked for our 'angle' and made sure that no other concessions were likely to be forthcoming." All these tendencies were magnified by Communist ideology and by the North Vietnamese conviction that they had been cheated by the Geneva Conferences of 1954 and 1962 (over Laos) and denied the proper fruits of their battlefield victories. Kissinger analyzed the negotiating style of Hanoi, and paid particular attention to "the careful planning, the subtle, indirect methods, the preference for opaque communications which keep open as many options as possible toward both foe and friend . . ." There were cycles of reconnaissance and withdrawal in North Vietnam's diplomacy, analogous to Viet Cong military strategy. Few moves were accidental; even the most obtuse communication served a purpose. Washington was not very good at dealing with such an adversary. The pragmatic, legal dissection of individual cases was not what was called for. Kissinger wrote: "Pronouncements that the United States is ready to negotiate do not guarantee that a negotiating position exists or that the U.S. Government has articulated its objectives." In the Washington bureaucracy there were some who equated negotiation with surrender. Those who advocated negotiation tended to avoid the issue, realizing that it would only rouse passions. As a consequence, there was a tendency to be very rigid before negotiations and to rely excessively on tactical considerations once the negotiations had started. The Americans tended to lack a negotiating program in the early phases of a conference and to hammer one out as the discussion proceeded. It was very difficult in these circumstances to judge progress.

Kissinger wrote of the lessons of the bombing halt. The United States in September 1967 announced that it was willing to stop an aerial and naval bombardment of North Vietnam in return for productive talks and reciprocal abandonment of military operations by the north. The North Vietnamese refused to give such an undertaking, and insisted on an unconditional cessation of bombing. Washington feared that if the bombing was once halted, it would be difficult politically to start it up again. Hanoi insisted on unconditional cessation precisely because it wanted to use this as a political weapon; for Hanoi, the bombing had always been "illegal"; it was determined that it be stopped, and that there be no conditions attached to the cessation. Kissinger wrote: "Hanoi did not want a formula under which the United States could resume bombing 'legally' by charging violations of an understanding. Finally, Hanoi was eager to give the impression to its supporters in the South that it had induced us to stop 'unconditionally' as a symbol of imminent victory. For the same reason, it was important to us that *both* sides in South Viet Nam believe there had been reciprocity."

Six months were spent trying to define a *quid pro quo* which could be represented as unconditional. Finally, when the bombing halt was announced, Johnson explained that Hanoi knew that it must not "take advantage." Hanoi never admitted that this was the case, but it knew that if it disregarded the points made by the President and the Secretary of State the bombings would probably resume. The United States insisted that Saigon be present at the conference, and North Vietnam made the same claim for the NLF. The Americans agreed. Kissinger wrote: "It is difficult to disentangle from public sources whether Saigon ever agreed to this formula and whether it understood that our formula amounted to giving the NLF equal status." Kissinger deplored the rift that developed between Washington and Saigon; he wrote: "Clearly, there is a point beyond which Saigon cannot be given a veto over negotiations. But equally, it is not preposterous for Saigon to insist on a major voice in decisions affecting its own country. And it cannot strengthen our position in Paris to *begin* the substantive discussions with a public row over the status of a government whose constitutionality we have insistently pressed on the world for the past two years. The impasse has demonstrated that to deal with issues on an ad hoc basis is too risky; before we go much further in negotiations, we need an agreed concept of ultimate goals and how to achieve them."

Kissinger asked whether in negotiating the object should be to proceed step by step, discussing individual items, or whether to seek agreement on some ultimate goals. He feared that the first strategy would lead to deadlock. This would be the case, for example, if one discussed a cease-fire —which was tantamount to establishing the preconditions of a political settlement—or if one discussed the possibilities of a coalition government. Kissinger wrote: "It is beyond imagination that parties that have been murdering and betraying each other for 25 years could work together as a team giving joint instructions to the entire country." If the Vietnamese freely negotiated for a coalition government, the United States should no nothing to impede such discussion. However, the United States should not itself sponsor the effort. Were it to do so, it would only be contributing to the collapse of the Saigon regime.

Kissinger recommended that agreement be reached first on ultimate goals; once those were decided, an effort could be made to fill in the details. Kissinger stopped to reflect on what the respective strengths and weaknesses of North Vietnam and the United States were. Hanoi was fighting on familiar territory; the United States was fighting a war distant from its own territorial base. Hanoi grasped the local situation better than the United States; it showed a greater capacity to design military operations for political ends. Relying heavily on world opinion and on American domestic political pressure, Hanoi believed that the unpopularity of the war would eventually force the Americans to withdraw. Hanoi was in no position to defeat the United States militarily; it could not by itself force the withdrawal of American forces. Eventually, Hanoi would require more foreign assistance to win, and yet it did not welcome any aid that threatened to compromise its autonomy. The Soviet invasion of Czechoslovakia had told North Vietnam how vulnerable it was whenever world opinion shifted to another area of the world. Kissinger said: "Hanoi is unable to gain a military victory. Since it cannot force our withdrawal, it must negotiate about it."

A favorable outcome of negotiations, according to Kissinger, depended on a clear definition of objectives. He wrote: "The limits of the American commitment can be expressed in two propositions: first, the United States cannot accept a military defeat, or a change in the political structure of South Viet Nam brought about by external military force; second, once North Vietnamese forces and pressures are removed, the United States has no obligation to maintain a government in Saigon by force." The United States, Kissinger wrote, "should concentrate on the subject of the mutual withdrawal of external forces and avoid negotiating about the internal structure of South Viet Nam for as long as possible. The primary responsibility for negotiating the internal structure of South Viet Nam should be left for direct negotiations among the South Vietnamese." Kissinger thought that tying "the bombing halt to Saigon's participation in the substantive discussions was probably unwise—all the more so as Hanoi seems to have been prepared to continue bilateral talks." He wondered also about the participation of Saigon and the NLF, which "raised issues about status that could have been better deferred; it made a discussion of the internal structure of South Viet Nam hard to avoid." These errors, however, did not, according to Kissinger, make impossible negotiations along the lines he had suggested. He added: "The tension between Washington and Saigon can even prove salutary if it forces both sides to learn that if they are to negotiate effectively they must confront the fundamental issues explicitly."

If the South Vietnamese appeared in Paris, as was probable, then the four-sided conferences should be viewed "primarily as a plenary session to legitimize the work of two negotiating committees which need not be formally established and could even meet secretly: (a) between Hanoi and the United States, and (b) between Saigon and the NLF. Hanoi and Washington would discuss mutual troop withdrawal and related subjects such as guarantees for the neutrality of Laos and Cambodia. . . . Saigon and the NLF would discuss the internal structure of South Viet Nam." Kissinger knew that the Saigon regime, "for understandable reasons," had consistently refused to deal with the NLF as an international entity, but he hoped that it would get over this view. A third forum would be "an international conference to work out guarantees and safeguards for the agreements arrived at in the other committees, including international peace-keeping machinery."

Why should Hanoi accept such a solution? Because it had no choice. It could not bring about a withdrawal of American forces by its own efforts, particularly if the United States "adopts a less impatient strategy—one better geared to the protection of the population and sustainable with substantially reduced casualties." Kissinger concluded: "No war in a century has aroused the passions of the conflict in Viet Nam. By turning

Viet Nam into a symbol of deeper resentments, many groups have de-feated the objective they profess to seek. However we got into Viet Nam, whatever the judgment of our actions, ending the war honorably is essential for the peace of the world. Any other solution must unloose forces that would complicate prospects of international order. A new Administration must be given the benefit of the doubt and a chance to move toward a peace which grants the people of Viet Nam what they have so long struggled to achieve: an opportunity to work out their own destiny in their own way."

For anyone who had given attention to Rockefeller's campaign statements on the Vietnam war, Kissinger's *Foreign Affairs* article would have seemed simply a confirmation of things he had already heard. How could it have been otherwise? The events of the spring and early summer had forced Kissinger to develop a concrete set of proposals for dealing with Vietnam. When he came to write about the subject in his own name, he could do nothing but reiterate what he had already advised Rockefeller to say. The question that an intrepid newspaper commentator would have asked was whether there was any reason to expect that Richard Nixon would be influenced by Henry Kissinger's views. There was no way to answer that question on January 20, 1969. The position in itself did not guarantee that kind of influence.

EPILOGUE
The Testing of Theory

Henry Kissinger, before he reached the White House, was an outspoken critic of American foreign policy. He criticized objectives, found fault with operating procedures, and complained constantly of the absence of subtlety and nuance. American foreign policy, in his view, was crisis-oriented. When a disaster threatened, resources were mobilized; rarely, if ever, did the American government anticipate events. Its policies were almost always short-range. Even when the United States could claim to have something like a "philosophy" undergirding its disparate foreign policy efforts, the doctrine was generally flawed, out of date, irrelevant, or simply inappropriate. Kissinger could point to relatively few instances in the years after World War II when American leaders performed at a level adequate to the challenges of the international system. Too few of those who conducted American foreign policy had any feeling for the enterprise; even fewer appreciated its intellectual character.

Between January 20, 1969, and July 15, 1971, a critic of Kissinger's own performance as Assistant to the President for National Security Affairs might have been forgiven if he had suggested that for all the vaunted reforms of the National Security Council, and despite the high-sounding prose of the first two "state of the world" reports, largely written by Kissinger for the President, there was not much to suggest that Nixon was doing anything except what his predecessors had also tried to do. He appeared to be mired in the crises of the moment, and it was not at all clear that he was resolving them. The Vietnam fighting was continuing; peace

271

seemed no closer; Cambodia was now an active theater of war; dissension in the country was scarcely different from what it had been in the days of Lyndon Johnson. Almost nine hundred days had passed since Nixon had taken his oath of office. What, in the area of foreign policy, could the administration point to if it wished to list its accomplishments?

On July 15, 1971, the first such accomplishment was announced. Nixon revealed, to everyone's surprise, that Kissinger had recently held discussions with Chou En-lai in Peking, and that he himself planned to visit Communist China before May 1972. The news suggested a dramatic turn in American foreign policy. In the days that followed, almost no one remarked on the tens of thousands of hours that had gone into the making of this new policy. Even fewer inquired into how the policy had been coordinated with new approaches to the Soviet Union, and what it portended for peace in Southeast Asia. Americans were so much in the habit of thinking of individual foreign policy initiatives that few saw reason to believe that this was part of a drastic overhaul of American priorities that would affect policies in every corner of the globe. Kissinger's hand was looked for in all of this, but since his works were so rarely consulted by those who wrote about him, there was no possibility of understanding what had happened. While the administration had spent more than its full quota of hours attending to every crisis, large and small, it had managed also to engage in long-range planning, on which Kissinger had always insisted. More significantly, it had done so on a global scale, realizing that no such major departure as that represented by the China policy could be undertaken in isolation. Many took note of the fact that the administration had not been very adroit in its handling of Japan; the criticism was justified. It tended to deflect attention, however, from other no less crucial questions. What did the change in policy portend? Were other changes to be expected? Was this the first expression of a major foreign policy shift—the great departure from the policies of the immediate postwar period that Kissinger had been proposing for over a decade?

Henry Kissinger, in his first two and a half years in the White House, lived as a fairly conspicuous and obviously influential presidential aide, but he had not become the subject of daily newspaper attention. All that was changed by the disclosures of July 15, 1971. The most bizarre conjectures began to circulate to account for Kissinger's purported influence on the President. Some chose to see him as the prince's mentor; others preferred to regard him as the devil's collaborator. Persistent efforts were made to distinguish between policies that were assumed to be Kissinger's and those that might more reasonably be attributed to the man he served. All such theorizing, while unobjectionable, contributed nothing to resolving the one question that ought to have been asked: was foreign policy under Richard Nixon shaped by theories and influenced by operational procedures that had some significant resemblance to what Kissinger had himself proposed before he assumed his governmental responsibilities?

On this point, the evidence is irrefutable: the foreign policy strategies and statements of the Nixon administration replicate or approximate procedures and policies recommended by Kissinger in all his published writings. The President of the United States—reputed to be a pragmatist—has not shied away from insisting on the centrality of philosophy, on the importance of doctrine. In each of his annual reports to Congress—largely prepared by Kissinger—he has emphasized the existence of what, in 1972, he called "the philosophy of a new American foreign policy." Nixon, like Kissinger, has wanted to distinguish between his policies and those of his predecessors. He has been equally concerned to distinguish between the premises that he is willing to accept in the foreign policy sphere and those that were once thought sufficient in this area.

When Richard Nixon assumed the presidency, the nation's attention was riveted on the war in Vietnam. No other foreign policy issue engaged the interest of the country. Kissinger's own theoretical leanings made it impossible for him to view the Vietnam conflict in the way that the news media did. The United States, in his system, was a major world power; it could never afford to become preoccupied with any single issue to the exclusion of all others. Its concern had to be the international environment in a larger sense. Kissinger, in everything that he had ever written about contemporary foreign policy, showed a continuing interest in five constituent elements: the arms equation; the condition of the Communist bloc; the state of America's alliances; the plight of the developing countries; America's internal domestic strengths and weaknesses. Policy, in his mind, depended on conjectures being made about the opportunities offered by all of these.

As he had made quite evident in speeches prepared for Nelson Rockefeller a few months before he entered the White House, Kissinger believed that the times were propitious for new initiatives to be taken vis-à-vis both the Soviet Union and Communist China. The Americans and the Soviets accepted the fact that a strategic balance existed between them; the Communist bloc seemed irrevocably split; both the Soviet Union and Communist China had ceased to be "revolutionary" states. That term had a very special meaning in Kissinger's lexicon. Since he had always believed that an international order demanded a certain acceptance by all of its members, the existence of any state pledged to its destruction created a serious hazard to world peace. It mattered very much, in Kissinger's mind, that neither Moscow nor Peking appeared any longer to entertain such ambitions. For Kissinger, this opened the possibility of meaningful discussions. He was too innately cautious to believe that the Communist states would remain committed to the existing order for all time. Kissinger, together with others in the administration, saw an opportunity in 1969 and 1970; they fastened on it.

Since access to information concerning the precise measures undertaken by the government to alter its relations with Communist China and the Soviet Union is currently restricted, and is likely to remain so for many years to come, it is quite impossible to describe in any detail the sequence of events that led to the dramatic reversal of policies with respect to Peking and the rapid improvement of relations with Moscow. On the basis of published information, however, certain significant elements of the long-range planning that went into the establishment of these policies become evident. Clearly, the strategy was based on an active diplomacy— much of it secret—and almost all of it involving Kissinger. Kissinger, while favoring diplomatic initiatives, was fully aware of the hazards involved. There was no way of knowing for certain how the Soviet Union would react when it learned of the approaches the United States had made to Peking. Clearly, the administration believed that the reaction would not be so unfavorable as to jeopardize the various concrete plans for improved relations that Kissinger and the Soviet Ambassador in Washington had been discussing for well over two years.

Kissinger, when he proposed diplomatic overtures in his published works, never pretended that he did so because he believed that either the Soviet Union or Communist China had in any significant respect deviated from its Marxist principles; he scorned those who thought it necessary to argue that they were becoming increasingly "bourgeois." Nor did he pretend to know very much about the specifics of their internal politics. He assumed that if American initiatives were responded to favorably, it was because the other side saw a potential gain in improved relations. Given the very substantial differences that existed, and that would continue to exist, and given the events of the postwar period, caution was the only safe policy. Kissinger accepted the possibility of failure; he never believed that the risk of failure justified inactivity.

Kissinger's object was to secure a stable international order. That purpose transcended all others; in his mind, it was the necessary precondition of peace. While the world tended to pay greater attention to the specific differences that separated the Soviet Union and the United States, and, not infrequently, pretended that they were less substantial than they appeared, Kissinger had no patience with that view. Issues that had not been settled for over twenty years would not suddenly succumb to his ministrations or to those of a new generation of leaders in the Kremlin. Kissinger did not believe in instant conversions; he did believe, however, in the educational possibilities of diplomacy, properly conceived. He was less interested in negotiating technique than in negotiating objectives. In his mind, the "statesman" was not a figure of history, consigned to a pantheon that included some of the most distinguished minds of the past. Kissinger thought that statesmanship was a twentieth-century possibility. The statesman's talents were primarily psychological; he had to know how to estimate the objectives of societies different from his own. He had to be able to judge correctly the real relationship of forces. He had to possess a "vision," and know how to translate that vision into reality. His failure to make his ideas credible to his own people would defeat him; so, also, would his failure to communicate his principles to others, including those who represented states that were hostile or neutral to his own.

It mattered immensely to Kissinger how a specific negotiation was entered upon; it mattered even more what proposals were communicated. Kissinger did not believe that negotiation was a good in itself; negotiation was useful only when there was some understanding of the objectives desired, and when one knew how to secure those objectives. In any international negotiation, it was impossible for one state to be entirely satisfied and another entirely frustrated. A successful negotiation demanded that all parties receive some satisfaction. Unless all could see the advantage of a specific agreement, the incentives to maintain it would be minimal. The statesman's task, therefore, was not only to know what one wanted for one's own country, but to understand something of what the representatives of the other negotiating parties also wanted, and to know how much to give in order to secure one's own principal objectives. The statesman was required to have what the eighteenth century called "sympathy," which was not so much a liking for the other as a capacity to place oneself in the position of the other. That kind of sympathy was a major psychological virtue, necessary to diplomacy, but only when accompanied by an accurate appraisal of the other's needs and resources, not to speak of one's own.

Kissinger knew that a state's options were always limited; a state could not simply opt for every possibility. However, a statesman generally recognized the existence of a greater number of options than were seen by those who lacked his vision. The statesman's skill was demonstrated in his capacity to choose well among the options that he detected. All choice involved risk; all choice was based on conjecture. When one chose option A rather than option B, one could not be certain of the results; one could only hope that one's analysis of the situation had been such that the expected results would in fact be achieved. The policy-maker was the risk-taker; there was no way to guarantee his success. Kissinger spoke openly of the risks taken in the decision to lay mines outside the principal North Vietnamese harbors; there was always a chance that the Soviet Union would view this as a "provocative act," and retaliate by suggesting that the President postpone his visit to Moscow, thereby undoing the work of more than three years. In this instance, as Kissinger admitted, the administration deemed the risk "acceptable." So, also, in the decision to bomb Hanoi after the disruption of the Paris peace talks, there were obvious risks involved. Again, the decision was made to run those risks, in the belief that the alternatives, while less dangerous, promised results that could not be satisfactory.

Kissinger had no illusion that he or others would be commended for what they had done. His knowledge of history told him that the most difficult decisions—those that often carried the greatest potentialities for improving a situation—were not infrequently condemned. Nor did he flatter himself that history would justify what his contemporaries judged adversely. Again, he knew sufficient history to realize that this did not always happen. The "statesman" who looked for "justice" either from his contemporaries or from history, and counted on receiving it, was almost certain to be disappointed. There was a deep pessimism in Kissinger's fundamental philosophy; with it, however, came the most insistent demands that risks be taken, and that opportunities be seized.

Repeatedly, Kissinger emphasized the importance of seeking and gaining domestic support for significant foreign policies. That, in his view, implied more than having legislative or popular support, though both were clearly essential, particularly in democratic societies. It meant having also the support of the bureaucracy and knowing how to treat the bureaucracy so that it did not interfere with policy-making or try to do what it was not equipped to do. The policy-maker was the artist who had to conceive and execute a large plan; the bureaucrat was the technician who made the plan work. It was dangerous to ask bureaucrats to do what only policy-makers could do; it was even more dangerous to ignore bureaucrats, acting as if anything could be done, even against their opposition.

The statesman had to accept that technical virtuosity was not enough; he had to admit that his first objective was to set goals. In setting goals, he had to realize that he could not become entirely dependent on the good will of others. He had to remain free, realizing that only in freedom was there the possibility of creative action. He had to know also that his best plans might be laid to nought by circumstances over which he had no control. A totally unforeseen accident might destroy everything that he had planned. This was the tragedy of states, as it was also the tragedy of individuals. There was no way for a state to prepare for every contingency.

Peace was the legitimating principle that made sense to twentieth-century men, who had reason to be frightened of the weapons of war. The slogan by itself, however, did not establish a reality. Even if the United States worked for a stable international order, and sought to persuade others of its necessity, that was no guarantee of success. Good intentions were not enough; other states had to be persuaded; in Kissinger's words, they had to be "reconciled"; they could not be manipulated. The world was constantly watching the United States, but the United States needed also to watch the world. The problem, obviously, was to know what to look for. This, in the best sense of the word, was an intellectual problem. It was the problem that Kissinger had spent the greatest part of his life studying.

When Richard Nixon came to write *Six Crises*, he spoke about lawyers in politics. It is interesting to note that he expressed certain of the same reservations about lawyers in high political office that Kissinger had expressed in his own books. Nixon wrote: "To the extent that the study of law disciplines the mind, it can be most helpful in politics as well as in other fields. But as a lawyer I should add a caveat at this point: lawyers tend to be 'nit-pickers.' Too often, when confronted with a problem, they approach it from the standpoint of 'how not to do it' rather than 'how to do it.' Lawyers in politics need non-lawyers around them to keep them from being too legalistic, too unimaginative." Nixon may have chosen Kissinger because he believed that he would be the non-lawyer in his entourage who would keep him from being "too legalistic, too unimaginative." If Nixon needed someone of a philosophical bent, he found that person in Kissinger.

Kissinger was made part of the White House staff because of his expert knowledge; no outside constituency pushed Kissinger on Nixon. He had been chosen by the President-elect and would remain with him so long as he felt that he was needed and so long as the President wanted to have him. Kissinger had spent many years of his life studying foreign policy. He believed that his knowledge of the subject equaled that of any other person in the country. His professorial life had given him the freedom to study. His associations with many in high places in government even before he entered the White House instructed him in certain of the fundamentals of American politics. His continuing relations with hundreds of foreigners told him something of the diversity of opinion that existed. Neither his study nor his experience guaranteed his success; each, however, made possible the formulation of a doctrine that now commended itself to the man who was President of the United States. It is impossible to know why Nixon found Kissinger's views so congenial, or how Nixon himself altered those views so that they more precisely coincided with his own, or whether he in fact did so; it is possible to say, however, that a man who came to the United States as a refugee, and spent most of his adult life reflecting and writing about foreign policy, enjoyed a remarkable success when he was given the opportunity to put his ideas into practice.

The years in academic life gave Kissinger the competence he required. He did not, however, simply borrow from his teachers. He incorporated what he learned into a system that gave great importance to ideas; words mattered immensely to him. In an age that put relatively little stock in the value of words—believing that they were generally intended to deceive, and therefore suspect—Kissinger argued the contrary. Words, in his mind, were precise; they merited attention; they revealed purpose and therefore gave evidence of the mind of another. Kissinger was never one to dismiss Marxist argument as "propaganda."

Even more, he repudiated what was implicit in the economic determinism of many who studied international relations in the West, particularly in the United States. Kissinger was never very partial to those arguments that insisted on the "inevitability" of certain developments because of certain undisputed facts. The facts were "undisputed" only in the minds of those who adduced them. Kissinger, at a time when such belief was unfashionable, asserted the importance of what the individual in high office was in a position to do. For him, the statesman was an artist, often working with intractable materials, but conscious always of some larger design. He believed that the statesman deserved to be celebrated. Because his own standards for judging performance were so high, he found few who achieved the distinction that he was looking for.

He never underestimated the difficulty of the statesman's task. In the first instance, it was intellectual; that, however, was only the beginning of the statesman's capabilities. He had to know how to communicate his purposes—in diplomatic negotiations, to other states; in daily political encounters, to his own fellow citizens. In Kissinger's mind, the statesman was always the educator, seeking to communicate his "vision" to others. It was imperative that he be aware of history—which meant more than simply knowing history. He had to know the limits of the perception of others, realizing how difficult it was for any society to view problems from a perspective that did not simply repeat what it had already learned. Kissinger knew that even the most accomplished statesman failed if he accepted to be a "solo" performer. Kissinger was looking not for heroes but for principles that would make it possible for states in the twentieth century to avoid the terrors of nuclear war.

BIBLIOGRAPHY
of Henry Kissinger's Works

BOOKS

A World Restored: Metternich, Castlereagh, and the Problems of Peace, 1812–1822, Houghton Mifflin, 1957.

Nuclear Weapons and Foreign Policy, Harper, 1957.

The Necessity for Choice: Prospects of American Foreign Policy, Harper, 1961.

The Troubled Partnership: A Reappraisal of the Atlantic Alliance, McGraw-Hill, 1965.

Problems of National Strategy: A Book of Readings, ed. Kissinger, Praeger, 1965.

American Foreign Policy: Three Essays, Norton, 1969.

ARTICLES

"Reflections on the Political Thought of Metternich," *American Political Science Review*, December 1954.

"American Policy and Preventive War," *Yale Review*, April 1955.

"Military Policy and the Defense of the 'Grey' Areas," *Foreign Affairs*, April 1955.

"Limitations of Diplomacy," *The New Republic*, May 6, 1955.

"Congress of Vienna," *World Politics*, January 1956.

"Force and Diplomacy in the Nuclear Age," *Foreign Affairs*, April 1956.

"Reflections on American Diplomacy," *Foreign Affairs*, October 1956.

"Strategy and Organization," *Foreign Affairs*, April 1957.

"Controls, Inspection and Limited War," *The Reporter*, June 13, 1957.

"Missiles and the Western Alliance," *Foreign Affairs*, April 1958.

"Nuclear Testing and the Problem of Peace," *Foreign Affairs*, October 1958.

"The Policymaker and the Intellectual," *The Reporter*, March 5, 1969.

"The Search for Stability," *Foreign Affairs*, July 1959.

"The Khrushchev Visit—Dangers and Hopes," *New York Times Magazine*, September 6, 1959.

"Arms Control, Inspection and Surprise Attack," *Foreign Affairs*, July 1960.

"Limited War: Nuclear or Conventional? A Reappraisal," *Daedalus*, Fall 1960.

"The New Cult of Neutralism," *The Reporter*, November 24, 1960.

"For an Atlantic Confederacy," *The Reporter*, February 2, 1961.

"The Unsolved Problems of European Defense," *Foreign Affairs*, July 1962.

"Reflections on Cuba," *The Reporter*, November 22, 1962.

"Strains on the Alliance," *Foreign Affairs*, January 1963.

"The Skybolt Affair," *The Reporter*, January 17, 1963.

"NATO's Nuclear Dilemma," *The Reporter*, March 28, 1963.

"Coalition Diplomacy in the Nuclear Age," *Foreign Affairs*, July 1964.

"Classical Diplomacy," in *Power & Order: Six Cases in World Politics*, Harcourt, Brace & World, 1964.

"The Price of German Unity," *The Reporter*, April 22, 1965.

"Domestic Structure and Foreign Policy," *Daedalus*, April 1966.

"For a New Atlantic Alliance," *The Reporter*, July 14, 1966.

"The White Revolutionary: Reflections on Bismarck," *Daedalus*, Summer 1968.

"Bureaucracy and Policy Making: The Effect of Insiders and Outsiders on the Policy Process," in *Bureaucracy, Politics, and Strategy*, Security Studies Paper No. 17, University of California, Los Angeles, 1968.

"Central Issues of American Foreign Policy," in *Agenda for the Nation*, Brookings Institution, 1968.

"The Vietnam Negotiations," *Foreign Affairs*, January 1969.

Acheson, Dean, 72, 73, 148
Adenauer, Konrad, 54, 155, 195, 197, 210–211
"Administrative and Policy Problems of the United States in the Field of Diplomacy" (seminar), 114
Advantageous strategy, American superiority and, 82
Agency for International Development (AID), 224
Agenda for the Nation, 254
Aggression, doctrine of, 66–68, 72, 84, 105, 134, 136, 260; local, dealing with, 159–160
Alexander I, Tsar, 29, 31, 32, 33, 34, 42, 44, 46; as a "prophet," 38, 47–48
Alliance for Progress, 178, 192
All-out war, strategy of, 74–75, 78, 79, 84, 87, 89, 134–135, 136, 138, 158, 181
America, discovery of, 39
Anderson, Robert, 108
Anti-ballistic missile system, 162–163
Anti-colonialism, neutralism and, 89
Aristocracy, eighteenth-century, 21, 40
Aristotle, 6
Armaments race, 83; preceding World War I, 147
Arms control, 138, 156–167; local aggression and, 159–160; need for positive evidence inspection, 158–159; negotiations, 132, 137, 139–140, 156–167; nth country problem, 160; and nuclear proliferation, 160–164; problem of surprise attack, 156–158; Pugwash discussions, 116–117; seminar (Center for International Affairs), 115–116, 127; tactics for negotiating, 139–140
"Arms Control, Inspection and Surprise Attack" (Kissinger), 127
Arms stockpiles, reducing, 84–85

Armstrong, Hamilton Fish, 60, 63
Army Specialized Training Program (A.S.T.P.), 2
Ascoli, Max, 119
Atlantic alliance, 179; purpose of, 146
Atlantic Policy Studies (Council on Foreign Relations), 203
Aubrac, Raymond, 246, 247, 248
Authority: conference system, 37–38; political process and, 11

Baghdad Pact, 148
Balance of forces, 39; international order and, 35–36
Balance of power, 48, 88
Baldwin, Hanson, 63
Ball, George, 199–200
Bargaining process, the, 216, 231–232; *see also* Diplomacy
Bay of Pigs invasion, 189
Beer, Samuel, 114
Berkner, Lloyd, 63
Berle, Adolf, Jr., 107, 109
Berlin crisis, xiv, 153
Berlin Wall, 177, 189, 211
Bernadotte, Marshal Jean Baptiste, 31
Bien Hoa province, 225
Binh Dinh province, 225
Bismarck, Otto von, x, xi, 21, 49; compared to de Gaulle, 238; foreign policy of, 224, 237–240
Bowie, Robert, 63, 115, 116
Bowles, Chester, 107
Brain trusts, 172
British Bomber Command, 185
Buchenwald, 8
Buckley, William, 58
Buddhists, 224
Bulganin, Nikolai, 120

281